Game Changers in Labour Law

Bulletin of Comparative Labour Relations

VOLUME 100

Founding Editor

The series started in 1970 under the dynamic editorship of Professor Roger Blanpain (Belgium), former President of the International Industrial Relations Association. Professor Blanpain, Professor Emeritus of Labour Law, Universities of Leuven and Tilburg, was also General Editor of the International Encyclopedia of Laws (with more than 1,600 collaborators worldwide) and President of the Association of Educative and Scientific Authors Authors. He passed away in October 2016.

General Editor

In 2015 Frank Hendrickx, Professor of labour law at the Faculty of Law of the University of Leuven (Belgium) joined as a co-Editor. Frank Hendrickx has published numerous articles and books and regularly advises governments, international institutions and private organisations in the area of labour law as well as in sports law. He is the Editor-in-Chief of the European Labour Law Journal and General Editor of the International Encyclopaedia of Laws.

Introduction

The Bulletins constitute a unique source of information and thought-provoking discussion, laying the groundwork for studies of employment relations in the 21st century, involving among much else the effects of globalization, new technologies, migration, and the greying of the population.

Contents/Subjects

Amongst other subjects the Bulletins frequently include the proceedings of international or regional conferences; reports from comparative projects devoted to salient issues in industrial relations, human resources management, and/or labour law; and specific issues underlying the multicultural aspects of our industrial societies.

Objective

The Bulletins offer a platform of expression and discussion on labour relations to scholars and practitioners worldwide, often featuring special guest editors.

The titles published in this series are listed at the end of this volume.

BULLETIN OF COMPARATIVE LABOUR RELATIONS – 100

Game Changers in Labour Law

Shaping the Future of Work

Editors

Frank Hendrickx
Valerio De Stefano

Contributors

Mariya Aleksynska
Janice R. Bellace
Janine Berg
Susan Bisom-Rapp
Valerio De Stefano
Michael Doherty
Merle Erikson
Mijke Houwerzijl
Martine Humblet

Barbara Kresal
David Mangan
Alan C. Neal
Jacques Rojot
Monika Schlachter
Achim Seifert
Michele Tiraboschi
Manfred Weiss
Mimi Zou

General Editor

Frank Hendrickx

Founding Editor

Roger Blanpain

Published by:
Kluwer Law International B.V.
PO Box 316
2400 AH Alphen aan den Rijn
The Netherlands
E-mail: international-sales@wolterskluwer.com
Website: lrus.wolterskluwer.com

Sold and distributed in North, Central and South America by:
Wolters Kluwer Legal & Regulatory U.S.
7201 McKinney Circle
Frederick, MD 21704
United States of America
Email: customer.service@wolterskluwer.com

Sold and distributed in all other countries by:
Air Business Subscriptions
Rockwood House
Haywards Heath
West Sussex
RH16 3DH
United Kingdom
Email: international-customerservice@wolterskluwer.com

Printed on acid-free paper.

ISBN 978-90-411-9953-9

e-Book: ISBN 978-90-411-9954-6
web-PDF: ISBN 978-90-411-9955-3

© 2018 Kluwer Law International BV, The Netherlands

All rights reserved. No part of this publication may be reproduced, stored in a retrieval system, or transmitted in any form or by any means, electronic, mechanical, photocopying, recording, or otherwise, without written permission from the publisher.

Permission to use this content must be obtained from the copyright owner. More information can be found at: lrus.wolterskluwer.com/policies/permissions-reprints-and-licensing

Printed in the United Kingdom.

Notes on Contributors

Mariya Aleksynska is an Economist, Labour Market Specialist at the International Labour Office, Switzerland.

Janice R. Bellace is Samuel Blank Professor of Legal Studies and Professor of Management, at The Wharton School, University of Pennsylvania, USA.

Janine Berg is a Senior Economist, Labour Market Specialist at the International Labour Office, Switzerland.

Susan Bisom-Rapp is Associate Dean and Professor of Law at the Thomas Jefferson School of Law, USA.

Valerio De Stefano is a BOZ-ZAP Research Professor of Labour Law at the Institute for Labour Law, KU Leuven, Belgium.

Michael Doherty is Professor of Law, Department of Law, Maynooth University, Ireland.

Merle Erikson is Professor of Law at the School of Law, University of Tartu, Estonia.

Frank Hendrickx is Professor of Labour Law at the Institute for Labour Law, KU Leuven, Belgium. He is the general editor of the Bulletin of Comparative Labour Relations of the International Encyclopaedia of Laws and the editor-in-chief of the *European Labour Law Journal*.

Mijke Houwerzijl is Professor of Labour Law at Tilburg University and Professor of European and Comparative Labour Law at the University of Groningen, the Netherlands.

Martine Humblet is a Legal Specialist on Working Conditions at the International Labour Office, Switzerland.

Notes on Contributors

Barbara Kresal is Professor of Labour Law and Social Security at the University of Ljubljana, Slovenia.

David Mangan is Lecturer in Law at City University of London and Adjunct Professor at Osgoode Hall Law School, Canada.

Alan C. Neal is Professor of Law at the University of Warwick, United Kingdom, and an Employment Judge in the London Central office of the Employment Tribunals of England and Wales. He is the Convenor of the European Association of Labour Court Judges.

Jacques Rojot is Professor Emeritus at the Université Paris II – Panthéon Assas, France.

Monika Schlachter is Professor of international and European Labour Law and Civil Law at the University of Trier, Germany.

Achim Seifert is Professor of Private Law, German and European Labour Law and Comparative Law at the Friedrich-Schiller-University Jena, Germany.

Michele Tiraboschi is Full Professor of Labour Law at the University of Modena and Reggio Emilia, and Scientific Coordinator of ADAPT, Italy.

Manfred Weiss is Professor Emeritus at the Law School of the J.W. Goethe University in Frankfurt, Germany.

Mimi Zou is the inaugural Fangda Fellow in Chinese Commercial Law at the University of Oxford, United Kingdom. She graduated with DPhil and BCL degrees from Oxford.

Summary of Contents

Notes on Contributors	v
Tributes to Marco Biagi and Roger Blanpain	xvii
Acknowledgements	xxi
Introduction *Frank Hendrickx & Valerio De Stefano*	1
PART I Shifting Labour Law	9
CHAPTER 1 The Changing Face of Capital: The Withering of the Employment Relationship in the Information Age *Janice R. Bellace*	11
CHAPTER 2 Non-standard Employment Around the World: Regulatory Answers to Face Its Challenges *Janine Berg, Mariya Aleksynska, Valerio De Stefano & Martine Humblet*	27
CHAPTER 3 European Labour Law and the Millennium Shift: From Post to (Social) Pillar *Frank Hendrickx*	49
CHAPTER 4 Labour Law: The Medium and the Message *David Mangan*	63

Summary of Contents

CHAPTER 5
Changing the Rules of the Game or Rearranging the Deckchairs on the Titanic: 'Brexit' and the Future of European Social Policy
Alan C. Neal   75

PART II
Industrial Relations and Labour Law   97

CHAPTER 6
Trade Unions and the 'Gig Economy'
Michael Doherty   99

CHAPTER 7
Strikes in Essential Services under International Law
Monika Schlachter   113

CHAPTER 8
Collective Bargaining and the All-China Federation of Trade Unions: A Game Changer in Governing Chinese Workplaces?
Mimi Zou   125

PART III
Fairness and Rights   137

CHAPTER 9
What We Know about Equal Employment Opportunity Law after Fifty Years of Trying
Susan Bisom-Rapp   139

CHAPTER 10
Expansion of Temporary Agency Work Across Borders and the Difficulties for Workers Involved, in Particular in Light of Their Work-Life Balance
Mijke Houwerzijl   153

CHAPTER 11
Protection Against Dismissal in Contemporary Labour Law
Barbara Kresal   165

CHAPTER 12
Employee Data Protection in the Transnational Company
Achim Seifert   177

PART IV
Pathways of Labour Law   193

CHAPTER 13
Regulating Labour Relations and a Changing Society: The Pathways of a
Baltic Country – Estonia
Merle Erikson 195

CHAPTER 14
Main Directions of Change in French Industrial Relations and Labor Law
Jacques Rojot 207

CHAPTER 15
Tradition and Innovation in Labour Law: The Ambiguous Case of 'Agile
Working' in Italy
Michele Tiraboschi 225

Table of Contents

Notes on Contributors	v
Tributes to Marco Biagi and Roger Blanpain	xvii
Acknowledgements	xxi
Introduction *Frank Hendrickx & Valerio De Stefano*	1

PART I
Shifting Labour Law   9

CHAPTER 1
The Changing Face of Capital: The Withering of the Employment Relationship
in the Information Age
Janice R. Bellace   11
§1.01   Introduction   11
§1.02   The Rise of Industrial Society and Labour Law   12
        [A]   The Emergence of Labour Law   13
§1.03   The Decline of Industrial Employment   14
§1.04   Changes in the Environment Impacting Industrial Relations   15
        [A]   Globalization   16
        [B]   Change in the Nature of Work   18
        [C]   Rise of the Individual and the Decline of Group Identity   19
        [D]   The Implications of Industrial Relations and Labour Law   20
§1.05   Algorithms and the Need for a New Labour Law   21
        [A]   The Reality of the Worker   22
        [B]   Core Values as a Basis for a New Labour Law   23

Table of Contents

CHAPTER 2
Non-standard Employment Around the World: Regulatory Answers to Face Its Challenges
Janine Berg, Mariya Aleksynska, Valerio De Stefano & Martine Humblet   27
§2.01   Understanding Trends in NSE   28
    [A]   Transformations in the World of Work   28
§2.02   What Are Some of the Effects of NSE on Firms, Workers and Labour Markets?   30
    [A]   Workers   31
    [B]   Implications for Firms, Labour Markets and Society   34
§2.03   Addressing Decent Work Deficits in NSE   36
    [A]   Legislative Responses: Plugging Regulatory Gaps   37
    [B]   Strengthening Collective Bargaining   43
§2.04   Conclusions   44
Bibliography   45

CHAPTER 3
European Labour Law and the Millennium Shift: From Post to (Social) Pillar
Frank Hendrickx   49
§3.01   Introduction   49
§3.02   What Is the Pillar?   50
§3.03   Previous 'Posts' for Labour Law   52
    [A]   The 1972 Paris Declaration   52
    [B]   The 1989 Community Charter   53
    [C]   In Search for a Legal Beacon: The CFREU   54
§3.04   How the Game Was Changed   55
    [A]   The Green Paper on European Social Policy (1993)   56
    [B]   The White Paper on Growth, Competitiveness and Employment (1993)   56
    [C]   The White Paper on European Social Policy (1994)   58
    [D]   Labour Law Initiative   58
    [E]   Economically Acceptable Social Integration   59
    [F]   The Economic Governance Agenda of Labour Law   59
§3.05   Assessing the Pillar as a Game Changer   60

CHAPTER 4
Labour Law: The Medium and the Message
David Mangan   63
§4.01   Introduction   63
§4.02   Discerning the Message from the Medium   64
    [A]   The 'Gig Economy' as a Challenge to Orthodoxy   66
    [B]   Employment Status Redux   67
        [1]   The Difficulty in Discerning Who Is a 'Gig' Worker   67
        [2]   'Gig' Work as Repackaging Jobs   69

| §4.03 | Regulation by Algorithm | 72 |
| §4.04 | Conclusion | 74 |

CHAPTER 5
Changing the Rules of the Game or Rearranging the Deckchairs on the Titanic: 'Brexit' and the Future of European Social Policy
Alan C. Neal — 75

§5.01	Introduction	75
§5.02	European Social Policy and the 'Bad Boy of Europe'	77
§5.03	Changing the Rules of the Game? A European Union Perspective	85
§5.04	Changing the Rules of the Game? A UK 'Brexit' Perspective	90

PART II
Industrial Relations and Labour Law — 97

CHAPTER 6
Trade Unions and the 'Gig Economy'
Michael Doherty — 99

§6.01	Introduction	99
§6.02	Competition, Cartels, and Collective Rights	100
	[A] EU Competition Law and Collective Bargaining	101
	[B] Orchestral Manoeuvres in the Dark or Spring Variations? The FNV Kunsten Decision	102
	[C] An Irish Jig: Collective Bargaining Rights for the Self-Employed	103
§6.03	Trade Unions and 'Gig Workers'	105
	[A] The Political Response: The Pillar of Social Rights	105
	[B] The Legal Response: Knowledge Is Power	106
	[C] The Grassroots Response: Organising for the Gig Economy	108
§6.04	Concluding Remarks	109

CHAPTER 7
Strikes in Essential Services under International Law
Monika Schlachter — 113

§7.01	Introduction	113
§7.02	Essential Services and Privatization	114
§7.03	The International Labour Organisations' Approach	115
	[A] The Legal Basis and Its Interpretation	115
	[B] Public Service	117
	[C] Essential Services in the Strict Sense of the Term	118
	[D] Forms of Restrictions That May Be Justified	119
	[E] Compensatory Guarantees for Workers	121
§7.04	Consequences for Balancing the Interests at National Level	122
§7.05	Conclusion	124

Table of Contents

CHAPTER 8
Collective Bargaining and the All-China Federation of Trade Unions: A Game Changer in Governing Chinese Workplaces?
Mimi Zou 125
§8.01 Introduction 125
§8.02 The ACFTU and the Party-State 126
§8.03 A Game Changer for Collective Bargaining? 128
    [A] National-Level Laws and Policies 128
    [B] Localised Experiments in Collective Bargaining 130
§8.04 Remaining Challenges 132
    [A] Top-Down, Control-Driven Approach by the Party-State 132
    [B] Legal Protections for Workers Engaging in Industrial Action 133
    [C] Room for Labour NGOs? 134
§8.05 Conclusion 135

PART III
Fairness and Rights 137

CHAPTER 9
What We Know about Equal Employment Opportunity Law after Fifty Years of Trying
Susan Bisom-Rapp 139
§9.01 Introduction 139
§9.02 The Costs to Victims of Pursuing EEO Claims and the Refusal to Acknowledge Their Harms 142
§9.03 Narrowing the Reach of EEO Law by Preserving Managerial Prerogatives 145
§9.04 Missing Discrimination That Occurs over Time and Allowing Disadvantage to Cumulate 147
§9.05 Conclusion: What Is the Way Forward When the Game Has Changed? 149

CHAPTER 10
Expansion of Temporary Agency Work Across Borders and the Difficulties for Workers Involved, in Particular in Light of Their Work-Life Balance
Mijke Houwerzijl 153
§10.01 Introduction 153
§10.02 The Evolution of a Global and EU Regulatory Framework on TAW 155
§10.03 TAW in the Context of Cross-Border Service Provision Within the EU 157
§10.04 Two Types of Cross-Border Temporary Agency Workers 158
§10.05 Transnational Agency Workers and Their Children: Who Cares? 160
§10.06 Concluding Remarks 163

Table of Contents

CHAPTER 11
Protection Against Dismissal in Contemporary Labour Law
Barbara Kresal   165
§11.01   Introduction   165
§11.02   Historical Developments and Recent Trends   167
§11.03   Relevant International and European Legal Instruments   170
§11.04   Conclusion   173
Bibliography   174

CHAPTER 12
Employee Data Protection in the Transnational Company
Achim Seifert   177
§12.01   Cross-Border Data Processing in the Employment Context   177
§12.02   Data Processing Within the Internal Market   179
      [A]   Consent of Employees   180
      [B]   Article 6(1)(b) GDPR   181
§12.03   Transfer of Employee Personal Data to Third Countries   182
      [A]   Data Transfers on the Basis of an Adequacy Decision of the Commission   183
      [B]   Appropriate Safeguards   185
           [1]   Standard Contract Clauses   185
           [2]   Binding Corporate Rules   186
           [3]   Approved Codes of Conduct   187
           [4]   Certification   187
§12.04   Toward a Transnational Collective Bargaining on Employee Data Transfers to Third Countries?   188
      [A]   Employee Data Protection: A New Field for European Works Councils   188
      [B]   International Framework Agreements   191
§12.05   Concluding Remarks   192

PART IV
Pathways of Labour Law   193

CHAPTER 13
Regulating Labour Relations and a Changing Society: The Pathways of a Baltic Country – Estonia
Merle Erikson   195
§13.01   Introduction   195
§13.02   Transition to a Market Economy   196
§13.03   Accession to the EU   198
      [A]   The Formal Aspects of Transposing the EU Law   198
      [B]   The Substantive Issues of the Transposition of the EU Law   200

	[1]	General Remarks	200
	[2]	Equal Treatment of Employees	200
	[3]	Employee Involvement	202
§13.04	The Development of Technology		204
§13.05	Concluding Remarks		205

CHAPTER 14
Main Directions of Change in French Industrial Relations and Labor Law
Jacques Rojot 207
§14.01 Introduction 207
§14.02 The Process 212
    [A] The Ordinances 212
    [B] The Ordinances Constitute Step One in a Series of Important Subjects 213
    [C] An Innovative Consultative Process 213
§14.03 A Point of Controversy 213
§14.04 Outline of the Contents of the Reform 214
    [A] Collective Bargaining 215
    [B] Collective Bargaining and Social Dialogue in SMEs 217
    [C] Labor Courts 218
    [D] Collective Breach of Contracts of Employment by Mutual Agreement 220
    [E] Simplification of the System of Employee Representatives 221
    [F] Telework 222
    [G] Other Minor Technical Provisions 223
§14.03 In lieu of a Conclusion 223

CHAPTER 15
Tradition and Innovation in Labour Law: The Ambiguous Case of 'Agile Working' in Italy
Michele Tiraboschi 225
§15.01 Looking at New Forms of Telework: Drawing on Roger Blanpain's Insights 225
§15.02 The Regulation of Agile Working in Italy as an Indirect and Devious Response to Legal and Trade Union Limitations to Telework? 227
§15.03 Agile Working and Telework: Definitions and Legal Framework 230
§15.04 The Reasons for a New Provision on Agile Working 233
§15.05 The Relevance Attached to Employee Subordination in a Changing World of Work: An Unsolved Issue 238

Tributes to Marco Biagi and Roger Blanpain

From Biagi to Blanpain: Fifteen Years Between Two milestones

Marco Biagi (24 November 1950–19 March 2002)	Roger Blanpain (5 November 1932–11 October 2016)

On 11 October 2016, Roger Blanpain passed away, at the age of 83. Soon after his death, the scholarly community realized that one of the major actors in labour law would be no more. From the academic scenery, somebody disappeared who had a huge impact on academic life and labour law scholarship. For this reason, Blanpain's passing away could be seen as a milestone. It also brings us to the life and death of Marco Biagi, his legacy and the role that different personalities have played over many years. It is thus appropriate to commemorate these two eminent scholars in one single tribute.

Quite a few decades ago, some scholars started working in close cooperation. The core group consisted of Alan Neal, Janice Bellace, Tadashi Hanami, Csilla Kollonay-Lehoczki, Jacques Rojot, Tiziano Treu and Manfred Weiss, led and inspired by two giants in our field whom we commemorate today: Marco Biagi and Roger Blanpain.

The group shared a common perspective, emphasizing the close link between labour law and industrial relations and focusing on law in action instead of law in books. This also is meant to be the spirit for the conference, "Game Changers in Labour Law: Shaping the Future of Work", in Leuven, Belgium where we discuss whether and in what way the labour law of the future will have to change in view of changed realities.

Commemorating the two protagonists of our group, we would like to say a few words first about our dear friend Marco Biagi who was assassinated in his home town Bologna by the Red Brigades on 19 March 2002 at the young age of 51.

Marco taught labour law in several Italian universities, starting at the University of Bologna, Italy via the universities of Pisa, Calabria, and Ferrara, ending up as professor of Italian and Comparative Labour Law and Industrial Relations at the University of Modena, Italy. Since 1986 he also was adjunct professor of Comparative Industrial Relations at the Dickinson College and member of the Academic Council of the John Hopkins University, Bologna Center, a true international figure.

Marco's merits in promoting the international and comparative perspective of labour law are extraordinary. This not only refers to his many publications but also and in particular to his efforts in establishing a forum for international scholarly exchange, first in Bologna and later on in Modena. Already in the eighties of the last century, he organized international seminars on comparative labour law and industrial relations at the John Hopkins University, United States and in the nineties the annual summer school on the same topic. Thereby, Bologna became a centre of international scholarly debate not only for scholars but also for many young researchers from all over the world. Later on he became the organizer of the famous conferences in Modena where Marco succeeded to not only stimulate scholarly debates on all kind of topics of comparative labour law and industrial relations but also integrate in these debates practitioners: trade unionists, business people, and politicians. And we should add that all these events were impressive not only because of their intellectual quality but also because of Marco's outstanding Italian hospitality.

Marco was a dedicated European. His contribution to the promotion of European labour law barely can be overestimated. Again this is not only shown by his many publications in this area but also by his efforts to directly influence the development of European labour law and the structure of the European labour market. In 1997, Marco was appointed as a representative of the Italian Government to the Committee for the employment and the labour market, and in 1999, he became the Vice President of the committee. His latest book, *Quality of Work and Employee Involvement in Europe*, published in 2002 by Kluwer, is somehow an account of his eminent task in this committee.

Marco, of course, was not only a promoter of labour law and industrial relations in a comparative and European perspective but also and foremost a leading figure in this field in the Italian context. And again not only his scholarly work in a narrow sense is characteristic for his approach but his involvement in shaping reality. He became President of the Italian Industrial Relations Research Association in 1994 and was appointed from 1995 as a special advisor to the Minister of Labour, Tiziano Treu, later on serving in the same capacity to Tiziano's successors. He developed a far-reaching reform agenda which even after his death led to legislative amendments bearing his name. It was this reform activity which provoked his cruel assassination. He died for his conviction.

The Fondazione Marco Biagi which has been founded in his honour in Modena promotes research in continuation of Marco's approach. And every year an international conference is held in commemoration of Marco, dealing with challenges for labour law and industrial relations. Thereby, Marco's legacy is kept alive every year shared not only by established scholars but also by an ever-increasing number of younger researchers from all over the world.

When we turn to Roger Blanpain, many things that we mentioned about Marco Biagi will come back, but of course, with each having had his own pathway.

Roger Blanpain was a living legend. Born in Belgium on 5 November 1932, he studied Law at the University of Leuven, Belgium. In this university, he obtained his doctoral degree in Law in 1956. In 1957, he obtained a Master of Arts degree from Columbia University, New York. In 1961, Blanpain became assistant and later professor at the Law Faculty of the University of Leuven where he held the chair in labour law until his retirement in 1998. For him, becoming an emeritus professor was not the end of his career, but the start of a new one. He continued teaching for many years at the Law Faculty of the University of Tilburg in the Netherlands, did not stop writing and stayed active in academic conferences and the wider media.

During his academic career, Blanpain took up various functions in Belgian academia and became dean of the law faculty, member of the Board of Directors of the University of Leuven, member of the Royal Academy of Arts and Sciences, and president of the Leuven law alumni-society. He also took up the presidency of the Belgian Association for Labour Relations for many years.

Just like has been said for Marco Biagi, Roger Blanpain studied labour law in a multi-dimensional way. His work had a strong international and comparative approach since the very beginning. Furthermore, he understood the study of labour law and industrial relations as one and the same academic undertaking.

Among Blanpain's well-known publications can be mentioned the *International Encyclopaedia of Laws*, a worldwide series of monographs that started with 'Labour Law and Industrial Relations' in the 1970s. Another reference work is his *Comparative Labour Law and Industrial Relations in Industrialized Market Economies*. We also know the many revised versions of his book *European Labour Law*.

Roger Blanpain witnessed and triggered the birth and the early years of international academic communities. He stood at the foundation of networks and later became president of the International Society for Labour Law and Social Security Law and of the International Industrial Relations Association (IIRA), now the International Labour and Employment Relations Association (ILERA). He was a visiting professor at various prestigious universities around the world.

Just like Marco Biagi, Blanpain was a scholar who saw his role much larger than the academic world. He had a strong sense of responsibility and wanted his ideas to have an impact on society. He took the step to politics in the 1980s. He became a Belgian senator between 1987 and 1989. However, the combination of political life and academic freedom was difficult and he left politics quite soon. Nevertheless, he managed to play a role in societal debate, by publications reaching out to a wider public and numerous media performances. He became a public figure, really putting weight on social questions. He strived for the abolition, in Belgian employment contract legislation, of the distinction between white-collar and blue-collar workers (a distinction found unconstitutional by the Belgian Constitutional Court in 2011), he took initiatives to have a smoking ban in workplaces, including restaurants and cafés, and he openly defended the rights of sportspeople and athletes. Blanpain's death was a national news in Belgium, and the media noted him as a professor who had reached than the average politician.

Looking back at the passing away of both Marco Biagi (2002) and Roger Blanpain (2017) and the timeframes in which it happened, we can really see to milestones. In the period of fifteen years separating the two moments, many things have happened. We have increased globalization, new technologies changing our societies and workplaces, migration and the multicultural question, issues of safety and security, many challenges in the European Union as well in world politics. We are sure that both Marco Biagi and Roger Blanpain would still have played their respective roles in guiding and discussing these developments.

It also leaves us with a great responsibility with confidence when looking ahead. Our labour law community is still there, growing and renewing, and young and old are now teaming up. We will continue the work that has been started by the early group of scholars, the core group we mentioned earlier, the pioneers. The spirit remains the same: we shared a common perspective. We want to know what is going, follow international developments, share our ideas and bring together people. Working together in a good spirit of cooperation, studying the law in books and the law in action, we foster the debate trying to give answers, using the light of the foundational goals and the great history and legacies of labour law and industrial relations.

Frank Hendrickx & Manfred Weiss

Acknowledgements

For this initiative, we are indebted to:
Manfred Weiss, Alan Neal, Jacques Rojot

Introduction

Frank Hendrickx & Valerio De Stefano

This volume aims to commemorate the late Emeritus Professor Roger Blanpain (°5 November 1932–†11 October 2016) by bringing together international scholars in setting up the 100th Bulletin of Comparative Labour Relations, a series started under his initiative in the 1970s. The scholars were brought together during an international conference organised by the Institute for Labour Law at the University of Leuven (Belgium) on 3 and 4 November 2017. This volume collects the papers presented at this conference.

As a professor of labour law at the University of Leuven (Belgium) and as one of the founding fathers of various international communities and networks, Roger Blanpain was a real pioneer. He believed very strongly in studying labour law in an international and comparative perspective and in close connection with the broader field of industrial relations. Blanpain was also a reformer, and he continuously searched for key challenges in the world of work and looked as far as possible into the future, engaging in critical reflection and rethinking the design of labour law. Based on his way of working, and together with his time-fellows, he laid the basis of how we approach and study labour law today. Taking it all together, Roger Blanpain has really been a 'game changer'.

It is in this spirit that this volume is looking to deal with 'game changers' in labour law. This means that the aim is to examine evolutions, concepts, ideas or new challenges that we identify as having (had) a major impact on the way how we (have to) understand and approach labour law. While seeking to identify the main game changers in labour law, we are looking for a better insight into problems and challenges and, where possible, we explore new pathways and answers, which may help to understand and shape the future of work.

For the organisation of the discussion, this volume has been divided into four main parts.

Part I looks into the main trends and shifts in the world of work and their interaction with approaches to labour law over time.

Janice Bellace starts with an overview of how the world of work and industrial relations have evolved over the years and by indicating key factors of change for labour law. She does this against the outlook of current challenges, including populations that perceive the outlook of the future as threatening for their jobs and their lifestyle. In making the analysis over time, Bellace points at three major changes: globalisation, changes in the way of working and the rise of the individual. These factors pose not only challenges for governments but also for trade unions. Important to note is that globalisation came together with trade liberalisation, as trade barriers are increasingly falling since 1995, with the creation of the World Trade Organisation. When Bellace discusses the new world of work, she also analyses the gig economy. Her point is that the problems arising from it are not new as – what Bellace calls – the 'basic economic fact' remains: capital buys labour and transfers risks to labour. Much of the work in the gig economy can be seen, according to Bellace, as the information age equivalent of industrial homework. In light of these developments, though, Bellace stresses the importance to make a vision of the future and to return to the basics and fundamental values. To the core values of labour law belong, in her view, economic security and health and safety at work. Bellace also mentions freedom of association. As in the gig economy, workers may find new ways of organising, Bellace suggests that organising workers cannot be locked into 'an industrial age view' of ILO Convention 87 on freedom of association and protection of the right to organise.

Janine Berg, Mariya Aleksynska, Valerio De Stefano and Martine Humblet draw insights from the recent ILO study on non-standard employment. New forms of work are on the rise as can be shown in the labour statistics. The International Labour Organisation has recognised these new forms of work, and the issue, from this perspective, is not to make all work standard but to make sure that all work is decent. Changes to new forms of work are explained by factors such as the rise of the service sector, globalisation, fragmentation of production and outsourcing. Also in this context, the authors refer to insecurities caused by new types of work. Temporary work, for example, does not often provide a 'transition' to the so-called permanent employment, although, if properly regulated, it may increase the chances of finding a regular job. Interestingly, not only the pure contractual forms of work are discussed, but attention is also paid to more traditional issues of labour law, such as working time (on-call work/zero-hours) and health and safety. It is clear that new forms of work also bring challenges in this field. The authors indicate how insecurity and poorer remuneration are the two key factors of non-standard employment. There is a repercussion between the type of job and a person's consumption and socialisation, including for example credit and housing possibilities. The relationship between work, decent work and daily life is well illustrated in this debate. The authors also pay attention to the policy responses and, in particular, to regulation. They point at the issue of thinking about proper regulation strategies, as they argue that some regulation might limit the rights and protection of non-standard workers. For the authors, it is clear that proper classification is needed, and they take note of the 'binary divide' between employment and self-employment as a basis for regulation. Not only the individual but also the collective aspects should be analysed, as the authors remind that possibilities for unionisation of non-standard workers should also be protected and promoted.

Introduction

Frank Hendrickx looks into the development of European labour law and pays attention to the European Pillar of Social Rights, adopted in 2017. He refers to the 'millennium shift', not one single moment but a game-changing time frame in which a new approach towards labour law took shape. Traditional understandings of labour law were confronted with an agenda of economic competitiveness and with the demands of supranational economic liberalisation. This shift resulted from policy responses to a complex reality of globalisation, new labour market realities and political challenges such as EU enlargement and Eurozone deepening. Hendrickx argues that the promise of creating an equally progressing economic and social Europe was reformulated – re-calibrated – by the Delors Commission in the 1990s. With regard to the Social Pillar, Hendrickx views it as a contribution to a renewed consensus on the relationship between economic development and social policies. It is seen as a positive message and it re-establishes the idea that social progress must also serve the purpose of fairness, and that European economic integration is subject to the respect of fundamental social rights.

David Mangan looks into changing patterns in the real world and how they have influenced labour law over time. A tool for discussing this is his phrase 'the medium is the message'. The idea is derived from communications theory where attention has also focused on technology through which 'gig' work relationships are conducted. Mangan points at the danger of overlooking what is really going on in labour law when looking into specific new phenomena. He therefore suggests to not just focus on 'regulating for the particular'. He looks into the issue of employment status and looks at how app-based work shapes and controls the scale and form of association in the personal work relationship.

Mangan puts forward how relevant it is to study the gig economy in the reality context and warns against the presumption that gig work is there mostly for workers really voluntarily involved in it and (or) receiving a supplementary income. In conceptualising gig work, he argues that it is closer to the idea of 'homework' or piece work where a worker is paid per item produced. That may be problematic as 'gig work renders the job more abstract insofar as it is packaged into tasks which are units of work, individually falling short of a job'. Furthermore, Mangan points at the emergence of algorithms in the workplace. He refers to the difficulties with algorithms and their design. In light of this, he implies the European Data Protection Regulation (GDPR) and, even in this light, raises questions on whether this instrument is up to making a proper response towards algorithms in the workplace.

Alan Neal reflects on the future of European social policy in light of the 'Brexit'. He draws a sketch of the evolution of European labour law and social policy and provides an outlook which is not very optimistic. In light of the challenge of bringing more harmony between the economic project and the social project, he describes the European Pillar of Social Rights as rather coming 'out of the blue' and 'with a remarkable speed'. It is indeed remarkable that while some argue for more Europe in the Union, there is our confrontation with a Brexit. However, this new European evolution may arise partly because of the emergence of anti-EU or populist movements in different countries in the European Union. Alan Neal also tries to look forward to see what would happen with labour and employment rights in the United Kingdom after exit day. Taken from this contribution, the question whether parts of the United Kingdom's 'floor of rights' for workers will remain, or will undergo an adjustment, seems to largely depend on domestic political will and capacity of the post-Brexit government. The question is also reversed. It remains to be seen what the impact of Brexit will be for the future of social policy at the level of the European Union.

Part II examines industrial relations and challenges in collective labour law.

Michael Doherty concentrates on the role of trade unions and the law in the gig economy. What soon emerges from his text is the intersection between collective bargaining rights and competition law. In a European context, there is case law of the Court of Justice of the European Union in this field. It seems that the issue does not only arise from the nature of collective bargaining, but also from the classification problem in labour law. Doherty shows that the issue of collective bargaining rights for freelancers has been the subject of controversy in Ireland. Legislative response there shows an interesting attempt to extend collective bargaining rights to vulnerable workers who do not fit in the classical definition of 'employee'. The Irish legislation clearly recognises that collective representation should not be denied to those who do not satisfy employee status.

Doherty refers to the European Social Pillar as a way to think further and improve rights in the gig economy. He would suggest that it requires European institutions to take a more cross-sectional mainstreaming approach and also pay attention to key labour rights in designing and realising connected policy areas, such as the 'digital single market' strategy. In other words, he argues that gig workers may be better protected when social pillar rights would be taken into account in all areas of law and policy in the European Union. Doherty would certainly think here about the intersection between market and social regulation.

Monika Schlachter looks into strikes in essential services in international law. She notes that strikes are not a necessary precondition for an effective system of collective bargaining. She nevertheless points at an important issue in or modernising economies, where more and more 'consumer' markets are at the core. When looking at 'essential services', not merely economic consequences for the undertaking are at stake but primarily the dependency of consumers on the provision of such services in practice, certainly in a world of further privatisation of formerly public services. This broader consumer interest in the right to strike discussion is certainly felt in public debates in different countries, where unions sometimes loose in the outside perception of their collective action. As Schlachter points out, it would be good to recall that collective bargaining without the possibility of collective action is only 'collective begging'.

Mimi Zou discusses collective bargaining in China. She describes China being in a transition to a market economy with 'Chinese characteristics' and argues that it has fundamentally transformed the foundations of its labour market and the relationship between state, labour, and capital. She shows that China has developed a formal regulatory framework for collective bargaining within a relatively short period of time. It showed an increase in the quantity of signed collective agreements. It has provided 'game-changing' opportunities for the ACFTU. In China, specific regional and rather experimental practices in collective bargaining practices emerged, which have led to

Introduction

certain interesting effects on wages and working conditions. There remain many challenges, including the outlook of top-down structures or, like in many other systems, the position of the right to take collective action. What is interesting is that, given the context and the proper characteristics of an industrial relations system, original strategies arise. For example, Mimi shows that labour NGOs have played an important role in labour dispute resolution and in network and capacity building in collective action in labour disputes. Whatever the sum may be, it is clear that collective bargaining is a growing issue in the developing Chinese economic context. This may already be game changing in itself.

Part III looks into major changes and patterns with regard to issues of fairness and rights.

Susan Bisom-Rapp discusses two issues that are very important for labour scholars, which is the law in action (versus the law in the books) and the principle of equal treatment. This exciting area of law is given a rather worrying outlook. Bisom-Rapp makes a review of equal opportunity law and its functioning in American society and her point is that the transformative potential of this law has been disabled over time. She argues that equality and inclusion are under assault. She points at certain problems in this area of law, including the 'managerialisation of civil rights law' and including the problem of missing the point of discrimination that occurs over time. In light of this, she argues for a life-course approach and to use a model of lifetime disadvantage, which she has proposed in former work. The change that Bisom-Rapp proposes is the construction of a comprehensive approach to regulation that takes account of vulnerability of people. The role of the state, she argues, is to promote the resilience of its people. States can do this by setting ground rules but also to monitor outcomes. So change should not be made in the margin. On the contrary, it should be radical.

Mijke Houwerzijl gives an account of the evolution of labour law towards the acceptance and regulation of temporary agency work. She makes an assessment of the role of temporary employment agencies in light of globalising and Europeanising labour markets. She shows that the (positive) correlation between regulation of agency work and its contribution to the performance of labour market has always been an issue in the debate. Houwerzijl also indicates the growing role of temporary agency work in facilitating transnational labour mobility. With this also come the concerns specific to moving – migrant – workers, such as the issue of equal treatment or the reconciliation of work and family life. She brings up the interesting idea to focus on 'bringing the work to the people instead of the people to the work'.

Barbara Kresal discusses a core issue of labour law, which is termination of the employment relationship. It is one of the key issues of the labour market and stands central in the globalisation and labour cost discourse. Kresal shows that employment termination is far from an outdated topic in contemporary labour law. Workers need secure and reasonably predictable employment engagements, perhaps now more than ever. However, she raises the issue that strong protection against dismissal may be a privilege for standard contracts and less available for rising and new forms of work or, what would be called, precarious work. Where this would often lead to arguments that the standard level of protection should be diminished in order to address labour market segmentation, Kresal suggests that it would be better to instead increase the protection offered to non-standard workers. She finally concludes that protection against termination of employment fulfils various essential functions and this includes a long-term life perspective and a human rights approach.

Achim Seifert focuses on cross-border processing of employee personal data within transnational companies or groups of companies. This issue becomes increasingly relevant in transnational companies. HR practices have discovered the possibilities of cloud computing, digital personnel files, skills inventories and so on, involving personal data processing of employees. Due to its nature, digital data can be processed globally, in cross-border context in the service chain. In the data protection context, the EU has adopted the well-known General Data Protection Regulation (GDPR). However, Seifert's argument is that the provisions of the GDPR on cross-border data processing are not sufficiently adapted to the employment context. They need to be supplemented by more specific rules on employee data protection. Moreover, he argues that transnational collective bargaining may fill the (legal protection) gap in the context of employee data protection in transnational business environments. In Europe, a role for the European Works Council is seen as an important option.

In **Part IV** attention is paid to developments and trends in labour law in representative national jurisdictions which have been the subject of reform.

Merle Erikson gives us an insight into the development of labour law in the Baltic countries. For a country like Estonia, which is studied in this contribution, the last decades have been quite revolutionary. Interestingly, Erikson not only refers to the transition of this country – and its legal system – to joining the European Union, but also to the changes in the world of work. She points out that the accession to the EU did not cause fundamental changes in the regulation of employment relations. It rather entailed the emergence of new topics, like the equal treatment of employees and the employee involvement. However, the biggest challenge facing Estonian labour law has been the technological development, impacting society and the world of work. This challenge seems to be the most difficult to deal with. In that sense, labour law challenges in Estonia are not different from what is happening in the rest of the European Union or wider on the globe.

Jacques Rojot discusses the reforms made to the French Labor Code in 2017. There is a clear attempt of the government to materially impact industrial relations in France. The reform of the French Labor code has gone through the technique of ordinances, based on a mandate given by the Parliament. However, not every reform seems a dramatic game changer. A major reform is probably the notion of representativeness of trade unions. In a low union-density country, the government has gone away from the traditional idea that representativeness would follow from affiliation with the five listed national union federations. The key to full representativeness and bargaining rights would be the audience resulting from the votes by employees in the elections of employee representatives. Another issue is the famous 'principle of favor', which has been severely modified. However, Rojot argues that this has never been a constitutionally or fundamentally anchored principle and interferences in this principle have been happening already since the late 1990s. Another change is that attempts are made to give the level of small and medium enterprises the same access to collective bargaining than the larger ones. Also at the level of individual employment law, there are some changes, but perhaps these are more technical. The industrial relations changes are clearly more important. Jacque Rojot makes an interesting point where he says that it might be the first time that government takes collective bargaining seriously as a general policy. He concludes that the real impact of the reform is in the hands of the social partners. As it often happens, it will depend on the laws in action how future industrial relations in France will be shaped for the future.

Michele Tiraboschi reminds us of the true historical function of labour law – safeguarding both employee protection and the employers' right to production – by offering a fascinating analysis of the evolution of remote work schemes. He focuses in particular on the Italian legislative landscape by giving a critical analysis of the new legislation on 'agile work', a remote work arrangement whereby work is performed in part on the employer's premises and in part remotely, without a fixed workstation. Tiraboschi looks closely at the new regulation and argues that the boundaries between agile work and traditional telework – a scheme that never actually got off the ground in Italy – are not easily identifiable. In his opinion, the obstacles that prevented telework from fully spreading in Italy were also left unaddressed. He also observes that the new regulation may be at odds with the EU directives on working time and occupational health and safety, which, in turn, may be in need of an update that takes into account technological and business evolution. The analysis of the Italian legislation on 'agile work' offers him the opportunity to discuss this evolution more broadly and to call for a general reflection on the current status of labour protection, which could be in need of an overhaul, to keep up with the historical functions of labour law.

The answer to the question what is – or has been – game changing in labour law is complex. What certainly stands in front is the changing world of work. Here, globalisation and technological development stand out. These factors are self-evidently mutually interdependent and interacting.

Patterns of change have influenced labour law, challenged its design and the way its regulation is perceived. The gig economy is certainly one of these challenges for labour law, where classic concepts come more under question. It also shows that labour law is not an isolated discipline but intersectional with economic or market law. This does not come as a surprise; it is, after all, a constant feature of labour law since its early days. It may bring us to the fact that some developments, indicated as radically new, are not necessarily triggering new questions. Some gig work is, in fact, comparable to home work or piece rated work and reminds of discussions from the late nineteenth and early twentieth century.

What also comes out is that policy responses are as crucial as the actual changes in the work reality. Not every technological evolution can, or should, be blocked. Liberalisation has come with globalisation, but the regulation of liberalisation remains a policy question. In different countries or areas of the world, the answers to evolutions are as much under discussion as the evolutions themselves. For example, we may look at minimum services in strike law differently, when confronted with consumer-driven markets; economic competitiveness may be important, but the social justice question within it is paramount; nor a business-modelled reasoning should be allowed to ignore the goals of equality law.

In a context of individualism and spread of new forms of work, industrial relations are under debate. But the contributions show that collective actors remain paramount. Unions may have to reinvent themselves or their methods. And we may have to look at the right to collective bargaining while thinking away from classic industrial patterns. Some reforms only make sense, or some labour law goals can only be achieved, if social partners are involved and forms of collective regulation are respected.

Roger Blanpain was the first to remind us that labour relations are power relations. Economic market forces are always around, and we have been reminded in some contributions about 'basic economic facts'. But we also have received emphasis on the importance of values. This also implies governance strategies, political will and the empowering of actors. Many contributions have reminded us of the fundamental values of labour law, the importance of creating economic security in societies, the need for equitable outcomes, for fairness, decent work and social justice. Even within times of change, these values are stable factors and stand as real cornerstones or 'pillars' of social rights.

We live in complex world and difficult times with enormous challenges are facing us. What is nevertheless very clear from this volume is that labour law can play a crucial role in our contemporary and future societies. What is also clear is that academia can help to understand, guide and shape the future of our societies, beginning with offering insights for shaping the future of work. We hope that this volume can be seen as a good contribution to this ambition.

PART I   Shifting Labour Law

CHAPTER 1
The Changing Face of Capital: The Withering of the Employment Relationship in the Information Age

Janice R. Bellace[*]

§1.01 INTRODUCTION

Our economy is at the point of a paradigm shift. Industrialization is over. Models from the Industrial Age are likely obsolete. We are firmly at the beginning of the Digital Age. In considering what are game changers in labour law, the first step is to identify how the game has changed.

Over the past five years, various articles have been written about the 'gig economy' and the problems this creates for labour law.[1] The issue normally is framed as one of employment; namely, that these workers do not fit the mould of traditional employees as erected by statutes and court decisions over the past century. As a result, they fall outside the perimeter of the area deemed employment and therefore do not benefit from the various protections of labour and social security law. There is a widespread distaste for this outcome because the claim that these persons are

---

[*] © Janice R. Bellace, 2017. This chapter was prepared at the International Conference in Commemoration of Roger Blanpain, 'Game Changers in Labour Law: Shaping the Future of Work', Institute for Labour Law, Law Faculty, University of Leuven, Belgium 3-4 November 2017.
1. Numerous articles could be cited. The Spring 2016 issue of the *Comparative Labor Law and Policy Journal* contained articles arising from a symposium on labour law and the gig economy that discussed various legal issues arising from non-standard work. See, e.g., Valerio De Stefano. Spring 2016. 'The Rise of the "Just-in-Time Workforce": On-Demand Work, Crowdwork, and Labor Protection in the "Gig Economy."' *Comparative Labor Law Journal & Policy Journal* 37.

independent contractors rings hollow.[2] The real problem may be that we are locked into a mode of analysis with its basis in the industrial era, and we are quickly leaving that behind. We are now in the information age and new modes of analysis need to emerge.

Yet, some things do not change and grasping that reality may enable us to consider how we can shape the future of work. Focusing on capital and labour, rather than employer and employee, may provide the path forward.

§1.02 THE RISE OF INDUSTRIAL SOCIETY AND LABOUR LAW

It is generally accepted that labour law arose as a reaction to industrialization. Often commentators point to the harsh conditions of factory life in the first stages of industrialization, with many of the early labour laws focused on working conditions. But the need for such laws arose from a paradigm shift. Before industrialization, the term 'employer' was basically unknown. Most persons who worked engaged in agricultural labour or worked as domestic servants. The face of capital was the owner. Although agricultural labourers and domestic servants might receive some cash compensation, their remuneration package was complex. Most lived on land and in housing that was the property of the owner. Workers may have paid some rent, but it did not equate with the market rate. The financial arrangement under which they lived in a house was tied to their work for the owner. In British English, the term 'tied cottage' graphically connotes this arrangement.

Those working on the lands or in the house of the owner did not have a 'contract of employment'. Rather, the owner set the rules. But the relationship between the owner and the worker was constrained by notions of status and of obligations to the other party. Generally, the relationship was expected to be of some considerable duration unless the worker broke the owner's rules. Much labour law scholarship looking back at early labour law cases focuses on the highly skilled worker, such as stone masons and carpenters who performed work or those who made and sold their own products, such as silversmiths and cordwainers. These, however, were the exceptional cases. The highly skilled were not in a long-term status relationship with an owner.[3] Typically, they performed specified work over a short term for a fee.

Industrialization, the harnessing of steam power leading to the establishment of factories, changed the way in which capital organized itself for the purpose of acquiring the necessary labour to make the products. The face of capital was now the employer.

---

2. The exact way in which the status of the worker is analysed depends on the legal system. For instance, in the US, there are only two choices: employee or independent contractor. In the UK, there are three choices: independent contractor, worker or employee. In November 2016, the UK government launched a review (the Taylor Review) to determine whether current legal categories are appropriate in light of modern employment practices.
3. The words used to describe these workers, such as 'journeyman' and 'master,' indicate the lack of a long-term relationship with an owner.

The immense difference was remuneration. Those who worked were paid wages – and nothing else. The employer felt no obligation to provide housing or food.[4] The reality was that employment was viewed as a cash-only transaction. There was no status relationship between employer and employee; only a contractual one.

The basic economic fact is that capital needs labour to make products and perform services. That had always been the case. Industrialization heightened workers' awareness that capital *buys* labour (a work-for-cash transaction). The market economy also drove the cost-cutting nature of capital in that capital buys no more labour than it needs, for no longer than it needs, and it shifts risk to labour where possible.

The implications of these drivers made industrial workers' lives in the early stages of industrialization much more insecure and unpredictable than those of earlier generations. An employer might offer only a few hours work a day or might demand fourteen hours work per day. Not even a day's employment was guaranteed, and dismissal could be instantaneous. There was no promise of employment tomorrow, let alone the following week. And, as workers came off the fields to the factories, the surplus of labour permitted employers to offer very low wages, often on a piece rate basis, which in turn caused workers to work very long hours in order to make enough to be able to afford housing and food. The risks inherent in manufacturing, such as the risk of delay from machinery malfunctioning or delays in receiving goods, or injury were all placed on the workers.

[A] The Emergence of Labour Law

It was the grim existence of workers who confronted harsh and dangerous working conditions that led the law to move from a master-servant orientation to an employer-employee orientation. In doing so, the law accepted that there no longer was a status relationship where certain obligations on both sides could be assumed. In its place, the law now saw a bargain whereby the employee agreed to work for the employer for a certain wage. But the contract of employment was not deemed to have any other enforceable promises unless they were expressly stated. Since factory workers individually usually had no bargaining power, the contract of employment served as legal backing for the workers' weak position. It was not until the latter half of the nineteenth century in Britain and Germany, and later in many other countries, that the legislature intervened, either to permit some form of collective action by workers or to stipulate certain minimum working conditions.

It is at this point that modern labour law emerges. Sir Otto Kahn-Freund in a series of lectures identified the purpose of labour law. He said its principal purpose was

---

4. Where the factory was located in some remote location, or in the case of mines, the employer might provide housing but usually the employer charged the workers for this housing. Also the employer set the rent (with the employees having no other rental options). It was not until the late nineteenth century that some companies, in an early manifestation of corporate social responsibility, decided to build decent, subsidized housing.

'to regulate, to support, and to restrain the power of management and the power of organised labour'.[5] In reading this, one must bear in mind that Kahn-Freund believed that there was inherent inequality in the bargaining relationship and he stressed that the primary force in labour relations is economic, pointing out that the law is secondary.[6] The critical point to bear in mind is that the bargaining relationship between capital and labour is inherently unequal because of economic forces. Thus, if one is to restrain the power of capital (exercised by management), one must understand what economic force is creating this power and what actions can usefully regulate or restrain that power. Throughout the twentieth century, many labour law scholars spoke of the 'employer' but in fact meant 'the modern company', and many assumed that national legislatures could regulate and restrain the inherent economic power of the company.

By the late twentieth century, these assumptions were being questioned in the face of the power of multinational corporations to avoid regulation simply by moving production to another country. But today, circumstances have changed to such an extent that the purpose of labour law itself demands re-examination because in 2018 we are not seeking to restrain the power of management, as much as the power of the platform (or more accurately, the power of capital as exercised by the platform).

§1.03 THE DECLINE OF INDUSTRIAL EMPLOYMENT

As demonstrated by recent elections in several advanced countries, many people perceive the outlook for the future to be threatening. Immigration as a threat to cultural identity may be one reason, but economic uncertainty is an over-riding concern in many countries. Average people know that their lifestyle depends on having a job, and preferably one with decent wages and working conditions and a modicum of security. Their anxiety, often based on anecdotal evidence, relates to the availability of such jobs. This anxiety is not unfounded. Central bankers have been perplexed by the failure of wages to rise even when unemployment levels are low. One highly respected institution has cited slack in the labour market as the explanation.[7] Commenting that country-level data appears to be understating involuntary part-time, the IMF also pointed to slow productivity growth.[8] The fact that the skill level of workers is not being fully utilized may explain the slow growth. This phenomenon does not jump out from the statistics because workers may be working full time, but at a job that does not call upon their skills. This is the barista-with-a-bachelor's-degree syndrome, where recent university graduates take a job that could be done by someone with much lower

---

5. Otto Kahn-Freund. *Labour and the Law* (London: Stevens and Sons, 1972). Page 5.
6. *Id.*, at 8.
7. International Monetary Fund (2017). *World Economic Outlook, October 2017. Seeking Sustainable Growth: Short-Term Recovery, Long-Term Challenges.* Chapter 2, pages 73–116.
8. *Id.*, at 90. The report notes that at the country level labour market slack, together with weak productivity growth and low inflation expectations are the main forces weighing on wage growth.

educational qualifications.[9] The sobering reality is that at the present time the supply of educated persons may be higher than the current demand in higher wage service industries.

This syndrome highlights another phenomenon. New information technologies have been eliminating middle-skill jobs. Studies on the long-term effects of new technologies automating mental work do not find across-the-board negative effects, but they do find larger effects on the wages of particular groups, such as middle-skilled workers.[10] The IMF analysis suggests that even low-skilled workers may have been negatively affected in that they seem to have experienced a larger decline in hours than other skill groups.[11]

This may be a transitional phase as societies move from the industrial era to the information age. Yet, a transitional stage may prove highly disruptive to democratic countries. Many of those displaced from their jobs by technology will find it difficult to secure employment. High-tech industries and industries now making greater use of information technology employ many fewer persons than conventional industrial firms. It may be necessary to raise the skill levels of many current workers or reskill them in new areas such as coding. This, however, will take substantial time and the success of the effort is far from guaranteed. Over the past fifty years, an era of deindustrialization, advanced countries have not demonstrated an ability to reskill workers who lose their jobs due to offshoring of production or technological innovation.

§1.04 CHANGES IN THE ENVIRONMENT IMPACTING INDUSTRIAL RELATIONS

Scholars in strategic management look at companies that were once successful and ask why they failed. Often the answer is that top management failed to spot a significant change in the external environment early enough to adapt. When they finally realized the seriousness of the threat, it was too late. That can apply to a country's legislators and to unions. For they also must ask what has changed, and to such an extent, that the actors in the industrial relations system must adopt new positions and strategies.

Looking at the past fifty years, there have been three major changes that have had an enormous impact on industrial relations systems: (1) globalization, (2) changes in the way most people work and (3) the rise of the individual and the decline of group identity. All three have one thing in common: technological innovation was the initial impetus for a series of developments.

---

9. Robert G. Valletta. 'Recent Flattening in the Higher Education Wage Premium: Polarization, Skill Downgrading, or Both?' NBER Working Paper 22935. Cambridge, MA: National Bureau of Economic Research, 2016.
10. David H. Autor and David Dorn. 2013. 'The Growth of Low-Skill Services Jobs and the Polarization of the US Labor Market'. *American Economic Review* 103 (5): 1553–1597.
11. International Monetary Fund, *supra* n. 7 at 92. The IMF notes that country level data by sector on hours by skill level are not readily available. It may be that there has been a decline in one sector, such as retail, but not in another, such as nursing homes/personal care.

[A] Globalization

Much has been written about globalization and its impact on industrial relations. Often, those discussing this concentrate on the inadequacy of national level bargaining to control the parameters within which employers and labour work. Forty years ago, some lamented that multinational companies were more powerful than the sovereign state, and attention was directed to supranational responses.[12] Within the past twenty years, attention has turned to global supply chains, wherein a company in an advanced economy buys materials or a finished product from an independently owned supplier company in a developing country where wages and labour conditions are often far inferior to that of the purchaser company. Human rights groups have argued that the purchaser company has the ability to require that the supplier company abide by internationally recognized labour standards and these should be included in contracts. This has led to the development of company codes of conduct, and in turn, since 2000 there has been increasing acceptance for the notion that companies, on their own, should comply with international labour standards in all their activities.[13]

There has been less discussion of the sobering implications for unions. A fundamental principle of union organization indicates the magnitude of the challenge. The great American labour economist, John R. Commons of the University of Wisconsin, famously remarked: 'a union must organize the length and breadth of the market'. In other words, a union must be able to take the price of labour out of competition, and it can only do that if it can organize all the workers making the product that will be sold in the same market. Commons realized that employers compete with each other, and if a company is selling its product in the same market at a higher price than the same product made by other companies, it will be in trouble. It will seek to lower its price, and one easy way to do this is to slash labour costs.

The corollary is also true: a union which has organized all the workers producing the same product for the same market can seek to raise wages; in other words, it can impose higher labour costs on employers. If all the employers belong to the same employers' association or if there is strong pattern bargaining, collective bargaining can achieve this result. Even if the union has not managed to persuade all employers making the product to sign a collective agreement, the legislature can compel all

---

12. Examples would be the OECD Guidelines for Multinational Enterprises, adopted in 1976 and most recently revised in May 2011, and the ILO'S Tripartite Principles Concerning Transnational Enterprises and Social Policy. The latter was adopted by the Governing Body of the International Labour Office at its 204th Session in November 1977, and was amended at its 279th Session in November 2000. http://www.ilo.org/wcmsp5/groups/public/@ed_emp/@emp_ent/documents/publication/wcms_101234.pdf.
13. The UN Global Compact was first announced by UN Secretary General Kofi Annan in a speech to the World Economic Forum in January 1999. It was launched in July 2000. http://www.unglobalcompact.org/. The UN Global Compact is described as 'a strategic policy initiative for businesses that are committed to aligning their operations and strategies with ten universally accepted principles' in relation to human rights, labour, the environment and an anti-corruption stance. Four of the ten principles specifically related to labour standards.

employers to abide by the terms of the collective agreement through extension of the collective agreement to non-signatory employers.[14]

Traditional industrial relations systems in many European countries were developed on the assumption that unions could impose higher labour costs on employers. National labour law regimes regulated and, in fact supported, national industrial relations systems built on that assumption. The most striking example is extension of collective agreements to non-signatory employers in an industry. In effect, the government agreed with unions and employers' associations that employers in the same country making the same product should not be allowed to compete on the basis of lower labour costs.

A problem immediately arises if companies can sell in the same market but produce in another country. A national legislature can only extend a collective agreement to employers within the boundaries of the country. From the moment the Treaty of Rome was signed there was an implicit threat to traditional industrial relations systems, but it was not widely recognized for more than thirty years.[15]

The greater threat arose from globalization. Technological advances in telecommunications and the increasing use of English as a business language made it feasible for North American and European companies easily to engage in business dealings with suppliers in faraway countries. The Uruguay Round of talks led to more bilateral trade treaties, and it became possible for products destined for the European market to be made in Asia where labour costs were a mere fraction of those in Europe. Barriers fell in 1995 when the World Trade Organization was created, with the mission of liberalizing international trade.

Since 1995, Commons' observation and its corollary have been proved correct. Unions in advanced countries cannot impose higher labour costs if they have not organized all the workers making the products that will be sold in their market. The response of employers, as they endeavour to remain price competitive, varies depending on the national context. Through employers' associations, there may be efforts to gain increased flexibility in the way labour is utilized, such as in Germany. There may be efforts to relax labour legislation, with the goal of permitting the employment of persons on more flexible terms (thus leading to an increase in precarious employment). Or, employers may pursue a strategy of operating without unions or being subject to a collective agreement, such as in the US and the UK.

---

14. This legal technique found in some European countries with a civil law system is completely unknown in common law countries. It may explain why unions in common law countries must devote significant resources in organizing workers at every company in the industry.
15. For the first twenty years of the EU's existence, the wage differences between the Member States were not substantial, and often higher wage countries had higher productivity, and thus could remain competitive. After the fall of the Berlin Wall, with the prospect of the entry into the EU of low wage countries from Eastern Europe, those in higher wage countries recognized the threat this posed.

[B] Change in the Nature of Work

Many of today's labour laws date back decades. They were written in the industrial age, and legislators often thought of industrial workers when the word 'worker' was used. The laws usually did apply to office workers and those who worked in shops, but the laws were designed around notions of industrial work and unions of factory workers. Today in most advanced market economies, only a minority of workers work in factories, and even office work has changed tremendously. Epochal change has occurred. The development of the computer at the end of World War II and the invention of the microprocessor in the early 1970s mark the beginning of the information age.

In 1974, Intel produced the first 8-bit microprocessor, the Intel 8080, which fuelled the development of the personal computer. The world of work was about to change from the factory floor to office suites. Contemporary commentary predicted what we have witnessed; namely, that the introduction of microprocessors would lead to various ways of automating manual work and even skilled work (e.g., by the use of CAD/CAM). Factories that once employed thousands now employed a couple hundred to produce the same amount.

First used in a retail setting in 1974, the barcode scanner was rapidly adopted by supermarket companies who saw that it could easily and cheaply identify a product (through the UPC code) and be used to track the movement of the product. Routine clerical jobs where people identified, tracked and tallied items disappeared.

The PC gained ascendancy over the mainframe computer not only when more powerful microprocessors were developed, but when it became possible for the average office worker to use them. The development of the World Wide Web in the early 1990s vastly sped up the introduction of computerized working methods in offices. Typists and secretaries who knew shorthand disappeared. Routine clerical jobs, such as file clerk, were eliminated. This was hastened by the widespread introduction of the World Wide Web to desktop computer users which vastly eased the individual's interface with computer programs.

These are only four of the major technological innovations of the past forty years that have affected employment. But they are sufficient to reveal a massive shift in the way people work. Instead of many people performing repetitive rote tasks, manual or mental, fewer people are producing the same amount of products or services through greater use of their minds and by interacting with computers.

It is not surprising that companies have reacted by paying much more attention to the individuals doing these jobs. Rather than workers seeming all of a sameness, with one worker interchangeable with another and another available if someone quit or was dismissed, the intelligence and engagement of individuals became important. With the nature of work changing, companies needed a new type of worker, one who exercised judgment, who could take ownership of tasks and who could work in teams. Seen in this light, the rise of human resource management and the decline of traditional industrial relations as managerial functions were inevitable.

[C] Rise of the Individual and the Decline of Group Identity

In the 1950s and 1960s, manual workers represented the bulk of union membership in most North American and European countries. Most of these workers would readily have identified themselves as working class and, as such, would have seen themselves as having different interests than the managerial or ownership classes in society. Most would have worked in establishments (such as factories, mines and docks) employing hundreds of people at one workplace. Typically they would live near where they worked, in working-class areas of a town or city. Often they socialized together in the local café or pub. Most importantly, they would have realized that as individuals they had no bargaining power, and that to the company they did not matter as individuals since workers were seen as much the same, and as such, interchangeable. These were natural supporters of unions and left-of-centre political parties.[16]

Over the past forty years, the change in the nature of how work is performed and the change in companies' expectations of what they expect of workers have had an effect on workers themselves, particularly those born after the 1970s. These are the persons born into smaller families (due to the birth control pill) and raised with an expectation of more individualized treatment. While still in school, they were introduced to technology and became comfortable with computers. As a generation, they are better educated than their parents and have higher career expectations. Many encountered a more difficult labour market, as thousands of well paying, unionized, full time, secure jobs were lost. But those who did find employment often found a job where they were treated as an individual and given a certain amount of autonomy in deciding how to perform their assigned tasks.

The result is a prime working age generation that no longer sees itself as working class, a generation that lives in scattered lower middle-class areas, and spends its leisure time playing video games, interacting with friends and family on Facebook and surfing the Web. It is a trend that sociologists have documented, perhaps most memorably in the 2000 book, *Bowling Alone*,[17] where Robert Putnam, drawing on social survey data for the prior twenty-five years, showed how Americans had become increasingly disconnected from family, friends, neighbours and social structures, whether the church, recreation clubs, political parties, unions or team sports (such as bowling leagues). Putnam observed that disconnected persons are much less likely to unite in communities for any purpose, even one which would be of direct benefit.

---

16. But it should be noted that even then, union support depended on a person's self-perception of identity and self-interest. Unions found it difficult to organize persons who had less attachment to the labour market, such as part-time female employees, or those working in small establishments, such as family-owned retail shops.
17. Robert D. Putnam, *Bowling Alone: The Collapse and Revival of American Community* (New York: Simon & Schuster, 2000). Putnam is a professor of government at Harvard University. The title of the book refers to an American recreational activity, vaguely like boules or bocce. An individual throws a heavy ball down a lane and attempts to knock down as many 'pins' as possible. As an activity, individuals usually play with others. In the years following World War II, it was common for people to form teams, and then for teams to join leagues. This required a high degree of social organization, with individuals willing to commit significant time simply to heighten group social activity.

Admittedly Putnam studied only the US, and the US may be an extreme case. It is more likely, however, that the US is further along the curve of social disorganization than European countries. Moreover, Putnam's study occurred before the advent of the smartphone and social media,[18] developments which likely have intensified the trends Putnam identified.

The change, from workers having strong group identity to workers seeing themselves as individuals, is unlikely to change. The millennial generation, called 'digital natives,' now entering the labour market is the one that has known technology from birth. Enthusiastic adopters of social media, they live (as Mark Zuckerman exhorts) part of their life online. They may feel part of an online community but it is not a community tied to geographic location or work or workplace communities.

[D] The Implications of Industrial Relations and Labour Law

These three factors – globalization, the change in the way most people work and the rise of the individual and the decline of group identity – did not occur in isolation. They occurred simultaneously, and one factor may have reinforced and heightened the impact of another factor. Formed in the late nineteenth and early twentieth century, many industrial relations systems relied on collective bargaining as a major way of promoting workers' interests. Most labour law frameworks related to the industrial relations system in the country and usually relied on collective bargaining to set wage rates for most workers.

In the private sector,[19] in those industries exposed to foreign competition or making use of outsourcing, unions effectively lost the ability to strike to improve the terms of employment. Statistics on union density reveal the negative impact, although there are significant differences among the advanced market economies,[20] due in part to the coordination of policy choices by governments, employers and unions.[21]

These changes since 1990 have overturned the assumptions upon which collective bargaining rests; namely, that workers can achieve bargaining power by joining together. As the Nobel Prize-winning economist Joseph E. Stiglitz has noted, 'the dearth of jobs and the asymmetries of globalization have created competition for jobs in which workers have lost and the owners of capital have won'.[22]

In the new digital economy, even if workers wanted to form unions and bargain collectively, it is difficult to see how they could strike when the platform and algorithms

---

18. Facebook was launched in the US in 2004. Apple marketed the first iPhone in 2007.
19. For the most part, globalization had an impact only on the private sector. In most countries, the public sector does not face the pressure of domestic competition, let alone with foreign competition.
20. Union Density in OECD countries 1960-2010. http://www.oecd.org/document/34/0,3746,en_2649_33927_40917154_1_1_1_1,00.html.
21. For a persuasive explanatory analytic framework, see Peter A. Hall and David Soskice (eds), *Varieties of Capitalism. The Institutional Foundations of Comparative Advantage*. (Oxford: Oxford University Press, 2001).
22. Joseph E. Stiglitz, *The Price of Inequality* (New York: W.W. Norton & Co., 2012).

operate automatically.²³ Thus, the conventional approach to improving terms and conditions of employment through collective bargaining simply no longer applies.

Other approaches are also failing. In the twentieth century, the traditional 'employer' paid for a period of time such as a day or a week or a month at the workplace – not for the work done. The 'employer' paid wages/salary, and other benefits, such as private pension and private health insurance. Moreover, to guarantee workers a minimum level of financial security, the State imposed obligations on 'employers' to include on top of regular pay additions such as maternity pay, holiday pay, redundancy pay and social security contribution. Depending on the country, these additional payments can add substantially to the cost of labour. But in the twenty-first century, capital is seeking to return to basics: to pay only for the work done – nothing more. Labour law's narrow focus on employee status as the hook on which to hang these obligations has incentivized companies to devise ways to utilize labour without creating an employment relationship.²⁴

§1.05 ALGORITHMS AND THE NEED FOR A NEW LABOUR LAW

The game changer in the last few years has been the rapid introduction of 'algorithms' in business. In mathematics, an algorithm is a step-by-step procedure for calculations. It is a method used by computer programmers for writing software. With the development of computers capable of handling vast amounts of data (often called 'big data') especially in real time, algorithms became a practical business tool for calculation, data processing and automated reasoning. This is artificial intelligence (AI), whereby a computer mimics the way humans think and make decisions. AI can be applied to machines themselves whereby machines access data relating to their results to learn from and improve on their own experience without being programmed by a person. Companies strive to develop a platform that permits software to be run on their hardware and which permits specialized software applications containing algorithms to run. This technological development has made possible the modern gig economy whereby someone desiring a service can be connected with a person willing to perform the service with both user and performer connecting through a platform driven by AI.

This has led to a paradigm shift in the orientation of capital. Once capital wore the face of the owner when it utilized labour; later it wore the face of the employer when it utilized labour. Today capital has begun to wear the face of 'the platform' when it utilizes labour.

Today a company seeking to make money by matching providers of service with the end users of a service no longer needs a human resources department that

---

23. They could attempt to disengage them but this would be act of sabotage which is unlawful in nearly all countries.
24. David Weill, *The Fissured Workplace: Why Work Became So Bad for So Many and What Can Be Done to Improve It* (Cambridge, MA: Harvard University Press, 2014). Weill examines trends in the American workplace and notes a fundamental restructuring that is not due to efficient production concerns but rather to a desire to escape directly employing persons. He takes the position that the misclassification of employees, by treating them as independent contractors instead of employees, pervades the modern 'fissured workplace'.

advertises jobs, screens applicants and selects from among them. Instead a description of the services wanted, and an application form is placed online. An algorithm selects who will be offered a position. Once selected, the worker has no supervisor and is subject to no performance reviews. An algorithm monitors the demand for the service and the providers willing to meet that demand at any given moment, and it sets the price the end user will pay. The providers know of work opportunities through an app. They are instructed on what to do (where to go) by the app. Their performance is rated by the end users through an app. The provider may be de-selected by the platform based on this ratings which are analysed by an algorithm.

Depending on the nature of the service, there is likely to be no workplace provided by the company. Workers may use their own car or bicycle, or their own computer, and often may work from home. The company, therefore, does not have the cost of providing a workplace or equipment nor does it have a responsibility for health and safety conditions.

This type of work, managed by an algorithm, usually does not require set working hours. Compensation is related to the unit of work performed (an Uber ride, a Grubhub food delivery, a task on Amazon Mechanical Turk). It is the work done on a piece rate basis, often with workers competing to secure the opportunity on a crowdsourcing basis. This in itself is acceptable, but the problem arises in determining whether working hours are excessive or unpredictable. Moreover, the work opportunities offered may be inadequate to provide the worker with minimum economic security.

Despite the protestations of some gig economy entrepreneurs, these are not new problems. This huge move into a radically new economy has re-surfaced patterns from a century ago – that capital buys labour, not paying for more than it needs, and capital transfers risk to labour. Noting that a 'gig economy' is not new, one commentator has termed its modern-day manifestation the 'tech enabled gig economy.'[25] It can also be viewed as the information age equivalent of industrial homework which was often banned not because it was dangerous but because there was no way to enforce minimum wage, overtime and child labour laws.[26]

[A] The Reality of the Worker

In the transitional phase of the digital economy, a first task is to dismantle the outmoded distinction between an independent contractor (contract for services) and an employee (contract of service). Presented with a challenge by a working person, such as an Uber driver, to his status as an independent contractor, courts often look at the degree of subordination or direct control. The quandary that arises is that this

---

25. Dubal, V.B., 2017. 'Winning the Battle, Losing the War?: Assessing the Impact of Misclassification Litigation on Workers in the Gig Economy', *Wisconsin Law Review* 739–802, 2017, no. 4.
26. The legislative prohibition of industrial homework typically applied in those industries, such as the garment industry, which utilized women working at home to perform specific non-skilled tasks, such as sewing buttons on a garment. This work could be done in factories but the company's costs were lower if people worked at home using their own equipment.

working person often has much more flexibility and discretion as to whether to work than an employee, at least an industrial age employee, has. The starting point should be whether the working person meets the criteria of an independent contractor. In this regard, the Court of Justice of the European Union (CJEU) in a case most definitely not from the gig economy,[27] succinctly listed three criteria for deciding whether the individual is a worker or a self-employed person.[28] The CJEU stated that a self-employed person works:

- outside any relationship of subordination concerning the choice of the economic activity, working conditions and conditions of remuneration;
- under that person's own responsibility; and
- in return for remuneration paid to that person directly and in full.

This is a persuasive common sense approach that would quickly dispel any notion that persons such as Uber drivers or Grubhub delivery persons are self-employed persons or independent contractors. It could be applied in most countries without any changes in labour law, but it would provoke discussion in some countries regarding the additional payment obligations imposed on companies because of the worker-employee distinction.[29] The persuasiveness of the CJEU approach is that it accords with the reality that Uber drivers are not capital, they are labour. The question then becomes one of how labour law responds to this reality in the information age.

[B] Core Values as a Basis for a New Labour Law

Although in certain countries litigation has been used to obtain worker or employee status for those working in the gig economy, this is likely only a stopgap measure in a time of transition. Surveying recent US cases and the workers' reactions, one commentator has concluded that litigation victories for employee rights in the gig economy are

---

27. Judgment of the Court of 20 November 2001. *Aldona Malgorzata Jany and Others v. Staatssecretaris van Justitie*. Case C-268/99. This decision of the CJEU combined four cases. *Jany* focused on the issue of whether a prostitute from an EU Eastern European Member State seeking the right of entry into the Netherlands had such a right based on the right to establish services.
28. This *Jany* case was not seen as a labour law case because it arose mainly in connection with internal migration within the EU, but the labour issue had to be decided since the provisions in the EU association agreements 'on the movement of workers are not as "generous" as those on the freedom of establishment of self-employed persons'. Ronald Van Ooik, 'Freedom of Movement of Self-Employed Persons and the Europe Agreements Comments on Case C-63/99, *Gloszczuk*; Case C-235/99, *Kondova*; Case C-257/99, *Barkoci and Malik* (judgments of 27 September 2001); and Case C-268/99, *Jany* (judgment of 20 November 2001).' *European Journal of Migration and Law* 4: 377–393, at 388 (2002).
29. For instance, in the UK a person can be deemed a 'worker' and entitled to some protections (such as paid holidays and sick pay) but not the full benefits of being deemed an employee (for instance protection against unfair dismissal or consultation rights with regard to redundancies). Unlike the UK, in the US, there is no intermediate category between employee and independent contractor. A proposal by Harris and Krueger would produce a result similar to the UK outcome. Seth D. Harris and Alan B. Krueger, *A Proposal for Modernizing Labor Laws for Twenty-First Century Work: the 'Independent Worker.'* Hamilton Project. December 2015. http://www.hamiltonproject.org/assets/files/modernizing_labor_laws_for_twenty_first_century_work_krueger_harris.pdf.

by themselves ineffective.[30] They do not bring economic security to workers. Dubal points out that supporters of these workers have almost solely relied on lawsuits, but the on-demand gig economy firms have mounted a politically integrated counterattack, not only vigorously defending lawsuits, but also lobbying for new laws to protect their independent contractor model, and initiating public relations campaigns by using social media to mobilize consumers.[31] This highlights the need of workers' rights supporters, such as academics, to have a vision for the future, to articulate this and to convey this vision to consumers who must also recognize that their interest in cheap services can conflict with their interest as workers. Just as capital in the information age has reverted to basics in its approach to labour, we must ask labour law to revert to basics, to its fundamental values.

A core value of labour law is economic security, both in the ability of work to provide a basis for a decent life for oneself and one's family, and in the need for the State to provide a social safety net when the individual cannot work. Before the digital economy, there were gig economy workers, and some were able to bring a measure of economic security to their work. The classic example is musicians who played 'gigs', that is, one-off performances of limited duration. Once they joined together to form a union, they accepted the reality that their work would never fit the model of a forty-hour week,[32] and instead set rates for units of work, and negotiated that they would receive an additional amount, calculated as percentage of the wage, to fund their sickness, disability, medical insurance and pension plans. Thus, there is a precedent for providers of services to many different users to achieve a modicum of economic security even though they are compensated on a piece rate basis. We must revive this search for ways of providing economic security to tech-enabled gig economy workers, whether it be some form of universal basic income or new ways of imposing additional costs on unit-based pay.

Another aspect of security relates to predictability which permits workers to schedule their working and personal lives, and to make arrangements for child and elder care. The rise of the tech-enabled company has led to zero-hour contracts and to workers being required to be on demand. Labour law must be changed to require some modicum of predictability.[33]

Another core value of labour law is safe and healthy work. National laws should be scrutinized to ensure that they apply to on-demand workers, tech-enabled gig economy workers and those utilizing their own equipment (such as cars, bicycles, computers) for work.

---

30. Dubal, *supra* n. 25 at 801.
31. *Id.*, at 802.
32. In the US, musicians in New York City who played at clubs and theatres followed this model. Such workers might have one hundred or more gigs per year. In contrast, musicians for major symphony orchestras were able to negotiate an annual salary with one entity.
33. New York's Governor Andrew Cuomo recently announced that the State's Labor Department would propose regulations on 'just in time', 'call-in' or 'on call' scheduling with the aim of setting an advance notice standard for scheduling, requiring extra pay for last-minute scheduling, and mandating a four-hour minimum if workers are called in to work. For 10 November 2017 announcement, *see* https://www.governor.ny.gov/news/governor-cuomo-announces-new-regulations-employee-scheduling.

Labour lawyers know the 1998 ILO Declaration of Fundamental Principles and Rights at Work. These are fundamental human rights principles applied to work and as such, they apply to information age workers. It cannot be assumed that the problems of the industrial age have disappeared in the information age. Two examples will suffice to show this. A fundamental principle is non-discrimination. Yet algorithms may produce discriminatory results. Unconscious bias may surface in the performance ratings users give providers; e.g., users may perceive black Uber drivers to be less courteous than white drivers, or female drivers to be less competent than male drivers. If the performance ratings are used by the company to de-select drivers without the algorithm taking into account unconscious bias, then impermissible discrimination has occurred. Similarly, child labour is prohibited with 14 the absolute minimum age in advanced countries for work of any duration. Experience has shown that in industrial homework, children often perform work (such as sewing) while the mother is doing housework tasks. This is not dangerous but it prevents children from engaging in activities that 12 year olds should do (such as school, doing homework assignments, rest). The use of computers in information age homework does not change the situation. Children should not be doing their parents' work.

Most importantly freedom of association for information age workers must be protected. The way in which workers will express this will change. Industrial era unionism, strikes and even collective bargaining may change. But it is likely that workers will want to communicate, that they will want to form online associations, and they may want to engage in concerted activities and they will want to do all these without being subjected to surveillance or monitoring. These will take new forms, and labour law cannot be locked into an industrial age view of ILO Convention No. 87. In 2020, a Facebook group may be the equivalent of a 1920 gathering of workers in the pub across the street from the factory. Manifestations of freedom of association may change, but the core value must remain a bulwark of labour law if labour law is to remain relevant. The president of MIT, noting that artificial intelligence and automation 'will transform our work, our lives, our society', expressed the challenge as 'building a future in which technology works for everyone'.[34] Labour law is at the forefront and must be at the forefront of this effort.

---

34. L. Rafael Reif, President of the Massachusetts Institute of Technology, 10 November 2017, *Boston Globe*. Statement accessible at https://www.bostonglobe.com/opinion/2017/11/10/transformative-automation-coming-the-impact/az0qppTvsUu5VUKJyQvoSN/story.html.

Chapter 2
Non-standard Employment Around the World: Regulatory Answers to Face Its Challenges

Janine Berg, Mariya Aleksynska, Valerio De Stefano & Martine Humblet[*]

In most parts of the world, the laws regulating employment have hinged on a type of work that is continuous, full-time and part of a subordinate and direct relationship between an employer and an employee – commonly referred to as the 'standard employment relationship'. The standard employment relationship provides not only important protections for workers, but also helps employers, who can rely on a stable workforce for their enterprise, retain and benefit from their workers' talents, and gain the managerial prerogative and authority to organize and direct their employees' work.

Over the past few decades, in both industrialized and developing countries, there has been a marked shift away from standard employment to non-standard employment (NSE). NSE is a grouping of different employment arrangements that deviate from standard employment. It includes temporary employment; part-time work; temporary agency work and other multiparty employment relationships; and disguised employment relationships and dependent self-employment.

The rise in these forms of work is evident in the employment statistics of many industrialized countries. In developing countries, non-standard workers have always constituted an important share of the labour force, as many of them are employed temporarily in casual work, but NSE has also grown in segments of the labour market previously associated with standard jobs. Some forms of NSE lack data to track trends,

---

[*] The Authors are the principal authors of the ILO Report, *Non-Standard Employment Around the World: Understanding Challenges, Shaping Prospects* (Geneva, ILO, 2016). The chapter draws on work done in preparation of the Report. The opinions expressed in this chapter, however, are the authors' only and do not necessarily represent the opinion of the ILO.

but an increase is still discernible in the growing anxiety that many workers have about their jobs, standard and non-standard alike.

The growth of NSE is a concern because these employment arrangements are associated with greater insecurity for workers when compared with standard employment. There are also important and under-appreciated consequences for firms, which may underestimate some of the managerial demands that NSE entails, particularly if significant parts of their workforce are in non-standard arrangements. In addition, what may be desirable and beneficial for the individual worker or enterprise, especially in the short run, can have negative consequences for the economy. These negative consequences include under-investment in innovation, a slowing of productivity growth, risks to the sustainability of social security systems, increased volatility in labour markets and poor economic performance. There are also important social consequences that require further attention.

The International Labour Organization (ILO) recognizes that work can have varied contractual forms. The goal is not to make all work standard but rather to make all work decent.[1] This chapter presents some of the main findings of the recent ILO report on NSE (2016). It focuses on three main aspects: the reason why there was an increase in NSE, the consequences of this for workers, enterprises and the economy and society at large, and regulatory proposals to improve NSE. The recommendations draw on international labour standards and national experiences to provide guidance to balance the needs of workers, enterprises and governments.

§2.01   UNDERSTANDING TRENDS IN NSE

Although it is unlikely that all workers will be employed in temporary, part-time or dependent self-employment arrangements in the future, NSE has nonetheless proliferated in sectors and occupations where it did not previously exist, and its overall importance in the labour market of most countries of the world has increased over the past several decades. The reasons for this proliferation are multifaceted and vary substantially across countries. Yet transformations in the world of work, regulatory changes and macroeconomic fluctuations and crises all contributed to the developments.

[A]   Transformations in the World of Work

Transformations in the world of work that affect the use of NSE include changes in the economic structure of economies from agriculture and manufacturing to services, increased pressure from globalization, technological change as well as resulting changes in organizational strategies of enterprises.

---

1. *See* the 'Conclusions of the Meeting of Experts on Non-Standard Forms of Employment', GB.323/POL/3, available at http://www.ilo.org/gb/GBSessions/GB323/pol/WCMS_354090/lang--en/index.htm.

Over the past several decades, there has been an expansion throughout the world in the services sector, which by 2015 comprised nearly half of all employment in the world.[2] In services, demand peaks can be more frequent and less predictable than in manufacturing, putting greater pressure on firms to ensure 'organizational flexibility'.[3] Some sub-sectors within services also have particular features that favour NSE, such as the hospitality and tourism sector, which is characterized by high fragmentation, global hotel chains and franchises, outsourcing, seasonality and the need to provide services outside of standard working hours.[4] In addition, the growth of the retail sector and the subsequent extension of opening hours have also spurred the use of part-time employment, as firms often hire workers on part-time hours to cover these additional shifts. This growth has had implications for women's employment, as women are more commonly found in service industries, particularly retail.[5]

At the same time, manufacturing has come under pressure from globalization, with a continuing intensification of international competition and pressure to reduce costs. The fragmentation of production, coupled with outsourcing, led to acceleration in trade of intermediate goods and proliferation of global supply chains. Fierce competition between suppliers and ever-growing pressure from buyers to reduce costs and ensure on-time production put further pressure on local suppliers to outsource and sub-contract labour and to use workers for short periods of time repeatedly hiring them on short-term contracts.[6] The expansion of services and global supply chains is inseparable from technological developments. New information technologies, higher quality and lower cost of infrastructure and improvements in logistics and transportation, enabled businesses to compare, organize and manage production scattered around the globe.[7]

While these global forces are important influences on firm practices, ultimately the choice of contractual arrangement rests with the firm. In the early 1990s, enterprises began increasing their use of outsourcing and other non-standard arrangements as a means for focusing on their 'core' competencies, with the stated goal of concentrating managerial resources on activities that were central to the firms' competitive advantage.[8] Office cleaning was one of the first tasks to be outsourced, followed by other office-support functions such as IT and payroll. Although many businesses restricted outsourcing to peripheral functions, some businesses came to rely on NSE arrangements for what were arguably 'core' functions.[9] Certain industries 'fissured' key functions, such as major hotel chains that outsourced front-desk services and cleaning to third-party management companies, and telecommunications companies

---

2. ILO, 2014.
3. Euwals and Hogerbrugge, 2006.
4. ILO, 2010z.
5. Tilly, 1991; Carré and Tilly, 2012; Euwals and Hoggerbrugge, 2006.
6. ILO, 2016.
7. ILO, 2016.
8. Prahalad and Hamel, 1990; Quinn and Hilmer, 1994.
9. *See*, for example, the discussion in Weil, 2014. Also, Rubery et al., 2002; Green, 2008.

that subcontracted installation and home-repair services to legions of 'self-employed' workers.[10]

Many enterprises use NSE arrangements as they are often cheaper, because of lower wage or non-wage costs.[11] In some instances, regulations may unintentionally – or deliberately – encourage the use of alternative arrangements, such as when part-time workers fall under the threshold of social security benefits, or when fixed-term contracts are allowed for permanent tasks. For example, prior to the reform in 2013, German employers paid a reduced rate for social security contributions for workers employed in 'mini-jobs'. In India, most labour laws apply solely to establishments with a minimum number of employees; as a result workers in small enterprises and most casual workers remain outside the scope of regulation.

Beginning in the 1970s, numerous European countries partly deregulated labour markets with the aim of increasing labour market flexibility and stimulating job growth. The reforms allowed for a wider use of temporary contracts, by expanding their scope of jobs that were not temporary in nature, and by increasing the allowed duration and number of renewals. As a result, temporary employment grew in many European countries. Similar reforms of the use of temporary labour were undertaken in some developing countries in the 1990s, particularly in the Andean region.[12] Since then, some European countries have implemented counter-reforms to constrain the growth of temporary employment, but in many instances, the process has not been easy to reverse.

Another change that is often overlooked is the decline of unionization that has occurred in some countries over the past several decades. This decline meant that fewer collective agreements were negotiated, especially in countries where the dominant form of collective bargaining is at the enterprise level. Moreover, the absence of unionization enabled firms to develop alternative employment arrangements, which were not in conflict with prevailing laws, but which ran counter to what had been prevailing practices. For example, the growth of 'zero-hours' contracts in the United Kingdom (UK), 'if and when' contracts in Ireland and 'just-in-time scheduling' in the United States (US) and Canada was not due to the introduction of new legislation, but rather to the realization by businesses that it was not necessary to provide guaranteed hours to workers within the employment contract, and that new arrangements could be introduced to increase businesses' scope for employing labour more flexibly.

§2.02 WHAT ARE SOME OF THE EFFECTS OF NSE ON FIRMS, WORKERS AND LABOUR MARKETS?

The decision by enterprises to use NSE has important consequences for the individual worker, but also for the firm itself, the labour market and the economy and society at large.

---

10. Weil, 2014.
11. Nesheim et al., 2007; von Hippel et al., 1997. *See also* the review on wage penalties addressed in Chapter 5 of the ILO, 2016.
12. Vega-Ruíz, 2005.

[A] Workers

NSE has implications for nearly all aspects of working conditions including employment, earnings, working hours, occupational safety and health (OSH), social security coverage, training, and representation and other fundamental principles and rights at work. While insecurities in these seven areas are also apparent in standard employment relationships, in general it presents fewer insecurities when compared with the different forms of NSE. Whether NSE workers experience insecurities in these seven areas depends on the attributes of the individual worker, as well as on the firm, industry and country setting. Importantly, the quality of NSE also depends on the extent to which engagement in NSE is voluntary. Some key findings regarding workers' insecurity are discussed below.

Employment security and labour market transitions. The ease of transiting between non-standard and regular employment is an issue of particular concern for temporary workers, workers in TAW and other multiparty employment relationships, and the dependent self-employed. It may be less of an issue for part-time workers if they are working under contracts of unlimited duration, although part-time workers are generally in a less favourable situation than their full-time counterparts with respect to job security.[13] Transitions from temporary to permanent employment are generally quite low, ranging from a yearly rate of under 10% to around 50%, in countries with available data. However, being in a temporary job, as opposed to being unemployed, can increase the probability of obtaining a regular job. Temporary employment can indeed act as a 'stepping stone' for young graduates, immigrants and workers initially disadvantaged in terms of either education or pay. These are the workers for whom the benefits of having lower initial screening, obtaining general rather than specific work experience, and expanding their network through non-standard jobs, are high. Nevertheless, when temporary work is more widespread, then longer-term evidence, such as for Spain or Japan, suggests that over a lifetime of working, those workers who started off with a temporary job have a greater chance of switching between non-standard work and unemployment, compared to workers who start with a permanent contract. In these cases, temporary work ceases to be a stepping stone. In the majority of countries considered, even where NSE functions as a stepping-stone, non-standard workers have a significantly higher rate of transition into unemployment or inactivity – sometimes nearly ten-fold – compared to standard workers.[14]

Wage differentials. Differences in wages arise when two similar workers performing similar work are paid differently. Temporary work usually results in wage penalties, which can vary between a few percentage points difference to 30 percentage points relative to comparable standard workers (Figure 2.1). In contrast, part-time employment can sometimes feature premiums. This is the case for formal employees in Latin America, although it is rarely the case in Europe and the US, where part-time employment is usually associated with wage penalties. Wage differentials for NSE also

---

13. OECD, 2010.
14. ILO, 2016.

vary across income levels. For example, in Italy, wage penalties associated with temporary jobs are substantially more pronounced among workers with lower salaries but are almost non-existent in high-wage jobs.[15] In some instances, wage gaps may widen with age, as is the case with Japanese fixed-term workers; or decrease with time spent in the sector, as is the case with temporary agency workers in Germany. In developing countries, while workers with written fixed-term contracts usually suffer a wage penalty when compared to those with permanent contracts, this penalty tends to be lower than that of workers who do not have a written contract.

Figure 2.1 Wage Penalties for Temporary Work, Selected Empirical Findings

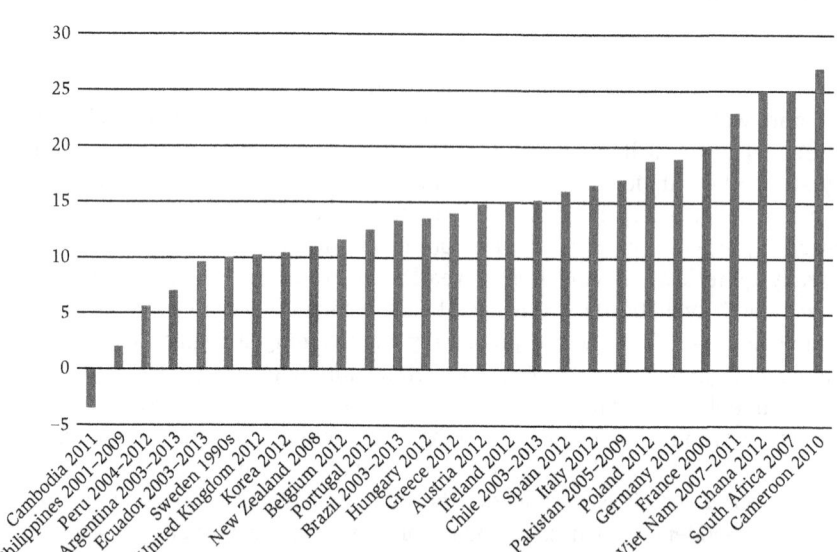

Note: Findings show wage penalties for being in temporary rather than in permanent work for men only. Partial coefficients from regression analysis, controlling at least for age, education, occupation and sector of activity (other controls vary across studies). Years refer to the years of data on which the analysis was based. 'Negative' penalty should be interpreted as a wage premium.*Source*: ILO, 2016.

Hours. Some forms of NSE, particularly temporary work, are associated with longer hours and work intensity. Findings from New Zealand, Switzerland, Thailand and Vietnam indicate that workers on fixed-term contracts and TAW are more likely to work unpaid overtime, often in anticipation of a renewal of their contract. In addition, to compensate for insufficient income, many workers in NSE hold multiple jobs. The other main concern with respect to working time is for on-call workers, including those on zero-hours contracts, and similar casual arrangements, as these workers typically have limited control over when they work, with implications for work-life balance, but

---

15. Bosio, 2014.

also income security, given that pay is uncertain. Variable schedules also make it difficult to take on a second job.

OSH. There are four broad categories of OSH risks associated with NSE: injury-related risks and accidents, mental health and harassment risks, exposure to poorer working conditions and hazards, and fatigue issues. These risks stem from a combination of poor induction, training and supervision, communication breakdowns (especially in multiparty employment arrangements) and fractured or disputed legal obligations.[16] In terms of injury rates, occupational injury rates among workers employed on temporary and TAW contracts can be significantly higher than those of permanent workers. They are almost twice as high in New Zealand, and substantially higher in Italy, India and Japan, even among NSE workers working side-by-side with standard workers.[17] Outsourcing and subcontracting have also been implicated in several catastrophic accidents.[18] In addition to physical health and safety issues, NSE is also associated with psychosocial factors that increase the risk of adverse health outcomes. Having an involuntary temporary or part-time job can aggravate subjective perceptions of job insecurity, especially among more vulnerable groups in the labour market, and when opportunities for shifting from temporary to open-ended contracts are low.[19] Greater job insecurity is associated with a range of negative outcomes adversely affecting work satisfaction, psychological and mental well-being and overall life satisfaction.

Social security. Workers in NSE often have inadequate social security coverage either because statutory provisions exclude them from entitlements to social security payments or because short tenure or low earnings or hours provide limited or no access to such entitlements. For example, in Japan, the Republic of Korea and South Africa, eligibility for unemployment benefits among employees is restricted to those working a minimum number of hours, with obvious consequences for part-time workers whose hours are below the minimum threshold.[20] In Europe, most temporary workers are legally eligible for unemployment insurance, but the higher rates of job rotation and greater likelihood of periods of unemployment due to non-renewal of temporary contracts make them less likely to be eligible for benefits.[21]

Training. The amount of training provided to temporary and temporary agency workers varies depending not only on the type of firm and the industry but also whether temporary contracts are combined with apprenticeship schemes or are used to screen potential workers for permanent positions (in which case the NSE worker will receive training) or whether production is highly standardized and jobs are easily replaceable, in which case little training, beyond the task at hand, is offered. Part-time

---

16. Quinlan, 2016.
17. Schweder, 2009; Fabiano et al., 2008; Bena et al., 2011. Maheshrengaraj and Vinodkumar, 2014.
18. Quinlan, Hampson and Gregson, 2013.
19. Dolado et al., 2012.
20. Fagan et al., 2014.
21. Leschke, 2007.

workers generally benefit from less training opportunities than their full-time counterparts.[22] These penalties may be linked to perceptions that part-timers are less career-oriented.

Representation and other fundamental principles and rights at work. Workers in NSE may be deprived of their freedom of association and collective bargaining rights either because the law prevents them from joining or because their more tenuous attachment to the workplace, makes it more difficult for them to join a union, especially if they fear retaliation from their employer.[23] Workers in multiparty employment relationships do not always have the right to engage in collective bargaining with the lead firm. In the Philippines, project employees in the construction sector can join the relevant industrial union but cannot constitute an appropriate collective bargaining unit.[24] Moreover, in Indonesia,[25] outsourced or subcontracted workers may not be part of the unions of regular workers, and in the Republic of Korea, they are only allowed to collectively negotiate with the subcontractor.[26] In some instances, thresholds can prevent workers from forming unions. For example, in Vietnam, workers with contracts shorter than six months cannot join unions.[27] Also, the self-employed are often excluded from the right to organize or from regulation protecting this right, which has consequences for workers in disguised employment relationships and dependent self-employment.[28] These challenges are confirmed by statistical evidence that workers in NSE have a lower rate of unionization.[29] Forced labour practices are sometimes concealed through the use of work arrangements involving multiple parties, and can be found in global supply chains, particularly at the lower subcontracted tiers.[30] The potentially discriminatory impact of 'atypical' forms of employment has been cited as a concern by ILO supervisory bodies, in cases concerning the Republic of Korea, Madagascar and Turkey.[31]

[B] Implications for Firms, Labour Markets and Society

With the growing incidence of NSE, it is important to understand what the implications are for firms. Firms that rely heavily on NSE need to adapt their human resource

---

22. Fagan et al., 2014; OECD, 2010.
23. Ebisui, 2012; De Stefano, 2017.
24. Vacotto, 2013.
25. Serrano et al., 2014.
26. Rubiano, 2013.
27. Landau, Mahy and Mitchell, 2015.
28. *See* ILO, 2016 for a detailed discussion of observations made by the Committee of Experts on the Application of Conventions and Recommendations (CEACR) and the Committee on Freedom of Association (CFA) on restrictions in law or practice on the right to freedom of association and collective bargaining.
29. ILO, 2016.
30. ILO, 2015.
31. *See* for instance, *Republic of Korea* – CEACR, direct request, C.111, published 2016; *Madagascar* – CEACR, direct request, C.111, published 2014; *Turkey* – CEACR, observation, C.111, published 2016. For a detailed analysis of sex discrimination in relation to fixed-term and part-time employment in Europe, *see* Burri and Aune, 2013.

strategies.[32] Management must shift its human resource strategies from training and development of employees within the organization to identifying the sets of skills that the firm needs to buy from the markets and procuring these skills in an efficient and timely manner.[33] This shift requires the organization to have good human resource systems that facilitate the timely recognition of the needs for particular types of skills or competencies in the organization.

Another important aspect is the possible impact on skills within companies. A dependence on procuring as opposed to cultivating the skills that the firm needs can affect organizations in two ways. First, it can result in a gradual erosion of firm-specific skills in the organization.[34] Organizations that describe their human resources as one of their key assets then have assets that are not very distinct from that of their competitors, thus diminishing the role of people as a source of competitive advantage. A second implication of the use of temporary or contract workers is that the firms' ability to respond to changing markets might be restricted. Since the focus is less on training-for-skills and more on hiring-for-skills, firms might be limited in the extent to which they can change by the availability of skills in the labour market.

NSE can bring positive benefits for firms in terms of cost savings and flexibility, particularly if the workers are performing tasks that are routine and highly structured. Nevertheless, the short-term cost and flexibility gains from using NSE may be outweighed by longer-term productivity losses induced either by lower productivity of workers in NSE, or negative spillover effects on the productivity of standard workers, or high transaction costs involved in the management of a 'blended' workforce (workforces where workers in standard and non-standard arrangements work side-by-side). If not well managed, blended workforces can result in conflicts and decreased morale.[35]

In addition, there is evidence that firms recurring to more non-standard labour underinvest in training, both for temporary and permanent employees, as well as in productivity-enhancing technologies and innovation.[36] Firm performance may also suffer from disruptions to accumulation of firm-specific knowledge and how it is transmitted to new employees, if the majority of employees are non-standard. Evidence from Italy and the Netherlands warns that firms using higher proportions of flexible labour experience lower labour productivity growth.[37] Similarly, an analysis of the use of temporary workers in firms in 132 developing and transition countries found that the firms that were less productive were also the same firms that used temporary labour 'intensively' in their operations (defined as 50% or more of the workforce on temporary contracts). These firms tended to use temporary labour to save on labour costs and did not invest in their training.[38]

---

32. Ashford et al., 2008.
33. Davis-Blake and Uzzi, 1993.
34. Lepak and Snell, 2002.
35. Davis-Blake et al., 2003. See also George and Chattopadhyay, 2016.
36. Nielen and Schiersch, 2014; Hirsch and Mueller, 2012; Dolado et al., 2012; Lucidi and Kleinknecht, 2010.
37. Kleinknecht et al., 2006; Lucidi and Kleinknecht, 2010.
38. Aleksynska and Berg, 2016.

For labour markets, widespread use of NSE may reinforce labour market segmentation, a situation in which one segment of the labour market (non-standard workers, or 'the less protected fringe') faces both inferior working conditions and vulnerable employment status, while the other segment enjoys more favourable working conditions – even if workers in both segments perform the same types of jobs. A key feature of segmented labour markets is that the transition from one segment to another is compromised. Labour market segmentation also means that there is unequal risk-sharing between standard and non-standard workers in terms of unemployment and income security – and also between non-standard workers and employers in terms of economic adjustment, because economic adjustment disproportionately results in job losses for workers in NSE. As a consequence, employment volatility is high, without any overall benefit for employment creation.[39] Labour market segmentation can also exacerbate wage and income inequality.

Two key aspects of NSE – employment insecurity and poorer remuneration – can have repercussions on the consumption and socialization patterns of workers. Research shows that for temporary and on-call workers, it is more difficult to get access to credit and housing, because banks and landlords usually prefer workers with stable jobs and regular incomes. Thus in France, young workers are more likely to live separately from their parents if they have stable jobs, compared to young workers on temporary contracts.[40] There is similar evidence for workers in NSE in the US.[41] Workers with temporary contracts who have difficulty transiting to permanent jobs also report having to delay marriage and childbearing until they can find stable employment.

§2.03 ADDRESSING DECENT WORK DEFICITS IN NSE

The world of work is not static and presents challenges that merit policy responses. Adapting regulations and policies to ensure decent work for all has to be an on-going effort. In addition, more effort needs to be made to ensure that regulations are effectively applied. This is particularly true for sectors and occupations where regulatory oversight has traditionally been weak and where collective bargaining coverage is limited.

To ensure decent work in NSE, the ILO (2016) proposes recommendations covering labour market regulation and policies supporting workers, regardless of their contractual status. This chapter details policy recommendations and the role of collective bargaining in achieving these objectives. However, as the ILO report highlights, it is also necessary to implement policies that strengthen social protection, accommodate labour market transitions and provide public services. These recommendations are based on the idea that a worker in an insecure job will likely feel less insecure if she or he lives in a country with a developed welfare state, where the

---

39. Bentolila and Saint-Paul, 1992; Boeri and Garibaldi, 2007.
40. Cahuc and Kramarz, 2004.
41. Wiens-Tuers, 2004.

person's basic needs are guaranteed through social protection and other social policies.[42]

[A] Legislative Responses: Plugging Regulatory Gaps

The analysis of legislative responses centres on five broad measures to plug existing regulatory gaps with respect to NSE. The objective of these measures is to align, to the extent possible, the labour protections of NSE with standard employment, so that workers in NSE arrangements receive better protection, as well as to mitigate abuses by employers in the use of these arrangements that undermine their legitimate purpose.[43] For many of these measures, there are international labour standards that provide guidance.

Equality of treatment. Ensuring equality of treatment for workers in NSE is important not only to avoid discrimination based on occupational status and as a matter of fairness, but also as a way of ensuring that NSE arrangements are not used solely to lower labour costs by offering worse terms and conditions to particular groups of workers. For this reason, ensuring equality of treatment is also a way of maintaining a level-playing field for employers. Given the over-representation of women, young people and migrants in NSE, it is important to ensure equal treatment for non-standard workers as this helps to combat discrimination in the workplace and in general. In addition to international labour standards that prohibit discrimination in the workplace, other standards address the specificities of workers in NSE and mandate non-discrimination of non-standard workers.[44] Equal treatment of fixed-term, temporary agency workers and part-time workers is established in EU Directives,[45] and is also present in national regulation, albeit its scope and functioning vary significantly among jurisdictions. Table 2.1 presents different examples of equal treatment entitlements for part-time workers.

---

42. *See also* Kalleberg and Hewison, 2013.
43. *See also* Adams and Deakin, 2014.
44. The two fundamental ILO Conventions that address discrimination at work are the Equal Remuneration Convention, 1951 (No. 100) and the Discrimination (Employment and Occupation) Convention, 1958 (No. 111). In addition, the protection of part-time workers against discrimination is ensured through two specific standards, the Part-Time Work Convention, 1994 (No. 175) and Recommendation (No. 182); other relevant standard include the Private Employment Agencies Convention, 1997 (No. 181) and the Employment Relationship Recommendation, 2006 (No. 198).
45. European Union Council Directive 1999/70/EC of 28 June 1999 concerning the Framework Agreement on Fixed-Term Work concluded by ETUC, UNICE and CEEP; European Directive 97/81/EC of 15 December 1997 concerning the Framework Agreement on part-time work concluded by UNICE, CEEP and the ETUC; Directive 2008/104/EC of the European Parliament and of the Council of 19 November 2008 on Temporary Agency Work.

Table 2.1 Principles of Equal Treatment for Part-Time Workers

Provision	Countries
General non-discrimination clause	Armenia, Bulgaria, Chile, France, Hungary (direct and indirect discrimination is prohibited), Italy, Latvia, Lithuania, Luxembourg (subject to specific provisions included in collective agreements), FYR of Macedonia, Mali, Moldova, Norway, Romania, Senegal, Slovakia, Slovenia, Spain, Tunisia (subject to particular provisions), Vietnam (right to equality in opportunities and treatment)
Equal treatment except for objective reasons	Austria, Belgium, Cape Verde, Cyprus, Estonia, Germany, Greece, Hungary, Iceland, Ireland, Malta, Mozambique, Netherlands, Portugal (objective reasons to be determined by collective agreement), Sweden, Turkey (prohibition of differentiated treatment solely because the worker is employed on a part-time basis and unless there is a justifiable cause), United Kingdom
Pro rata cash benefits	Argentina, Austria, Brazil, Cape Verde, Cyprus, Ecuador, France, Germany, Greece, Iceland, Iran, Ireland, Italy, Republic of Korea, Lithuania, Luxembourg, Mali, Malta, Mauritius (with an increase of at least 5%), Mozambique, Portugal, Romania, Russian Federation, Senegal, Seychelles, Slovakia, Spain, Tunisia, Turkey, Bolivarian Republic of Venezuela

Even when the principle of equal treatment is provided, however, exceptions or legal loopholes may be in place that limit its scope and effectiveness. Thus, a good practice is to re-examine exclusions from this principle on a regular basis to verify whether they are still justified by monitoring the effects of such exclusions.

In some cases, regulation limits the rights and protection of non-standard workers. For example, the provision of qualification periods and minimum continuity of employment can deprive some workers, particularly those whose work is intermittent, from acceding to important labour protections even when their relationship with a same employer has lasted for a considerable amount of time, albeit on a discontinuous basis.[46] Legislation adopted on casual work in some developing countries such as the Philippines, addressing continuity of employment of workers whose work is discontinuous, provides examples for tackling similar problems in industrialized economies.[47]

Minimum hours and other safeguards for part-time, on-call and casual workers. Part-time workers sometimes work very short hours and may therefore have low

---

46. Landau, et al., 2015. De Stefano, 2016.
47. De Stefano, 2016.

income, particularly if they do not benefit from equal treatment with full-time workers in terms of remuneration. When on-call and casual workers can be called in at the employer's discretion and are not guaranteed a minimum amount of hours or payment, their income security and work-life balance suffers. These problems are exacerbated if workers fear they may not to be offered more work if they turn down an offer for a particular shift or task, or if they are called and report for work but their shift is cancelled at the last minute.

Measures to provide workers with a minimum number of guaranteed hours and to give workers a say in their work schedules, including by limiting the variability of working hours, are therefore important protective tools. Only a few countries, however, have established a minimum working hours for part-time employees to ensure them a minimum income. In the 2010s, French legislation was amended to ensure, with certain exceptions, that part-time workers would have a minimum of twenty-four hours per week. In Germany, Ghana, the Netherlands, Papua New Guinea and the US (limited to the District of Columbia and eight states), regulations require employers to pay their workers for a minimum number of hours when they report to work for a scheduled shift or are called in to work, even if the work is cancelled or its duration reduced.[48]

Addressing employment misclassification. In the vast majority of legal systems across the world, a 'binary divide' between employment and self-employment exists, with 'employment' serving as the basis for labour regulation.[49] This makes the definition of employment and the classification of a work relationship as an 'employment relationship' central to the provision of labour protection.

The ILO Employment Relationship Recommendation, 2006 (No. 198) provides guidance on how to regulate the scope of the employment relationship and deter circumvention of the labour and social protection that the relationship entails.[50] It contains a far-reaching series of principles that can guide countries on devising policies to address employment misclassification, including:

(a) Establishing the principle of 'primacy of facts', according to which the determination of the existence of an employment relationship should be guided by the facts relating to the actual performance of work and not on the basis of how the parties describe the relationship. Many jurisdictions in the world provide for such a principle either statutorily or via case law. It can be found in civil law and common law systems and can be expressly stated in laws (e.g., Argentina, Mexico, Poland, Panama, Venezuela), even at the constitutional level (e.g., Colombia), in some cases as a general principle of contract law (e.g., Bulgaria, Italy), or set out by the courts (e.g., Ireland).[51]

---

48. ILO, 2016.
49. *See* ILO, 2003 and ILO, 2006.
50. *See* Casale, 2011.
51. Ameglio and Villasmil, 2011; ILO and European Labour Law Network, 2013.

(b) Allowing a broad range of means for determining the existence of an employment relationship. Multifactor approaches are followed in the following common law countries: Australia, India, the UK and the US. Similar approaches are also followed in some civil law countries, including France and Greece.[52]

(c) Providing for a legal presumption that an employment relationship exists where one or more relevant indicators are present. Such a legal instrument may be found in various jurisdictions across the world and may take the form of a broad presumption under which working relationship are presumed to be employment relationships (e.g., Colombia, Dominican Republic, the Netherlands, Panama, Bolivarian Republic of Venezuela). Alternatively, the law may specify some indicators that may trigger a presumption or a reclassification under an employment relationship (e.g., Malta, South Africa, United Republic of Tanzania).

(d) Determining, following prior consultations with the most representative organizations of employers and workers, that workers with certain characteristics, in general or in a particular sector, must be deemed to be either employed or self-employed. This is done in France, for example, concerning professional journalists, certain performing artists, fashion models and sales representatives.

Restricting the use of NSE. In addition to improving the conditions of workers in non-standard arrangements, there are also situations where restricting or limiting the use of NSE is needed. By limiting its use, employers and workers can enter into non-standard arrangements to benefit from the flexibility that these forms of work offer while avoiding that non-standard jobs unnecessarily replace standard jobs. In other cases, limitation may be aimed at avoiding abuses or mitigating particular risks associated with their use, for instance by restricting their use in some sectors or occupations or when industrial disputes are ongoing. Existing international labour standards as well as national practices offer examples of restrictions.

Prohibition of using fixed-term work for permanent needs of the enterprise. More than half of the countries for which information is available limit recourse to fixed-term work to tasks of a temporary nature, as suggested by the ILO Termination of Employment Recommendation, 1982 (No. 166). Figure 2.2 is a map illustrating the national legal prohibition of the use of fixed-term contracts for permanent tasks. This measure has been shown to be effective in mitigating the use of fixed-term contracts.[53]

---

52. Countouris, 2011.
53. Aleksynska and Berg, 2016.

Figure 2.2 Legal Prohibition of the Use of Fixed-Term Contracts for Permanent Tasks

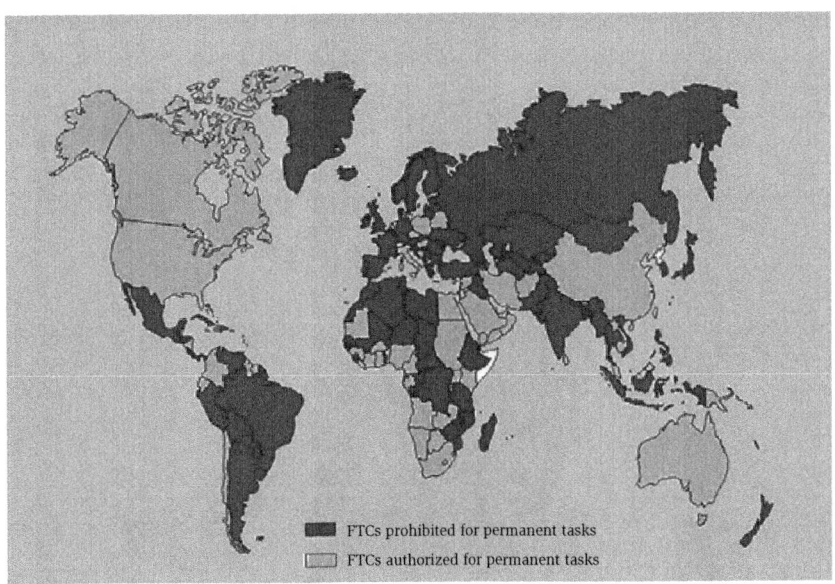

Source: Aleksynska and Muller (2015).

Limitation to recourse to temporary agency work. Recourse to TAW may be prohibited or restricted by national regulations for several reasons. For instance, TAW may be allowed only in case an objective or temporary reason exists. A very common limitation concerns prohibiting its use to replace workers on strike, as indicated in the ILO Private Employment Agencies Recommendation, 1997 (No. 188). Many national laws establish this restriction either by statutory measures (e.g., Argentina, Bulgaria, Chile, Hungary, Israel, Lithuania, Morocco, Namibia, New Zealand, Poland, Romania, Spain) or via collective bargaining (e.g., Denmark, Norway, Sweden). The World Employment Confederation sets out a similar provision in its code of conduct. Several countries, moreover, limit or prohibit TAW for hazardous work. National regulations also prohibit recourse to this form of work shortly after dismissals for business reason or collective dismissals.

Limitation on renewals or overall duration of fixed-term work, casual work and temporary agency work. Many jurisdictions have measures to ensure that recourse to fixed-term work, casual work or TAW is only temporary. It is common to provide for a maximum overall duration for these forms of work or limit the number or the renewal of successive contracts or assignments. A comparative analysis shows, for instance, that around half of the 193 countries for which information is available limit the maximum cumulative duration of temporary contracts to two to five years (*see* Figure 2.3).

Figure 2.3   Maximum Legal Duration of Fixed-Term Contracts, Including Renewals

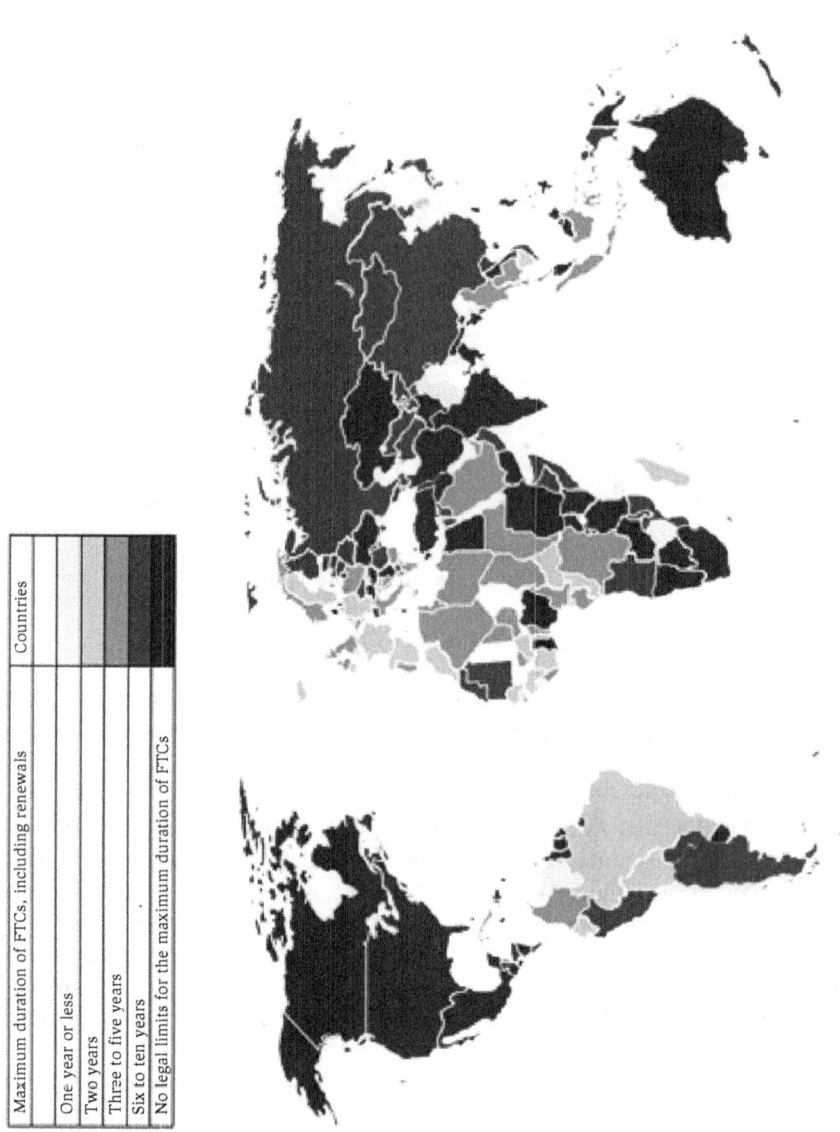

Source: Adapted from Aleksynska and Muller (2015).

Restricting or prohibiting the use of on-call employment contracts. On-call work and more specifically zero-hours contracts were recently the subject of heavy criticism in a number of countries. Some regulatory responses have been developed in response to these calls for a better protection of the workers concerned, including New Zealand, which in 2016 prohibited zero-hours contracts that require workers to remain at the disposal of their employer.

Limiting the percentage of non-standard workers. A limitation on the proportion of non-standard workers in the enterprise's total workforce is also established in some countries, such as China, Italy and Norway, including in collective bargaining agreements, to avoid abuses in their use.

Limiting NSE to non-core activities. This is one of the most common criteria used by national regulation in the definition of casual work. Some countries, such as Ecuador and Indonesia, also limit or prohibit recourse to subcontracting for core business activities.

Assigning obligations and liabilities in contractual arrangements involving multiple parties. The multilayered structure of these work arrangements can make it difficult for workers to effectively exercise their rights, including making it difficult for them to identify the subject responsible for ensuring that their working conditions comply with the law. Moreover, they face the additional risk of not being able to take action against subjects who are legally not their employers.[54]

An important remedy is to establish shared liabilities in contractual arrangements involving multiples parties, as this gives principal firms the incentive to select reliable counterparts when entering into such arrangements. Shared liability between the user firm and the agency is provided, for instance, in Argentina, France, India, Italy, the Netherlands, Namibia, Ontario (Canada) and South Africa.[55] Similarly, shared liability is critical for OSH, since, when workers involved in these arrangements work at the principal's premises, their direct employer may not control the workplace and may thus not be in a position on their own to provide for occupational health and safety and compliance with relevant obligations.

[B] Strengthening Collective Bargaining

The second set of policy measures concerns a different regulatory tool: collective bargaining. Collective agreements can be tailored to consider particular circumstances of the sector or the enterprise, and are thus well-suited for addressing decent work deficits in NSE. It can be used to advance regulatory provisions aiming at lessening insecurities, but efforts are needed to build the capacity of unions to do so, including through the organization and representation of workers in non-standard work arrangements. In countries where collective bargaining is extended to cover all workers in a sector or occupational category, collective bargaining can be an effective means for protecting non-standard workers, thus mitigating differences in treatment among workers in different employment arrangements. In Switzerland and the Netherlands,

---

54. Weil, 2014; Prassl, 2015.
55. For European Countries, *see* Spattini, 2012. For India, *see* Landau et al., 2015. Comprehensive information on the establishment of this protection in Namibia is provided in Bamu, forthcoming; Art. 29 BIS, Ley de Contrato de Trabajo, Argentina; Art. 35; Ontario (Canada), Stronger Workplaces for a Stronger Economy Act and Employment Standards Act 2000; South Africa, Labour Relations Act.

collective agreements have been extended to workers in vulnerable sectors including contract cleaning, security services, waste disposal and personal care. This is a potent policy tool, as these sectors have a large share of migrant workers and temporary agency workers with high levels of mobility, which usually results in low levels of unionization.[56] In addition, alliances between unions and other organizations can also be useful for developing effective collective responses to issues of concern to non-standard and standard workers alike.

Yet, to begin with, it is necessary to ensure that the legislative framework protects and promotes the freedom of association and collective bargaining rights of all workers. Establishing a legislative framework that effectively allows workers' organizations operating freely and choosing the level at which they are structured as well as removing impediments to the affiliation of all workers is a prerequisite in ensuring inclusive union strategies and actions in favour of non-standard workers. A measure that supports this objective is to extend the right to collective bargaining beyond the scope of the employment relationship. Examples of countries explicitly providing this right to dependent self-employed workers include Canada, Germany and Spain. It is also essential that practical barriers to unionization are eliminated, such as the fear of retaliation that some non-standard workers have about joining a union. This regulatory gap can be filled by extending protection against discriminatory dismissal to the non-renewal of temporary contracts, as is done in France.

Examples abound of collective agreements negotiated by the social partners that improve the terms and conditions of work of non-standard workers.[57] Key issues include: securing regular employment; providing equal pay for work of equal value; scheduling of hours, including guaranteeing minimum working hours for on-call workers; ensuring a safe working environment; extending maternity protection; as well as addressing specific interests and needs of non-standard workers.[58] Because these agreements are the outcome of negotiation by the social partners, they are also more likely to be implemented, also because unions play an important enforcement role.

§2.04 CONCLUSIONS

The world of work today is marked by differences in the use of contractual forms. Temporary employment, part-time work, multiparty employment relationships, disguised employment and economically dependent self-employment have increased worldwide. The reasons for this increase are linked to economic and technological transformations, but also to regulatory and social changes. This development has had a major impact on workers and companies. When its use is widespread throughout the labour market, there are also significant consequences for the economy and society.

The ILO's objective is not that all work should follow the standard-employment model, but rather that all work should be decent. To achieve this objective, the Office has recently proposed a set of legislative recommendations to improve NSE work,

---

56. Visser, 2017.
57. ILO, 2016.
58. *See* Xhafa, 2015; Ebisui, 2012.

based on international labour standards and good practice from national experiences. The role of collective bargaining in achieving this objective has also been emphasized.

While the focus of this article is on NSE, policies are needed to ensure that all forms of work are decent, as no contractual form is immune to the on-going transformations in the world of work. The years ahead will undoubtedly bring new changes. Yet the dependence on work for one's livelihood and the effect of work on a person's overall well-being will not change. It is thus incumbent on governments, as well as employers, workers and their organizations, through national, regional and international efforts, to come together to address the challenges in the world of work, with the goal of promoting decent work for all.

Bibliography

Adams, Z.; Deakin, S. 2014. 'Institutional solutions to precariousness and inequality in labour markets', in *British Journal of Industrial Relations* (Vol. 52, No. 4), pages 779–809.

Aleksnyska, M.; Berg, J. 2016. *'Firms' demand for temporary labour in developing countries: Necessity or strategy?'* Conditions of Work and Employment Series No. 77 (Geneva, ILO).

Aleksynska, M.; Muller, A. 2015. *Nothing more permanent than temporary? Understanding fixed-term contracts,* INWORK and GOVERNACE Policy Brief No. 6 (Geneva, ILO, 2015).

Ameglio, E.J.; Villasmil, U. 2011. 'Selected countries in Latin America and the Caribbean' in G. Casale (ed.): *The employment relationship – a comparative overview* (Geneva, ILO).

Ashford, S.J., E. George; Blatt, R. 2008. 'Old assumptions, new work: The opportunities and challenges of research on nonstandard employment', in J.P. Walsh and A.P. Brief (eds): *Annals of the Academy of Management,* Vol. 1 (Mahwah, NJ, Lawrence Erlbaum), pages 65–118.

Bamu, P. Forthcoming. *The regulation of non-standard forms of employment in Guinea, Namibia, Tanzania,* Condition of Work and Employment Series (Geneva, ILO).

Bentolila, S.; Saint-Paul, G. 1992 'The macroeconomic impact of flexible labor contracts, with an application to Spain', in *European Economic Review* (Vol. 36, No. 5), pages 1013–1047.

Boeri, T.; Garibaldi P. 2007. 'Two tier reforms of employment protection legislation. A honeymoon effect?' in *The Economic Journal* (Vol. 117, No. 521, 2007), pages 357–385.

Bosio, G. 2014. 'The implications of temporary jobs on the distribution of wages in Italy: An unconditional IVQTE approach', in *Labour* (Vol. 28, No. 1), pages 64–86.

Burri, S.; Aune H. 2013. *Sex discrimination in relation to part-time and fixed-term work: The application of EU and national law in practice in 33 European countries* (European Commission, European Network of Legal Experts in the Field of Gender Equality).

Cahuc, P.; Kramarz; F. 2004. *De la précarité à la mobilité: vers une sécurité sociale Professionnelle*. Rapport au Ministre de l'Economie, des finances et de l'industrie et au Ministre de l'Emploi, du travail et de la cohésion sociale (Paris, La Documentation Française).

Carré, F.; Tilly, C. 2012. 'Part-time and short hours in retail in the United States, Canada and Mexico: How institutions matter', in *Employment Research* (Vol. 19, No. 4), pages 4–6.

Casale, G. 2011. 'The employment relationship: A general introduction', in G. Casale (ed.): *The employment relationship – a comparative overview* (Geneva, ILO).

Countouris, N. 2011. 'The employment relationship: A comparative analysis of national judicial approaches', in G. Casale (ed.): *The employment relationship – a comparative overview* (Geneva, ILO, 2011).

Davis-Blake, A; Uzzi, B. 1993. 'Determinants of employment externalization: A study of temporary workers and independent contractors', in *Administrative Science Quarterly* (Vol. 38, No. 2), pages 195–223.

Davis-Blake, A., Broschak, J.P.; George, E. 2003. 'Happy together? How using non-standard workers affects exit, voice, and loyalty among standard employees', in *Academy of Management Journal* (Vol. 46, No. 4), pages 475–485.

De Stefano, V. 2017. 'Non-standard work and limits on freedom of association: A human rights based approach', in *Industrial Law Journal* (Vol. 46, No. 2), pages 185–207.

De Stefano, V. 2016. 'Casual work beyond casual work in the EU: The underground casualization of the European workforce – and what to do about it', *European Labour Law Journal* (Vol. 7, No. 3) pages 421–442.

Dolado, J.J., S. Ortigueira; Stucchi R. 2016. 'Does dual employment protection affect TFP? Evidence from Spanish manufacturing firms', *SERIEs* (Vol. 7, No. 4), pages 421–459.

Ebisui, M. 2012. *'Non-Standard Workers: Good Practices of Social Dialogue and Collective Bargaining'*, ILO Dialogue Working Paper No. 36 (Geneva, ILO).

Euwals, R.; Hogerbrugge, M. 2006. 'Explaining the growth of part-time employment: Factors of supply and demand' in *LABOUR* (Vol. 20, No. 3), pages 533–557.

Fagan, C. et al. 2014. *'In search of good quality part-time employment'*, Conditions of Work and Employment Series No. 43 (Geneva, ILO).

George, E.; Chattopadhyay, P. 2016. *'Non-standard work and workers: Organizational implications'*, Conditions of Work and Employment Series No. 61 (Geneva, ILO).

Hirsch, B.; Mueller, S. 2012. 'The productivity effect of temporary agency work: Evidence from German panel data' in *The Economic Journal* (Vol. 122), pages 562–569.

ILO and European Labour Law Network. 2013. *Regulating the employment relationship in Europe: A guide to Recommendation No. 198* (Geneva and Frankfurt, ILO and ELLN).

ILO. 2003. *The scope of the employment relationship*, Report V, International Labour Conference, 91st Session, Geneva, 2003, page 25.

ILO. 2006. *The employment relationship*, Report V (1), International Labour Conference, 95th Session, Geneva, 2006.

ILO. 2014. *Global Employment Trends 2014* (Geneva, ILO).

ILO. 2015. Conclusions of the Meeting of Experts on Non Standard Forms of Employment, Governing Body, 323rd Session, Geneva, March 2015 GB.323/POL/3.

ILO. 2016. Non-Standard Employment around the world: Understanding challenges, shaping prospects (Geneva, ILO).

Kalleberg, A.; Hewison. K. 2013. 'Precarious work and the challenge for Asia', in *American Behavioural Scientist* (Vol. 57, No. 3, 2013), pages 271-288.

Kleinknecht, A. et al. 2006. 'Flexible labour, firm performance and the Dutch job creation miracle', in *International Review of Applied Economics* (Vol. 20, No. 2, 2006), pages 171-187.

Landau, I., Mahy, P.; Mitchell, R. 2015. *The regulation of non-standard forms of employment in India, Indonesia and Vietnam*, ILO Conditions of Work and Employment Series Working Paper No. 63 (Geneva, ILO).

Lepak, D.P.; Snell, S.A. 2002. 'Examining the human resource architecture: The relationships among human capital, employment, and human resource', in *Journal of Management* (Vol. 28, No. 4) pages 517-543.

Leschke, J. 2007. *Are unemployment insurance systems in Europe adapting to new risks arising from non-standard employment?*, DULBEA Working Paper N°07-05.RS (Brussels, ULB).

Lucidi, F.; Kleinknecht, A. 2010. 'Little innovation, many jobs: An econometric analysis of the Italian labour productivity crisis', in *Cambridge Journal of Economics* (Vol. 34, No. 3), pages 525-546.

Nesheim, T et al. 2007. 'Externalizing the core: Firms' use of employment intermediaries in the information and communication technology industries', in *Human Resource Management* (Vol. 46, No. 2), pages 247-264.

Nielen, S.; Schiersch, A. 2014. 'Temporary agency work and firm competitiveness: Evidence from German manufacturing firms' in *Industrial Relations* (Vol. 53, No. 3, 2014), pages 365-375.

OECD. 2010. *Employment Outlook 2010: Moving beyond the jobs crisis* (Paris, 2010).

Prahalad, C.K.; Hamel G. 1990. 'The core competence of the corporation', in *Harvard Business Review* (1 May-June), pages 1-15.

Prassl, J. 2015. *The concept of the employer* (Oxford, Oxford University Press).

Quinlan, M. 2016. *The effects of non-standard forms of employment on worker health and safety*, Conditions of Work and Employment Series No. 67 (Geneva, ILO, 2016).

Quinlan, M., I. Hampson; S. Gregson, S. 2013. 'Outsourcing and offshoring aircraft maintenance in the US: Implications for safety', in *Safety Science* (Vol. 57), pages 283-292.

Quinn, J.; Hilmer, F. 1994. 'Strategic outsourcing', in *Sloan Management Review* (Vol. 35, No. 4), pages 43-55.

Rubery, J. et al. 2002. 'Changing organizational forms and the employment relationship', in *Journal of Management Studies* (Vol. 39, No. 5), pages 645-672.

Rubiano, C. 2013. 'Precarious work and access to collective bargaining. What are the obstacles?' in *International Journal of Labour Research* (Vol. 5, No. 1, 2013), pages 133-151.

Tilly, C. 1991. 'Reasons for the continuing growth of part-time employment' in *Monthly Labor Review* (March), pages 10–18.

Vacotto, B. 2013. 'Precarious work and the exercise of freedom of association and collective bargaining: Current ILO jurisprudence', in *International Journal of Labour Research* (Vol. 5, No. 1), pages 117–131.

Visser, J. 2017. 'The extension of collective agreements in Finland, the Netherlands, Norway and Switzerland', in *International Labour Review* (Vol. 156, 2017).

Von Hippel, C. et al. 1997. 'Temporary employment: Can organizations and employees both win?', in *Academy of Management Executive* (Vol. 11, No. 1, 1997), pages 93–104.

Weil, D. 2014. *The fissured workplace: Why work became so bad for so many and what can be done to improve it* (Cambridge, MA, London, Harvard University Press).

Wiens-Tuers, B. 2004. 'There's no place like home: The relationship of nonstandard employment and home ownership over the 1990s', in *The American Journal of Economics and Sociology* (Vol. 63, No. 4), pages 881–896.

Xhafa, E. 2015. Collective bargaining and non-standard forms of employment: Practices that reduce vulnerability and ensure work is decent. ILO INWORK Issue Brief No. 3. (Geneva, ILO).

CHAPTER 3
European Labour Law and the Millennium Shift: From Post to (Social) Pillar

Frank Hendrickx

§3.01 INTRODUCTION

On 17 November 2017, the 'European Pillar of Social Rights' was officially proclaimed by the European Union (EU) leaders at the occasion of the Social Summit held in Gothenburg, Sweden. When the 'Pillar' was officially proposed on 26 April 2017, the accompanying Commission Recommendation indicated that it 'expresses principles and rights essential for fair and well-functioning labour markets and welfare systems in 21st century Europe'.[1] The 'Pillar' contains twenty themes with rights and principles.

As we are looking in this contribution for 'game changers' in an EU labour law context, it is obvious that the 'European Social Pillar' stands out. The 'European Social Pillar' seems to have the aspiration of introducing a real game-changing momentum in European policy in general and with regard to the social Europe question in particular. Its strong rights discourse could also have an impact on labour law. However, we need to be critical and the question is whether we would need to single out this Pillar as *the* real game changer for European labour law. This question will be examined hereafter. It will be proposed that the Pillar can deliver a real game-changing momentum. However, it would need to overcome the problematic approaches towards European labour law and the difficult tension between the European economic and social dimensions.

In light of this, we wish to refer to what we propose as European labour law's millennium shift. It does not concern one single moment, but rather a game-changing time frame, close before and after the rise of the new millennium, in which a new approach towards labour law took shape. Traditional understandings of labour law

---

1. Brussels, 26.4.2017 C(2017) 2600 final.

were confronted with an agenda of economic competitiveness and with the demands of supranational economic liberalisation. This shift resulted from policy responses to a complex reality of globalisation, new labour market realities and political challenges such as EU enlargement and Eurozone deepening. Against this broad background, it is proposed that the promise of creating an equally progressing economic and social Europe was reformulated, rather recalibrated, by Delors' European Commission in the 1990s. It laid the basis for a new and dominant view with regard to labour law which could further be applied in the European employment strategy and developed by the EU institutions in policy and legal strategies.

The European Social Pillar has strong aspirations. However, the question is whether it can be seen as a new and game-changing context for European social policy and labour law. In order to come to an answer, this contribution first gives an insight into the content and background of the European Pillar of Social Rights. Second, it will connect the Social Pillar with past initiatives in EU labour law and social policy, such as the 1972 Paris Declaration and the 1989 Community Charter. These initiatives are applied methods showing similar ambitions or characteristics as the Pillar. Third, labour law's millennium shift is further explained and elaborated. It is shown that, while the former initiatives were fitting well into the European social rights tradition, a game-changing approach towards labour law became apparent in the course of the 1990s. Finally, an evaluation is made of the European Pillar of Social Rights, in light of the past developments and drawing further on its intrinsic characteristics and potential.

§3.02 WHAT IS THE PILLAR?

The initiative for a European Pillar of Social Rights was announced by President Jean-Claude Juncker during his first State of the Union before the European Parliament on 9 September 2015. In his speech, Juncker argued for 'a fair and truly pan-European labour market' and the development of 'a European Pillar of Social rights, which takes account of the changing realities of Europe's societies and the world of work. And which can serve as a compass for the renewed convergence within the euro area'. He also specified that the pillar 'should complement what we have already jointly achieved when it comes to the protection of workers in the EU. I will expect social partners to play a central role in this process. I believe we do well to start with this initiative within the euro area, while allowing other EU Member States to join in if they want to do so'.[2] After having organised a wide consultation of the Member States, the social partners and broader actors in society, the European Commission proposed the European Pillar of Social Rights on 26 April 2017. It was politically agreed that the Pillar would be 'inter-institutionally' proclaimed.

The Pillar initiative, as it came out on 26 April 2017, contained a set of documents:

---

2. Jean-Claude Juncker, President of the European Commission, State of the Union 2015: Time for Honesty, Unity and Solidarity, Strasbourg, 9 September 2015, SPEECH/15/5614 (http://europa.eu/rapid/press-release_SPEECH-15-5614_en.htm – consulted 1 November 2017).

- Commission Communication on the European Pillar of Social Rights:[3] explains background, process, purposes and rationale of the Pillar.
- Commission Recommendation on the European Pillar of Social Rights:[4] recommends the Pillar on behalf of the European Commission and lists the twenty rubrics of rights and principles contained in the Pillar.
- Proposal for an Interinstitutional Proclamation endorsing the European Pillar of Social Rights:[5] contains a proposed draft of the solemn declaration of the Pillar with the twenty rubrics of rights and principles.
- Commission Staff Working Document:[6] details the contents and scope of each principle or right of the Pillar, referring to the existing social acquis and making suggestions with regard to its implementation.
- Commission Staff Working Document: Report of the public consultation:[7] summarises the feedback and findings following the public consultation concerning the Pillar.

On 17 November 2017 the 'European Pillar of Social Rights' was officially proclaimed by the EU leaders at the occasion of the Social Summit held in Gothenburg, Sweden. It was signed by Jean-Claude Juncker (President of the European Commission), Antonio Tajani (President of the European Parliament) and Prime Minister Jüri Ratas (on behalf of the Presidency of the Council of the EU).[8]

Together with launching the Social Pillar, the European Commission made a proposal on work-life balance with minimum standards for parental, paternity and carer's leave, initiated consultations on the Written Statement Directive (91/533/EEC)

---

3. Communication from the Commission to the European Parliament, the Council, the European Economic and Social Committee and the Committee of the Regions, Establishing a European Pillar of Social Rights, Brussels, 26.4.2017, COM(2017) 250 final (http://eur-lex.europa.eu/legal-content/EN/ALL/?uri = COM:2017:0250:FIN – consulted 31 October 2017).
4. Commission Recommendation of 26.4.2017 on the European Pillar of Social Rights, Brussels 26.4.2017, C(2017) 2600 final (http://eur-lex.europa.eu/legal-content/EN/ALL/?uri = COM:2017:0250:FIN – consulted 31 October 2017).
5. COM(2017) 251 final; Text of the Interinstitutional Proclamation on the European Pillar of Social Rights as agreed in Coreper on 20 October with a view to the Council (EPSCO) on 23 October 2017 (https://ec.europa.eu/commission/sites/beta-political/files/proposal_for_an_interinstitutional_proclamation_endorsing_the_european_pillar_of_social_rights.pdf – consulted 31 October 2017).
6. Commission Staff Working Document Accompanying the document Communication from the Commission to the European Parliament, the Council, the European Economic and Social Committee and the Committee of the Regions, Establishing a European Pillar of Social Rights, Brussels, 26.4.2017, SWD(2017) 201 final (http://eur-lex.europa.eu/legal-content/EN/TXT/HTML/?uri = CELEX:52017SC0201&from = EN – consulted 31 October 2017).
7. Commission Staff Working Document. Report of the public consultation, Accompanying the document Communication from the Commission to the European Parliament, the Council, the European Economic and Social Committee and the Committee of the Regions, Establishing a European Pillar of Social Rights, Brussels 26.4.2017, SWD(2017) 206 final (http://eur-lex.europa.eu/legal-content/EN/TXT/HTML/?uri = CELEX:52017SC0206&from = EN – consulted 31 October 2017).
8. *See* the booklet: https://ec.europa.eu/commission/sites/beta-political/files/social-summit-european-pillar-social-rights-booklet_en.pdf; a brief discussion has also been made on the Regulating for Globalization Blog of Kluwer Law International: F. HENDRICKX, 'The European Social Pillar: labour law not only needs rights', 29.11.2017 (http://regulatingforglobalization.com).

and on access to social protection, and an interpretative communication on the Working Time Directive (2003/88/EC).[9] Against this Pillar background, the European Commission also proposed a revision of the rules on posting of workers in the EU.

The fact that the Pillar formulates rights seems logical, since it is entitled Pillar of Social Rights. However, the legal impact of the Pillar remains very vague and rather limited, as will be discussed below.

§3.03 PREVIOUS 'POSTS' FOR LABOUR LAW

The European Pillar of Social Rights resembles a methodology of the past. Two major declarations – posted by the EU institutions – need to be reminded as they had, given their timeframe, arguably similar game-changing potential as the European Social Pillar. It concerns the Paris Declaration (1972) and the Community Charter of Fundamental Rights of Worker (1989). They had the ambition of being main references for the development of labour law and social policy at the level of the EU (or, at the time, European Community).

[A] The 1972 Paris Declaration

While social policy was only embryonically present in the Treaty of Rome (1957), quite European integration project received an important impulse for the adoption of social policies. In 1971, the European Commission issued guidelines for a community social action programme. Six founding Member States shared rather similar traditions, but they faced the first enlargement of the European integration project: three new Member States, among which the United Kingdom, were in the process of joining. A political climate in favour of a bigger role for the European policy level gave rise to the Paris Declaration of 1972. The heads of state or government held their 'First Summit Conference of the Enlarged Community' between 19 and 21 October 1972. They not only 'assigned themselves the objective of converting, before the end of this decade and in absolute conformity with the signed Treaties, all the relationships between Member States into a European Union'. They also declared 'that vigorous action the social sphere is to them just as important as achieving economic and monetary union'.[10]

The Paris Declaration is methodologically interesting. It was political declaration, involving the founding states as well as the new Member States. It created a strong political message for increased European cooperation and for strong social policy action at the level of the European institutions. It not only made clear that the European project was more than a mere economic project, but the Member States' heads of state

---

9. Cf. Press release IP/17/1006.
10. *Bull. EC*, 10-1972, p. 19.

or government underlined the idea that European social policy needs to be equally important as the realisation of the economic and monetary goals.[11]

Although no specific rights or other precise social policy measures were formulated, the Paris conclusions resulted in the social action programme, officially adopted by a Council Resolution on 21 January 1974,[12] which gave rise to a series of legislative initiatives of the European Commission in the field of labour law. This announced the so-called golden period of harmonisation.[13] There remained, nevertheless, some problems. Only a limited amount of initiatives resulted in legislation. There was not only an issue with (the absence of) political consensus, but there was also a lack of sufficient legal basis in the treaty to make labour law.

The political meaning of the Paris Declaration kept of course its worth. It learnt that a big political declaration can be necessary to give new impetus to European policies, although it also showed that a political momentum bringing real change is likely to be dependent on other factors, including a supporting consensus and a proper legal and institutional framework.

The notion that the integration process was not only economic, but also social, would bring Europe to the 1980s, when a quest for more flexibility and deregulatory forces came through.[14] It created a setting that was symptomatic for the tension between economic and social progress. In that time, deregulation and in particular flexibility became important slogans in the fight against the economic and social crisis, in order to address the issues of decreasing economic growth and rising unemployment. The social aspirations of the European project could keep the idea of serving as a counterforce to economic developments.

[B] The 1989 Community Charter

In the mid-1980s, a new European Commission took office under the presidency of Jacques Delors, with renewed ambitions for social policy.[15] The idea was to realise a Europe with a human face, the creation of *'l'Europe sociale'*. Somewhere in the background, the 1972 Paris Declaration remained important. At the 1989 Madrid Summit, the European Council repeated the 1972 principle that as much importance must be given to the social dimension as to economic policies.

The strategy of the 'Delors Commission' was fitting well with a traditional labour law approach. Social policy aspirations would require a rights-based approach. Quite soon, a ground floor of fundamental rights for workers became part of the ambition.

---

11. PH. VAN PRAAG, 'Trends and achievements in the field of social policy in the European Communities', *Bulletin of Comparative Labour Relations*, nr. 4, 1973, 150.
12. 'Social Action Programme. Resolution of the Council of 21 January 1974', *Bulletin of Comparative Labour Relations*, nr. 5, 1974, 135-187.
13. R. BLANPAIN, *Europees arbeidsrecht*, Brugge, die Keure, 2001, 135.
14. B. HEPPLE, 'European rules on dismissal law?' in ISLLSS, *Proceedings of the 5th European Regional Congress for Labour Law and Social Security, 17-21 September 1996, Leiden, The Netherlands*, 2.
15. President of the Commission of the European Communities (1985-1995).

On 9 November 1988, the Commission invited the Economic and Social Committee (ESC) to engage in a general discussion on the possible content of a Community Charter of Fundamental Social Rights for Workers. The ESC's opinion was adopted on 22 February 1989[16] and outlined the framework of the basic Community social rights, which they considered to be established in conjunction with the completion of the single market. However, the question as to what procedures were to be adopted with a view to establishing social rights in the Community was left open. On 15 March 1989, the European Parliament adopted a resolution on 'the social dimension of the single market'. It called for 'the adoption at Community level of the fundamental social rights which should not be jeopardized because of the pressure of competition or the search for increased competitiveness, and could be taken as the basis for the dialogue between management and labour' and expressed the need to ensure the social dimension of the internal market by implementing a programme of concrete measures comprising a timetable.[17] On 9 December 1989, at the Strasbourg Summit, the Heads of State of Government of eleven Member States (all except the U.K.) finally adopted, in the form of a declaration, the text of the Community Charter.

The comparison with the European Social Pillar initiative is apparent. The 1989 Charter is similarly interesting for it being promulgated as a political declaration, although it used the language of fundamental rights. Turning the document into a real and actual enforceable legal instrument remained uncertain and problematic. The ambiguous name (Charter) and its origin and purpose seemed to imply that the Charter was not seen as a legally binding instrument.

Also for this Charter – or was it to be called a 'declaration' – a new and major political momentum was created. The perspective of developing European social policy and the adoption of a series of 'rights' was a groundbreaking policy step. Furthermore, the Charter was followed by an *Action Programme*, thus requiring implementation by European action.[18] It contained a number of measures proposed by the Commission to be developed in order to implement the Charter. Finally, the real labour law impact of the Charter perhaps appeared some years later, as political consensus grew in favour of European social policy competences and a major amendment to the EC Treaty including competences for labour law, although an opt-out for the United Kingdom was arranged.

[C] In Search for a Legal Beacon: The CFREU

The weak legal status of the Charter – not seen as a binding legal document – became an issue in a later stage. A desire for a real legal beacon became apparent. It happened at the verge of the new millennium. In March 1996, a 'Comité des Sages' was appointed by the European Commission. This Comité des Sages was an initiative following from the 1995 Medium-Term Social Action Programme and its initial task was to address the issue of how to transform the 1989 Charter into a more institutionalised and effective

---

16. *O.J.* 23 May 1989, C126, 4.
17. *O.J.* 17 April 1989, C96, 61.
18. COM(89) 568 final.

floor of rights for workers within the Union.[19] In its 1996 Report, the Comité des Sages indicated that the moment was come to consolidate past achievements in the social field and to set about realising the aspirations and needs of the people of Europe.[20] The Comité brought the discussion to a more comprehensive level and proposed to conclude a real 'Bill of Rights' for the EU, including wide series of fundamental rights. At a later stage, the Charter of Fundamental Rights of the EU was prepared, after a Convention which fulfilled its mandate from the European Council, which, in turn, unanimously accepted the draft Charter at Biarritz on 13/14 October 2000. After having received the affirmation of the European Parliament (14 November 2000) and Commission (6 December 2000), as well as that of several national parliaments, the Charter was solemnly proclaimed by the presidents of the three EU institutions at Nice on 7 December 2000.

Even with the adoption of this new and clear fundamental rights Charter, a large vagueness rested on the legal status of the document. Since the Lisbon Treaty, and according to Article 6, 1 of the Treaty on EU, the Charter of Fundamental Rights of the EU shall have the same legal value as the Treaties. The inherent limits of the Charter do not give it the full potential compared to the originally conceived idea of an 'EU bill or rights'. However, this binding Charter on Fundamental Rights assures that it is applied throughout the Union by the institutions and Member States that are addressed.

§3.04 HOW THE GAME WAS CHANGED

The initiatives of the 1970s and 1980s, and their major 'posts', created a firm basis for furthering the development of the social dimension of Europe. During times in which the need was felt to address the tension between economic and social integration in Europe, a declaration, or the method of a charter, seemed a strategy to ease the pathway to Treaty amendments and secondary hard law initiatives. The fit with a logic of labour law seemed also present. The aspirations were directed towards a political view in favour of a more balanced project, with 'socially acceptable economic integration'. Furthermore, Delors' views on the involvement of management and labour in social policy-making confirmed a European 'tradition of inclusion of unions and workers' interests in the shaping of industrial relations and political regulations in general'.[21] Likewise, the Delors strategy accommodated a tradition of government activity and social policy intervention in the (integrating) economy in Europe.

In sum, the adoption of the 1989 Charter of Fundamental Rights and the introduction of the Maastricht Protocol on Social Policy in 1991 marked a major development for European labour law and social policy. However, three sets of policy papers would mark a new era, in which views on economic and social progress can be

---

19. A. NEAL, 'Stimulating the debate over fundamental social rights at work in the European Community', in A. NEAL, *Fundamental social rights at work in the European Community*, Aldershot, Darmouth, 1999, 14.
20. For a Europe of Civic and Social Rights (1996), Foreword.
21. P. ZILTENER, 'EC social policy: the defeat of the Delorist project' in V. BORNSCHIER (ed.), *State-building in Europe. The revitalization of Western European integration*, Cambridge, Cambridge University Press, 2000, 165.

seen to start moving forward in a slightly, or is it a significantly, different manner. It concerns the adoption of the 'Green Paper on European Social Policy – Options for the Future',[22] presented by Commissioner Flynn on 17 November 1993; the White Paper on Growth, competitiveness, and employment, adopted on 5 December 1993;[23] and the White Paper on European Social Policy, adopted on 27 July 1994.[24]

[A] The Green Paper on European Social Policy (1993)

According to this 1993 Green Paper, European social policy entered into a 'critical phase'. The existing social action programme was reaching its natural end; the entry into force of the Treaty on EU opened up new possibilities for European action in the social field, and the changing socio-economic situation, reflected notably in the serious levels of unemployment, required, as the Green Paper explained, a new look at the link between economic and social policies, both at national and at European level. The Commission considered that this situation required the launching of a wide-ranging debate about the future direction of social policy (and that would include labour law).

The 1993 Green Paper was not only important for the development of European social policy in general. The reflection that it stimulated debate about the future direction of labour law also displayed a concern for the reconciliation of labour laws and labour markets with economic objectives. In particular, the Green Paper stated that 'this process will be taking place at a moment when the attention of the Community is focused on the whole issue of how to reconcile economic and social objectives in the face of rising unemployment and growing concern about Europe's ability to remain competitive into the 21st century'.

[B] The White Paper on Growth, Competitiveness and Employment (1993)

With this White Paper, the economy came back on centre stage. The Copenhagen European Council (June 1993) invited the European Commission to present a white paper on a medium-term strategy for growth, competitiveness and employment. That decision followed an in-depth discussion between the Heads of State or Government based on an analysis by the President of the Commission of the weaknesses of the European economies. The 1993 White Paper that followed drew in large part on the contributions from the Member States. It was also guided by the discussions between governments and social partners.

The White Paper, as its title suggests, was clear on the priority in European policy at the time: the issue of employment. It announced that, in order to reverse the course of unemployment, the EU should aim to create 15 million jobs by the end of the

---

22. COM(1993)551.
23. EUROPEAN COMMISSION, *Growth, competitiveness, and employment. The challenges and ways forward into the 21st century*, COM(93) 700 final, Brussels, 5 December 1993.
24. COMMISSION OF THE EUROPEAN COMMUNITIES, *European Social Policy – A way forward for the Union*, COM(1994) 333 final, 27 July 1994.

century. Equally, the White Paper's primary angle was made clear: 'It is the economy which can provide the necessary pointers to a reappraisal of principles inherited from an age in which manpower resources were scarce, technological innovation was made possible through imitation, and natural resources could be exploited at will. We are thus setting out a number of broad guidelines which have a predominantly economic basis.'[25]

Nevertheless, the White Paper showed, at the same time, that the economic approach could not be dissociated from other major policy objectives, such as, for example, quality of life and values of solidarity. In this way, a balanced approach of social and economic integration remained the underlying idea.

Interesting is the fact that the 1993 White Paper also refers to labour law. The paper suggested that labour law as well as labour markets needed modernisation, and mentioned issues such as flexibility of enterprises, training and modernised social protection systems.[26] The White Paper clearly suggested that the economic problems and the high unemployment figures throughout Europe could be explained by the inflexibility of the labour market and specific institutional, legal (labour law and social security law) circumstances in each country.[27]

When looking back to the 1993 White Paper's ingredients for future action, an early, perhaps unpronounced, concept of flexicurity can be read, at least where it combines a need for internal and external flexibility with training and labour market mobility.[28]

It is clear that the main concept used in the paper was flexibility, understood in various forms.[29] Within this focus on flexibility, the White Paper addressed other major points of attention that also come back in a flexicurity debate, such as training, the

---

25. COM(93) 700 final, 11.
26. COM(93) 700 final, 11: 'Our employment systems have aged: by this term we mean the whole complex of issues made up nowadays by the labour market, labour legislation, employment policy, the possibilities of flexibility within or outside enterprises, the opportunities provided or not provided by the education and training systems, and social protection.'
27. COM(93) 700 final, 16: 'In a general manner, they show that growth is not in itself the solution to unemployment, that vigorous action is needed to create jobs. However, such action must take account of national circumstances. More specifically, the inflexibility of the labour market, which is responsible for a large part of Europe's structural unemployment, can be traced back to specific institutional, legal and contractual circumstances in each country. The educational system, labour laws, work contracts, contractual negotiation systems, the social security system, and business management (including internal work management) form the pillars of the "employment environment" in each Member State and combine to give each of them a distinctive appearance. In each case, the entire environment must be mobilized to improve the functioning of the labour market. This goes to show, once again, that there is no miracle solution; nothing short of coordinated action by the various players responsible for the components of these environments can effect the necessary transformation. Moreover, in each country the methods of social dialogue will reflect national traditions.'
28. COM(93) 700 final, 17: 'The question of labour flexibility needs to be examined from two angles: that of the external labour market, where supply meets demand, and that of the market internal to each business, i.e. the human resources at its disposal which it adjusts according to its needs, and the chosen forms of work organization and working hours.'
29. *Cf.* COM(93) 700 final, 17. For example internal and external flexibility; geographical mobility; contractual flexibility; organisational flexibility: 'staff versatility, the integrated organization of work'; working time flexibility; pay flexibility.

insiders/outsider problem, active labour market policies and adjustment of income guarantee mechanisms.

[C] The White Paper on European Social Policy (1994)

The wide-ranging debate, initiated by the 1993 Green Paper on Social Policy, was followed by the White Paper on European Social Policy of 27 July 1994,[30] setting out the Commission's approach to the next phase of social policy development and, in fact, a strategy for consolidating and developing the Union's action on social policy for the future.

It is clear from the outset of the social policy White Paper that the social policy thoughts needed to be brought in line with the economically oriented analysis as presented in the 1993 White Paper on Growth, Competitiveness and Employment. Therefore, the 1994 White Paper went back into the core debate of the economic and social balancing act. It also referred back to the issue of labour law and the pressure on labour standards from the viewpoint of economic competitiveness. The 1994 White Paper did not conceal the real issue: 'A substantial base of labour standards has been consolidated in European law. The question of where to go from there is complex and controversial because the issue of labour standards is at the heart of the debate about the relationship between competitiveness, growth and job creation. (...) On the one hand, there are those who argue that excessively high labour standards result in costs which blunt the competitive edge of companies in one country or region as compared with others. On the other hand, many believe that productivity is the key to competitiveness and that high labour standards have always been an integral part of the competitive formula. (...) It must be said that there is no clear consensus on this point and that Member States and others remain divided in their opinions about the need for further legislative action on labour standards at European level.'[31]

[D] Labour Law Initiative

The issue of the role of labour law in light of an economic performance agenda was also reflected in the exercise by the Union of its hard European social policy competences. Under the rubric of 'economic issues', the conclusions of the Essen European Council (9-10 December 1994) emphasised the need to take steps to improve the employment situation, and called for measures aimed at 'increasing the employment-intensiveness of growth, in particular by more flexible organisation of work in a way which fulfils both the wishes of employees and the requirements of competition'. A hard law approach for flexible work is followed with the involvement of the European social partners.[32] The European initiatives were explained as accommodating the need for

---

30. COMMISSION OF THE EUROPEAN COMMUNITIES, *European Social Policy – A way forward for the Union*, COM(1994) 333 final, 27 July 1994.
31. COM(1994) 333 final, 23.
32. *Cf.* T. TREU and M. BIAGI, 'The role of a European social policy' in *Labour law and industrial relations in the European Union, Bulletin of Comparative Labour Relations* 1998, vol. 32, 217.

flexibility (of employers) and security (of workers).[33] Steps towards the development of a policy concept of flexicurity would later be elaborated by the European employment strategy around the millennium change.

[E] Economically Acceptable Social Integration

Although the idea was reflected that 'social progress must go into retreat in order for economic competitiveness to recover' and that 'the Community is fully committed to ensuring that economic and social progress go hand in hand' (*see* the Green Paper), it nevertheless left a different impression. The new developments, through the Green and White Papers, gave all the signs that the phrase that economic and social progress goes hand in hand, first seen as 'socially acceptable economic integration', could now be explained as 'economically acceptable social integration'. It seemed to enshrine the European Commission's, later the whole EU's, new blueprint view.

It would of course turn labour law into a new dilemma and to a new test. While in principle labour law is conceived as a *corrigendum* to the market forces or a counterforce to the economy, now labour law was viewed as a competitiveness factor. This certainly changed the approach towards labour law and created a dilemma of making a compromise, or even a choice, between protection versus economic competitiveness.

[F] The Economic Governance Agenda of Labour Law

The economic challenges for labour law were also triggered in the EU's employment policy agenda. The Employment Title, adopted in the 1997 Amsterdam Treaty, gave the EU employment policy competences through an 'open method of coordination'. In general, the European employment strategy was perceived as a soft law mechanism. However, not only became the blurring of social and economic policies more and more apparent. In addition the logic and dynamics of economic policy seemed to strongly dominate social objectives.

The tensions between labour law and economic policies became stronger when employment policies and labour law debate became part of the new 'EU economic governance'. Critics of economic governance claim that the EU demands its Member States to dismantle acquired social rights in a one-sided crusade for austerity and economic growth.[34]

---

33. *Cf.* EUROPEAN COMMISSION, *Background paper for first-stage consultations with the social partners, flexibility in working time and security for workers*, Sec(95)1540/3, 4; Y. SUWA, 'How to regulate the fixed-term work: a trade-off relationship in employment', *International Journal of Comparative Labour Law and Industrial Relations* 1999, vol. 15(2), 175-178.
34. C. BARNARD, 'The Social Partners and the Governance Agenda', *E.L.J.* 2002 vol. 8, nr. 1, 86; C. CROUCH, 'Entrenching neo-liberalism' in N. CONTOURIS en M. FREEDLAND (eds), *Resocialising Europe*, Cambridge, Cambridge University Press, 2013, 43-44; M. DE VOS, 'Interne Markt en eurocrisis: arbeidsrecht in de tang van de Europese Unie', *Tijdschrift voor Sociaal Recht* 2013, no. 3, 694-697; J. FUDGE, 'The way forward for social Europe: how do we get there from here?', book

§3.05 ASSESSING THE PILLAR AS A GAME CHANGER

The Pillar has many positive aspects. The Pillar reemphasises the commitment of the EU with regard to social policy and social rights. However, the Pillar also leaves some questions and doubts.

When looking at the content of the Social Pillar, itself, a couple of remarks can be made. It is clear that the Pillar is an interesting document, also from a legal point of view. The Pillar reads like a rights charter. It contains twenty rubrics under which various social rights are formulated. The fact that the Pillar formulates rights seems logical, since it is entitled Pillar of Social Rights. The Pillar departs from existing EU competences, although it goes quite deep into crucial areas of labour law. For example, although the EU has not yet been able to address (individual) dismissal law through legislation, it formulates the principle (or right?) that 'prior to any dismissal, workers have the right to be informed of the reasons and be granted a reasonable period of notice. They have the right to access to effective and impartial dispute resolution and, in case of unjustified dismissal, a right to redress, including adequate compensation'. Or, knowing the problematic exclusion of pay from the social chapter's regulatory competence, the Pillar states that 'adequate minimum wages shall be ensured, in a way that provide for the satisfaction of the needs of the worker and his / her family in the light of national economic and social conditions, whilst safeguarding access to employment and incentives to seek work. In-work poverty shall be prevented'.

Some of these provisions not only go further than what EU law currently provides. They also go further than the level of protection found in some EU Member States. The content thus appears to be quite modern and exciting.

The legal nature of the Social Pillar will certainly be subject of debate. While the Pillar gives the impression to create new rights, nothing is pointing in the direction of a legally enforceable instrument. On the contrary, the Pillar is expressly referred to as being 'designed as a compass' and 'to serve as a guide' (Preamble 12), as also expressed in the Interinstitutional Pillar Proposal of 26 April 2017. In the accompanying Commission Working Staff document it is mentioned that 'given the legal nature of the Pillar, these principles and rights are not directly enforceable and will require a translation into dedicated action and/or separate pieces of legislation, at the appropriate level'.[35] About its own content, the Pillar's 14th Preamble mentions 'for them to be legally enforceable, the principles and rights first require dedicated measures or legislation to be adopted at the appropriate level'.

Nevertheless, many of the rights mentioned in the Pillar are *in se* sufficiently clearly formulated. Take for example the Pillar's provision that 'prior to any dismissal, workers have the right to be informed of the reasons'. It is not excluded that both national courts and the Court of Justice of the EU start to draw inspiration from the Pillar's rights and promote it as interpretative guidelines or as general principles of Union law.

---

review of N. Contouris en M. Freedland (eds), *Resocialising Europe*, Cambridge, Cambridge University Press, 2013 in *M.L.R.* 2014, vol. 77, no. 5, 811.
35. SWD(2017) 201 final, p. 3.

What is causing some confusion is that, according to the Pillar's 14th preamble 'the European Pillar of Social Rights expresses principles and rights'. 'It reaffirms some of the rights already present in the Union acquis. It adds new principles which address the challenges arising from societal, technological and economic developments.'[36] The reference to both rights as well as principles is a terminology which we know from the Charter of Fundamental Rights of the EU, although we would read only rights.

As the Pillar's legal profile is rather low, scepticism on its impact may become high. And we must indeed be critical. However, the Pillar obviously has the potential of bringing about a new policy dynamic. And within an EU context, labour law needs more than just new labour rights.

The Pillar has been linked to concrete legislative initiatives in the area of labour law, such as a revised EU Written Statement Directive or a new EU Posting Directive. Obviously, these initiatives are taken on the basis of existing EU competences. A Pillar is not required for this, nor expanding the EU's competences. But the political consensus building is perhaps more crucial than the legal basis.

Furthermore, the Pillar's potential may be highest in areas where the EU institutions itself hold a large degree of control. One of those fields concerns the European economic governance mechanism. This system, strongly driven by the European Commission itself, is under criticism as it is encouraging or even requiring national labour law reform, based on economic and financial parameters rather than social policy deliberation. The Pillar may lead to improvement in this field. As the Commission now suggests itself, in the annual cycle of economic policy coordination 'the euro area and country analysis and recommendations will reflect and promote the development of social rights'.[37] This may result in a positive impact on national labour law.

There are thus reasons to be optimistic. The Pillar's message is positive. It builds on a renewed consensus. It reestablishes the idea that social progress must also serve the purpose of fairness and that European economic integration is subject to the respect of fundamental social rights. The Pillar reminds somewhat at the Community Charter of Fundamental Social Rights for Workers, adopted in 1989. That Charter also created a new momentum, although not legally binding rights. The 1989 Charter laid a basis for new Treaty changes. It also started a reflection on fundamental rights in the EU and this led to our current (binding) Charter of Fundamental Rights of the EU, legally much more important than the Social Pillar. So where the Pillar will lead us may be more than we could expect.

From this perspective, the European Pillar of Social Rights is great. But is it great enough? Some nuance needs to be made. Notwithstanding the positive flow the Pillar creates, it draws on a methodology comparable to the 1989 Community Charter. This Charter was ultimately seen as too weak but, partly due to its existence and need for improvement, it helped building the pathway to the Charter on Fundamental Rights of the EU, now having the same legal value as the Treaties. This EU Fundamental Rights

---

36. Preamble 14 of the European Pillar of Social Rights.
37. COM(2017) 250 final, p. 3.

Charter is a real legally binding beacon for social rights, although with intrinsic limitations, and legally speaking much more important.

Words are not enough. For the Pillar to be real game-changing, strong political will and consensus will be necessary. It might then be able to really influence EU labour law's millennium shift and the game-changing views on the relationship between economic and social progress, as sketched above.

In one of his later writings, Roger Blanpain repeated his argument for more EU legal competences in the area of labour law in order to bring Europe's social aspirations really forward. Blanpain analysed how 'the political will to give the EU more social competences is lacking. And that will be necessary to advance decent work on a supra-national basis'.[38] A competence shift could indeed bring more change than another big declaration. However, we would make two nuances to this proposition. First, the EU competences in labour law are not too modest and are not yet fully explored. The European institutions introduced new legislative initiatives in labour law (revision of the Written Statement Directive 91/533/EEC) addressing the new work relationship, even in light of a European concept of worker. So the secondary and indirect impact of the Pillar in the (revision of the) existing legal 'acquis' may be more worthwhile than the direct legal consequences arising from the Pillar document(s) itself. But there is also a second point to be made. Labour and social progress may also effectively proceed through small legal steps. The Pillar will certainly be subject of further legal debate and, quite likely, be used in legal interpretation. Every new formula with potential legal relevance, even if it goes through a Social Pillar, gives new potential to build up a legal system that responds to the logic of labour law and the aspirations of real social policy. This means that, besides the Pillar's political effects, the power of its words should not be underestimated.

---

38. R. BLANPAIN, 'Decent work in the European Union: hard goals, soft results', *Employee Rights and Employment Policy Journal*, 2011, 40.

CHAPTER 4
Labour Law: The Medium and the Message

David Mangan[*]

From the contract of employment to the 'gig economy', attention in the United Kingdom (UK) has been fixed on the medium through which personal work relationships have been facilitated. Fragmentation and the associated decline in trade unions (the most evident medium in labour law) have been evident. 'Gig' work does not warrant 'game changer' standing because it is a continuation of the enduring issue of employment status. Still, innovations in information technology prompt further reflection, such as the lure of app-based work. Conversely, algorithms as a tool of workplace management may be perceived as 'game changers'. Appealing to the concept of 'scientific management', algorithms ostensibly promise an objective means through which to measure workplace performance.

§4.01 INTRODUCTION

Contemporary challenges in labour law have historical precursors. There is a continuity of message connecting past endeavours with the present circumstances. A tool for detecting these connections is the phrase 'the medium is the message'. It emerged first in Marshall McLuhan's 1964 book *Understanding Media: The Extensions of Man*.[1] McLuhan gained widespread attention for his work, and this phrase (as well as the concept of the global village) is perhaps the touchstone. For the present analysis, the exact meaning of McLuhan's seminal notion is not the focus. Instead, McLuhan is utilized as an instrument in exploring contemporary personal work relations. He identified the message of any medium as 'the change of scale or pace or pattern that it

---

[*] This chapter has benefitted from the comments of Janice Bellace, Maria Murphy and the participants at the International Conference in Commemoration of Roger Blanpain held at KU Leuven (3-4 November 2017).
1. Toronto: McGraw Hill, 1964.

introduces into human affairs'.[2] Relying on a pioneer in communications theory focuses attention on the use of information technology through which 'gig' work relationships have been conducted. The salience of McLuhan's analysis further emerges when considering the theme of game changers in labour law. With the implicit challenge to discern what is a game changer, labour law has a penchant for being diverted by the novelties and overlooking of what that item may be an emblem. The 'gig economy'[3] has been such a diversion; drawing attention away from substantive changes to the employment relationship. Consequently, app-based work (a hallmark of the gig economy) has shaped and controlled the scale and form of association in the personal work relationship.

The use of algorithms in the workplace, however, may pose a more profound challenge to personal work relationships because they offer the potential of a neutral means for measuring workers' performance. Although a history can be traced to Frederick Winslow Taylor's 'scientific management' from the early twentieth century,[4] there may be something approaching game changer status with algorithms. Overarching the discussion are innovations in applicable technologies coupled with the regulatory framework of the General Data Protection Regulation (GDPR). The challenges of algorithms as well as the difficulty in discerning protections for workers under the GDPR mean that these systems may constitute a medium through which the message of scientific management may be actualized.

§4.02 DISCERNING THE MESSAGE FROM THE MEDIUM

In labour law, trade union action stands out as one of the most evident media for workers. Trade unions are the medium through which workers channel efforts to resolve workplace issues and to effect workplace change. It is the conglomerate of worker decision-making being the majority decision of the membership. The perception of the union as a medium requiring constraint stands out in UK labour law.[5] Unions have been fragmented over a lengthy period. The Trade Union Act 2016[6] serves as a recent example of constraint. These changes are set within the context of the ongoing influence of non-standard work on trade unions.[7] The union as medium has dwindled over time and so turning attention to the more individualized means of

---

2. *Ibid.*, 1.
3. Differing understandings of what this term means range from economic practices to labour arrangements. Here a working definition applies to employment exclusively: 'participants who trade their time and skills through the Internet and online platforms, providing a service to a third party as a form of paid employment': CIPD, *To gig or not to gig: stories from the modern economy* (March 2017), 3. Different names have also been used such as the sharing economy or the on-demand economy. Miriam Cherry uses 'virtual work' as a collective term: Miriam Cherry, *A Taxonomy of Virtual Work*, 45 GA. L. Rev. 951 (2011).
4. Frederick Winslow Taylor, *The Principles of Scientific Management* (Harper Brothers, 1919).
5. David Mangan, *No Longer. Not Yet. The Promise of Labour Law*, 26 KLJ 129 (2015).
6. For further commentary, see Michael Ford QC and Tonia Novitz, *An Absence of Fairness … Restrictions on Industrial Action and Protest in the Trade Union Bill 2015*, 44 ILJ 522 (2015).
7. *See* Valerio De Stefano, *Non-standard Work and Limits on Freedom of Association: A Human Rights-Based Approach*, 46 ILJ 185 (2017).

redress garners greater reflection. For this reason, the introduction of tribunal fees instituted an added challenge. If the effectiveness of trade unions was curbed, then the most viable alternative has been through the individual (or group) claim to enforce employment protections. While the original fee scheme introduced was found by the UK Supreme Court to be unlawful,[8] this does not mean that the debate regarding charging has been abandoned. Now, the 'gig economy' is perhaps the most overt example for labour law of the message in a medium.

Roger Blanpain wrote in 1999 about globalization and technological innovation 'causing enterprises to explode into networks of teams where work will be done on a project basis, fundamentally altering the employment relationship, the role of the social partners and the like'.[9] As we reflect on the entirety of his work, Blanpain once again anticipated contemporary developments. The 'gig economy' represents a network of individuals occupied by discrete projects.

The term 'gig' refers to the use of wireless communication applications through which work relationships have been formed. In the English language, there is another meaning, from the music industry, referring to a paid performance. This connotation emphasizes the individuals who are electing to take on work through these app-based opportunities.

The 'gig economy' is not the only influence on forms of work that has enacted a nomenclature of fragmentation. Part-time work has long been an example. Between 1951 and 1989, the ratio of part-time to full-time workers grew from 1:25 to approximately 1:4.[10] Short-time working has also arisen as a response to fluctuations in demand. In the UK, steps were taken in order to extend certain protections to this cohort to the effect that short-time working 'assumed a special and technical meaning'.[11] Gig work dissects the components of full-time work into smaller parts. Unsurprisingly, remuneration is apportioned in relation to a job.[12] The query is whether or not there should be (and, if so, to what extent) legislation pertaining to this workforce. The question is not new.[13] Gig work falls within the parameters of non-standard employment (NSE) as outlined by De Stefano *et al* in this volume: 'Non-standard employment (NSE) is a grouping of different employment arrangements that deviate from standard employment. It includes temporary employment; part-time work; temporary agency work and other multiparty employment relationships; and disguised

---

8. *R (on the application of UNISON) (Appellant) v. Lord Chancellor (Respondent)* [2017] UKSC 51.
9. Roger Blanpain, European Social Policies: One Bridge Too Short, 20 Comp. Lab. L. & Pol'y J. 497 (1999).
10. Lord Wedderburn *The Social Charter in Britain: Labour Law – And Labour Courts?* (Lord Wedderburn (ed.), *Employment Rights in Britain and Europe – Selected Papers in Labour Law*, Lawrence & Wishart, 1991), 361.
11. Erika Szyszczak, *Employment Protection and Social Security* (Roy Lewis (ed.), *Labour Law in Britain*, Blackwell, 1986), 372.
12. Usual terms like work or labour are not mentioned: Valerio De Stefano, *The Rise of the Just-in-Time Workforce: On-Demand Work, Crowdwork, and Labor Protection in the Gig-Economy*, 37 Comp. Lab. L. & Pol'y J. 471, 477–478 (2016).
13. It was posed in 2007 regarding non-standard work in Paul Davies and Mark Freedland, *Towards a Flexible Labour Market* (OUP, 2007), 2.2.3.

employment relationships and dependent self-employment.' While terminology remains contested, the 'sharing economy' has developed with support from innovations in information technology where digital intermediaries connect 'self-employed' individuals with clients. App-based work also recalls the persistent challenge to employment status.

[A] The 'Gig Economy' as a Challenge to Orthodoxy

Despite criticism of the 'gig economy' as an exploitation of workers, the continued attraction to this form of work remains a matter for further attention. A positive dimension has been advocated that sees individuals avoiding the traditional detractions of workplaces (such as not being watched at work) and enjoying the associated flexibility. The difference in message may depend on how one dissects the medium. The argument regarding positives in app-based work may be contingent on how the 'gig economy' is construed. In the UK, the *Taylor Review*[14] noted testimony in support of the gig economy.[15] Anticipating the *Review*'s contention, the Chartered Institute of Personnel and Development (CIPD) has found that a minority of workers (14%) participated in it because they could not find full-time work.[16] This figure appears to be subject to interpretation. A significant number of individuals take on this work because of the absence of full-time, traditional employment opportunities.[17] The CIPD contend the 'gig economy' is of particular value to those seeking supplementary income.[18] This view, though, reveals part of the struggle with nomenclature. While there are different names for the shared economy, these are collective terms referencing work by platforms such as Deliveroo and Airbnb. Gig workers are not a uniform cohort and neither are these platforms. Airbnb illustrates an income generating opportunity that is not necessarily related to taking on remunerated work. Associated factors remain relatively untouched, such as socio-economic status, gender and race of gig workers.

Convenience and control are two aspects of the message that can be extracted from app-based work. For the consumer, food delivery from any outlet (as one example) represents a significant convenience. There can also be expediency for individuals (viewing app-based work more generally than just food delivery) seeking work on-demand. The possibility of working from home and the opportunity to

---

14. Matthew Taylor (chair), *Good Work: The Taylor Review of Modern Working Practices* (July 2017).
15. Though no reference was given in the *Taylor Report*, 'gig' companies have contended that the flexibility of 'gig' work has been part of the appeal to work with them: Work and Pensions Committee, *Self-employment and the gig economy* HC 847 (1 May 2017), para. 12. To this same Committee, company and worker representatives from Uber and Deliveroo asserted that the flexibility was pivotal.
16. CIPD, *To Gig or Not to Gig: Stories from the Modern Economy* (March 2017).
17. For example, 30% of temporary employees took on this form of work because no permanent position could be found: Office for National Statistics, *Labour market release.* (ONS, 2016).
18. The variation in interpretation underscores the diversity in definition of the term 'gig' worker – illustrated further in Full Fact, *Who's Working in the 'Gig Economy'?* (10 July 2017) https://fullfact.org/economy/whos-working-gig-economy/ (accessed 29 November 2017).

supplement income stand out as examples.[19] There is an element of choice that the worker in the traditional workplace does not have. In choosing the specific task, the individual can exert greater control over the execution of the task. This form of 'self-employment' may be enticing to those 'who might feel that the system doesn't accommodate the reality of their working relationships'.[20] Whether this is in fact the case will be discussed in the next section. Still, in a time of contesting the orthodoxies of contemporary life, there is reason to be alert to similar attitudes for change in personal work relationships.

[B] Employment Status Redux

'Gig' work is another aspect of the 'common doctrinal'[21] employment status issue. Arguments surrounding its benefits tap into the arguments often associated with labour regulation. There is an imminent importance, then, in mapping this 'digital transformation'[22] because misclassifying 'gig' work poses the potential of deepening the spectrum of precarity that has been a gradual outcome of a neoliberal policy shift.

[1] The Difficulty in Discerning Who Is a 'Gig' Worker

Alluded to above, there are taxonomical questions, such as who are 'gig' workers and how many are there? The importance of these queries emerges when unpacking the range of interpretations of the collective term 'gig economy' as well as the varied conclusions drawn. Part of the stated appeal for engaging in 'gig' work is that 'most gig economy workers see their gig economy income as supplementary rather than as their main source of income'. Around 51% of those in a CIPD survey expressed satisfaction with their income from 'gig' work.[23] It seems difficult to determine with sufficient precision how many individuals in the UK are supplementing their income through 'gig' work. In the United States (US), the impression of widespread uptake included figures combining both users and suppliers.[24] In the UK, the Labour Force Survey (LFS) identifies the number of individuals in employment. 32.136 million in employment and 1.119 million workers with second jobs comprised the total September 2017 LFS figure of 33.254 million.[25] The measurement from Workforce Jobs (WFJ) is the number of jobs, instead of the number of individuals in work. This figure for June 2017 was 34.949 million leaving a difference between the two surveys of 1.695 million (the LFS being

---

19. Janice Berg, *Income Security in the On-Demand Economy: Findings and Policy Lessons from a Survey of Crowdworkers*, 37 Comp. Lab. L. & Pol'y J. 543, 552 (2016).
20. *Taylor Review, supra* n. 14 at 7.
21. Miriam Cherry, *Beyond Misclassification: The Digital Transformation of Work*, 37 Comp. Lab. L. & Pol'y J. 577, 578 (2016).
22. *Ibid.*, 579.
23. CIPD, *supra* n. 16, at 13.
24. Katy Steinmetz, 'See How Big the Gig Economy Really Is' (6 January 2016) http://time.com/4169532/sharing-economy-poll/ (accessed 29 November 2017).
25. ONS, *Reconciliation of Estimates of Jobs: September 2017* (13 September 2017), 2.

lower). Adjusted for measurable differences, this figure was 1.016 million.[26] Part of the trouble in assessing the number of workers supplementing their income through 'gig' work is that the numbers are hard to reconcile; let alone determining the total number of 'gig' workers. Therefore, it is hard to suggest that this figure represents the total number of workers earning a supplemental income from 'gig' work.

App-based companies contend that 'gig' workers are self-employed. Looking at the available data, innovations in information technology have developed rapidly and overlap with the time since the Great Recession. UK employment since 2008 has predominantly increased as a result of self-employment: between the first quarter of 2008 and the second quarter of 2014, employment rose by 1.1 million, with 732,000 being self-employed.[27] Self-employment has been estimated at 4.8 million,[28] constituting approximately 15% of the workforce.[29] When at 4.6 million, the Office of National Statistics characterized this figure as indicative of 'strong performance' and as being 'among the defining characteristics of the UK's economic recovery'.[30] The aforementioned CIPD figure of 14% may be at the lower end of a range, considering a survey by the Royal Society for the Encouragement of Arts, Manufactures and Commerce (RSA) which found, in the five years leading to 2014, that 27% of 'gig' workers started self-employment in order to escape unemployment.[31] A 2017 RSA survey estimated there were 1.1 million 'gig' workers.[32] It may be that there is a smaller portion of 'gig' workers if the figure is based upon self-employment. The age range for the gig cohort tends to be 16–30 year old.[33] Based on the Office of National Statistics data, 35–54-year-old workers comprise the majority of the self-employed.[34] The growth in self-employment had also been located in two notably different areas, construction (30%) and finance/business (20%). These are not the typical locales for 'gig' work such as Uber or Deliveroo. However, it may be that these roles fit within discrete task-oriented platforms such as TaskRabbit. An RSA survey also noted that about 80% of 'gig' workers worked what (using a traditional concept of a job) equated to part-time hours.[35] It may be that in fragmenting portions of what would have been called a job into discrete tasks, the 'gig economy' has created a larger pool of part-time work. This work may be classified as part-time simply because it is a default term for work falling outside of the orthodox job.

---

26. Ibid., 4.
27. ONS, *Self-Employed Workers in the UK – 2014* (2014).
28. In contrast, there are about 5.44 million workers in the UK public sector: ONS, *UK Labour Market: November 2017* (15 November 2017), 10.
29. ONS, *UK Labour Market: October 2017* (18 October 2017); ONS, *UK Labour Market: November 2017* (15 November 2017). The majority of this growth (since 2001) has come from full-time self-employment: ONS, *Trends in Self-Employment in the UK: 2001 to 2015* (13 July 2016), 44.
30. ONS, *Trends in Self-Employment in the UK: 2001 to 2015* (13 July 2016), 2.
31. RSA, *Salvation in a Start-Up?* (May 2014).
32. RSA, *Good Gigs: A Fairer Future for the UK's Gig Economy* (April 2017), 13.
33. Full Fact https://fullfact.org/economy/whos-working-gig-economy/ (accessed 29 November 2017).
34. ONS, *Trends in Self-Employment in the UK: 2001 to 2015* (13 July 2016): 2.3% among those 45–54; 2.5% among those 35–44.
35. RSA, *Good Gigs: A Fairer Future for the UK's Gig Economy* (April 2017), 20.

The question of who is a 'gig' worker and the classification of that work reveals that the 'gig economy' may be a repackaging of existing jobs in a manner that: (1) deconstructs the orthodox job into discrete tasks and as a result (2) reconfigures the remuneration scheme and relationship between service provider and service user. On the latter point, the importance of the intermediary (the one connecting the service provider and the service user) stands out as pivotal. The intermediary connects the two, but it also has much to gain by this type of arrangement.

[2] 'Gig' Work as Repackaging Jobs

The lure of greater individual control suggests an absence of subordination that inaccurately characterizes work in the 'gig economy'. Instead, the pursuit of increased control over work recalls the tests for employment status that started with the 'control test' (itself crumbling soon after adoption in the nineteenth century UK[36]). With the 'gig economy', contract continues to be the cornerstone; but with an amendment that the message remains the limitation of a worker's control over her work.

Consider this statement by CrowdFlower's CEO: 'Before the Internet, it would be really difficult to find someone, sit them down for ten minutes and get them to work for you, and then fire them after those ten minutes. But with technology, you can actually find them, pay them the tiny amount of money, and then get rid of them when you don't need them anymore.'[37] Although intermediaries are in the most desirable position, it is still better to be the one seeking work to be done than the one performing the task: the underlying theme of app-based work. This disposition recalls common notions of the employment relationship in which the worker is in most ways subordinate.

The distinct nature of app-based work reveals some of its nuances. A brief comparison with 'homework' assists in unpacking these aspects. 'Gig' work is closer to the idea of 'homework' or piecework where a worker is paid per item produced. Finkin explored useful examples where the concern was 'only with the price and quality of the product turned in [and not] time and money in the supervision of the work process. ... the pace of work need not be monitored, so long as a product of acceptable quality is produced on time'.[38] Gig work renders the job more abstract insofar as it splinters tasks into components individually falling short of a job. A departure from the orthodox form of labour, there is a ready argument that since it is digital work, there should be other

---

36. Lord Wedderburn, *Labour Law – From Here to Autonomy? A Franco-British Comparison* (Lord Wedderburn (ed), *Employment Rights in Britain and Europe – Selected Papers in Labour Law*, Lawrence & Wishart, 1991), 110.
37. Of interest, this quotation was cited in the following: European Parliament, *The Situation of Workers in the Collaborative Economy* (October 2016), 15. http://www.europarl.europa.eu/RegData/etudes/IDAN/2016/587316/IPOL_IDA(2016)587316_EN.pdf (accessed 29 November 2017). This same CEO's comments proved deleterious to employment status litigation in the United States; though these comments also yielded further investment: Cherry, *supra* n. 21, at 592–593.
38. Matthew W. Finkin, *Beclouded Work, Beclouded Workers in Historical Perspective*, 37 Comp. Lab. L. & Pol'y J. 603, 609 (2016) [references omitted].

differences. Recall that this work is composed of discrete tasks; that is, components of a job, but never the entirety. It is not even the equivalent of a part-time job.

The business model depends upon the flexibility of employment status: 'by characterizing the relationship as one of arms-length dealing with self-employed independent contractors, not employees'.[39] Flexibility is the message of the medium for 'gig' companies and its value can be seen in the numerous employment status cases involving gig companies. The singular motive ascribed to this framework by a House of Commons committee was profit.[40]

Employment law has seen flexible work in different forms for some time. 'Gig' work has been found, so far, to be questionable on the analysis of mutual flexibility.[41] An insightful simplicity comes from the blunt statement of the District Court of Northern California in relation to Uber claiming to be a technology and not a taxi company:

> Uber is no more a 'technology company' than Yellow Cab is a 'technology company' because it uses CB radios to dispatch taxi cabs, John Deere is a 'technology company' because it uses computers and robots to manufacture lawn mowers, or Domino Sugar is a 'technology company' because it uses modern irrigation techniques to grow its sugar cane. Indeed, very few (if any) firms are *not* technology companies if one focuses solely on *how* they create or distribute their products. If, however, the focus is on the substance of what the firm actually does (*e.g.*, sells cab rides, lawn mowers, or sugar), it is clear that Uber is most certainly a transportation company, albeit a technologically sophisticated one.[42]

When considering (what might be called) the philosophy underpinning Uber's argument, the premise quickly falls apart. It is tantamount to stating: 'I use technology therefore I am a technology company.' This premise entirely ignores the fact of a networked society in which technology has become ubiquitous, in day-to-day business as well as social communications. The above-cited passage may well become a plain language reference in the future for arguments that seek to distract from the fact of change and its impact.

Although it may be said that the 'gig worker' has more autonomy, for example over when to work, this is first a question turning on the particular facts of a case. Second, where there may be autonomy it is more a matter of degree. Finally, there is a cost to the work autonomy obtained in the 'gig economy': the fragmentation of work coupled with the commensurate fragmentation of remuneration. The larger picture is that 'gig' work contributes to the ongoing decline of the standard employment relationship. If the development of currency contributed to the 'recoding' of labour as

---

39. *Ibid.*, 611.
40. House of Commons Work and Pensions Committee, *Self-Employment and the Gig Economy* HC 847 (1 May 2017), para. 19.
41. *See Pimlico Plumbers v. Smith* [2017] EWCA Civ 51 (permission to appeal to the UKSC granted 9 August 2017; hearing 20–21 February 2018) and *Uber v. Aslam* [2017] UKEAT 0056_17_1011.
42. *O'Connor et al v. Uber Technologies, Inc.*, C.A. No. 13-03826-EMC (N.D. Cal.), 10.

a commodity,[43] the 'gig economy' adds another layer of code that further whittles away the notion of standard employment.

A supplementary note on the concept of the 'gig economy' is that analysis can replicate past constructs. App-based work has tended so far to focus on manual homework. With a platform such as TaskRabbit, application to cognitive homework is easily perceivable. The difficulty here is that cognitive work has been underdeveloped in labour law in comparison with the orthodoxy of industrial work. Professional work, such as legal services, has been repackaged into discrete tasks undertaken by a global workforce which in itself can drive down the associated workplace costs.

Concerns have been voiced at government level regarding the growth of self-employed workers. The tension is apparent when considering citizen demands on public funds (whether that is during times of low income or at retirement).[44] There is a likelihood of a tipping point at which time the state cannot accommodate the range of calls on it. Furthermore, 'gig' work may, like some NSE such as temporary work,[45] not even be a stepping stone to an improved financial situation. The more recent disquiet also reveals the absence of effective government action.[46] It has not been unprecedented to regulate this type of work. 'Homework' was the subject of regulation in the US pursuant to the *Fair Labor Standards Act* of the 1930s which provided the Secretary of Labor with the authority to restrict or prohibit industrial homework to 'prevent the circumvention or evasion of and to safeguard the minimum wage rate prescribed in this chapter, and all existing regulations or orders'.[47] A query to be answered is whether or not the foreseeable calls on public funds of those who find 'gig' work to be insufficient for meeting financial obligations will be sufficient to compel a sustainable government response. On this point, the Work and Pensions Committee and the Business, Energy and Industrial Strategy Committee have published *A Framework for Modern Employment*[48] which contains a draft bill. Among other points, the bill requires: individuals to be classified as either employees or workers, creating a default worker status[49] (where the burden of proof has been placed on employers to establish individuals are self-employed); as well as a premium hourly rate for non-guaranteed work,[50] targeting zero-hours contracts.[51]

---

43. A Aneesh, *Global Labor: Algocratic Modes of Organization*, 27 Socio. Theory 347 (2009), 365.
44. This point has been mooted in House of Commons Work and Pensions Committee, *Self-employment and the gig economy* HC 847 (1 May 2017).
45. On temporary work *see* De Stefano et al., in this volume.
46. Susan Bisom-Rapp has called this 'the paradoxical role [played by government] in the growth of nonstandard work and increasing precariousness': Susan Bisom-Rapp and Urwana Coiquaud *The Role of the State Towards the Grey Zone of Employment: Eyes on Canada and the United States*, 58 Rev. Inter. Econom. (2017), para. 5.
47. Finkin, *supra* n. 38, at 607 citing 29 U.S.C. §211(d).
48. HC 352 (20 November 2017). This report takes into consideration testimony before the committees as well as the *Taylor Review*.
49. Amending the Employment Rights Act 1996.
50. Amending the National Minimum Wage Act 1998.
51. The draft bill can be found at https://publications.parliament.uk/pa/cm201719/cmselect/cmworpen/352/35209.htm#_idTextAnchor048 (accessed 29 November 2017).

§4.03 REGULATION BY ALGORITHM

As presently perceived, algorithms provide all the certainty that numbers ostensibly offer. And so, they could be game changers in labour law. Algorithms in the workplace recall the spirit of Frederick Winslow Taylor's 'scientific management', where workers required an unusual amount of cajoling.[52] Algorithms afford the metrics to coax optimal effort.[53] To Taylor's chagrin, algorithms are immune from neither critical analysis nor scrutiny. Viewing them as potential sources of information, instead of solutions in themselves, can yield a better understanding of technology in the workplace. Moreover, further investigation can contribute to 'a more nuanced anticipation of future developments'[54] as well as assist in avoiding the 'transparency fallacy'.[55] A message to be derived from the medium of algorithms is that the workplace is not devoid of social considerations.[56]

One of the difficulties with algorithms is their design. For example, an algorithm that assigns gendered pronouns according to the individual's title (Mr or Ms) may be set as the male default for titles outside of those two, such as Professor. This discrimination instance is a simple illustration but it is not the focus here. This discussion centres around design aspects related to worker monitoring in regulating the personal work relationship.

The GDPR[57] overarches this topic. Within this framework, employers fall under the definition of 'controller'.[58] The GDPR contemplates 'profiling' algorithms for workplace outputs.[59] Article 22 provides the data subject with a right to avoid a decision based solely on automated processing that carries a legal effect. The distinction targeted here is between automated decision support (where a person would make the final decision) and automated decision-making (where there is no human judgement involved). Article 22 does not apply where the decision arrived at by automated processing 'is necessary for entering into, or performance of, a contract between the data subject and a data controller'. The Article 29 Working Party, in its *Opinion 2/2017 on data processing at work,*[60] explained that 'performance of a contract and legitimate interests can sometimes be invoked, provided the processing is strictly necessary for a

---

52. Taylor called 'underworking' the 'greatest evil with which working-people in both America and England were afflicted': Taylor, *supra* n. 4, at 13-14.
53. Algorithms can be used at any point in the employment process, such as hiring. The focus here is on work performance algorithms. Algorithms may also present costs savings at management level on tasks such as scheduling: Cherry, *supra* n. 21, at 596-597.
54. Daithí Mac Síthigh, *Medium Law* (Routledge, 2018), 16.
55. Lilian Edwards and Michael Veale, *Slave to the Algorithm? Why a 'Right to an Explanation' Is Probably Not the Remedy You Are Looking For,* 16 Duke L. & Tech. Rev. (2017) 18
56. There is a more pronounced interconnectedness in labour law to facets of human life than may be as evident in other legal disciplines.
57. Regulation (EU) 2016/679. An overview of the GDPR is found in Rónán Kennedy and Maria Helen Murphy, *Information and Communications Technology Law in Ireland* (Clarus Press, 2017).
58. GDPR Art. 4(7).
59. Article 4(4) (profiling).
60. WP 249 (8 June 2017).

legitimate purpose and complies with the principles of proportionality and subsidiarity'. It remains unclear what qualifies as performance of a contract.

Employer monitoring of employees serves as an instructive scenario for exploring the GDPR, which contains an expansive definition of 'processing'.[61] Additionally, lawful processing of data includes that 'necessary for the performance of a contract to which the data subject is party'.[62] When an employer has referenced, for example, a social media policy within the employment contract, it may form part of the parameters for performance of the contract. Consequently, the rights outlined within the GDPR may be attenuated more than at first appearance. Perhaps, there will need to be a distinction made (such as monitoring the content of communications, duration or volume of data traffic).[63] The decision in *Bărbulescu v. Romania*[64] illustrates how monitoring of employees intersects with the processing of personal data. Based on the Grand Chamber's ruling, at work monitoring may be permissible in order to ensure that workers are performing contractual duties. In order to do so, an employer must put into place certain safeguards.[65] The employee must be 'informed in advance of the extent and nature of his employer's monitoring activities, or of the possibility that the employer might have access to the actual contents of his communications'.[66] With the blending of social and work lives through social media,[67] the challenge of monitoring via algorithms is compounded. Even in the workplace, there is scope for protection of privacy.[68] Any conduct of an employer as a data controller must be proportionate. As such, the ruling anticipates the consent provisions of the GDPR in Article 7.

Employers have relied upon employee consent to the employment contract at the point of hiring to justify a range of subsequent activities that can take place during the life of the employment relationship. The GDPR scrutinizes this type of consent. Article 7(2) emphasizes clarity, accessibility and plain language when consent is sought.[69] Based on this provision, an employer would likely need to draw the worker's attention specifically to a distinct part of the contract that deals with special categories of personal data processing. Article 7(4) reiterates the importance of defining consent to processing of personal data necessary for the performance of a contract. Although the consent provisions endeavour to protect the individual, the GDPR has simultaneously galloped into a long-held debate by creating a potentially impractical expectation. Consent in contract law has long been a matter of debate because of the inherent difficulty in determining what constitutes voluntary consent within the context of contemporary circumstances. There may be motivating factors for consenting to a

---

61. GDPR, Art. 4(2).
62. GDPR, Art. 6(1)(b).
63. The latter points being noted in Directive 2002/58/EC of the European Parliament and of the Council of 12 July 2002 concerning the processing of personal data and the protection of privacy in the electronic communications sector.
64. Application 61496/08 (5 September 2017).
65. These are enumerated at *ibid.*, para. 121.
66. *Ibid.*, paras 78, 121.
67. *Ibid.*, para. 71.
68. *Ibid.*, para. 80.
69. Article 7 would be read in conjunction with Art. 9 (processing of special categories of personal data). In particular Art. 9(1), (2)(a), (b) would be applicable.

contract which could well be more generally characterized as coercion of the will[70] and yet still not vitiate consent.[71] The rapid entrenchment of new technology within the day-to-day of any business queries the viability of obtaining the stipulated form of workers' permission.

Additionally, the framework of the GDPR raises a question about the separation between ancillary function and regular systematic processing. The matter of monitoring based on algorithms that keep track of (for example) the number of times social media platforms are accessed at work and for how long is problematic. If the demarcation point is data processing that is regular versus irregular, employer monitoring raises some issues. Although the remarks were made in the context of appointing a Data Protection Officer pursuant to Article 37 of the GDPR, the Article 29 Working Party touches on the present query. It interpreted 'regular' and 'systematic' (respectively): 'Ongoing or occurring at particular intervals for a particular period; Recurring or repeated at fixed times; Constantly or periodically taking place'; and 'Occurring according to a system; Pre-arranged, organised or methodical; Taking place as part of a general plan for data collection; Carried out as part of a strategy.'[72] Monitoring workers' online activity would seem to fall within this spectrum. The framework of the GDPR, in this instance, demonstrates the intricate nature of the outlined obligations and protections. It also compels concerted attention in order to map out important points of distinction.

§4.04 CONCLUSION

This chapter emphasizes the way labour law has been recently diverted by the means instead of the effect. Workplace metrics constitute a significant challenge: the search for a 'scientific' way in which to manage the workforce. Algorithms have been imbued with this potential. The message in this medium rests in the same predisposition that we can trace to Frederick Winslow Taylor; that is, the presumption of underperformance and the correlative necessity in worker cajoling mechanisms.

---

70. Considered in the labour law context in Lord Wedderburn, *Economic Duress*, 45 Mod. L. Rev. 556 (1982).
71. The common law debate has been defined by the mental state and contextual approaches where the former describes what is going on in an individual's mind and the latter references complete freedom to consent absent any pressure: Stephen A. Smith, *Atiyah's Introduction to the Law of Contract* (OUP, 2006), 275. In response, responsible use has been suggested as an alternative framework: Executive Office of the President of the United States, 'Big Data: Seizing Opportunities, Preserving Values' (May 2014) https://obamawhitehouse.archives.gov/sites/default/files/docs/big_data_privacy_report_5.1.14_final_print.pdf (accessed 29 November 2017).
72. Article 29 Working Party, *Guidelines on Data Protection Officers*, WP243 (13 December 2016), 8.

CHAPTER 5
Changing the Rules of the Game or Rearranging the Deckchairs on the Titanic: 'Brexit' and the Future of European Social Policy

Alan C. Neal

§5.01 INTRODUCTION

When the British Prime Minister David Cameron formally declared that a 'referendum' was to be held,[1] in which citizens of the United Kingdom (UK) were to be presented with an opportunity to vote 'on an in/out basis' whether to continue the country's four-decade membership of the European Union, a train of events began to unfold which has stimulated unprecedented social and political division, set the backdrop to a fall in the value of Sterling against the Euro in the order of 15%, and continued to provoke bitter recrimination both within the UK and in relation to that country's relations with her European 'partner' Member States.

Following an election victory for the Conservative Party which had been widely thought highly unlikely, a European Union Referendum Bill was duly announced,[2] and that proposed measure was eventually passed by Parliament as the European Union

---

1. On 22 January 2015, the United Kingdom Prime Minister had announced, in a context of the run-up to a pending General Election in May 2015, that, if the Conservative Party under his leadership were to win that election, they would seek to renegotiate the United Kingdom's relationship with the European Union, and would follow this by giving the electorate a chance to vote in a referendum on the terms of that renegotiation.
2. The proposed measure was included in the Queen's Speech on 27 May 2015.

Referendum Act 2015.³ In due course,⁴ it was determined that the eventual referendum should take place on 23 June 2016.

At the European Council meeting on 25-26 June 2015, the Prime Minister set out his ambitions for a negotiated 'package' which could be put to the UK electorate by way of the forthcoming referendum. However, little apparent response was forthcoming to that statement of ambitions,⁵ and it was only at the European Council summit of 17-18 December 2015 that initial discussion of those negotiating objects was undertaken. The failure to find a way forward at this stage, particularly given the realisation that time was fast running out in which to formulate a 'package' which could be presented to the UK electorate in time for the June referendum, provoked a flurry of activity in the New Year 2016, with the result that, on 2 February 2016, the European Council published a draft 'blueprint' for a potential agreement with the UK. Indeed, a so-called 'package of reforms' was then duly agreed between Prime Minister Cameron and the other twenty-seven Member States at a European Council summit held on 18-19 February 2016 in Brussels, and it was this that formed the basis for judgment by the electorate in the following June.

In response to the eventual question posed to the electorate - 'Should the United Kingdom remain a member of the European Union or leave the European Union?' - 51.9% of the votes cast on 23 June were for the 'leave' option, while 48.1% of those voting favoured the 'remain' option.⁶

The referendum outcome - which flew in the face of almost all forecasts prior to the vote - immediately gave rise to the resignation of Prime Minister Cameron, and the arrival of Mrs Theresa May as his successor in office. Thereafter, following the outcome of controversial litigation before the Supreme Court,⁷ the UK government gave formal notice of withdrawal, in accordance with Article 50(2) of the Treaty of Lisbon, on 29 March 2017.⁸ In consequence, the UK is due to leave membership of the European

---

3. The measure received its Royal Assent on 17 December 2015.
4. As announced in a speech given on 20 February 2016.
5. Not entirely surprisingly, given that priority European concern was at that time being directed to a dramatic migration crisis unfolding from the south of the Union, along with continuing crisis economic management in relation to the Greek economy. Arguably the most significant progress made at that stage had been the establishment by the European Commission of a Brussels 'task force' to handle issues arising in the context of the forthcoming United Kingdom referendum. For the outcome of the June Summit, see *European Council meeting (25 and 26 June 2015) - Conclusions* (EUCO 22/15, CO EUR 8 CONCL 3, Brussels 26 June 2015).
6. More than 30 million United Kingdom citizens cast their vote in the referendum, reflecting an electoral turn-out figure of 71.8%.
7. See *R. (on the application of Miller and another) v. Secretary of State for Exiting the European Union*, [2017] UKSC 5. Proceedings in that case were extended to facilitate treatment of the same Art. 50 issues in relation to Northern Ireland. Conclusion of this litigation paved the way for Parliament to enact the European Union (Notification of Withdrawal) Act 2017, giving the United Kingdom Prime Minister power to notify, under Art. 50(2) of the Treaty on European Union, the United Kingdom's intention to withdraw from the EU.
8. Article 50 provides that: '(1) Any Member State may decide to withdraw from the Union in accordance with its own constitutional requirements; (2) A Member State which decides to withdraw shall notify the European Council of its intention. In the light of the guidelines provided by the European Council, the Union shall negotiate and conclude an agreement with that State, setting out the arrangements for its withdrawal, taking account of the framework for its future relationship with the Union. That agreement shall be negotiated in accordance with

Union on 29 March 2019.[9] In the aftermath of triggering the Article 50 procedure, Prime Minister May decided to call an unscheduled General Election, held on 8 June 2017. That election resulted in a return to office for Prime Minister May, but without an overall working majority in the House of Commons.[10]

Since then, negotiations within the framework prescribed by Article 50 have progressed through a 'Stage 1', with agreement having now been reached for a 'Stage 2' phase to proceed after a meeting held in conjunction with the European Summit held on 14 December 2017.[11] Meanwhile, domestic Parliamentary activity has concentrated upon attempts to enact legislation to provide for the consequences of UK departure from the European Union – in the form of a European Union Withdrawal Bill 2017–2019.

The following comments relate to a few of the issues raised in the context of this 'Brexit' process which are thought to be of concern to the world of work, and which are regarded by some as 'game changers' for labour law and social policy in both the UK and the European Union.

§5.02 EUROPEAN SOCIAL POLICY AND THE 'BAD BOY OF EUROPE'

The field of social policy has rarely been a 'comfort zone' for relations between the European Union and the UK. Right from the time that the UK became a member in 1973, the unique character and institutions of British labour relations have made it problematic to integrate within structures which reflect fundamentally different approaches to 'social dialogue' and constitutionally orientated 'fundamental workers' rights'.[12] Nor has the British approach to statutory draftsmanship always sat comfortably alongside systems which are accustomed to developing rights and protections couched in the form of grand declarations of principle, rather than with detailed

---

Article 218(3) of the Treaty on the Functioning of the European Union. It shall be concluded on behalf of the Union by the Council, acting by a qualified majority, after obtaining the consent of the European Parliament; (3) The Treaties shall cease to apply to the State in question from the date of entry into force of the withdrawal agreement or, failing that, two years after the notification referred to in paragraph 2, unless the European Council, in agreement with the Member State concerned, unanimously decides to extend this period; and (4) For the purposes of paragraphs 2 and 3, the member of the European Council or of the Council representing the withdrawing Member State shall not participate in the discussions of the European Council or Council or in decisions concerning it. A qualified majority shall be defined in accordance with Art. 238(3)(b) of the Treaty on the Functioning of the European Union.' The Article also provides that: '(5) If a State which has withdrawn from the Union asks to rejoin, its request shall be subject to the procedure referred to in Article 49.'

9. The so-called 'exit day'. This is defined by Clause 14(1) of the European Union Withdrawal Bill 2017–2019, in terms that: 'exit day' means 29 March 2019 at 11.00 p.m.
10. The ruling Conservative Party is currently governing under the terms of an agreement struck with the Democratic Unionist Party, a Northern Ireland political party currently holding ten seats in the Westminster Parliament.
11. *See European Council meeting (14 December 2017) – Conclusions* (EUCO 19/1/17 REV 1, CO EUR 24, CONCL 7, Brussels, 14 December 2017), and, in relation to the 'Brexit' discussions, *see European Council (Art. 50) meeting (15 December 2017) – Guidelines* (EUCO XT 20011/17, BXT 69, CO EUR 27, CONCL 8, Brussels, 15 December 2017).
12. Something which has, on occasions, also been the case for Ireland, which joined the (then) European Economic Community at the same time as the United Kingdom.

concern for linguistic certainty and clear boundaries of justiciability for regulatory arrangements introduced to deal with the challenges of labour market activity and worker protection.

To a large extent, it has appeared that the UK has found it easier to embrace the predominantly 'economic' dimension of the European Economic Community established by the Treaty of Rome in 1957, as compared with any overtly 'social' dimension – something more in keeping with the sentiments expressly articulated in the words of Article 2 of that 1957 instrument, to the effect that:[13]

> The Community shall have as its task, by establishing a common market and progressively approximating the economic policies of Member States, to promote throughout the Community a harmonious development of economic activities, a continuous and balanced expansion, an increase in stability, an accelerated raising of the standard of living and closer relations between the States belonging to it.

Nevertheless, the Treaty of Rome to which the UK signed up did contain some limited seeds for what quickly came to be described as 'Social Policy' provisions.[14] Indeed, a significant 'first step' on the journey to recognising an explicit 'social dimension' within this newly established EEC framework had already been witnessed in the form of a 'Joint Statement' issued by the six founding Member States at their Paris Summit of 1972,[15] to the effect that:

> The Heads of State or Heads of Government emphasized that they attached as much importance to vigorous action in the social fields as to the achievement of the Economic and Monetary Union. They thought it essential to ensure the increasing involvement of labour and management in the economic and social decisions of the Community.

Such a commitment to recognising the importance of 'vigorous action' in the social fields thus reflected the established attitude of the Member States at the time of the first enlargement, on the occasion of the accession of Denmark, Ireland and the UK with effect from 1 January 1973.

The initial period following enlargement of the EEC to nine Member States saw the earliest examples of social policy legislation at the European level. This was the era which witnessed the introduction of directives dealing with individual rights in the context of collective dismissals, transfers in the ownership of undertakings, and

---

13. Treaty of Rome, 20 March 1957, Art. 2. As has often been pointed out, this overwhelmingly 'economic' approach to the new institution of the EEC contrasted markedly with the underlying values embraced by the International Labour Organisation, whose relaunched ethos in 1944 proceeded from the proposition in the Declaration of Philadelphia (1944), Point I, that: 'The Conference reaffirms the fundamental principles on which the Organization is based and, in particular, that – (a) labour is not a commodity; ... .'
14. In Arts 117–122 – even though those provisions (with the exception of Art. 119, dealing with equal pay between men and women) were almost entirely concerned with technical collaboration and consistency in labour market data, and, in particular, the recording basis upon which mutual arrangements for social security provision were to be founded.
15. Joint statement published after the Paris European Summit, 19–21 October 1972, Point 6.

insolvency on the part of the employing enterprise.[16] The measures adopted during that period reflected a scheme of work set out in the first Social Action Programme adopted by the European Commission in 1974,[17] and it is noteworthy that the legislative instruments adopted during this period were enacted with unanimity, under the powers contained in Article 100 of the Treaty of Rome.

In this early phase of social policy development, therefore, one witnessed the UK government – led by a Labour Prime Minister between 1974 and 1979 – demonstrating active participation in, and enthusiasm for, the (admittedly limited) labour law and social policy initiatives developing at the level of the EEC.

By the time gradual expansion of the EEC had been achieved, to include Greece, in 1981, and Spain and Portugal in 1986, the Labour governments of Prime Ministers Wilson and Callaghan had been replaced by a significantly more 'market-orientated' administration under the leadership of Mrs Margaret Thatcher. At this time, too, in the early years of the 1980s, moves were well on foot towards amendment of the original Treaty of Rome – including an expansion of treaty powers relating to regulation of the labour market and the world of work. Thus, in addition to the general treaty power introduced by Article 100A for measures concerning completion of the 'single market', specifically social policy matters were addressed in the context of new Articles 118A and 118B, introduced by the Single European Act with effect from 1 January 1987.

Utilisation of the new Treaty powers proved highly controversial with the UK government. Yet, in spite of regular clashes over the proper scope of these new legislative powers, a substantial amount of social policy legislation came into being during the following half-decade. Many of these new measures involved the swiftly expanding area of health, safety and hygiene at work, in relation to which the newly introduced Article 118A had opened the way for measures to be adopted through 'qualified majority voting'. This provided opportunities to authorise legislation notwithstanding opposition from a single Member State – such as the UK – rather than through what had been the prevailing situation for measures adopted by unanimity under the Treaty power contained in Article 100 of the original Treaty of Rome, where an effective 'veto' was held by any and each of the Member States.

It therefore came as rather less of a surprise that might hitherto have been the case when, as part of the 1989 Madrid Summit Conclusions, the Member States (at this point including the UK) declared that:[18]

---

16. *See*, in particular, Council Directive 75/129/EEC of 17 February 1975 on the approximation of the laws of the Member States relating to collective redundancies, Council Directive 77/187/EEC of 14 February 1977 on the approximation of the laws of the Member States relating to the safeguarding of employees' rights in the event of transfers of undertakings, businesses or parts of businesses, and Council Directive 80/987/EEC of 20 October 1980 on the approximation of the laws of the Member States relating to the protection of employees in the event of the insolvency of their employer.
17. *See* Council Resolution of 21 January 1974 concerning a social action programme (*OJ C 13, 12.2.1974, pp. 1–4*). An Annex to that Resolution set out the programme of action – COM(73) 1600, 24 October 1973. *See Bulletin of the European Communities*, Supplement 2/74.
18. Madrid Summit 'Conclusions', 26/27 June 1989, Point 2.

in the course of the construction of the single European market, social aspects should be given the same importance as the economic aspects and should accordingly be developed in a balanced fashion.

It has been suggested that the express commitment to a 'balanced' development of social policy, enjoying 'the same importance' as the economic dimension of the EEC, in the 1989 Madrid declaration marked a historical 'high water mark' for social policy and labour law at the level of the European Union. Certainly, that explicit reference, just prior to the completion of the Single Market and in the immediate run-up to the adoption of the Maastricht Treaty, brought to an end the first period of development for European (EEC) labour law and social policy, and was to herald a sharp shift in approach from the UK government.

Signs of growing tension had already come to the surface in the context of a Charter of Fundamental Social Rights of Workers, from which the UK chose to distance itself in 1989.[19] Eventually, however, a fully fledged 'opt-out' from the newly introduced 'Social Chapter' of the Treaties agreed at Maastricht lit the touch-paper for an increasingly incendiary relationship between that particular Member State (regularly aided and abetted by Denmark and Ireland) and the more 'integrationist' tendencies developing within the six founding Member States who had shared the earliest developments since their signing of the Treaty of Rome in 1957.[20]

The post-Maastricht fall-out from the failure to incorporate the proposed 'Social Chapter' into the body of the Treaties undoubtedly served to rein back a number of the more ambitious social policy initiatives which had been emerging around this time. Meanwhile, and arguably of more concern, the UK 'opt-out' from almost all things social raised the level of political tensions between the Member States at a time when negotiations were approaching their final stages for the admission of four new entrant Member States.[21] Indeed, a remarkably vivid illustration of the increasingly divergent paths for the 'economic' and the 'social' dimensions of the (now renamed) European Union was provided by the development and publication of two important policy documents under the Commission leadership of Jacques Delors – one concerned with 'growth, competitiveness and employment', and the other with the related challenges of social policy.[22]

In the meantime, the already-mentioned gradual expansion in the number of Member States was beginning to place strains upon the ability politically of those

---

19. See the Charter of Fundamental Social Rights of Workers, adopted by declaration of the Member States, with the exception of the United Kingdom, on 9 December 1989.
20. See the resulting Protocol on Social Policy, together with an annexed Agreement on Social Policy, between eleven Member States with the exception of the United Kingdom, appended to the Treaty on European Union, signed by the Member States of the European Community on 7 February 1992.
21. Austria, Finland, Norway and Sweden. Of these, Norway eventually decided not to proceed towards full membership, following rejection of a proposal to that effect in a popular referendum. That referendum, which was held on 26–27 November 1994, resulted in 52.2% of the voters opting for the 'No' option, on a turnout of 88.6%.
22. That sharpening split was evident even from the titles of the documents: the 'economic dimension' blueprint, under the title of 'Growth, Competitiveness, Employment – The Challenges and Ways Forward into the 21st Century' (COM (93) 700 final) and its 'social dimension' counterpart, 'European Social Policy: A Way Forward for the Union' (COM (94) 333 final).

Member States to reach sufficient consensus to adopt meaningful labour law and social policy measures at the European level.

Even by the time the Single European Act brought into effect the first major amendments to the original 1957 Treaty of Rome,[23] there had been further enlargement of the EEC to accommodate the former dictatorships of Greece (1981), Portugal and Spain (both 1986). Use of the enlargement process to promote political and ideological coherence across the European continent could thus already be discerned, while encouragement for that process was coming enthusiastically from an unlikely quarter – the UK of Mrs Thatcher. Indeed, it has been suggested that, for the British Prime Minister, an enlarged Community, with an amalgamation of more sharply contrasting historical, political and social traditions, opened up interesting prospects for diluting the push towards an ever-broader 'Social Europe'.[24] By this time, therefore, the trajectory in favour of rapid enlargement was well established, and – notwithstanding a referendum outcome in Norway which brought that country's aspirations to membership to an end – 1995 saw the accession of Austria, Finland and Sweden, bringing the total membership to fifteen Member States.

Even as expansion to embrace these new economies was in train, however, the strategic planning basis upon which EU social policy had up until then proceeded received a severe shock, with a breakdown in the ability of the European Commission to put forward an acceptable five-year social policy action plan for the run-up to the Millennium. A Medium-term Social Action Programme was eventually put in place for the period 1995–1997,[25] and only fraught negotiation and compromise enabled a subsequent Social Action Programme to be adopted for 1998–2000.[26]

Nevertheless, this period of post-Maastricht 'opt-out' witnessed the first of a number of so-called 'social dialogue' measures – including concern to address problems associated with 'a-typical forms of employment' and the issue of parental leave[27]

---

23. From 1 January 1987.
24. A little-remarked upon, but highly significant, example of this 'creeping enlargement' was witnessed in 1990, when the former German Democratic Republic ('East Germany') became assimilated into the EEC under the umbrella of German 're-unification'. The longer-term implications of an overnight enlargement – to the tune of some 16.1 million new citizens – in this way have contributed, it has been suggested, to an underlying political suspicion and instability amongst the Member States faced with that unilateral German act of expansionism.
25. Communication from the Commission to the Council, the European Parliament, the Economic and Social Committee and the Committee of the Regions, *Medium term social action programme 1995-1997* (COM (95) 134 final, 12 April 1995).
26. *See* Communication from the Commission, *Social Action Programme 1998-2000* (COM(1998) 259 final, 29 April 1998).
27. Through the Framework agreement on part-time work (6 June 1997), the Framework agreement on fixed-term work (18 March 1999), and the Framework agreement on parental leave (14 December 1995). These 'framework agreements' eventually found their way into legislation, through, respectively, Council Directive 97/81/EC of 15 December 1997 concerning the Framework Agreement on part-time work concluded by UNICE, CEEP and the ETUC; Council Directive 1999/70/EC of 28 June 1999 concerning the framework agreement on fixed-term work concluded by ETUC, UNICE and CEEP; and Council Directive 96/34/EC of 3 June 1996 on the framework agreement on parental leave concluded by UNICE, CEEP and the ETUC.

– along with intervention in the field of working time,[28] and, significantly, the introduction of the 'European Works Council' as a new institution on the scene.[29]

Much of the underlying instability which had been introduced into this area had its roots in the widening dispute between the UK and the European Commission over the appropriate scope and approach to be taken in relation to European social policy. In particular, the parallel legislative powers to be found in: (a) the Treaties to which all fifteen Member States were party and (b) the Social Policy Agreement to which only fourteen had subscribed introduced significant controversy and confusion into the legislative process.

Indeed, only the field of health, safety and hygiene at work saw a strong linear development during this period[30] – although, as mentioned, valiant attempts to utilise the 'social dialogue' route to legislative norm creation saw the emergence of 'framework agreements' designed to address employment protection issues in a limited range of areas. Meanwhile, the degree of compromise 'dilution' which eventually enabled a Working Time Directive to be agreed in 1993 confirmed the extent to which markedly varied notions of 'social policy' were being pursued by different Member States.[31]

That being the case, therefore, it might perhaps have appeared surprising that eventual progress in relation to the establishment of a directive on 'European Works Councils' (EWCs) came to fruition in 1994 – although it should be noted that the UK was kept very much 'in the loop' during the legislative phases of that instrument.[32] This paradoxical situation perhaps owed something to the reality involved with recognition that the target enterprises sought to be brought within the net of the regulatory requirements for EWCs were largely headquartered in the UK and subject to that particular Member State's company laws. In consequence, a formal stance of 'lofty indifference' on the part of the UK Conservative government did not entirely reflect the reality of contacts, co-operation, and carefully balanced development which characterised the legislative phases leading up to the adoption of the 1994 directive.

Eventually, however, following the election to office of a 'new Labour' government in the UK in 1997, steps could be taken to paper over some of the cracks which had opened up in connection with European Commission activism in the context of the 'qualified majority vote' ('QMV') legislative powers introduced by Article 118A through the Single European Act; the declaration of the 'Charter of Fundamental Social Rights of Workers' in 1989; the introduction of the fourteen-Member State Social Policy

---

28. Council Directive 93/104/EC of 23 November 1993 concerning certain aspects of the organisation of working time.
29. Council Directive 94/45/EC of 22 September 1994 on the establishment of a European Works Council or a procedure in Community-scale undertakings and Community-scale groups of undertakings for the purposes of informing and consulting employees.
30. Particularly once the important 'framework directive' of 1989 had been adopted. *See* Council Directive 89/391/EEC of 12 June 1989 on the introduction of measures to encourage improvements in the safety and health of workers at work.
31. Ever since the enactment of the original version of the working time directive, substantial efforts have been expended (notably, on a 'sectoral' basis) with a view to 'plugging the gaps' to which that political compromise had given rise.
32. *See* the comments of this author in Alan C. Neal, 'European Works Councils: The United Kingdom Point of View', (1998) 32 *Bulletin of Comparative Labour Relations* 163.

Agreement at Maastricht; and the embracing of the 'social dialogue' route to social policy legislation. Nevertheless, to suggest that the twentieth century ended with harmony between the UK and the other Member States in the field of social policy and labour law would be a gross exaggeration. The best that can be suggested with any degree of justification might be that a greater atmosphere of co-operation had been engendered on the eve of the new Millennium than had hitherto characterised relations in this area over the previous decade and a half.

With the turn of the Millennium, however, the field of social policy in general at the European level found itself increasingly lacking the necessary political will for the launching of meaningful new initiatives. Instead, the field found itself under sustained pressure to shift its focus from 'social protection' to economic 'efficiency'. Louder and louder demands were voiced for 'flexible' labour markets and for 'competition' to be prioritised in the context of increasing globalisation – making it extremely difficult for the European Commission effectively to put forward realistic proposals for new regulation in this area. Nor had the replacement of the former Conservative administration by a 'new Labour' government under Prime Minister Tony Blair marked any significant departure from the fundamental focus upon the 'economic dimension' which had characterised the period of 'Thatcherism' and beyond from 1979 onwards.[33]

At the same time, institutional weaknesses within a still enlarging European Union were starting to become more apparent. In relation to the Treaties, the saga of the failed attempt to reach agreement on a proposed 2004 Treaty establishing a Constitution for Europe witnessed clear dissent expressed by public opinion in both France and the Netherlands from the trajectory favoured by Europe's increasingly out of touch leadership.[34] Defeats for the ruling governments in both countries during referenda to confirm ratification of the proposed Treaty modifications brought an abrupt halt to efforts directed towards 'ever-closer union'. Even the routine institutional response to such a setback, of simply returning the question time and again to the Member State electorate until a weary populace eventually conceded 'the right answer',[35] would not suffice on this occasion.

Some of the problem underlying the failure to take public opinion with the views of the European Union's increasingly unrepresentative bureaucracy lay in an attempt to convert what had previously been a declaratory 2000 'Charter of Fundamental Rights of Citizens' into a 'Part II' of the modified Treaties with legislative effect.

---

33. Notwithstanding occasional examples of domestic regulation being introduced with a view to improving the protective arrangements for workers in the United Kingdom. *See*, for instance, the introduction of a 'national minimum wage', by way of the National Minimum Wage Act 1998.
34. *See* the Treaty establishing a Constitution for Europe (OJ C 310, 16 December 2004), signed by the twenty-five Member States on 29 October 2004. Rejection of the proposed new Treaty by voters in referenda held in France (29 May 2005) and The Netherlands (1 June 2005) made it impossible to achieve the necessary ratifications, and the project was abandoned before the issue was put to the United Kingdom public by way of a referendum which had been announced by Prime Minister Blair.
35. As had already happened in Denmark (1992) with regard to the Treaty of Maastricht, and in Ireland in relation to ratification of the Nice Treaty (2001). Ireland was subsequently to be obligated, once again, to take a 'second bite of the cherry' in 2008 in relation to ratification of the Treaty of Lisbon.

Following the abrupt rebuff by the French and Dutch electorates to that initiative, the institutions of the European Union concentrated their efforts upon developing what was to become the Treaty of Lisbon, but without incorporation of the provisions of that 2000 Charter. Instead, with much fanfare a new 'Charter' was signed in Strasbourg in 2007 – although the bankruptcy of the modern European Union social policy was laid embarrassingly bare with the realisation that, remarkably, this gleaming new 2007 instrument simply repeated word for word the content of the earlier 2000 document.

Meanwhile, in the context of developing European monetary union, the transition from the ECU – which had been in use between 1979 and 1999 – and launch of the Euro with effect from 1 January 1999, provided important momentum towards the promised goal of a 'Euro-land'. The UK studiously refrained from participation in this new development – a stance which only hardened when further systemic weaknesses in the regulatory authority of the European Union were revealed. In particular, evidence emerged of a stubborn willingness to 'paper over the cracks' between aspiration and reality for the sake of maintaining momentum on the parts of the majority of Member States in the direction dictated by the EU's political and bureaucratic leaders. Thus, when it came to applying the so-called 'convergence criteria' for entry into the monetary union,[36] critics pointed to an alleged willingness to 'distort' economic data and to undertake some 'remarkable sleight of hand' in order to ensure that 'problem economies', such as Belgium, France and Italy, and weak economies with poor governance, such as Greece, might be kept within the fold.[37]

At the same time, the relentless march towards further twenty-first century enlargements was proceeding apace. The year 2004 saw the most dramatic step in that direction, with the accession of ten new Member States,[38] including a number of countries which had formerly been part of the Eastern European socialist *bloc* before the fall of the Berlin Wall. With the 'European club' already standing at twenty-five Member States, the further accession of Bulgaria and Romania in 2007 heralded a short pause, before the accession of Croatia in 2013 as the twenty-eighth Member State of the European Union brought about the present pre-'Brexit' composition.

Yet, in the end, it was the 2007/2008 global recession and financial crash which eventually hammered the most potent nails into the coffin of hopes for a revitalised 'Social Europe' and a resurgence of 'the golden age' of labour law regulation at the European level. In particular, the hitherto carefully concealed weaknesses in the eventual monetary union precipitated a catastrophic 'Euro-zone' crisis and set the scene for some of the most dramatic economic interventions into the economic management of ostensibly Sovereign States ever seen outside wartime occupation. Thus, Greece, Ireland and Portugal were formally made subject to the so-called 'Memoranda of Understanding on specific economic policy conditionality', while Italy

---

36. As established in the course of negotiating the Treaty of Maastricht in 1992. These related to (1) price stability; (2) government finance; (3) exchange rate; and (4) long-term interest rates.
37. For a contemporary critique of the 'convergence criteria' and their application in practice, *see* 'Maastricht Follies', *The Economist* (9 April 1998).
38. The so-called 'EU-10', comprising Cyprus, the Czech Republic, Estonia, Hungary, Latvia, Lithuania, Malta, Poland, Slovakia, and Slovenia.

was effectively also made subject to such oversight by way of an exchange of letters between the European Central Bank and the relevant Italian authorities.[39]

§5.03 CHANGING THE RULES OF THE GAME? A EUROPEAN UNION PERSPECTIVE

Against the increasingly pessimistic backdrop for European labour law and social policy by the turn of the Millennium, it had become clear that popular sentiment in the UK was not alone in regarding European Union activity in the social field with less than unbounded enthusiasm.

This was not only a problem of endeavouring to grant 'the social dimension' anything like the same standing as 'the economic dimension' of the Union. By the time of the 2007/2008 economic crisis there had also been witnessed an almost complete disappearance of coherent political will for action on the social front. That loss of political will had been paralysing the prospects for new initiatives[40] and leading the European Commission to adopt ever more instruments restating, adjusting, or seeking to ensure compliance with existing normative provisions making up the EU's framework of labour law. At the same time, the hugely enlarged membership of the European 'club' had served to create dramatic logistical obstacles in the way of the necessary political agreement. So, too, had this highlighted fundamental attitudinal differences of approach between the 'old Europe' established market economies, the 'former Dictatorship' economies of Greece, Portugal and Spain, and the former European socialist *bloc* Member States.

So serious has this tendency become that it may be argued that the modern institutional, political and regulatory framework of the European Union is unsuited to further development and strengthening of a normative regulatory social policy framework which can deliver enforceable social (particularly 'labour law') rights while at the same time respecting the particularities of national industrial relations and legal cultures/systems. This state of affairs, it may be suggested, has arisen by reason of a number of tendencies coming together in a period of economic uncertainty and social unease.

The first of these can be seen at the political level, where two components feed into the underlying weaknesses and problems at that level. The first has already been adverted to – the successive and dramatic steps to 'enlargement' of the European

---

39. *See* Greece: *Memorandum of Understanding on Specific Economic Policy Conditionality, May 2, 2010*; Ireland: *Memorandum of Understanding on Specific Economic Policy Conditionality, November 28, 2010*; Portugal: *Memorandum of Understanding on Specific Economic Policy Conditionality, 3 May 2011*; and the Letter of 5 August 2011, from Mario Draghi (at that time the Governor of the Bank of Italy) and Jean-Claude Trichet (the then President of the European Central Bank) to the (then) Italian Prime Minister, Silvio Berlusconi.
40. With the 'last leg' of the initiatives to deal with 'a-typical work forms' – the initiative which eventually became Directive 2008/104/EC of the European Parliament and of the Council of 19 November 2008 on temporary agency work – constituting the only truly 'fresh' development in the social field.

creature. The second arises out of the increasingly destabilising economic and ideological divergences between that enlarged 'community' of Member States.

Enlargement, it has to be noted, is not something which has come about suddenly or only recently. Notwithstanding some of the generalised rhetoric aspiring to a wider scope for the emerging EEC/EC, the real push along this road came during the mid-1980s, when *inter alia* the UK government under Prime Minister Margaret Thatcher showed remarkable enthusiasm for such a trend – cynically, it was suggested by commentators at the time, in the hope of splintering the tight consensus which had hitherto enabled regulation by unanimity of like-minded nations and their leaders.

In this context, legislative powers relating to social policy were very much to the fore, with significant battles being fought between the UK and the European Commission over (in particular) the scope of the 'non-unanimity' arrangements introduced through the 1986 Single European Act. Thus, while a substantial 'dyke-buster' was perceived in the new Treaty power contained in Article 100A for measures constituting part of the framework required to complete the single market by 1992, the provision of so-called 'qualified majority voting' in relation to social matters touching health and safety at work made the new Article 118A a particular focus for tensions in this area. Indeed, as was revealed by UK government evaluations in the wake of agreement on the 'framework' health and safety Directive 89/391/EEC, a strong sense of 'ultra vires activity' and 'dirty work at the crossroads' developed – particularly in relation to the Greek Presidency of the time, in a context when the Commissioner for Social Affairs was also of Greek origin.[41]

If, indeed, there was any conscious or thought-through strategy to press for faster and broader 'enlargement', with a view to achieving a situation in which there might be a political inability to find even the required level of 'non-consensus' legislative agreement facilitated by QMV and 'social partner' mechanisms introduced in the wake of the Maastricht social policy innovations at the level of the treaties, there is little doubt that this has been the result. In any event, whether or not there might have been any such conscious strategic push, the fact remains that the current position in terms of assembling a workable majority to push through anything but the most diluted of social policy regulatory initiatives can be said to reflect an entirely predictable 'post-Thatcherite' outcome.

Nor should it be overlooked that the incumbency of the European Commissionership for social affairs (in whatever semantic guise it might currently manifest itself)[42] by Commissioners from, respectively, the Czech Republic and Hungary, for the Barroso Commissions during the decade following the 2004 enlargement has coincided with a period in which the balance has been dramatically in favour of 'soft law', marginal

---

41. In the person of Vasso Papandreou, who held that office during the second Delors Commission, between 1989–1992.
42. Currently, the nomenclature is that of the Commissioner for Employment, Social Affairs, Skills and Labour Mobility. Since 2014, this post has been held by the Belgian national, Marianne Thyssen.

adjustments, and 'strengthening of enforcement' for existing regulatory arrangements.[43]

Indeed, this period of highly disappointing 'non-activity' in the social sphere has been regarded in some quarters as reflecting the relative weakness, in policy-making initiative terms, of the newcomer (especially former Socialist) Member States and officials whose backgrounds have been steeped in a very different developmental history from that of the Nordic economies, the Common Law countries, or the 'Old Europe' founder Member States.

Whether such a criticism can be made out as strongly as some have suggested may be open to interpretation, but there is no doubt that the increasingly evident economic and ideological divergence between the current twenty-eight Member States (especially as between the 'Old Europe' Member States, the former 'Dictatorship' countries, and the former socialist countries of Central and Eastern Europe) plays out in dramatic terms when it comes to balancing on the high wire between the social and economic dimensions of the European Union. Certainly, the lack of tangible product in the area of social policy has been taken by some as confirming that there is currently an inability to find common ground on which to develop social protection in the context of continuing and worsening economic deterioration in national labour markets.

A second tendency can be perceived at the regulatory level – and, in particular, with the intellectual 'love-affair' pursued by (most notably) the European Commission with 'soft law' instruments, rather than any sense that more direct and effectively enforced regulation might be required in order to facilitate and ensure adequate protective arrangements for citizens engaged in the world of work.

This trend can be seen to have gathered pace particularly since the adoption of such 'soft' mechanisms as 'the open method of co-ordination' in relation to 'employment policy' targets under the 1997 'Luxembourg' arrangements.[44] Indeed, for almost two decades this 'soft' approach has increasingly been championed in the context of EU-level 'labour law' regulatory initiatives, to such an extent that it now arguably constitutes a sad proxy for any protective regulatory intervention worthy of the name.

At the same time, the shift away from a 'floor of rights' approach to the declaration of social rights by reference to 'the principle of equal treatment' has also, it may be suggested, contributed to a dilution of effective enforceable labour protective rights. Rather, this operates in favour of broad concepts which offer little by way of certainty to employers, and whose protective coverage is increasingly subject to complicated technical qualification criteria to be satisfied on the parts of workers. Such a shift has developed out of (primarily) gender-related anti-discrimination arrangements. In that context, experience of 'gender mainstreaming', the development of the legal notion of 'indirect discrimination', use of a so-called 'reversed burden of proof',

---

43. Between 2004 and 2010, the 'Commissioner for Employment, Social Affairs and Equal Opportunities' was the Czech Vladimír Špidla, with László Andor, from Hungary, succeeding him for the period 2010–2014 as 'Commissioner for Employment, Social Affairs and Inclusion'.
44. See the agreement reached at the European Council meeting held in Luxembourg on 20–21 November 1997, giving effect to the new 'Employment Title' in the (yet to be ratified) Treaty of Amsterdam (Arts 128 and 129).

and a focus upon techniques such as 'gender pay gap reporting' have undoubtedly served to identify 'hidden' areas of discriminatory behaviour, as well as making access to 'effective recourse' less daunting than might otherwise be the case. However, as that approach has been extended to embrace an increasing number of areas involving the treatment of those in employment relations, it has also served, in some areas, to open a door to the 'blanket' lowering of standards by enterprise employers, in the name of (and under the cover of) 'equality of treatment'.

Meanwhile, at the level of the Social Partners, there has been a continued inability to develop the 'social dialogue' (and the agreements to which that can give rise) beyond the confines of 'non-controversial' subject-matter. This, indeed, has been a manifest weakness ever since the old 'Val Duchesse' arrangements which gave rise to the introduction of Article 118B through the Single European Act in 1986. Thus, while there have undoubtedly been some valuable declarations in respect of health and safety, teleworking, and the like, these declarations have acquired no real 'teeth' since the 'halcyon days' of the Italian Presidency at the end of the 1990s.

Finally, at the level of the European Commission, for the first decade and a half of the twenty-first century, there has been an embarrassing lack of leadership and social policy ambition on the parts of successive Commissioners responsible for this field. One has only to observe the remarkably limp commitments for this area contained in the 'Europe 2020' agenda to appreciate just how little impetus has existed for meaningful development in the labour law and social policy area.[45] So, too, has there been a lack of meaningful innovative regulatory proposals, other than continual 'tinkering' with existing instruments such as the Posted Workers Directive[46] or the Working Time Directive.[47]

---

45. *See* Communication from the Commission, *Europe 2020: A strategy for smart, sustainable and inclusive growth* (COM(2010) 2020, Brussels, 3 March 2010). The strategy is implemented and monitored through the wonderfully Euro-jargonistic 'European Semester'.
46. The original Directive 96/71/EC of the European Parliament and of the Council of 16 December 1996 concerning the posting of workers in the framework of the provision of services, has been supplemented by a so-called 'enforcement directive', Directive 2014/67/EU of the European Parliament and of the Council of 15 May 2014 on the enforcement of Directive 96/71/EC concerning the posting of workers in the framework of the provision of services and amending Regulation (EU) No 1024/2012 on administrative co-operation through the Internal Market Information System ('the IMI Regulation'), and is currently the object of a Proposal for a Directive of the European Parliament and of the Council amending Directive 96/71/EC of The European Parliament and of the Council of 16 December 1996 concerning the posting of workers in the framework of the provision of services (Interinstitutional File: 2016/0070 (COD), Brussels, 24 October 2017).
47. Council Directive 93/104/EC of 23 November 1993, concerning certain aspects of the organisation of working time has been overtaken by Directive 2003/88/EC of the European Parliament and of the Council of 4 November 2003 concerning certain aspects of the organisation of working time, while a series of 'sectoral' Directives have extended the regulatory scope in respect of working time to air, rail, sea and road transport, as well as to areas encompassed by Directive 2000/34/EC of the European Parliament and of the Council of 22 June 2000 amending Council Directive 93/104/EC concerning certain aspects of the organisation of working time to cover sectors and activities excluded from that Directive.

Yet, now, out of the blue, and apparently as a result of a speech delivered by the President of the European Commission on 9 September 2015,[48] social policy enthusiasts and commentators have suddenly been transported into paroxysms of delight by the proposition that, 'There is not enough Europe in this Union. And there is not enough Union in this Union', coupled with the announcement of the launch of a so-called 'European pillar of social rights'.[49]

That heralding of the social rights 'pillar' has sparked a quite remarkable flurry of activity – of an intensity almost unknown in the field of social policy for nearly two decades – culminating, on 16 November 2017, in the proclamation of 'a set of twenty principles and rights'.[50]

One might be forgiven for raising an eyebrow at the remarkable speed with which this 'pillar' has been conceived, developed and proclaimed, after so many years of inertia on the parts of those responsible for overseeing and driving forward labour law and social policy at the level of the European Union. Indeed, one might also conjecture that the emergence into 'mainstream politics' of (broadly anti-EU) populist movements in countries such as Austria, Hungary, Italy, Poland, Spain and the Netherlands – as well as in the UK – could have something to do with this new-found zeal to ensure social rights for European citizens. So, too, might the very fact of a 'Brexit' process taking place – itself a potential driver for the expression of dissent in relation to the trajectory of European Union activity over recent years – have contributed to concentrating attention upon the need to recognise that, when it comes to social rights and protection, fine words are not enough in the face of 'austerity' politics, widespread social exclusion, and a general sense of losing out to primarily 'economic' policy priorities in a globalised world of work.

Strangely, therefore, it may prove to be the case that 'Brexit' has contributed to a 'game-changing' reassessment of the role to be played by the European Union in the field of labour law and social policy. Certainly, reflection upon the shortcomings which

---

48. Under the title 'Time for honesty, unity and solidarity'.
49. The Commission President declared that, 'I will want to develop a European pillar of social rights, which takes account of the changing realities of Europe's societies and the world of work. And which can serve as a compass for the renewed convergence within the euro area. This European pillar of social rights should complement what we have already jointly achieved when it comes to the protection of workers in the EU. I will expect social partners to play a central role in this process. I believe we do well to start with this initiative within the euro area, while allowing other EU Member States to join in if they want to do so.'
50. From a starting point of a Communication from the Commission to the European Parliament, the Council, the European Economic and Social Committee and the Committee of the Regions, Launching a consultation on a European Pillar of Social Rights (COM/2016/0127 final, Strasbourg 8 March 2016), a period of little more than eighteen months has seen a plethora of staff working documents and background briefing papers, including an expedited process of consultation, before publication of a *Commission Recommendation of 26 April 2017 on the European Pillar of Social Rights* (C(2017) 2600 final, Brussels, 26 April 2017) and, on the same day, a Communication from the Commission to the European Parliament, the Council, the European Economic and Social Committee and the Committee of the Regions, *Establishing a European Pillar of Social Rights* (COM/2017/0250 final, Brussels 26 April 2017). This has given rise to a *Proposal for an Interinstitutional Proclamation on the European Pillar of Social Rights* (13129/17, SOC 634 EMPL 482 EDUC 365 SAN 350 ECOFIN 816, Brussels, 20 October 2017), and the eventual Proclamation of the European Pillar of Social Rights on 16 November 2017.

contributed to the 'Leave' vote of the UK electorate on 23 June 2016 might provoke a greater sense of urgency in addressing fast-developing issues in relation to the type of work now expected in European labour markets, problems associated with the inability of regulatory mechanisms (especially those of a 'legal' kind) to keep up with those rapid developments, and the gulf which continues to exist between 'theoretical'/'conceptual' policy-making at the heart of Europe and practical problems and challenges faced by the working citizenry of the present twenty-eight Member States.

§5.04 CHANGING THE RULES OF THE GAME? A UK 'BREXIT' PERSPECTIVE

Turning briefly to the impact of the 'Brexit' process upon domestic labour law and social policy in the UK, a few words may be said about the situation to date in terms of regulating the world of work for life after 'exit day'.

By way of introduction, it might be pointed out that UK employment law is no stranger to dramatic upheaval. Indeed, the current European Union (Withdrawal) Bill 2017–2019 – which is being developed by the Parliament as the instrument for regulating the statutory process and consequences of 'Brexit' – bears remarkable parallels to events forty years ago.[51] At that time, the Industrial Relations Act 1971 was the target for repeal, and a new Trade Union and Labour Relations Act 1974 was the instrument developed to replace that ill-fated predecessor.[52]

Current controversy rages around the practical extent of the stated ambition for the Bill to repeal the European Communities Act 1972, to provide a mechanism for reintroduction into domestic law of the relevant residual *acquis communitaire*, and to do away with the Court of Justice of the European Union as the judicial institution dealing with post-'Brexit' matters concerning the UK. Particular controversy abounds in respect of the extent of powers for Ministers to reintroduce current secondary legislative provisions which would otherwise fall away with the repeal of the 1972 Act.

Much of the difficulty faced by the drafters of the Withdrawal Bill arises out of the fact that in UK law, as a normal rule, 'secondary legislation' (usually so-called 'Statutory Instruments') enacted under powers contained in a 'primary' piece of legislation (normally, an Act of Parliament) will cease to have validity if the primary instrument itself is repealed. Since the normal instrument for establishing labour law and social policy rights and protections at the European level has historically been the directive, and the UK's obligation to give effect to the content of any such directive (in

---

51. The European Union (Withdrawal) Bill 2017-19 was presented to Parliament on 13 July 2017, and has been working through the parliamentary legislative procedure since then. Following detailed scrutiny in Committee, during the course of which a number of amendments were introduced into the draft text, the most recent version of the Bill at the time of writing is that published on 21 December 2017.
52. Section 1(1) of the Trade Union and Labour Relations Act 1974 declared: 'The Industrial Relations Act 1971 is hereby repealed.'; section 1(2) provided a mechanism for reintroducing large parts of the duly repealed statute; section 1(3) did away with a much criticised judicial institution, the National Industrial Relations Court.

accordance with what is now Article 288 of the Treaty on the Functioning of the European Union)[53] has generally been discharged by way of regulations contained in Statutory Instruments enacted under powers contained in the European Communities Act 1972, this problem of the 'knock-on effect' of repealing the 1972 Act is of major significance in this field.[54]

The heart of the procedures under the 1972 Act lies in its section 2, whereby subsection (1) provides for Treaties, Regulations, etc., to become directly applicable for the UK without the need for implementing legislation, while subsection (2) sets out the powers to enact 'delegated legislation' (thus facilitating the enactment of Statutory Instruments to give effect *inter alia* to the content of European Union directives).

The European Union (Withdrawal) Bill 2017–2019 seeks to deal with this situation by providing (in Clause 1) that 'The European Communities Act 1972 is repealed on exit day', and (in Clause 2(1)) that 'EU-derived domestic legislation, as it has effect in domestic law immediately before exit day, continues to have effect in domestic law on and after exit day.'

Thereafter Clause 5(1) stipulates that 'The principle of the supremacy of EU law does not apply to any enactment or rule of law passed or made on or after exit day', while Clause 6(1) provides that 'A court or tribunal – (a) is not bound by any principles laid down, or any decisions made, on or after exit day by the European Court, and (b) cannot refer any matter to the European Court on or after exit day.'

It may also be noted, in passing, that there is provision, in Clause 5(4) of the Bill, to the effect that 'The Charter of Fundamental Rights is not part of domestic law on or after exit day.'

In addition to the provision for retaining EU-derived domestic legislation under the provisions of Clause 2(1) of the Bill, it is also stipulated (in Clause 7(1)) that 'A Minister of the Crown may by regulations make such provision as the Minister considers appropriate to prevent, remedy or mitigate – (a) any failure of retained EU law to operate effectively, or (b) any other deficiency in retained EU law, arising from the withdrawal of the United Kingdom from the EU.'[55]

Faced with these provisions in the draft Withdrawal Bill, heated debate has been generated over whether 'Brexit' and the terms of the Bill as currently drafted, could pose a serious threat to the integrity of employment protection rights developed over

---

53. Article 288 of the Treaty on the Functioning of the European Union provides that, 'A directive shall be binding, as to the result to be achieved, upon each Member State to which it is addressed, but shall leave to the national authorities the choice of form and methods.'
54. Indeed, in this area – notwithstanding any reputation which the United Kingdom may have acquired over the years for being 'difficult' in relation to the enactment of social policy measures within the framework of membership of the European Union – practice within government, once a Directive is adopted, has consistently been to endeavour to give effect to its provisions within the designated time provided and in full compliance with the expectations of the Directive. A similar comment may be made in respect of the loyalty shown by United Kingdom courts and tribunals to judgments delivered by the Court of Justice of the European Union, particularly on preliminary references made under the provisions of Art. 267.
55. This procedure has been a key target for critics during the course of the passage of the Bill through its Committee stage up until 21 December 2017, and a number of amendments have been inserted into the text – which may or may not be reamended at a later stage in the Bill's progress through Parliament.

decades, to the detriment of workers in the UK. On the one hand, the Trades Union Congress (seeking to represent organised labour in the UK), along with a number of 'academics',[56] fear that the proposed withdrawal legislation will be used as a 'smokescreen' to facilitate attacks on existing labour law rights at large. As against that, the current 'received wisdom' would appear to be that the genuine (and politically practicable) intention is to 'hold the *status quo*' as of exit day; so that primary legislation (such as the Equality Act 2010) probably remains as it is,[57] while secondary legislation is not 'untouchable'.

As the European Union Withdrawal Bill is currently framed, there are good grounds for maintaining that fears expressed for the continued integrity of much of the individual 'floor of rights' for workers in the UK are probably over-stated, since large areas of this have always lain outside the scope of EU competence. That said, however, attention may be drawn to potential practical consequences of removing 'employee voice', through institutions such as EWCs, as well as certain specific 'information and consultation' rights – which owe their existence to the exercise of EU-level powers.

Thus, at first glance, one might not expect areas such as unfair dismissal,[58] or the regulation of wages,[59] to be affected directly by 'Brexit'. These are not, in themselves, areas in which the EU has enjoyed competence, and such rights consequently owe everything to domestic political will exercised through the sovereign power of the UK Parliament.

However, fields such as working time (maximum hours of work, paid vacation entitlement, etc.) derive from regulations introduced to implement rights introduced by EU directives,[60] and, as popular targets for criticism in the pre-'Brexit' era, would certainly be anticipated as 'being in the firing line' for potential repeal or wateringdown.

Whatever the differences as constituting 'home-grown' rights or 'EU-derived' residual rights, however, in practice the issue of whether any of these employment protections will be amended or removed turns entirely upon domestic political will and capacity after 'exit day'.[61] Is it, one may ask, seriously open to a political party struggling to command a voting majority in Parliament to propose abolition of annual

---

56. Largely drawing their propositions from an 'Advice' drafted by Michael Ford QC (dated 10 March 2016) for the TUC, under the heading 'Workers' Rights from Europe: The Impact of Brexit'. *See also* that author's revised version of his arguments published as M. Ford, 'The Impact of Brexit on UK Labour Law', (2016) 32 *International Journal of Comparative Labour Law and Industrial Relations* 473.
57. Something which relates particularly to the Equality Act 2010 – which contains the framework for, and the majority of provisions dealing with, anti-discrimination, equal opportunities, and related matters at work – over which considerable argument has been generated.
58. Regulated through primary legislation such as the Employment Rights Act 1996.
59. Unlawful deductions, minimum wage, etc – also regulated through primary legislation in, respectively, the Employment Rights Act 1996 and the National Minimum Wage Act 1998.
60. Council Directive 93/104/EC concerning certain aspects of the organisation of working time and Council Directive 94/33/EC on the protection of young people at work.
61. Such must also be the case irrespective of whether those rights satisfy the requirement in the current Clause 7 of the Bill that Ministerial powers to act by regulation to rectify 'deficiencies' in the legislation must arise where the 'deficiency' in question arises 'from the withdrawal of the United Kingdom from the EU', or whether any proposed adjustments can be said to be justified by 'necessity' or their no longer being 'appropriate'.

paid leave entitlement for UK workers? Or, given the practical benefits derived by public bodies such as HMRC[62] from obligations upon employers to keep records of hours worked and payments made, does one really anticipate a clear-out of all such arrangements, simply on the ground that their origins owe something to previous membership of the European Union?

On the other hand, one area in which soul-searching might take place would be in relation to individual protections afforded workers who carry out functions within collective employment relations institutions such as 'EWCs' or bodies established to facilitate information, consultation and participation for workers, or relating to issues of health, safety and hygiene at work.

As witnessed during the period of the UK opt-out from the post-Maastricht Social Policy Agreement (between 1992–1997),[63] UK enterprises will continue to be directly affected by the EWCs directive through the 'qualifying thresholds' provisions relating to size and numbers of employees in two or more EU Member States.[64] It is undoubtedly realistic to envisage that, once such EWCs are established (or, in reality, continue to function) in a transnational undertaking, there is unlikely to be any practical prospect that workers in a (now non-EU Member State) UK division of that undertaking would be excluded from participating in the activities of the enterprise's EWC. Such employees currently enjoy protection under UK labour law against dismissal or other detrimental treatment by reason of their membership of or participation in the activities of a body such as the EWC.[65] Are we now to anticipate repeal of the specific protections by reason that they are no longer 'appropriate' for an institution no longer recognised formally in UK post-'Brexit' labour law?[66]

In essence, therefore, the question of whether parts of the UK's 'floor of rights' for workers will remain broadly as they have been to date, or will undergo adjustment (or even repeal), comes down to a matter of domestic political will and capacity on the part of the governing parliamentary party post-'Brexit'.[67]

---

62. Her Majesty's Revenue and Customs – the public authority responsible for collection of taxes and enforcement of related duties.
63. Agreement on Social Policy (2 February 1992) annexed to the Maastricht Treaty's Protocol on Social Policy.
64. For consideration of the impact of the Directive upon United Kingdom circumstances, see Alan C. Neal, 'European Works Councils: The United Kingdom Point of View', (1998) 32 Bulletin of Comparative Labour Relations 163.
65. See The Transnational Information and Consultation of Employees Regulations 1999 (S.I. 1999 No. 3323).
66. Certainly, a case could be made to that effect. However, where, then, does this leave such individuals – given that, as seen so often in litigation before the Employment Tribunals, an 'enthusiastic' worker representative can very quickly become a 'thorn in the side' of HR, with eventual consequences of a more or less direct kind?
67. Only constraints such as those which might follow from the European Convention on Human Rights 1950 – to which regard must be had by reason of the provisions of the Human Rights Act 1998 – will continue to operate, and, unless it can be argued that Art. 11 on 'freedom of association' operates to prevent any such adjustment, even these are likely to prove relatively limited constraints.

Yet that latter point certainly raises a much broader issue in relation to 'collective' employment relations in the UK. In particular, it begs the question of whether the institutional arrangements designed to facilitate 'employee voice' in the British system of industrial relations might see significant amendment as a direct consequence of 'Brexit'.

Here, the position is much more nuanced. Notwithstanding that the plains of 'free collective bargaining' have, for the half century following publication of the report of the Donovan Commission,[68] been largely trespassed upon by legal regulation and lawyers, normative regulation in this area takes on a much greater significance than half a century ago. Consequently, one now finds provisions on 'recognition' of trade unions (which stem from domestic legislative initiatives), rules on disclosure of information and the giving of advance notice in cases of collective dismissals or transfers in the ownership of enterprises (many of which derive directly from obligations established by EU directives), and institutional arrangements for conducting consultation with representatives of workers (again, deriving largely from EU-level provisions).

At one extreme, one could well envisage institutions such as the 'European Company', European limited partnerships, and a host of parallel creatures, being at the front of the queue for a 'bonfire of the regulations' following 'exit day'. The strange situation of EWCs has already been mentioned. Indeed, having regard also to the linkages with individual protections constituting the 'floor of rights', might we see the abolition of protective provisions currently supporting workers' representatives in the context of collective dismissal, enterprise transfers, or changes to working practices with 'health and safety' implications – and could the opportunity be taken also to remove similar (non-EU-inspired) protections for trustees of pension funds, persons averse to Sunday working, 'whistle-blowers', or the like?

If nothing else, this serves to underline a number of truths which are only now beginning to be recognised with their full force. First, the legislative techniques used to implement EU-derived obligations into UK domestic law can be seen to have been remarkably successful in scrambling together the eggs of European social policy in the industrial relations architecture of a post-Donovan UK. Unscrambling that omelette has become almost an impossibility, with the consequence that 'clear-cut' prophesies of particular outcomes are equally rendered well-nigh impossible. Second, the political willingness to embark upon delivering dramatic 'swings' in labour law and industrial relations regulation as between 'labour' and 'employers' has all but vanished – as the maintenance of the reformed legal straightjacket imposed upon the freedom to undertake industrial action has demonstrated during the currency of successive administrations of widely varying political hue.

Without such a preparedness (or the political ability) to undertake thoroughgoing reform and to introduce a dramatic shift in the industrial balance of power, the immediate post-'Brexit' scenery may turn out to be rather unlikely to suffer dramatic redrawing solely as a consequence of the UK's withdrawal from membership of the

---

68. Report of the Royal Commission on Trade Unions and Employers' Associations (Chairman Lord Donovan), Cmnd. 3623, HMSO 1968.

European Union. To such an extent, therefore, the 'game-changing' impact of 'Brexit' may turn out to be of more significance for the future of social policy at the level of the European union than for the domestic enjoyment of labour law rights and protections in the labour market of a post-'Brexit' UK.

PART II Industrial Relations and Labour Law

CHAPTER 6
Trade Unions and the 'Gig Economy'

Michael Doherty

§6.01 INTRODUCTION

In 2001, Roger Blanpain edited an edition of the *Bulletin of Comparative Industrial Relations* entitled *The Evolving Employment Relationship and the New Economy: The Role of Labour Law & Industrial Relations*. The Bulletin addressed questions like:

- Do globalisation and high technology necessarily go hand in hand?
- Are contingent and partly dependent workers protected in a fair way?
- To what degree can the employment contract be stabilised?
- How can we tackle the erosion of social security provisions?

Contributors came from across the globe (Belgium, Germany, Italy, Spain, the United Kingdom, Australia, Japan, South Africa, Latin America, and the United States). It would be almost a decade before, in July 2008, Apple launched the App Store, officially introducing third-party application development and distribution to its platform, and some more years before app use became the all-pervasive basis of mobile technology it is today.[1] Blanpain, as ever, was ahead of his time in spotting, and interrogating, the issues that now confront labour relations actors, and regulators, when considering what is referred to as 'gig work', although even he was probably unlikely to have foreseen the rapid pace of technological change since 2001.[2]

---

1. http://appleinsider.com/articles/08/07/10/apples_app_store_launches_with_more_than_500_apps (accessed 17 November 2017).
2. There are various ways used to describe such work (*see* Valerio De Stefano, *Crowdsourcing, the Gig-Economy, and the Law*, 37 Comp. Lab. L. & Pol'y J. 461, 470 (2016)), and, to this author, 'platform work' seems possibly the most accurate, but, for ease of reference, I will use the term 'gig' throughout the chapter. This should be taken to refer to temporary assignments that a person takes on, in order to fulfil a service for others, and which depends on collaborative platforms that aim to bring together two actors (the service provider and the end-user/customer).

This chapter does not purport to tackle all of the multifaceted, and hugely complex, economic, political, social, and cultural implications of gig work.[3] Its rather more modest ambition is to take as a starting point the fact that there are 'gig workers', whose working conditions are relatively precarious, and for whom protection of their terms and conditions of employment is, or should be, a concern for labour relations actors. The chapter focuses on the means by which trade unions in Europe can act to protect such workers. In this regard, three avenues are explored. First, the chapter looks at the extent to which gig workers can be brought within the scope of collective bargaining coverage, examining the interaction between collective bargaining rights and competition rules. In this regard, recent judicial developments at the level of the EU and legislative developments at the level of one Member State (Ireland) are examined. Second, using the newly proclaimed European Pillar of Social Rights (EPSR) as a framework, the chapter considers measures, legal and political, that might aid trade unions in protecting vulnerable gig workers. Third, the chapter looks at how trade unions might adapt to the new organising challenge of gig work.

§6.02 COMPETITION, CARTELS, AND COLLECTIVE RIGHTS

A key source of controversy in relation to gig work relates to the employment status of gig workers. In most legal systems, the 'starting point for the analysis of legal obligations arising in the context of working relations must always be the terms of any contractual arrangement'.[4] Crucial are the questions, in law, of 'who is an employee?' and 'who is an employer?'. This is because, as Davidov et al. point out, the approach to determining the coverage of labour law tends to be the same throughout the world, in being defined by reference to 'employee' and 'employer' (or similar terms); being categorised in these groups, therefore, carries important implications in terms of labour rights and obligations.[5] For example, in most jurisdictions access to a range of statutory protections (e.g., minimum wage laws, unjust dismissal laws, working time laws) will generally depend on an individual's employment classification.

For the purposes of this chapter, a key point of controversy in Europe lies in the intersection between a key labour right – the right to bargain collectively – and competition/antitrust law. Article 101 of the Treaty on the Functioning of the European Union (TFEU) prohibits:

> all agreements between undertakings, decisions by associations of undertakings and concerted practices which may affect trade between Member States and which

---

3. For this, *see* the wonderful account in Jeremias Prassl, *Humans as a Service* (OUP, 2018, forthcoming).
4. Hugh Collins, K.D Ewing, and Aileen McColgan, *Labour Law: Text and Materials*, 70 (2nd ed., Hart, 2005).
5. Guy Davidov, Mark Freedland, and Nicola Kountouris, 'The Subjects of Labour Law: "Employees" and Other Workers' in Matthew Finkin and Greg Mundlak (eds) *Research Handbook in Comparative Labour Law* (Edward Elgar 2015). Of course, there are examples of 'intermediate' categories such as 'worker' in the UK; Alan Neal, 'The Protection of Working Relationships under United Kingdom Law' in Frans Pennings and Claire Bosse (eds) *The Protection of Working Relations* (Kluwer 2011).

have as their object or effect the prevention, restriction or distortion of competition within the internal market, and in particular those which…(a) directly or indirectly fix purchase or selling prices or any other trading conditions…. .

As noted by Schiek et al. this provision restricting cartel action was originally addressed to private actors ('undertakings'), but the Court of Justice has expanded its scope by holding Member States bound by those rules:[6]

> Member States must not introduce or maintain in force measures, even of a legislative or regulatory nature, which may render ineffective the competition rules applicable to undertakings.[7]

Collective bargaining processes, however, are based precisely on combining employees to fix wages (prices) in order to alleviate the pressure to undercut the price of each other's labour, sometimes in bargaining with single employers, and sometimes in bargaining with associations of employers. This is justified by the need to remedy the structural imbalance and asymmetries of labour markets, as most workers do not have any alternative to earning their main income on the labour market; if wages fall below a certain level, they simply expand supply (e.g., by taking up another occupation, or working overtime).[8] Therefore, competition rules which, at their core, prohibit cartels, or agreements between undertakings which distort competition, clearly conflict with the right to conclude binding collective agreements (often referred to as 'wage cartels'), the purpose of which is to set prices (wages). This conflict is one with which courts, and legislatures, must grapple. Some solutions are to exclude collective agreements from the scope of competition/antitrust laws altogether; to exclude such agreements only if they fulfil certain objectives (e.g., directly contribute to the improvement of working conditions); or to restrict or prohibit binding collective agreements.[9] In the next section, the choice of the Court of Justice will be analysed.

[A] EU Competition Law and Collective Bargaining

The intersection between collective bargaining rights and competition rules has been the subject of many decisions of the Court of Justice, and the tensions inherent in this intersection have been aired. In *Albany*, Advocate General Jacobs emphasised it is generally accepted that 'collective agreements between management and labour prevent costly labour conflicts, reduce transaction costs through a collective and rule-based negotiation process and promote predictability and transparency'.[10] In *FNV*

---

6. Dagmar Schiek, Liz Oliver, Chris Forde, and Gabriella Alberti, *EU Social and Labour Rights and EU Internal Market Law: Study for the EMPL Committee* ((http://www.europarl.europa.eu/RegData/etudes/STUD/2015/563457/IPOL_STU(2015)563457_EN.pdf; accessed 17 November 2017), 26.
7. Case C-96/94 *Centro Serviczi Spediporto* ECLI:EU:C:1998:454 [1995] E.C.R I-2883, para. 20.
8. Dagmar Schiek et al., *supra* n. 6, 18.
9. *See*, for discussion, Valerio de Stefano, *Non-Standard Work and Limits on Freedom of Association: A Human. Rights-Based Approach*, 46 ILJ 185 (2017).
10. Case C-67/96 *Albany International BV v. Stichting Bedrijfspensioenfonds Textielindustrie* EU:C:1999:28 [1999] E.C.R I- 5751, points 181 and 232.

Kunsten, Advocate General Wahl also noted the 'good socio-economic reasons to restrict, or even to eliminate, wage competition among workers through collective bargaining', adding that 'I also believe that the promotion of social peace and the establishment of a system of social protection which is equitable for all citizens are aims of the greatest significance in any modern society'.[11]

However, the jurisprudence of the Court of Justice has tended to emphasise the dichotomy in the position of 'employees', on the one hand, and the 'self-employed' on the other. So, In *Albany*, the Court held that collective agreements do *not* fall within the scope of Article 101 TFEU when two cumulative conditions are met: (i) they are entered into the framework of collective bargaining between employers and employees, and (ii) they contribute directly to improving the employment and working conditions of workers. As the Court's case law refers explicitly to 'employees', collective agreements involving the self-employed fall outside of the *'Albany* exception'. The Court's position, then, is that, unless a worker has 'employee' status, s/he is an independent undertaking and forbidden from coming to mutual arrangements over basic terms such as minimum payments.

This position of the Court has come in for criticism. Under EU Law, the right to bargain collectively is a fundamental right protected by the Court[12] and outlined in Article 28 of the Charter of Fundamental Rights. Given this status, it has been argued that the autonomous nature of collective bargaining must also be protected:

> the right to collective bargaining is infringed in its essence if the parties negotiating a collective agreement are subjected to a detailed control of the process, or if the content of the demands they may make is prescribed.[13]

Thus, control of the process, or content, of collective agreements by Competition Authorities arguably infringes the right to collective bargaining.

[B] Orchestral Manoeuvres in the Dark or Spring Variations? The FNV Kunsten Decision

This issue came before the Court again recently in *FNV Kunsten*,[14] where the question was whether EU competition rules applied to a Dutch collective labour agreement, which contained provisions on the minimum fees to be paid not only to *employees* of an orchestra, but also to *self-employed musicians* who work for orchestras on an occasional basis as substitutes for employed musicians. The Court held that a self-employed musician should 'in principle' be treated as an 'undertaking', and that an organisation negotiating on behalf of self-employed service providers should not be

---

11. Case C-413/13 *FNV Kunsten Informatie en Media v. Staat der Nederlanden* ECLI::EU:C:2014:2215, para. 33, and footnote 14.
12. Case C-341/05 *Laval v. Svenska Byggnadsarbetareförbundet* ECLI:EU:C:2007:809 [2007] E.C.R I-11767.
13. Dagmar Schiek et al., *supra* n. 6, 17.
14. Case C-413/13 *FNV Kunsten Informatie en Media v. Staat der Nederlanden* ECLI::EU:C:2014:2215.

treated as a social partner but should be characterised as an 'association of undertakings'.[15] Therefore, the agreement in question could not fall under the *Albany* exception'. However, the Court went on to note that the boundaries between the self-employed (as undertakings) and employees are not so easy to determine in a fluid employment market, and it identified a category of workers which it called the 'false self-employed'; namely 'service providers [who are] in a situation comparable to that of employees' who, subject to certain conditions, *can* benefit from an *Albany*-type exemption.[16]

The Court did not engage with Advocate General Wahl's much more nuanced balancing of the interests of collective bargaining and competition rules. The Advocate General also concluded that the '*Albany* exception' could not cover contractual provisions concluded on behalf of self-employed persons. He did accept, however, the argument that the provisions of the collective agreement *did* improve the working conditions of the employees concerned (the musicians employed directly by the Orchestra), by aiming to prevent social dumping.[17] Applying the terms of the agreement to the self-employed musicians would help ensure orchestra employees could not be replaced by lower-cost self-employed workers; not applying it to the self-employed, equally, would weaken the *collective bargaining power of employees* in negotiations.

[C] An Irish Jig: Collective Bargaining Rights for the Self-Employed

This issue of collective bargaining rights for 'freelance' workers has been a source of controversy in Ireland for many years. In 2004, the Irish Competition Authority (now the Competition and Consumer Protection Commission) issued a decision that an agreement between the trade union Actors' Equity SIPTU and the Institute of Advertising Practitioners (an association of advertising agencies) setting out specific fees for services rendered and various other terms and conditions, amounted to price-fixing.[18] The issue was one of great concern to the Irish Congress of Trade Unions (Ireland's only trade union confederation), which lobbied for change for many years on behalf of voice-over actors, session musicians, and freelance journalists; the matter was even one of conflict with the 'Troika' in the context of Irelands EU-IMF 'bail out'.[19] In 2017, legislation was finally passed to address the issue; the *Competition (Amendment) Act 2017*. The Act provides that section 4 of the *Competition Act 2002* (prohibiting cartel action) shall not apply to collective bargaining and agreements in respect of certain categories of workers. There are three such categories. First, the Act specifically applies to voice-over actors, session musicians, and freelance journalists. Second, the Act

---

15. *Ibid.*, paras 27–28.
16. *Ibid.*, paras 31–32. The factors to be considered in establishing 'false' self-employment would include the extent to which the worker acts under the direction of another; whether the worker shares in the employer's commercial risks, and whether, for the duration of the relationship, the worker forms an integral part of the employer's undertaking (para. 36).
17. *Ibid.*, paras 74–79.
18. Competition Authority Decision E/04/002.
19. https://www.ictu.ie/download/pdf/executive_council_report_2013.pdf (p. 36; accessed 17 November 2017).

introduces the concept of the 'false self-employed' worker; this is defined, in section 15(D), as an individual who:

(a) performs for another person, under a contract (whether express or implied and if express, whether orally or in writing), the same activity or service as an employee of the other person,
(b) has a relationship of subordination in relation to the other person for the duration of the contractual relationship,
(c) is required to follow the instructions of the other person regarding the time, place and content of his or her work,
(d) does not share in the other person's commercial risk,
(e) has no independence as regards the determination of the time schedule, place and manner of performing the tasks assigned to him or her, and
(f) for the duration of the contractual relationship, forms an integral part of the other person's undertaking.

Third, the Act introduces the concept of the 'fully dependent self-employed worker', defined, in section 15(D), as an individual:

(a) who performs services for another person (whether or not the person for whom the service is being performed is also an employer of employees) under a contract (whether express or implied, and if express, whether orally or in writing), and
(b) whose main income in respect of the performance of such services under contract is derived from not more than 2 persons.

In both of these last cases, a trade union which represents a class of false self-employed, or fully dependent self-employed, worker may apply to the Minister to include the class of worker in question as falling within the scope of the Act, in order to allow the union to bargain collectively, and conclude collective agreements, on behalf of the workers. The union must provide evidence under section 15(F) that the workers who are the subject of the application do fall within the relevant definitions. The application must also be accompanied by evidence that extending the Act's provisions to the class of workers in question will:

(i) have no or minimal economic effect on the market in which the class of self-employed worker concerned operates,
(ii) not lead to or result in significant costs to the State, and
(iii) not otherwise contravene the requirements of (the Competition Acts) or any other enactment or rule of law (including the law in relation to the European Union) relating to the prohibition on the prevention, restriction or distortion of competition in trade in any goods or services.

The Minister must also be satisfied that extending the scope of the Act's provisions to the class of workers in question is 'appropriate'.

The legislation represents an innovative attempt to extend collective bargaining rights to vulnerable workers, who do not fit within the classic 'employee' definition. While the provisions of section 15(F), in particular the requirement that extending the Act's provisions will have 'no or minimal economic effect' on the market are somewhat concerning, and may well be in breach of ILO standards, the Act does clearly set out the principle that collective representation should not be automatically denied to those who cannot satisfy traditional tests of employee status. Clearly, the legislation could be extended to certain categories of gig workers; it will be an interesting challenge for Irish trade unions to frame applications aimed at extending the protections in the Act to classes of workers other than those specifically covered in the legislation. We await the outcomes.

In the next section, the chapter goes on to look at the challenges of gig work for the trade union movement more generally.

§6.03   TRADE UNIONS AND 'GIG WORKERS'

It was argued above that one means of protecting vulnerable gig workers is to extend the scope of collective bargaining rights beyond traditionally defined 'employees'. In this section, the chapter looks at other means by which trade unions can seek to protect such workers. First, the potential of the EPSR, as a political tool on which the labour movement might capitalise, is referenced. Second, the section looks at how legal protections for gig workers might be strengthened in the short-term, via a focus on the REFIT of the Written Statements Directive. Third, the section concludes with some brief thoughts on how trade unions might seek to organise, and mobilise, gig workers.

[A]   The Political Response: The Pillar of Social Rights

In November 2017, EU leaders gathered in Stockholm to 'proclaim' the EPSR. The Pillar, and its potential impact on labour and social rights in the EU, has already been much debated, and we can expect this debate to loom large in the coming years.[20] For the purposes of this chapter, a relatively simple point may be made about the Pillar. While it is clear that, initially, at least, the Pillar lacks any legal force, its importance in this context lies perhaps more in the political signal it represents, notably to the EU Institutions.

The Digital Single Market (DSM) strategy adopted in 2015 is a key legislative and policy priority for the Commission and the Union.[21] However, perhaps predictably, to date the DSM has focused almost exclusively on the interests of digital business; discussion of the impact on workers (other than the claims that the DSM will lead to employment growth) and society more generally has been extremely limited. Similarly, and relatedly, the Commission work programme for 2017 announced an initiative on company law to facilitate the use of digital technologies throughout a company's

---

20. Zane Rasnača, *Bridging the Gaps or Falling Short? The European Pillar of Social Rights and What It Can Bring to EU-Level Policymaking* (ETUI 2017); Daniel Seikel, *The European Pillar of Social Rights – No 'Social Triple A' for Europe* (https://www.socialeurope.eu/european-pillar-social-rights-no-social-triple-europe; accessed 17 November 2017); Klaus Lörcher and Isabelle Schömann, *The European Pillar of Social Rights: Critical Legal Analysis and Proposals* (ETUI 2017).
21. *A Digital Single Market Strategy for Europe* COM(2015) 192 final.

lifecycle and cross-border mergers and divisions; again, the impacts on labour have not formed a large part of the debate.[22]

The argument here is that, while the EPSR should, and is explicitly designed to, have an impact on legislative developments explicitly within the field of social policy (*see* next section), it should also have a 'mainstreaming' dimension in EU law- and policy-making more generally. As noted by Rasnača:

> Member States should be able to rely upon the fact that the Union institutions will not breach or facilitate breaches of the rights and principles embedded in the EPSR, not only within but also outside the scope of social policy (for example, in the internal market or EMU).[23]

Indeed the EPSR itself makes explicit reference to Article 9TFEU, which states that in 'defining and implementing its policies and activities, the Union shall take into account requirements linked to the promotion of a high level of employment, the guarantee of adequate social protection, the fight against social exclusion, and a high level of education, training and protection of human health'. Thus, the impact of the Pillar on Union future law and policy developments cannot simply be limited to the social sphere, in which, as the Commission is fond of pointing out, legislative competence is relatively limited. Therefore, measures in relation to the DSM, or the digital economy more generally, must take into account social concerns.

[B]   The Legal Response: Knowledge Is Power

In launching the Pillar, the Commission noted that it 'flanks' the EPSR with a number of concrete legislative and non-legislative initiatives, such as on the work-life balance of parents and carers, on the information of workers, and on access to social protection and on working time.[24] All of these initiatives, clearly, do not 'derive' from the EPSR, as they were already in train before the launch of the Pillar, but, to take the Commission at its word, they 'illustrate both the nature of the issues covered by the Pillar as well as the way in which its principles and rights can be implemented'.[25] In terms of gig work, the potential legislative change in respect of the Written Statements Directive could well be significant.[26]

First, it is clear that there is uncertainty throughout the Member States on the scope of the Directive, and the extent to which atypical workers, including, of course, gig workers, are covered. Therefore, a revision of the Directive (notably Article 1) to extend the scope of its coverage to either explicitly include a definition of 'gig workers', or to extend the scope more generally, in the context of the 'blurred lines' between

---

22. *Commission Work Programme 2017 Delivering a Europe that protects, empowers and defends* COM(2016) 710 final.
23. Zane Rasnača, *supra* n. 20, 30.
24. http://europa.eu/rapid/press-release_IP-17-1007_en.htm (accessed 17 November 2017).
25. *Ibid.*
26. Council Directive 91/533/EEC of 14 October 1991 on an employer's obligation to inform employees of the conditions applicable to the contract or employment relationship (OJ L288/32).

employment and self-employment noted in the *FNV* decision, would be welcome. It should be noted that in *Jany*, the CJEU held that an economic activity is pursued by a *self-employed person* where it is being carried on by the person providing the service:

- outside any relationship of subordination concerning the choice of that activity, working conditions and conditions of remuneration;
- under that person's own responsibility;
- and in return for *remuneration paid to that person directly and in full.*[27]

This last condition is unlikely to be satisfied in the context of gig work, where the platform normally acts as intermediary for the payment by the end-user and generally deducts a commission of some sort.

Second, Article 2 of the Directive requires an employer to notify the worker to whom the Directive applies, 'of the essential aspects of the contract or employment relationship'. In the context of gig work, some of the aspects listed in the Article become crucial, for example, the identities of the parties; the registered place of business or, where appropriate, the domicile of the employer; and the initial basic amount, the other component elements and the frequency of payment of the remuneration to which the worker is entitled. Without knowledge of the basic components of the employment relationship, details of which can become very difficult to ascertain in the context of digital work, the ability of workers to access, and enforce, their rights becomes almost impossible. It may be, too, that other core elements of the employment relationship need to form part of the notification to the worker; for example, details of the social security rights and obligations of both parties, or a right to tightly defined 'hours of work', including, perhaps, rights to minimum paid hours.[28]

Third, Article 3 of the Directive provides that the information referred to in Article 2 may be given 'not later than two months after the commencement of employment'. Given the temporary nature of, and fluctuating demand for, some forms of gig work, it seems appropriate that the Directive should require basic information on, at least, remuneration and working hours, be given earlier than this two-month period. Second, it should be very clear in the Directive that the form of this communication must be transparent, and easy to read; this is crucial in the context of the manner in which many platforms operate. In litigation involving the transportation platform Uber, for example, the Employment Tribunal in London remarked that any organisation that

---

27. Case C-268/99 *Jany and Others v. Staatssecretaris van Justitie* ECLI:EU:C:2001:616 [2001] ECR I-8615, para. 70 (emphasis added).
28. In this respect, *see* the soon to be enacted Irish legislation on 'banded' hours, where workers on low hour contracts, who consistently work more hours each week than provided for in their contracts of employment, will be entitled to be placed in a band of hours that reflects the reality of the hours they have worked over an extended reference period (eighteen months); https://www.workplacerelations.ie/en/news-media/Workplace_Relations_Notices/Priority_Legislation_May_2017.html (accessed 17 November 2017).

resorted in 'its documentation to fictions, twisted language and even brand new terminology, merits, we think, a degree of scepticism'.[29]

Fourth, and relatedly, Article 5 of the Directive states that any change of the referred details must be given to the worker in written form at the earliest opportunity, and not later than one month after the date of entry into effect of the change in question. In the context of gig work, this must clearly apply to any changes of the terms and conditions of the platforms; it must also be ensured, again, that platforms cannot 'cloak' changes in complicated legal language, and in the 'fine print' of their terms and conditions.

Finally, we can return again to the EPSR. Article 8 of the Written Statements Directive provides that Member States must ensure an effective means of redress for those whose rights under the Directive have been breached. In the context of some forms of gig work, where the worker, the platform, and the end-user may all be located in different jurisdictions, the need for effective cross-border enforcement becomes crucial. While accepting the difficulties of enforcing labour rights in a global context, we should, and must, at least ensure effective cross-border enforcement with the EU. In this context, the announcement by Commission President Juncker of the need to establish a European Labour Authority (which, again, does not require the EPSR to be feasible, but has been explicitly linked with the Pillar) is promising.[30] As President Juncker noted, 'it is absurd to have a Banking Authority to police banking standards, but no common Labour Authority for ensuring fairness in our single market'.[31] As argued above, it is no less absurd to have proclaimed a Pillar of Social Rights, and then not to have its principles inform EU law- and policy-making in *all* areas.

[C] The Grassroots Response: Organising for the Gig Economy

The focus of this chapter is the protection that trade unions can give to vulnerable gig workers. Above, the emphasis has been on political measures, and legal changes, that can have an impact in this regard. However, ultimately, trade unions will also need to master the challenge of organising these workers. This, of course, will be challenging. Trade unions traditionally thrive where there exist large workforces, with identifiable common interests and employers, and which are physically and geographically bounded. The characteristics of much gig work are that workers are often isolated (and, often, of course, are argued to be self-employed), the question of who bears the traditional 'employer' function in relation to specific employment obligations is often unclear,[32] and there is usually no physical workplace, as the work can be done via apps from anywhere, and for end-users who may be located in any part of the globe. The obstacles to organisation, and mobilisation, therefore, are considerable.

---

29. *Aslam and others v. Uber BV and others* (28 October 2016, para. 87; https://www.judiciary.gov.uk/wp-content/uploads/2016/10/aslam-and-farrar-v-uber-reasons-20161028.pdf; accessed 17 November 2017).
30. President Juncker's State of the Union Address 2017 (http://europa.eu/rapid/press-release_SPEECH-17-3165_en.htm; accessed 17 November 2017).
31. *Ibid.*
32. Jeremias Prassl, *The Function of the Employer* (OUP, 2015).

Nonetheless, trade unions are beginning to come to terms with these challenges and strategies are beginning to be developed.[33] Following on from the discussion of the Written Statements Directive, above, the focus again is on how trade unions can work to inform, and therefore empower, gig workers. One implication of the growth of digital work, and a key means by which gig workers can be monitored and controlled by platforms, is that vast quantities of data (information) are collected, stored, and accessed instantaneously. It is relatively easy, therefore, for regulators and other actors to seek access to information on working time, remuneration rates, and so on. It is even easier to be able to compare these across workers, tasks, sectors, and geographical boundaries. If knowledge is power, those concerned with the enforcement of basic labour standards have potentially more access to power than ever before. So, for example, platforms offering similar services can more easily be compared; online remuneration calculators can more easily be established, and accessed, by gig workers, wherever they are; and trade unions themselves can even be established in 'virtual' form ('crowd' or 'pop-up' unions). Trade unions have long fought, and in many jurisdictions continue to fight, to gain access to physical workspaces in order to police employment standards. Now, the fight must move to the digital space; 'virtual access' to platforms, and the data that there reside, similarly, is key in order to police employment standards for 'gig work'.[34]

§6.04 CONCLUDING REMARKS

This chapter has taken as its starting point that, while gig work is vastly heterogeneous, there are undoubtedly gig workers who are in precarious, and vulnerable, working situations, and to whom trade unions should seek to offer support and, where necessary, protection. The chapter suggests a number of ways in which this might occur.

First is the question of collective bargaining rights. It was argued that such workers often do not fall neatly into the binary categories of 'employee' or 'self-employed'. Therefore, the manner in which the Court of Justice has determined the application of competition rules to collective agreements (that only employees can be covered by collective agreements) may need to be reconsidered. Ultimately, the fundamental right to bargain collectively is only meaningful if the full autonomy of the parties is respected and guaranteed. The current position, where collective agreements are subject to the control of competition authorities at EU, and national, level, undermines this right to autonomy. The decision of the Irish competition authorities in

---

33. *See*, for example, Samuel Engblom, *Atypical Work in the Digital Age – Outline of a Trade Union Strategy for the Gig Economy* (http://www.academia.edu/32900838/Atypical_Work_in_the_Digital_Age_Outline_of_a_Trade_Union_Strategy_for_the_Gig_Economy; accessed 17 November 2017); the special editions of Transfer: European Review of Labour and Research (issues 2 and 3 2017) on *The Digital Economy and Its Implications for Labour*; and the ETUC *Resolution on tackling new digital challenges to the world of labour* (https://www.etuc.org/documents/tackling-new-digital-challenges-world-labour-particular-crowdwork#.Wg7jrohBrIU; accessed 17 November 2017).
34. I am indebted to Prof. Barbara Kresal (University of Ljubljana) for this conceptualisation.

relation to certain freelance workers was referenced above.[35] In the course of the decision, the Competition Authority made the following comment:[36]

> If one were to take a wooden approach and find that all trade union members were exempt from the Act, the protections afforded Irish consumers by the [Irish Parliament] in enacting the *Competition Act 2002* could easily be rendered illusory. Associations of independent pharmacists, publicans, and barristers – to name only a few – would shortly obtain safe haven for their members by adding 'union' to their name and obtaining a negotiation license (*sic*).

The argument here is that this stance misses the point completely. If *genuinely* independent pharmacists, publicans, and barristers are seeking to invoke collective bargaining rights in order to circumvent competition rules, this is an abuse of such rules, which competition authorities should detect, and prohibit. However, why should the collective bargaining rights of those who are *not* genuinely independent contractors should be rendered 'illusory' *a priori*?

In the context of where this remains the rather unsatisfactory legal position, the chapter outlined above a rather innovative approach to the question recently enacted by the Irish legislature. While, ultimately, the granting of collective bargaining rights to a class of 'false self-employed', or 'fully dependent self-employed', workers remain a matter for the Minister, and the factors to be taken into account are predominantly economic, the legislation at least allows, first, trade unions to outline the case for granting such workers collective bargaining rights, and, second, opens the Minister's decision to a level of public scrutiny not generally given to decisions of competition authorities.

Second, the chapter used the recently proclaimed EPSR as a framework for suggesting how gig workers might be better protected at EU level. Politically, this would mean a recognition that the provisions of the social pillar relating to, for example, decent employment standards, and social security protection, should inform all areas of law-, and policy-, making with the EU. Specific focus was given to one of the concrete legislative proposals accompanying the EPSR; the REFIT of the Written Statements Directive. Here, it was argued, the clarity and transparency afforded to, for example, *consumer* rights in the EU should be afforded in the same manner to gig workers; in short, guarantees that the basic details of the employment relationship should be notified to gig workers must be secured. The maxim 'knowledge is power' was employed here, and in the previous section, which argued that trade unions must also utilise the opportunities inherent in the digitalisation of work to shine a light on any abuses, or erosion, of employment standards.

In essence, the chapter argues that the political and regulatory will to ensure decent employment standards in the gig economy, aligned with concrete legal reforms, must be accompanied by grassroots action by labour actors (note that while the chapter focused on trade unions, action by 'good' employers is also necessary).

---

35. Competition Authority Decision E/04/002.
36. *Ibid.* (para. 2.12).

In conclusion, it is often noted, not least by the Commission, that 'gig work' remains a very minority form of work in the EU; the implication being that to express too much concern about the phenomenon is excessive. However, witnessing the number of articles, books, conferences, and seminars on this topic in recent times, one can only conclude that labour law academics are very exercised indeed by the implications of such work. It might be said, therefore, that this is an instance where labour law academics are somewhat 'ahead of the curve'; of this, one can only assume Prof. Roger Blanpain would have approved.

CHAPTER 7
Strikes in Essential Services under International Law

*Monika Schlachter**

§7.01 INTRODUCTION

The increasingly difficult conditions for conducting effective collective actions rank high among circumstances influencing the future of work and therefore may legitimately be counted among 'game changers' for industrial relations. It may suffice to recall professor Blanpains' globally acknowledged insight that collective bargaining without the option of conducting collective action represents no more than 'collective begging'. This famous notion presents in a nutshell why the possibility of resorting to collective action is, despite the economic losses caused, so important for the industrial relations system at large. Not only is collective action the most fundamental means available to workers and their organizations for promoting their economic and social interests.[1] In parallel, it represents the one instrument allowing using the advantages of contractual over statutory regulations also in labour relations without compromising necessary standards of protection. A state responsible for securing social rights in the world of work would have to refrain from applying the principle of freedom of contract to aspects of labour relations where the general imbalance of bargaining power is likely to result in insecure substandard working conditions. However, once the power imbalance can be effectively overcome by conducting the bargaining process collectively instead of individually, the many advantages of regulations created by those

---

* The article is based on a compilation of international law materials produced by Diana Balanescu, temporary lawyer at the Council of Europe's department on the European Social Charter.
1. T. Novitz, *The Restricted Freedom to Strike: 'Far Reaching' ILO – Jurisprudence on the Public Sector and Essential Services*, Comparative Labour Law and Policy Journal 38, 353, 355 (2017); M. Sädevirta, *Freedom of Association and the Right to Strike*, Europäische Zeitschrift für Arbeitsrecht, 445, 447 (2016).

directly involved in their application promote the contract as a means of self-regulation.

Collective bargaining can effectively replace protective labour legislation, once equal bargaining power is established, as indicated by the labour relations in Northern Europe. The workers' side needs an effective means to counterbalance the managerial prerogative to just decline all attempts at improving working conditions. In short, once collective action loses its ability to effectively pressure undertakings to compromise, the results of bargaining collectively will not lead to better standards than bargaining individually, which would make the whole system pointless. However, collective bargaining is under pressure, changing social and economic developments under conditions of globalization have led to declining membership rates in both, unions and employer organizations, in most European states. As a consequence, the regulative capacity of collective bargaining is generally weakened, including the capacity of unions to conduct successful strikes. This chapter concentrates on one specific aspect of such general problem, i.e., conducting strikes in essential services negatively affecting third parties.

§7.02 ESSENTIAL SERVICES AND PRIVATIZATION

Strike action is generally the most visible and controversial form of collective action and mostly seen as the last resort of workers' organizations in pursuit of their demands.[2] This generally rather reluctant degree of acceptance is regularly even lower once the strike concerns activities which may be counted among 'essential services' impacting the general public interest. However, strike action in recent times tends to happen more frequently in areas which might be included in such category. In earlier decades, such services used to be part of a public service guaranteeing 'essential' features to the whole of the population. The 'essentiality' of the service, however, is not dependent on a public or private organization of the service provider. It much rather refers to the dependency of consumers unable to satisfy their needs because alternative services are either totally unavailable or much too costly.[3] As privatization of formerly public functions became a dominant feature of economic policy, also services previously considered to be the responsibility of the state were turned into an issue of private supply and demand.[4] Consumers were made to believe that this manoeuvre would be beneficial to them in reducing costs and furthering competitive innovations.

Effects of cost reduction, however, were to be borne by the employees. They lost the status and any privileges that may have been attached to a public service employment relationship. Public service collective agreements rarely remain applicable; the bargaining process regularly takes place at enterprise level which is harder for unions to organize than the larger public service level. What remains unchanged, however, is the dependency of the general public on the reliable flow of such services.

---

2. J.-M. Servais, *ILO Law and the Right to Strike*, Canadian Labour & Employment Law Journal, 148 (2008).
3. G. Morris, *Strikes in Essential Services*, 1 (1986).
4. T. Novitz, *ibid.*, 353, 358 (2017); W. Hänsle, *Streik und Daseinsvorsoge* 189 et seq. (2016).

Therefore, the states continue to maintain specific rules governing the possibility to withhold services for the purpose of improving working conditions, even if the state has given up the position of the service provider.[5] Not only have transferees to the private sector lost the public services' larger bargaining power, they anyhow remain under restrictive mechanisms applied to activities still considered of public interest: while potentially existing previous privileges have been lost, previous restrictions remain.

Restrictions to services deemed 'essential' can emerge in many different ways. Legislation may establish a general definition of essential services or provide a list of activities included in such notion and leave its interpretation in specific cases to a public authority or the courts. Or a procedure for determining whether an activity should be deemed essential may be established; e.g., with the participation of employers' and workers' organizations. Any such definition, however, will result in restrictions to the right to strike, be it that for some services work stoppages are totally precluded or that narrower preconditions than for other sectors apply. This may amount to including the general publics' or the consumers' interest in the continuous flow of specific services in determining the legality of a strike. Strikes may also become illegal due to eventually harsh economic consequences, or due to their potential detriment to public order or to the general or national interest.[6] Given the dependency of fruitful collective bargaining on the existence of an effective right to strike, such development may bear unintended negative consequences for the bargaining system at large. For ways and means to secure the effectiveness of collective bargaining in essential services even under the condition of privatization and globalization, it might be useful to include the guarantees of a right to strike in international law when determining justified restrictions to this right. Certainly, no prompt solution should be expected from international law guarantees: Which criteria are appropriate to assess the essential nature of a service has not been precisely established on an international level,[7] and states possess a large degree of discretion in defining acceptable means for securing the public interest in reliable essential services. However, some preconditions have been developed internationally that might be useful for balancing also domestically the rights and interests of all parties concerned.

§7.03 THE INTERNATIONAL LABOUR ORGANISATIONS' APPROACH

[A] The Legal Basis and Its Interpretation

The right to strike is recognized by the International Labour Organisations' (ILO) supervisory bodies, the Committee on Freedom of Association (CFA) and Committee of

---

5. T. Cohen &R. le Roux, *Limitations of the Right to Strike in the Public Sector and Essential Services*, 127, 129 et seq. (2015).
6. ILO CEACR, General Survey on the fundamental Conventions concerning rights at work in light of the ILO Declaration on Social Justice for a Fair Globalisation (2008), International Labour Conference 101st Session, para. 132 (2012).
7. G. Morris, *ibid.*, 188 (1986); A. Pankert, *Settlement of Labour Disputes in Essential Services*, International Labour Review 119, 723, 731 (1980).

Experts on the Application of Conventions and Recommendation (CEACR), as *an intrinsic corollary of the right to organise protected by Convention No. 87* (Freedom of Association and Protection of the Right to Organise Convention, 1948).[8] Its connection to the right to bargain collectively is strong, even though a situation of collective bargaining is as such not conditional for collective action; however, the potential recourse to collective action in concrete bargaining situations is an effective means for rendering bargaining a 'meaningful' process.[9] Under Convention No. 87, the right to strike is derived from the right of workers' organizations to formulate their programmes of activities to further and defend the economic and social interests of their members.[10]

However, the right to strike is not considered absolute. It may be subject to certain legal conditions or restrictions and even denied completely in exceptional circumstances. As for the exceptions, first, Article 9 of ILO Convention No. 87 states that 'the extent to which the guarantees provided for in this Convention shall apply to the armed forces and the police shall be determined by national laws or regulations'. As a result, the CFA did not object legislation which denies the right to strike to such groups of workers.[11] Second, the CFA did accept exceptions to be imposed for (1) public servants exercising authority in the name of the State and (2) workers in essential services in the strict sense of the term.[12] The two concepts, public service and essential services, both of which are in principle able to justify restrictions to the right to strike, are considered as having a partly overlapping scope. Third, the CFA has further considered a general prohibition of strikes to be justified 'in the event of an acute national crisis and for a limited period of time'.[13] The existence of an 'acute national crisis', however, is dependent on extremely severe circumstances such as a *coup d'état* against a constitutional government leading to the declaration of a state of emergency in accordance with the national constitution.[14] Such national emergency may also be of an economic nature, once the severity of the situation is comparably harsh. The CEACR has emphasized that the acknowledgement of a crisis situation depends on circumstances such as serious conflicts, insurrections, natural, sanitary or humanitarian disasters, in which normal conditions for the functioning of societies are lacking.[15] In essence, out of the three alternatives, only those concerning public service or essential services may apply for restrictions to the right to strike in the cases described above.

---

8. How such recognition of the right to strike has been fiercely attacked by the employers' group has been extensively debated; for details: T. Novitz, *ibid.*, 353 (2017).
9. M. Weiss, *International Labour Standards: A Complex Public-Private Mix*, International Journal of Comparative Labour Law and Industrial Relations 29, 7 (2013); N. Smit, *International Developments Regarding the Implementation of the Right to Strike*, Comparative Labour Law and Policy Journal 38, 395, 400 (2017).
10. Freedom of Association and Protection of the Right to Organise Convention, Art. 3 (No. 87, 1948); ILO CEACR, General Survey on Freedom of Association and Collective Bargaining, para. 151.
11. ILO Principles Concerning the Right to Strike, 17.
12. Digest CFA, Chapter 10, para. 576 (2006); and CFA Report No. 337, Case No. 2244, para. 1268.
13. Digest CFA, Chapter 10, paras 570 and 571 (2006).
14. CFA, Report No. 284, Case no. 1626, para. 91.
15. ILO CEACR, General Survey, para. 140 (2012).

[B] Public Service

In some countries, the concept of essential services is used in legislation to refer to services in which strikes are not prohibited but where a minimum operational service may be required; in other countries, the related notion of public service justifies a total prohibition of strike action. Therefore, it has been essential for the ILO supervisory bodies to give an autonomous definition to certain expressions when developing its case law. Self-evidently, states are not required to use these terms in their national law in the same sense. It is up to the national legislation to determine, e.g., who qualifies as a 'public servant'. Yet, when applying restrictions or measures, which the supervisory bodies have found permissible only for 'public servants' exercising authority in the name of the State,[16] states must ensure to limit their use to those persons who would also fulfil the ILO's definition; the mere categorization of certain workers as public servants under national law will, as such, not be sufficient for restricting their right to strike.[17] The nature of the functions that employees actually carry out is conditional for determining who may be excluded. This may include officials working in the administration of justice and the judiciary[18] and customs officers,[19] but not public servants in state-owned commercial or industrial enterprises,[20] in oil, banking and metropolitan transport undertakings or employed in the education sector.[21]

With a slightly different approach, the CEACR has held that despite the different legal and social traditions of each country, uniform criteria must be established for examining the compatibility of national legislation with the provisions of Convention No. 87. This can, however, not be achieved by drawing up an exhaustive and universally applicable list of categories of public servants who may be denied the right to strike. To establish that specific functions or professions do always or do never fall in the categories of public service deems impossible as it disrespects the specific situation in the country concerned. For this reason, the CEACR has suggested to not impose any total prohibition on strikes in public service, but rather to provide for a defined and limited category of staff maintaining a negotiated minimum service when a total and prolonged stoppage of a public service might result in serious consequences for the public.[22] This would amount to disallowing a total prohibition of strikes in public service while allowing restrictions to the number of employees entitled to withdraw their labour. When excluding all or merely a part of public service employees from the right to strike, states must, however, establish sufficient guarantees to protect their interests, including appropriate, impartial and prompt conciliation and arbitration

---

16. Digest CFA, Chapter 10, para. 574 (2006); CFA Report No. 338, Case No. 2363 para. 731 and Case No. 2364 para. 975.
17. T. Novitz, *International and European Protection of the Right to Strike*, 305 (2003).
18. Digest CFA, Chapter 10, para. 578 (2006); CFA Report No. 336, Case No. 2383, para. 763.
19. Digest CFA, Chapter 10, para. 579 (2006); CFA Report No. 304, Case No. 1719, para. 413.
20. Digest CFA, Chapter 10, para. 577 (2006); CFA Report No. 338, Case No. 2348, para. 997.
21. ILO, 1984a, Report No. 233 para. 668; ILO, 1983b, Report No. 226, para. 343; and ILO, 1996d, note to para. 492.
22. ILO, 1994a, para. 158.

procedures to ensure that all parties may participate at all stages, and in which arbitration decisions are binding on both parties and are fully and promptly applied.

[C] Essential Services in the Strict Sense of the Term

The ILO's supervisory bodies have taken the position that it might also be admissible to limit or prohibit the right to strike in essential services once the concept of essential services applied includes merely essential services in the strict sense of the term.[23] This category is defined as those services 'the interruption of which would endanger the life, personal safety or health of the whole or part of the population'.[24]

The CFA established that what is meant by essential services in the strict sense of the term depends to a large extent on the particular circumstances of the concrete case. Specific services that may not regularly be labelled 'essential' in absolute terms, may become essential if the strike affecting it exceeds a certain time or extends beyond a certain scope, thus endangering the life, personal safety or health of the whole or part of the population.[25] By way of example, the CFA has listed as essential in the strict sense services such as:[26] the hospital and ambulance services; electricity services; water supply services; the telephone service; the police and the armed forces; the fire-fighting services; public or private prison services. Such list, however, is not representing an absolute categorization of the services concerned as the context of the specific case is to be considered. The fact of being employed by a hospital does not justify to include the services of a gardener into the category of 'essential services'.[27] By the same token, also a list of examples provided for services generally not to be considered essential[28] is understood as not being definitive: the interruption of certain services which in some countries might at worst cause economic hardship could prove disastrous in other countries and rapidly lead to conditions endangering the life, personal safety and health of the population. For example, a strike in the port or maritime transport services might cause serious disruptions for an island heavily dependent on such services to provide basic supplies to its population.[29]

Once a strike would interrupt a service, the withdrawal of which, under concrete circumstances of the case, would endanger the life, health or safety of the whole or part of the population,[30] prohibiting such action is justified (if accompanied by compensatory measures). However, a total prohibition of strike action should be avoided whenever possible. The workers' fundamental right to strike must not be restricted any

---

23. J.-M. Servais, *ibid.*, 147, 153 (2008).
24. ILO, 1983b, para. 214; Digest CFA, Chapter 10, para. 581 (2006); and CFA Report No. 338, Case No. 2326, para. 446 and Case No. 2329, para. 1275.
25. Digest CFA, Chapter 10, paras 582 and 591 (2006); and CFA Report No. 309 Case No. 1916, para. 100.
26. Digest CFA, Chapter 10, para. 585 (2006).
27. Digest CFA, Chapter 10, para. 593 (2006); and CFA Report No. 333, Case No. 2277, para. 274; and CFA Report No. 338, Case No. 2403, para. 601; CFA Report No. 374, Case No. 3057, para. 215.
28. Digest CFA, Chapter 10, paras 587–590 (2006).
29. ILO, 1994a, paras 159 and 160.
30. ILO, 1984a, Report No. 233, paras 668 and 669.

further unless necessary and appropriate for the protection of the interests of the users of such services. Therefore, services not qualifying as essential in the strict sense just described but nevertheless being of fundamental importance should be treated differently. While strikes may not be banned for this category, a system of minimum service may be imposed establishing limited operations of the undertaking or institution in question.

[D] Forms of Restrictions That May Be Justified

A state may resort to replacing the prohibition of strikes by mere procedural limitations to strike actions. Should such restriction suffice for eliminating the danger to life, health or safety, a total ban of the strike action would be disproportionate and therefore unjustified. Consequently, the application of such means must be considered before a strike may be banned. Different procedural limitations have been reviewed by the ILO Committees.

A procedural means for restricting strike action widely used at national level requires the parties to a possible conflict to undergo a mediation or conciliation process *prior* to calling a strike or to give advance notice to the other party. Both amount to *'cooling-off'* periods during which action has to be delayed. Such restriction is deemed acceptable as both parties may go back to bargaining, possibly reaching an agreement without having recourse to a strike.[31] However, the required waiting period should not be so long as to unduly restrict the right to strike. Depending on the individual circumstances a twenty-day notice period in the case of services of social or public interest does not undermine the principles of freedom of association,[32] whereas the requirement of an advance notice of sixty days is excessive.[33]

The retention of a *'minimum service'* – i.e., the continued provision of service by a part of the workforce – represents a substantive restriction to the right to strike as employees in principle willing to take collective action are thereby prevented from doing so. According to the ILO supervisory bodies, it nevertheless may be required in situations in which it is necessary to ensure that users' basic needs are met and that facilities operate safely.[34] For avoiding damages which are irreversible or out of proportion to the occupational interests of the parties to the dispute, as well as damages to third parties, namely the users or consumers who suffer the economic effects of collective disputes, a minimum service may be imposed instead of outright banning strikes.[35] While to workers concerned, this difference may deem insignificant, for securing the interests of the population such restriction may nevertheless be unavoidable. The conditions of legitimacy for substantive restrictions to the right to strike must, however, be comparable to those for an outright ban, given that the consequences of both measures are, at an individual level, identical. The CFA has stated that the

---

31. Digest CFA, Chapter 10, para. 554 (2006).
32. Digest CFA, Chapter 10, para. 553 (2006); and CFA Report No. 309, Case No. 1912, para. 365.
33. ILO CEACR, Observation 2011, United Republic of Tanzania.
34. ILO, 1994a, para. 162.
35. ILO, 1994a, paras 159 and 160.

establishment of minimum services should only be possible in: (1) essential services in the strict sense of the term; (2) services which are not essential in the strict sense, but where the extent and duration of a strike might be such as to result in an acute national crisis; and (3) public services of fundamental importance.[36]

In the language of the CEACR, a minimum service should meet at least two requirements. First, it must genuinely and exclusively be a *minimum service*, that is, one which is limited to the operations which are strictly necessary to meet the basic needs of the population or the minimum requirements of the service, while maintaining the effectiveness of the pressure brought to bear.[37] Second, since this system restricts one of the essential means of pressure available to workers to defend their economic and social interests, their organizations should be able, if they so wish, to participate in defining such a service, along with employers and the public authorities.[38] Concerning the determination of minimum services to be maintained and the minimum number of workers providing them, the CFA has considered that this should guarantee that the scope of the minimum service does not result in the strike becoming ineffective in practice because of its limited impact, and to dissipating possible impressions on the trade union organizations that the strike has come to nothing because of over-generous and unilaterally fixed minimum services.[39]

The CFA has also pointed out that it is important for provisions regarding the minimum service to be established clearly, to be applied strictly and made known to those concerned in due time.[40] If there is any disagreement between the parties as to the number and duties of the workers concerned by a minimum service during a strike, the Committee states that legislation should provide for any such disagreement to be settled by an independent body and not by the ministry.[41] Moreover, an appeal to judicial authorities must be possible.[42] The CEACR noted with concern that in practice governments frequently determine unilaterally, without consultation, the level of minimum services required demanding a specific percentage of services to be provided during strikes.[43]

Comparably strict preconditions apply in case of requisitioning of workers, that is, a *back-to-work order*. The CFA ruled that, in case a total and prolonged strike in a vital sector of the economy might cause a situation in which the life, health or personal safety of the population might be endangered, a back-to-work order can be justified. However, it must be applied to a specific category of staff in the event of a strike the

---

36. Digest CFA, Chapter 10, para. 606 (2006).
37. ILO CEACR, General Survey on the fundamental Conventions concerning rights at work in light of the ILO Declaration on Social Justice for a Fair Globalisation (2008), International Labour Conference 101st Session, paras 136–139 (2012).
38. ILO, 1994a, para. 161.
39. Digest CFA, Chapter 10, para. 612 (2006); and CFA Report No. 338, Case No. 2373 para. 381.
40. Digest CFA, Chapter 10, para. 611 (2006); and CFA Report No. 330, Case No. 2212, para. 751.
41. Digest CFA, Chapter 10, para. 613 (2006); and CFA Report No. 320, Case No. 2044, para. 753; CFA Report No. 376, Case No. 3096, para. 890.
42. Digest CFA, Chapter 10, para. 614 (2006); CFA Report No. 304, Case No. 1866, para. 114; CFA Report No. 376, Case No. 3096, para. 891.
43. CEACR, General Survey, para. 138 (2012); CEACR Observations 2011, Bulgaria; CEACR Observations 2011, Romania.

scope and duration of which is likely to cause such situation. Back-to-work requirements outside such cases must be refrained from.[44] The use of the military or of requisitioning orders to break a strike over occupational claims, unless these actions aim at maintaining essential services in circumstances of the utmost gravity, constitute a serious violation of freedom of association.[45] The intensely debated strikes in public transport may be used as an example for such case: While a stoppage in transport companies or railways might disturb the normal life of the community, it can hardly be claimed that such stoppage could cause a state of acute national emergency. The Committee has therefore considered that requisition measures in services of this kind are not justified in restricting the workers' right to strike.[46] Also the CEACR accepted requisitioning only in circumstances of utmost gravity or ensuring the operation of essential services in the strict sense; apart from that requisitioning is to be avoided for the risk of abusing it as a means of settling labour disputes.[47]

An alternative means of securing essential services to the general public during collective action aims at annihilating the effects of a strike by replacing the workers withdrawing their labour. Such measures are capable of generally undermining any collective action and therefore in principle not acceptable. The CFA has considered the replacement of strikers to be justified only under very narrow preconditions: (a) in an essential service in which strikes are forbidden by law[48] and (b) in a situation of acute national crisis.[49]

Also the CEACR has considered it especially problematic when legislation or practice allows enterprises to recruit workers to replace their own employees on *legal* strike. The action is even more serious if strikers do not, as of right, find their job waiting for them at the end of the dispute. The Committee considered that this type of provision or practice seriously impairs the right to strike and affects the free exercise of trade union rights and the legislation should provide for genuine protection in this respect.[50] In principle, the CEACR recalled that the maintaining of the employment relationship is a normal legal consequence of recognition of the right to strike.[51]

[E] Compensatory Guarantees for Workers

Where the right to strike is restricted or denied in essential services or the public service, adequate compensation should be provided to workers.[52] This should include a corresponding denial of the right to lock out. Furthermore, restrictions should be

---

44. Digest CFA Chapter 10, para. 634 (2006); and CFA Report No. 333, Case No. 2281, para. 634.
45. Digest CFA Chapter 10, para. 635 (2006); and CFA Report No. 333, Case No. 2288, para. 831.
46. Digest CFA Chapter 10, para. 637 (2006); and CFA Report No. 337, Case No. 2249, para. 1478.
47. ILO, 1994a, para. 163.
48. Digest CFA, Chapter 10, para. 639 (2006).
49. ILO, 1996d, paras 570 and 574.
50. ILO, 1994a, para. 175.
51. ILO CEACR, General Survey on the fundamental Conventions concerning rights at work in light of the ILO Declaration on Social Justice for a Fair Globalisation (2008), International Labour Conference 101st Session, paras 151-152 (2012).
52. Digest CFA, Chapter 10, para. 595 (2006); CFA Report No. 337, Case No. 1244, para. 1269.

'accompanied by adequate, impartial and speedy conciliation and arbitration proceedings in which the parties concerned can take part at every stage and in which the awards, once made, are fully and promptly implemented'.[53]

The CFA has generally accepted that provision may be made for recourse to conciliation, mediation and voluntary arbitration procedures in industrial disputes *before* a strike may be called, provided that the guarantees just mentioned are in place.[54] According to the CFA case law, *compulsory arbitration to end a strike* is usually not adequate, the exception being strikes in essential services in the strict sense of the term, an acute national crisis, or in the public service:[55] Apart from this, the substitution of strike action by compulsory arbitration at the initiative of the authorities or one party is not considered compatible with international guarantees.[56] Where governments hold specific services as being essential, this is not always supported by the facts of the case; an inconvenience to some part of the population, such as lacking the services of metropolitan transport, should rather be diminished by the establishment of a minimum service.[57] Therefore, compulsory arbitration is acceptable only if it is provided for in the collective agreement as a means of settling disputes or is approved by the parties during bargaining carried out regarding the problems which gave rise to the industrial dispute in question.

§7.04 CONSEQUENCES FOR BALANCING THE INTERESTS AT NATIONAL LEVEL

The exercise of the right to strike in essential services is specifically complex as it involves not only the usual process of coordinating the fundamental rights of the parties to the collective conflict, employers and employees. Much rather, in services considered essential due to the relevance of their uninterrupted flow to the general public, the main bearer of negative effects of a work stoppage are the consumers. While not being formally involved in the conflict, they suffer from consequences of a strike without having any influence in the solution process. Even if the national law might provide financial compensation for a failure to fulfil contractual service obligations, this might not solve consumers' problems as they regularly depend on the availability of the service in kind. In such triangular contractual situations, the balancing process cannot disregard the consumers' interest. However, by generally attaching a decisive weight to such interests, the continuation of services would essentially rank above workers' right to collective action, so that in collective bargaining employers would lose any incentive to compromise for ending the conflict. It would be equally inappropriate for the state to hide behind the consumers' needs for abolishing a right

---

53. Digest CFA, Chapter 10, para. 596 (2006); CFA Report No. 336, Case No. 2340, para. 649.
54. ILO, 1194a, para. 171.
55. Digest CFA, Chapter 10, paras 564–565 (2006); and CFA Report No. 338, Case No. 2329, para. 1275; CFA Report No. 380 Case No. 3126, para. 722.
56. ILO, 1984c, Report No. 236, para. 144.
57. CFA Report No. 377, Case No. 3107, paras 340–343.

Chapter 7: Strikes in Essential Services under International Law   §7.04

to strike as privatization measures taken by the public institutions contributed greatly to intensifying the need for collective measures on the part of workers.

The right balance between the fundamental right to conduct collective action, which is a necessary precondition for a labour relations system based on collective agreements, and the interests of the general public therefore cannot be reached by interventions of the state such as setting up a list of 'essential' services for which the right to strike is generally inapplicable. Such measures would provide the advantage of legal certainty and foreseeability for all parties concerned. They would, however, render collective bargaining pointless in the respective sectors. The state would become responsible for securing working conditions and participating in the financial gain of enterprises; governments mainly would have to resort to establishing relevant contractual conditions by law. Given that the services concerned have been privatized with the goal of shrinking economic activities of public entities, such solution would not fit into the prevailing economic theory of the superiority of private contractual solutions over public regulations.

For alternative solutions to this pertinent difficulty, inspiration may be gained from experiences at international level. The ILO supervisory bodies provide case law on the right to strike that aims at securing fundamental rights of workers while taking account of the diversity of national legal systems. The insights in the process of balancing rights of workers, employers and the general public gained in the cause of developing such case law are highly valuable for constructing sensible solutions also at domestic level, – over and above the fact that countries having ratified the relevant ILO Conventions are legally obliged to guarantee workers' rights enshrined in such Conventions. Different aspects of a possible solution can be extracted from ILO case law:

- Guaranteeing a right to strike and securing that it remains effective in practice is essential for any legal system basing the establishment of main working conditions on collective bargaining. Therefore, such right should be protected and given the widest possible personal scope of application, independent from the existence of a contract of employment.
- *Exclusion* of certain groups from the right to strike due to their status, such as soldiers, secret service members, must be justified by prevention of emergency situations threatening the security of the state. Other workers may be denied the right to strike according to their individual functions, such as exercising authority in the name of the state or providing services that are essential for the life, health or safety of the population at large. For the latter group, their exclusion from the right to strike should be avoided as far as possible and be replaced by minimum services provisions. A list of sectors, economic activities or professions presumed to be essential may merely establish an incidence to this effect, but creates no absolute ground for disallowing collective action.
- The justification of *restrictions* to the right to strike for persons providing services of fundamental importance but not so essential as to justify a total ban on their right to strike also depends on considering all the circumstances of a concrete case. This may include factors such as the services' relevance for

securing basic consumer needs or social policy, the number of affected persons, the duration of strike action or potentially high damages caused.
- Due to the fundamentality of the right to strike for the collective bargaining system at large, restrictions must be applied in a proportionate manner; therefore, substantive restrictions such as imposing minimum services, restricting the total duration of strike measures, back-to-work orders or requisitioning may be only justified in case a vital public interest cannot be secured by other means. Procedural restrictions such as balloting/quorum requirements/notice periods/ pre-dispute mediation/ cooling-off periods may be legitimate once they are applied proportionally, i.e., that collective measures are not delayed for too long.
- Restrictive measures are conditional upon *involving* the conflicting parties in defining such means. This may include 'no strike' agreements, stating preconditions to collective action in collective agreements; jointly organizing minimum services. Furthermore, *judicial review* of restrictions to the right to strike must be guaranteed.
- Where the right to strike has legitimately been restricted or even banned, *compensatory measures* must be provided for stabilizing the effectiveness of the collective bargaining system or replacing it with institutional guarantees. Such measures may include: Automatic indexation of wages or working conditions; independent pay review; mediation or conciliation systems and a final arbitration.

§7.05 CONCLUSION

Despite their detrimental economic consequences, strikes are not merely unavoidable but represent a necessary precondition for an effective system of collective bargaining. Where 'essential services' are concerned by strike action, not merely economic consequences for the undertaking are at stake but primarily the dependency of consumers on the provision of such services in practice. In determining the legitimacy of strike action, also the consumers' dependency on the continuous flow of such services must be taken into account. This may justify restrictions to the right to strike. In such case, the restriction must not go beyond what is absolutely necessary to reach the legitimate goal. As a consequence, procedural restrictions may not become so severe that they in fact obstruct the possibility of conducting a strike. Where substantive restrictions are set up, this must involve the parties to the bargaining process remain strictly proportionate and be open to judicial review. Additionally, the diminished effectiveness of a bargaining process without a full right to collective action must be fully compensated. If such preconditions are not respected, the whole system of collective bargaining may be endangered.

CHAPTER 8
Collective Bargaining and the All-China Federation of Trade Unions: A Game Changer in Governing Chinese Workplaces?

Mimi Zou

China's transition to a market economy with 'Chinese characteristics' has fundamentally transformed the foundations of its labour market and the relationship between state, labour, and capital. Since the 2000s, there has been a proliferation of labour laws, policies, and institutions for promoting 'collective consultation' (collective bargaining) against the backdrop of growing labour unrest. Attempts to resolve labour disputes through collective bargaining have revealed a top-down approach by the state and the All-China Federation of Trade Unions (ACFTU) on the one hand and bottom-up pressures from workers for shop floor representation on the other hand. This chapter examines the role of Chinese trade unions in light of these regulatory developments and assesses the 'game changing' aspects as well as existing problems and challenges confronting collective labour relations and workers' voice in China today. As the state seeks to 'build harmonious labour relations' as a key pillar of its economic development while maintaining social stability, the ACFTU has played an important role in expanding collective consultation institutions at various levels over the past decade. Nevertheless, the potential of the ACFTU as a 'game changer' in worker representation remains institutionally and systemically limited.

§8.01 INTRODUCTION

Reforms to labour laws and labour market institutions in China over the past decade have taken place in the wider backdrop of policymakers' attempts to reorient the country's economic development strategy since the mid-2000s. Concerns over the sustainability of an unbalanced, high growth model and its implications for the Party-state's goal of maintaining social stability (and ultimately, its legitimacy) have emerged in the context of labour relations. The number and scale of labour disputes through formal and unofficial channels have been on the rise. Growing inequality, insecurity, and conflict in a rapidly changing and increasingly complex labour market have seen policymakers prioritise the goal of 'building harmonious labour relations' over the past decade. The expansion of formal collective consultation (*jitixieshang*) or collective bargaining[1] institutions has become an important policy tool for pursuing this goal.

As I have argued in an earlier article (in a book on China and ILO Fundamental Principles that was edited by the late Roger Blanpain and colleagues),[2] collective labour laws and labour market institutions that could provide workers with greater voice and the ability to genuinely bargain with employers can have a longer-term, systemic impact on labour relations in China. Such laws and institutions have become particularly important in light of the Party-state's pursuit of a more balanced and sustainable model of economic development. This new model entails a structural shift from export-led growth based on low-cost labour to an economy that is driven by domestic consumption, which requires the raising of average household wage and income levels.

In this contribution to the special volume of BCLR, I explore some 'game-changing' developments in China's collective bargaining regime in recent years, which have seen some materialisation of reform prospects within the official trade union, the ACFTU. The ACFTU and its local branches have a monopoly on the representation of Chinese workers.[3] Section §8.02 of the chapter starts with an overview of the institutional relationship between the ACFTU and Party-state. Section §8.03 examines a number of important legal and institutional developments in China's collective bargaining regime, including local experimentation in recent years that have signalled some potential on the part of the ACFTU to enhance its worker representation role. Finally, section §8.04 looks at the major challenges facing the 'game changer' prospect of Chinese trade unions in the governance of work in the world's most populous country.

§8.02 THE ACFTU AND THE PARTY-STATE

Prior to the market-based economy in China, almost all enterprises under the centrally planned system were state-owned. A dual system of control by the Party and the management was the basis of enterprise leadership. The basic institutional structure at

---

1. The literal Chinese-English translation of '*jitixieshang*' (the term found in formal legal and policy documents) is 'collective consultation'. This term is used in the official discourse instead of 'collective bargaining'. In this article, both terms are used interchangeably.
2. M. Zou, *The Evolution of Collective Labour Law with 'Chinese Characteristics': Crossing the river by feeling the stones?*, in R. Blanpain, U. Liukkunen & Y. Chen (eds) China and ILO Fundamental Principles and Rights at Work (Kluwer Law International, 2014).
3. M. Gallagher, *The Limits of Civil Society in a Late Leninist State*, in M. Alagappa (ed.) Civil Society and Political Change in Asia, 419 (Stanford University Press, 2005).

the enterprise level consisted of the Party committee, the trade union, and the workers' congress that was led by the trade union. The work-unit (*danwei*) represented the basic level organisation that linked workers to the Party and enabled the Party to directly exert political control over workplaces. The regime mandates trade unions' role as a 'transmission belt' between Party and workers: relaying party edicts and policies to workers while conveying workers' concerns and suggestions to the party leadership.

The 1992 Trade Union Law stipulated the nature and structure of trade unions and the rights and obligations of trade unions and their members. The legislation did not explicitly include any roles or duties of trade unions to represent and safeguard workers' rights and interests. Instead, their basic duty was linked to the 'overall interests of the entire Chinese people'. A new Trade Union Law was promulgated in 2001. This legislation did not alter the political environment for Chinese trade unions' operation nor did it address their representational deficiencies in the workplace. Nevertheless, it opened up important institutional opportunities for the ACFTU.

First, the 2001 Trade Union Law stated the goal of 'safeguarding the legitimate rights and interests of workers' as the basic duty of trade unions. Second, it provided for the establishment of joint trade unions in small enterprises (employing less than twenty-five workers), thereby expanding the scope for sectoral and regional union organising and collective consultation beyond the enterprise level. Third, tripartite consultations were introduced to improve coordination on labour relations among the state, ACFTU, and the officially designated employers' association, the China Enterprise Confederation. Since then, the All China Federation of Industry and Commerce, representing the private sector, has played an increasingly important role in the tripartite consultations.

Nevertheless, the 2001 Trade Union Law did not alter certain constraints for trade unions in representing workers' interests when it comes to resolving the growing number of labour disputes. For example, the role of unions under the law includes mediating an end to industrial action: 'When a work-stoppage or slow-down occurs in an enterprise or institution, the trade union shall ... assist the enterprise or institution in its work so as to enable the normal production process to be resumed as quickly as possible.'[4] This provision reflects the institutionally challenged role of Chinese trade unions as the formal reconciler of conflicting interests between employers and workers.

There is still a prevailing practice of local union officials being appointed by Party officials, with a tendency for managers to concurrently serve in union leadership positions.[5] In these situations, unions' ability to represent their actual constituency when bargaining with management and their capacity to monitor management decisions and enforce observance with the law become highly compromised. Official unions at the enterprise level commonly lack credibility with workers who perceive

---

4. Zhonghua Renmin Gongheguo Gonghuifa (PRC Trade Union Law), Art. 27 (27 October 2001).
5. Qiao Jian, *Zai Guojia, Qiye he Laogong Zhijian: Gonghuixiang Shichangjingji zhuangxingzhongde Duozhong Juese* (Between State, Enterprise and Workers: Multiple Roles of Trade Unions during Market Economy Transition), in China Industrial Relations Institute, *2007 Beijing Gonghui Luntan Lunwenji* (2007 Beijing Trade Union Forum) China Industrial Relations Institute.

these unions as the 'administrative local union' or the 'bosses' union'.[6] Howell argues that the dysfunctional structure of the ACFTU has undermined its identity among workers as the 'representative' of their interests.[7]

When evaluating the extent to which Chinese unions are a workers' representative organisation instead of merely 'an arm of state bureaucracy',[8] it is important to consider the political structure in which the ACFTU is embedded.[9] The Leninist regime mandates trade unions' role as a 'transmission belt' between Party and workers at the grassroots: relaying party edicts and policies to workers, while conveying worker concerns and suggestions to the party leadership.[10] Inherently, the ACFTU must remain supportive of the Party-state rule.

Collective labour disputes entailing industrial action organised by workers without trade unions have been on the rise, particularly interest-based disputes. The changing nature of such disputes has been described as a shift from 'defensive' to increasingly 'offensive'.[11] The emergence of labour shortages in coastal and inland regions also helped to enhance some workers' bargaining power. A notable example was the strikes that took place at the Nanhai Honda Auto Parts Manufacturing plants in 2010, which also triggered 'copycat' strikes in other factories. Along with demands for wage increases, workers also sought to elect their own representatives to negotiate with management. The credibility of their enterprise union was severely undermined by its heavy control by management and its inaction in supporting the workers' claims.[12]

The next section examines how the development and expansion of laws and institutions for collective bargaining have provided some 'game-changing' opportunities for the ACFTU.

§8.03 A GAME CHANGER FOR COLLECTIVE BARGAINING?

[A] National-Level Laws and Policies

At a national level, the conclusion of collective contracts between the employing entity and trade unions on behalf of the employees or an elected staff representative was formally recognised in the Labour Law 1994. The few provisions of the Labour Law

---

6. B. Taylor and L. Qi, *Is the ACFTU a Union and Does It Matter?*, 49 Journal of Industrial Relations. 701-715 (2007).
7. J. Howell, *Trade Unionism in China: Sinking or Swimming?*, 19 Journal of Communist Studies and Transition Politics 102 (2003); J. Howell, *All-China Federation of Trade Unions Beyond Reform? The Slow March to Direct Elections*, 196 The China Quarterly 845 (2008).
8. S. Cooney, *China's Labour Law, Compliance and Flaws in Implementing Institutions*, 49 Journal of Industrial Relations 673, 681 (2007).
9. S. Clarke, *Post-Socialist Trade Unions: China and Russia*, 36 Industrial Relations Journal 2 (2005).
10. M. Gallagher, *The Limits of Civil Society in a Late Leninist State*, supra n. 3.
11. M. Elfstrom & S. Kuruvilla, *The Changing Nature of Labor Unrest in China*, 67 Industrial and Labor Relations Review 453 (2014).
12. Liu Yang & Chen Zhigang, *Nanhai Honda Labour Dispute, the Experience of Shishan Union Reform*, Nanfang Wang (4 July 2011), consulted at the time of writing via http://www.jttp.cn/a/report/news/union/2011/0704/1649.html.

regarding collective contracts did not address issues of scope, content, coverage, process, and dispute settlement arising from collective bargaining. In 1995, the former Ministry of Labour and Social Security issued the Regulations Governing Collective Contracts ('1995 Regulations') to supplement the few provisions in the Labour Law. However, the 1995 Regulations were on the whole vaguely drafted and failed to address many procedural and substantial aspects of collective bargaining.[13]

From 2000 onwards, there has been an accelerated expansion of formal laws and institutions concerning collective bargaining. In 2000, the then Ministry of Labour and Social Security promulgated the Interim Measures for Collective Consultation on Wages. The Interim Measures laid out the subject matters of wage collective consultation, which includes a system of wage distribution, level of annual adjustment on wages, payment of allowances and bonuses, and conditions for terminating a wage agreement. It also lists the factors that should be considered in the determination of wage levels, such as the economic efficiency of the enterprise and local consumer price index.

In 2004, the then Ministry of Labour and Social Security adopted the Provisions on Collective Contracts ('2004 Provisions'), which laid out more detailed rules on the conduct of and relationship between the parties in collective consultation. For example, Article 24 stipulates that no person may concurrently act as representatives of both the employer and employees. The employer must also treat employee representatives' participation in collective bargaining as 'having worked normally' (Article 27). Such representatives shall not be dismissed except in very limited circumstances (Article 28). Importantly, either party, upon receiving a written request, 'shall not refuse to conduct negotiations on signing a collective contract without justifiable reasons' (Article 32). This provision differs from the 1995 Regulations, which limited the requests of either party to 'amend' or 'negotiate in regards to the execution' of preexisting collective contracts.

Furthermore, there was a wave of worker-protective labour law reforms in 2007, which represented an endeavour by policymakers to 'reverse the deregulation agenda' of the 1990s and to 're-regulate' the labour market with the overarching goal of 'building harmonious labour relations'.[14] The 2007 Labour Contracts Law (LCL) contained numerous provisions regulating collective contracts, such as defining the scope of a valid collective contract, for parties to enter into specific collective agreements regarding the specific issues. The LCL also formally recognised sectoral level collective contracts concluded below the county level.

There has also been growing regulatory emphasis on concluding collective contracts at the sectoral and regional levels. In 2006, the ACFTU, China Enterprise Confederation, and China Enterprise Management Association jointly issued an Opinion recommending the development of regional and sectoral collective bargaining. In 2010, the Ministry of Human Resources and Social Security, the China Enterprise Management Association, and the ACFTU further issued a circular setting out specific

---

13. S. Cooney, S. Biddulph & Y. Zhu, *Law and Fair Work in China* (1st ed., Routledge 2013).
14. C. Lee, W. Brown & X. Wen, *What Sort of Collective Bargaining is Emerging in China?*, British Journal of Industrial Relations (2014).

targets of 60% and 80% in collective contract coverage in 2010 and 2011 respectively.[15] It additionally proposed a focus on developing collective wage bargaining and sectoral collective bargaining. The most recent ACFTU Work Plan on Improving Collective Consultation (2014-2018) has emphasised that the main function of collective bargaining is to increase workers' incomes and narrow the income distribution gap.

Overall, China has quickly developed a formal regulatory framework for collective bargaining within a relatively short period of time. A concerted push by policymakers and the ACFTU has seen a dramatic increase in the quantity of signed collective contracts in recent years, with numerical targets set for local ACFTU federations and government officials. It has been observed that the quality of many collective contracts, particularly at the enterprise level, is generally weak in terms of substantive outcomes (such as simply replicating the statutory minima) as well as the absence of worker participation in the process.[16] Nevertheless, some localised experiments in law-making and institutional building around collective bargaining have taken place in specific regions and sectors, which have signalled potential 'game changing' opportunities for the ACFTU.

[B] Localised Experiments in Collective Bargaining

Institutional building around multi-employer and sectoral collective bargaining has seen some progress since the mid-2000s. Sectoral bargaining has been promoted partly based on the well-known 'Wenling model'. In 2003, a group of knitwear employers in Wenling city of Zhejiang Province saw the need to organise an association for standardising wages in order to curb excessive competition and maintain stable labour relations. It has been observed that the 'Wenling model', which was driven by employers' collective self-interest, departed from the usual state-driven approach to collective bargaining (at least initially).[17] Subsequently, the local government and regional federation of the ACFTU became heavily involved in establishing a sector collective bargaining mechanism.[18] The 'Wenling model' was subsequently incorporated into the amended Regulations of Zhejiang Province on Collective Contracts 2010. Under these Regulations, regional federations of trade unions could request, on behalf of employees in enterprises without an enterprise union, the employing unit to engage in collective bargaining.

Another notable example of sectoral and regional collective wage negotiations has emerged from the food and beverage industry in Wuhan municipality – which

---

15. Circular on Deeply Promoting the Implementation of a Rainbow Plan in Collective Contract System 2010.
16. C. Lee, *Recent Industrial Relations Developments in China and Vietnam: The Transformation of Industrial Relations in East Asian Transition Economies*, 48(3) The Journal of Industrial Relations 415-429 (2006).
17. Lee, Brown & Wen, *supra* n. 14.
18. X. Wen & K. Lin, *Restructuring China's State Corporatist Industrial Relations System: The Wenling Experience* 24.94 Journal of Contemporary China 665-683 (2015).

some have referred to as the 'Wuhan model'.[19] Collective negotiations on matters of sectoral minimum wages, annual wage growth, and overtime have been conducted between the Wuhan Municipal Food and Beverages union and employer representatives since 2011. These negotiations purportedly cover 500,000 food and beverage 'frontline' employees in the city. The latest agreement concluded in 2015 stipulated that the industry's basic wage increase this year would not be less than 7%, and the minimum sectoral wage in the main areas of Wuhan city shall be RMB 1,700 and in new parts of the city RMB 1,450.[20]

Furthermore, there have been efforts to introduce limited forms of 'direct' elections of workers' representatives in collective consultation at the enterprise level, the process of which has been carefully guided and supervised by local trade union federations.[21] The Nanhai strikes in 2010 have also given major impetus to this direction. Fan and Gahan have observed that subsequent reform of Nanhai Honda's union was associated with more active rank-and-file member involvement and greater internal union democracy that strengthened the union's worker representation role. A reconstituted enterprise union leadership at Nanhai was organised under the guidance of the Guangdong provincial trade union federation but involved the direct participation of workers at the preliminary stages of collective consultation. A new collective agreement was concluded that nearly doubled the workers' monthly wage rates.[22]

Field studies of collective bargaining in automotive and electronic companies in Guangdong province have revealed a 'dual-track' representation mechanism underpinning workplace election practices. The mechanism involves the participation of rank-and-file workers on the one hand and the continued supervision of enterprise unions by the local trade union federation on the other.[23] Designed to enhance the effectiveness and perceived legitimacy of the collective bargaining process, the arrangement resulted in a mixture of managerial staff and rank-and-file workers in the enterprise union committees. A 'hybrid representational structure' gave workers some institutional space for voice and negotiations with management, albeit under the stewardship of local trade union federations. These practices saw substantive effects on wages and working conditions, as well as revised wage structures in ways that reflected workers preferences.[24]

It remains to be seen whether such localised and ad hoc experimentation can develop into more systemic changes to the wider regulatory system. As the next section examines, there remain significant institutional constraints for Chinese trade unions to

---

19. C. Chan & E. Hui, *The Development of Collective Bargaining in China: From 'Collective Bargaining by Riot' to 'Party State-Led Wage Bargaining'*, The China Quarterly 221–242 (2014).
20. Y.M. Zhang, *Wuhan: Food Industry Workers to Collective Negotiation Basic Wage Increases of Not Less Than 7%*, Xinhua (8 August 2015), http://news.xinhuanet.com/fortune/2015-08/08/c_11 16188473.htm.
21. W. Zhang, *Candidates Running for Union Chair Elections Should Give an Address*, Nanfang Daily (2 August 2012), http://epaper.southcn.com/nfdaily/html/2012-08/02/content_7109968.htm.
22. Y. Fan & P. Gahan, *What Are Chinese Unions Doing? Explaining Innovation & Change in Grassroots Unions* (29 June 2012) http://ssrn.com/abstract=2113221.
23. C. Lee, W. Brown & X. Wen, *What Sort of Collective Bargaining is Emerging in China?*, British Journal of Industrial Relations (2014).
24. Ibid.

evolve beyond a 'transmission belt' of the Party-State to genuinely become a 'game changer' in representing workers in collective bargaining at Chinese workplaces.

§8.04 REMAINING CHALLENGES

[A] Top-Down, Control-Driven Approach by the Party-State

It could be said that developments in collective bargaining laws and institutions over the past two decades reflect a top-down, interventionist approach taken by the Party-state through the 'transmission belt' of the ACFTU. Higher-level trade unions have often played a 'directing and instructing' role in collective consultation at the enterprise level, with little participation from workers in the process. Clegg argues that 'state intervention may... be a powerful influence if it comes at a sufficiently early stage in the development of collective bargaining'.[25] However, significant involvement of the state can hinder the development of a mature collective bargaining system. Chan and Hui have described the phenomenon as 'Party state-led collective bargaining'.[26]

There have only been limited forms of direct involvement by workers in collective bargaining and the resolution of collective labour disputes.[27] Commentators have expressed doubt over the potential for genuine reform of trade union elections.[28] As Chan pointed out, the underlying agenda of the state is to maintain a collective bargaining system 'without being confrontational, and without politically independent unionism'.[29] A study by Hui and Chan also shows that although the Party-state may be more open to limited forms of trade union elections, it is also attempting to manipulate such elections.[30] Liu and Kuruvilla argue that the state's responses to labour unrest in recent times – namely the re-regulation of the labour market and revival of corporatist employment relations arrangements – have constrained the development of genuine trade unionism, therefore propelling 'greater worker demand for voice and justice' in the workplace.[31]

This top-down approach can be gleaned from the most recent reform of the ACFTU, initiated and sponsored by the Party in November 2015.[32] The reform is aimed

---

25. C.H. Armstrong, *Trade Unionism Under Collective Bargaining: A Theory Based on Comparisons of Six Countries*, 10 (1st ed., Blackwell Publishers 1976).
26. Chan and Hui, *supra* n. 19.
27. *See*, for example, Guangdong Regulations 2015, Arts 12, and 13; Zhejiang Amendment 2010, Arts 10–12; Shanghai Regulations 2015, Arts 6, and 7; Shenzhen Regulations 2008, Art. 11.
28. C. Chan & E. Hui, *The Development of Collective Bargaining in China: From 'Collective Bargaining by Riot' to 'Party State-Led Wage Bargaining'*, 217 The China Quarterly 239 (2014).
29. A. Chan, *Labour Relations in Foreign-Funded Ventures, Chinese Trade Unions, and the Prospects for Collective Bargaining*, in Greg O'Leary (ed.) *Adjusting to Capitalism: Chinese Workers and the State*, 124 (Armonk, NY; M.E. Sharpe, London, 1998).
30. C. Chan & E. Hui, *The Development of Collective Bargaining in China: From 'Collective Bargaining by Riot' to 'Party State-Led Wage Bargaining'*, 217 The China Quarterly 622 (2014).
31. M. Liu & S. Kuruvilla, *The State, the Unions and Collective Bargaining in China: The Good, the Bad, and the Ugly*, 38 Comparative Labor Law & Policy Journal (2017).
32. Central Committee of the Communist Party of China. *Central Committee of the Communist Party of China Opinion about Strengthening and Improving the Party's Mass Organisation Works* (People's Publishing House, Beijing 2015).

at strengthening the Party-state's top-down approach to enhancing the effectiveness of its 'transmission belt' when handling labour disputes, leaving little room for trade union autonomy. Notably, there is no mention of collective bargaining in the ACFTU's reform plan – instead, the emphasis seems to be on a pre-emptive mediation role by trade unions in labour disputes and incorporating rank-and-file workers into the ACFTU leadership structure.[33]

[B] **Legal Protections for Workers Engaging in Industrial Action**

For effective collective bargaining to take place, it has been recognised by the ILO that workers must have channels for exerting industrial pressure on the employer.[34] The right to strike has an ambiguous legal status in China. Since the right to strike was removed from China's Constitution in 1982, there has not been any explicit legal protection of such a right. There is also no clear prohibition of strikes in the law. Nevertheless, legal protection for striking workers in the form of criminal and civil immunity is absent under national and local laws. Such safeguards have been considered by the ILO as necessary to ensure respect for workers' right to strike.[35] Some have therefore argued that there should be a positive recognition of the right to strike in Chinese law.[36]

Furthermore, a lack of regulation governing industrial action makes it difficult for the Party-state to systematically respond to the growing number and scale of unofficial, 'wildcat' strikes undertaken by workers (since official trade unions will not organise any form of industrial action). Such strikes are usually handled on an ad hoc, case-by-case basis by local governments and ACFTU local affiliates.

An important attempt to regulate strike activity is the Guangdong Province Enterprise Collective Contract Regulations 2015 (Guangdong Regulations). It directly sets out certain restrictions on industrial action. It has been widely criticised by labour advocates for lacking adequate protections for workers who strike in response to breakdown in negotiations. It prevents workers from effectively resorting to industrial action during a designated three-month negotiating period, by prohibiting them from 'violating the labour contract and failing to complete job tasks', 'violating labour discipline', or 'obstructing access to the enterprise... or damaging the enterprise's normal regular operation procedures and public order' (Articles 13 and 24).

---

33. All-China Federation of Trade Unions, *Reform experiment plan of national trade unions* (ACFTU, Beijing 2015).
34. International Labour Organization, *Freedom of Association: Digest of Decisions and Principles of the Freedom of Association Committee of the Governing Body of the ILO*, paras 526–527. (ILO, 2006).
35. Committee on Economic, Social and Cultural Rights, United Kingdom, (2010) Observation (CEACR): Freedom of Association and Protection of the Right to Organise Convention, 1948 (No. 87) – United Kingdom, http://www.ilo.org/dyn/normlex/en/f?p = 1000:13100:0::NO:13100:P1 3100_COMMENT_ID:2322470.
36. K. Chang & F. Cooke, *Legislating the Right to Strike in China: Historical Development and Prospects*, 57(3) Journal of Industrial Relations, 449 (2015); E. Friedman, *Insurgency Trap: Labor Politics in Postsocialist China* (Cornell University Press 2014).

It has been common for employers to 'take a tough stand' against workers on strike and retaliate against strike leaders.[37] Employers may dismiss an employee based on alleging that the worker has seriously violated the company's regulations.[38] Based on the relevant provisions in the Guangdong Regulations (and other local regulations),[39] protections against employer retaliation are limited to the workers' representatives for the purpose of collective bargaining and do not extend to workers who want to impose industrial pressure on the company by going on strike.

[C] Room for Labour NGOs?

The law does not tolerate competing grassroots unions that are independent of the official ACFTU structure. The legal monopoly of ACFTU as the sole representative of workers' interests does not allow workers to establish any alternative institutional apparatus.[40] Despite the absence of an official role in labour dispute settlement, the activities of non-governmental organisations (NGOs) in providing various forms of assistance to workers in labour disputes have expanded in recent years. To circumvent a variety of political and legal constraints, many grassroots labour NGOs register as commercial entities or operate without formal legal status.[41]

Labour NGOs have played an important role in labour dispute resolution to date. They have acted as a representative negotiator for workers by means of network building and capacity building in collective action in labour disputes.[42] These organisations have stepped in to fill the gap of much-needed services for workers such as advising and assisting workers in day-to-day labour disputes as well as acting as 'legal representatives' for workers in administrative proceedings (such as in labour inspections) and in civil proceedings (such as mediation, arbitration, and litigation). Since many grassroots NGOs' personnel were once migrant workers themselves, they are often more effective than trade union officials in developing and maintaining close communications with workers.[43]

There are inevitably conflicts in the relationship between the ACFTU and NGOs. The latter poses a challenge to the former with regards to worker representation. An underlying reason of the 2015 ACFTU reforms is to counteract the growth of 'independent' labour NGOs.[44] It could be said that the latest ACFTU reforms involve a 'carrot

---

37. China Labour Bulletin, *Searching for the Union: The Workers' Movement in China 2011-13*, 21–22, http://www.clb.org.hk/sites/default/files/archive/en/File/research_reports/searching%20for%20the%20union%201.pdf.
38. Such reason is allowed under the Labour Contract Law, Art. 39(2). *See also* CLB (2014a: 23).
39. Guangdong Regulations 2015, Art. 16; Zhejiang Amendment 2010, Art. 14; Shanghai Regulations 2015, Art. 10; Shenzhen Regulations 2008, Art. 27.
40. F. Chen, *Union Power in China: Source, Operation and Constraints*, 35 Modern China 662 (2009).
41. D. Lee, *Legal Reform in China: A Role for Non-governmental Organisations*, 25 The Yale Journal of International Law 363 (2000).
42. M. Zou, X.M. Pan & S. Han, *Regulating Collective Labour Disputes in China: A Tale of Two Actors*, 10 Journal of Comparative Law 276 (2016).
43. *Ibid.*
44. X. Wen, *Typology and Institutional Construction of Collective Consultation in Chinese Transition* (Social Sciences Academic Press, 2016).

and stick' strategy. First, two new departments have been created within the ACFTU. The Social Liaison Department is a newly established body that monitors and deals with labour NGOs and other social actors involved in labour relations. A second newly created body, the Network Affairs Department, is responsible for handling labour-related discussions online and on social media. It appears that the Network Affairs Department's work is oriented towards creating positive publicity for the ACFTU and directing public sentiment away from independent labour organising. Second, a warning system of collective labour action has been established under the reforms. Trade unions are urged to increase their visibility among workers and take the responsibility for representing workers in mediation when a wildcat strike occurs. If a labour NGO is on site, unions should resort to the Trade Union Law – which recognises their legal status as the official (and only) workers' representative – and work with the local government and police to prevent the NGO and any independent labour organisers from communicating with the workers. Finally, the ACFTU can 'sponsor' labour NGOs that accept the supervision of official trade unions. The Social Liaison Department of the ACFTU will review annual work plans of these labour NGOs and monitor their daily operations. Funding could also be provided to these NGOs for service work (not organising work) that assist the ACFTU.

§8.05 CONCLUSION

Collective bargaining has become an important in the repertoire of Chinese labour relations policies over the past fifteen years. Compared to the 1990s, there has been a rapid development of formal laws and institutions around collective bargaining and collective agreements at various levels. Local experimentation in rulemaking and institution building has partly filled in the gaps of national laws and sometimes served as testing grounds for wider regulatory reform – providing 'game changing' opportunities for the ACFTU to go beyond its traditional 'transmission belt' role.

Nevertheless, there remain important limitations to this potential transformation of the sole state-sanctioned trade union, namely the continued emphasis of a top-down, control-driven approach by the Party-state, the ambiguous legal status of the right to strike and a lack of legal protections for workers engaged in industrial action, and the restricted institutional space that labour NGOs operate in. The most recent reform of the ACFTU, initiated by the Party, illustrates some of these constraints.

The stakes are high. The effectiveness of the ACFTU's representation of Chinese workers in collective bargaining can have far-reaching and systemic effects on the Party-state's commonly espoused goal of building 'harmonious labour relations'. This is a goal that faces considerable hurdles as the country seeks to deepen structural reform in its recent economic slowdown, with ever-greater possibilities for social and political instability. The Party-state's priority of maintaining stability ('*weiwen*') will most likely mean the continuation of a top-down, control-driven approach to labour relations. As Estlund argues: 'The powers-that-be in China fear that, if workers were permitted to organize themselves autonomously, they would pose a significant threat to the stability of the political-economic status quo. That fear puts sharp limits on the liberalization of collective labour activity and the democratization of the official union.'[45]

---

45. C. Estlund, *A New Deal for Chinese Workers*, 23 (Harvard University Press 2017).

PART III Fairness and Rights

CHAPTER 9
What We Know about Equal Employment Opportunity Law after Fifty Years of Trying

Susan Bisom-Rapp

§9.01 INTRODUCTION

Roger Blanpain cared deeply about equality, calling it a "one of the most fundamental aspirations of mankind... ."[1] The equality principle, he noted, is embodied in international declarations and treaties, supranational charters, and in the laws, constitutional and statutory, of many countries. Yet Blanpain also understood that discrimination is an intrinsic part of the human condition, and embedded in the way institutions and organizations function. And he knew, and was troubled by the fact, that as societies become more diverse, achieving equality becomes more complicated and difficult.[2] He worried about the tensions that increase as the demographics of a country change and expressed concern about the extent to which racism, sexism, and ageism, for example, continue to exist despite laws that ban discrimination.

Ten years ago, at the International Forum on Diversity, Equality and Integration, which he hosted and was held in the Palace of the Royal Flemish Academy of Belgium, Blanpain issued a plea. He exhorted researchers and policymakers to continue examining how equal employment opportunity (EEO) law and policy operates in action. Because "law on the books in itself may mean absolutely nothing," we need to look beyond the law as written. As he put it:

> [W]e need to find out what people do believe, what they are expecting, how they are organised and how societal institutions function, because discrimination, as the ILO says, is inherent in human nature. We thus need the input of sociologists,

---

1. Roger Blanpain, "Diversity Equality and Integration," in *Diversity Equality and Integration: Beyond the Law—A Comparative Study* 15 (Roger Blanpain, ed., Vanden Broele 2008).
2. *Id.*, at 17-18.

economists, psychologists, and other social scientists, describing the realities of society, discrimination and equality. A multidisciplinary approach is necessary providing transparency about where we are and where we are going....By carefully assessing the problem, we can craft appropriate responses it.[3]

Such an examination is necessary, said Blanpain, because "equality in reality" must be the goal if we are to achieve social justice and peaceful societies.

This is an especially opportune moment to embrace Blanpain's appeal. From an academic standpoint, five books published between 2016 and 2017 provide valuable legal and social scientific perspectives on why employment discrimination law has failed to eliminate workplace bias.[4] Read together, these books are game changing in the sense that they call not only for understanding present conditions but also for rethinking legal and organizational approaches to creating fair workplaces and decent work. These works, with one exception, concern themselves solely with the failure of EEO law in the United States (U.S.), a country that half a century ago was a leader in embracing workplace equality law.[5] Even so, many of the findings may be generalizable to other countries, and to the extent that they are, these books offer a number of important lessons to law- and policymakers not only in the U.S. but also in other nations.

From a political perspective, this is also a particularly good time to take up Blanpain's entreaty to examine how EEO law functions in reality. The rise of nationalism and xenophobia in the U.S. and in European Union Member States presents a significant challenge to the idea of the harmonious, multicultural society, which Blanpain viewed as ideal.

In the U.S., equality, inclusion, and civil rights are under assault. President Donald Trump's policy agenda, shaped by a cabinet close to devoid of the representation of women and of racial and ethnic minorities, is extreme and regressive.[6] The Trump administration, for example, in just its first eight months on the job, issued a travel ban to the U.S. aimed at Muslims,[7] proposed cutting legal immigration to the country in half,[8] advocated banning transgender individuals from the military,[9] took steps to argue that federal law does not prohibit employment discrimination against

---

3. Roger Blanpain & Susan Bisom-Rapp, "General Conclusion," in *Diversity Equality and Integration: Beyond the Law—A Comparative Study* 423 (Roger Blanpain, ed., Vanden Broele 2008).
4. This author makes no claim that these five books are the only important recent publications on the subject. Rather, they are books receiving a fair amount of notice in the United States and, as will be discussed herein, intersect in interesting, important, and game-changing ways.
5. One of the books is a comparative treatment of EEO law and policy in the United States *and* the United Kingdom. *See* Susan Bisom-Rapp & Malcolm Sargeant, *Lifetime Disadvantage, Discrimination and the Gendered Workforce* (Cambridge University Press 2016) [hereinafter *Lifetime Disadvantage*].
6. *See* Lilly Goren, "Few Women Hold Key Positions in the Trump Administration," Brookings, May 12, 2017; Molly Redden, "Trump Is Assembling the Most Male-Dominated Government in Decades," The Guardian, Sept. 21, 2017; Allison Graves, "Is Trump's Cabinet More White and Male Than Any First Cabinet since Reagan?," Politifact, Apr. 26, 2017.
7. Nahall Toosi, Ted Hesson & Sarah Frostenson, "Muslim Nations Targeted by Trump's Travel Ban See Steep Visa Drop," Politico, Sept. 28, 2017.
8. *See* Brian Naylor, "Trump Unveils Legislation Limiting Legal Immigration," NPR, Aug. 2, 2017.
9. *See* W.J. Hennigan, "Trump Orders Pentagon to Reinstate Ban on Transgender People in the Military," L.A. Times, Aug. 25, 2017.

Chapter 9: Equal Employment Opportunity Law after Fifty Years of Trying §9.01

LGBTQ people,[10] halted implementation of a rule aimed at tackling pay disparities that would have required large employers to report salary and wage data by gender, race, and ethnicity,[11] and launched an examination of university admissions policies intimating that they may discriminate against white people.[12] Trump was also widely criticized for failing to issue a timely and robust condemnation of a rally of neo-Nazis and white supremacists in Charlottesville, Virginia, after that event resulted in the death of one and the injury of many other counter-protesters.[13] The false premise behind the Trump campaign slogan "Make America Great Again" is that diversity and the quest for equality have harmed the American polity, and that white, native-born men are its primary victims.[14]

This chapter, by reviewing how EEO law after half a century is functioning in American society, will demonstrate the fallacy of claims that the law has provided advantages to women and people of color that damage the interests of white men. If anything, the transformative potential of EEO law has over time been disabled. The five books considered in this chapter are:

(1) *Rights on Trial* by Ellen Berrey, Robert Nelson, and Laura Beth Nielsen.[15]
(2) *Lifetime Disadvantage and the Gendered Workforce* by Susan Bisom-Rapp and Malcolm Sargeant.[16]
(3) *Working Law* by Lauren Edelman.[17]
(4) *Discrimination Laundering* by Tristin Green.[18]
(5) *Unequal* by Sandra Sperino and Suja Thomas.[19]

Rather than discuss each one in turn, as one might in a typical book review, this chapter teases out three key insights gleaned from them in three separate sections. Section §9.02 covers the first insight, which is a considerable drawback to using EEO law to vindicate one's rights: the adversarial process imposes significant emotional and

---

10. *See* Fred Barbash, "Trump Administration Intervening in Major LGBT Case, Says Job Bias Law Does Not Cover Sexual Orientation," Washington Post, Jul. 27, 2017.
11. *See* Danielle Paquette, "Trump Administration Halts Obama Era Rule to Shrink the Gender Wage Gap," Chicago Tribune, Aug. 30, 2017.
12. *See* Charlie Savage, "Justice Dept. to Take on Affirmative Action in College Admissions," N.Y. Times, Aug. 1, 2017 (noting that the Justice Department is preparing to investigate and sue universities for discriminating against white applicants for admission).
13. *See* Ronald Brownstein, "How Trump's Reaction to Charlottesville Threatens the GOP," The Atlantic, Aug. 17, 2017.
14. *See generally*, Ta-Nehisi Coates, "The First White President," The Atlantic, October 2017.
15. Ellen Berrey, Robert L. Nelson, & Laura Beth Nielsen, *Rights on Trial: How Workplace Discrimination Law Perpetuates Inequality* (University of Chicago Press 2017) [hereinafter *Rights on Trial*].
16. Bisom-Rapp & Sargeant, *Lifetime Disadvantage*, *supra* note 5.
17. Lauren B. Edelman, *Working Law: Courts, Corporations, and Symbolic Civil Rights* (University of Chicago Press 2017) [hereinafter *Working Law*].
18. Tristin K. Green, *Discrimination Laundering: The Rise of Organizational Innocence and the Crisis of Equal Opportunity Law* (Cambridge University Press 2017) [hereinafter *Discrimination Laundering*].
19. Sandra F. Sperino & Suja A. Thomas, *Unequal: How America's Courts Undermine Discrimination Law* (Oxford University Press 2017) [hereinafter *Unequal*].

financial costs on those employees who engage with it and leaves many uncompensated injuries clearly linked to discrimination. Section §9.03 details the way in which courts narrow the reach of employment discrimination law by preserving managerial prerogatives. Section §9.04 notes that the law frequently misses discrimination that accrues over time and describes the cumulative disadvantage that results. Following these three sections, a brief conclusion offers thoughts on legal and policy reform for diverse societies that wish to promote an antidiscrimination agenda along with fairness and decent work.

§9.02 THE COSTS TO VICTIMS OF PURSUING EEO CLAIMS AND THE REFUSAL TO ACKNOWLEDGE THEIR HARMS

The U.S., like its counterparts in the developed world and many countries in the developing world, has laws on the books prohibiting employment discrimination on a number of bases. On the national level, those bases include race, color, religion, national origin, sex or gender (including pregnancy),[20] age,[21] and disability.[22] Indeed, the civil rights revolution in the American workplace dates back over half a century when legislation aimed at dismantling virulent racism and overwhelming sexism in the labor market was first enacted. To understand why, despite the existence of these laws, explicit and implicit forms of racism, sexism, xenophobia, ethnocentrism, ageism, and ableism continue to affect the working lives of millions of Americans, one must examine how the promise non-discriminatory treatment is operationalized in practice.

American EEO statutes provide those aggrieved with a legal right of action against their employers. Employees must first seek the assistance of a government agency, a process known as the requirement of exhaustion of one's administrative remedies. Exhaustion envisions government investigation, and ideally, voluntary mediation and resolution of the dispute. After exhaustion, however, the statutes allow employees to sue their employers in a court of general jurisdiction. Hence, in great part, a system of rights-based litigation aims to vanquish workplace discrimination and, by doing so, effectuate transformative social change. Sociologists Ellen Berrey, Robert Nelson, and Laura Beth Nielsen in their book *Rights on Trial* interrogate this system in two ways. First, the authors examine what happens to plaintiffs who attempt to litigate their EEO claims. Second, the researchers scrutinize the adversarial system as a whole to reveal the way in which employers are advantaged within it. Based on close to "1,800 court filings with one-hundred in-depth interviews of parties and their attorneys,"[23] their analysis reveals the tremendous costs to victims of pursuing their claims and illuminates the barriers to victims' success in litigation.

Berrey, Nelson, and Nielsen's second point will be examined in section §9.03 below. Their first point of examination—what happens to plaintiffs—results in a powerful indictment of our system of EEO rights-based litigation. More specifically, the

---

20. Civil Rights Act of 1964, Title VII, 42 U.S.C. §§2000-e et seq.
21. Age Discrimination in Employment Act of 1967, 29 U.S.C. §§621 et seq.
22. Americans with Disabilities Act of 1990, 42 U.S.C. §§12101 et seq.
23. Berry, Nelson & Nielsen, *Rights on Trial, supra* note 15, at 10.

interviews reveal that when an employee files an EEO Commission charge or a lawsuit in court, he or she is transformed in the employer's eyes from an employee into an adversary. This is so even when there are indications that a claim of discrimination may be valid. From the employer's perspective, minimization of damage to the enterprise is at a premium and the well-being of the aggrieved employee fades to irrelevance. Within the organization, plaintiff employees report that colleagues shun and even lie about them.[24] Managers increase critical scrutiny of the plaintiff employee's performance. The employer's lawyers, who must as a professional duty zealously represent their client, are motivated to win by any legal means. As a defense strategy, this often results in the attorneys framing the facts in ways that denigrate the employee, question the employee's competence and loyalty, and characterize as naïve and incorrect the employee's views about what constitutes legally actionable discrimination.

The employee-plaintiff typically experiences these actions as a personal attack. Defense tactics take a high personal toll. Many of the plaintiff interviewees suffered not only job loss but also "depression, alcoholism, and divorce as a result of the experience of litigation."[25] Many came away from the process believing they were treated unfairly and suffered great financial costs. Most troubling, these costs were most evident for African Americans and other racial minorities bringing claims, a painful irony since the impetus for American EEO law—what our historic Civil Rights Movement sought to achieve—was the promise of racial justice. So punishing is the American system of EEO rights-based litigation that even victorious plaintiffs—those relatively few who win a substantial monetary settlement or successfully avoid claim dismissal or are awarded money damages at the conclusion of a trial—are left with a sense of emotional injury and the sense that the workplace practices they challenged remain essentially unchanged.

Legal scholars Sandra Sperino and Suja Thomas in their book *Unequal* also find that the adversarial process produces perverse outcomes in EEO litigation. Like Berrey, Nelson, and Nielsen, they observe that lawyers zealously representing employers use every possible argument to vanquish the employee-plaintiff or, at the very least, settle the lawsuit on monetary terms very favorable to their client even if the result is to hobble the reach of EEO law. Sperino and Thomas's focus, however, is on the harm caused by the actions of the judiciary. They argue that federal judges have created "legal frameworks, rules and inferences" to assist them in evaluating claims of individual disparate treatment (direct discrimination), retaliation (victimization), and harassment.[26] Using these analytical devices, judges "slice and dice" the operative facts so that in a shocking number of cases, they conclude no discrimination has occurred—even in cases where most people would consider that discrimination is clear.[27] From a comparative law perspective, the book represents an invitation to those from other countries to observe how the judging of workplace discrimination law

---

24. *Id.*, at 265.
25. *Id.*, at 266.
26. Sperino & Thomas, *Unequal, supra* note 19, at 1–2.
27. *Id.*, at 151–152.

claims may go astray when judges employ constructs that actually prevent them from discerning bias.

One particularly troublesome rule in U.S. cases is the adverse action doctrine, which holds that even if conduct is driven by discrimination, if the employer does not take what the court considers to be an "adverse action" against the plaintiff—an action such as a termination, a refusal to hire or promote, a reduction in pay—the plaintiff will lose. Under this rule, Sperino and Thomas found that courts often find employer conduct such as giving the plaintiff a negative performance review, refusing to transfer the employee to a different department or location, transferring the plaintiff laterally to a less favorable work site, threating to take disciplinary action or to sack the employee but not taking those actions, and assigning more difficult work cannot be considered "adverse actions" within the meaning of the EEO statutes. Thus, the harm visited upon the employee, even though driven by animus tied to a protected trait (e.g., race, sex), is not legally actionable.[28]

Another judicial creation is the "severe or pervasive" requirement in sexual harassment cases. Using this requirement, created by the U.S. Supreme Court although not found anywhere in the statute the Court was interpreting, courts frequently find behavior that would shock or make a person blush is not serious enough to constitute harassment. Hence, in cases, repeated requests for dates, brushing up against the plaintiff employee's breasts or buttocks, making comments about wanting to rape the plaintiff, rubbing the employee's stomach and saying it is sexy, trying to kiss the plaintiff on numerous occasions, asking the plaintiff to accompany a supervisor to a hotel, were all actions held not to constitute harassment. In other words, they were deemed insufficiently severe or pervasive to be actionable. These rulings refuse to acknowledge the illegality of obviously gender-driven conduct and, as such, the judicial decisions themselves may be experienced as emotionally injurious by victims. Moreover, such parsimonious readings of the facts leave harms clearly linked to bias without legal redress.[29]

Courts also use the "stray remarks" doctrine to cut the causal connection between what would seem to be direct evidence of discrimination and an adverse action. Under this doctrine, if an obviously discriminatory remark by a supervisor is not made very close in time to a negative employment decision, such as a decision to terminate, or not to promote, or not to hire, the employer's action is held to be unconnected to the comment. Thus, clearly biased supervisor statements are viewed as nothing more than harmless stray remarks, and cannot possibly have tainted employment decisions being challenged by employees as discriminatory.[30]

These rules, and others discussed by Sperino and Thomas, prevent judges from viewing discrimination in context, create "an alternate reality" where obviously discriminatory conduct is rendered beyond the reach of EEO law, and leave employee harm uncompensated.[31] As the authors note, the rules "favor employers and disfavor

---

28. *Id.*, at 40–41.
29. *Id.*, at 33–40.
30. *Id.*, at 87–88.
31. *Id.*, at 2.

workers" and result in a system where "[j]udges do not protect the core of the discrimination statutes."[32] But why are such frameworks, rules, and inferences created, and what causes judges to view actionable discrimination so narrowly? Section §9.03 below reveals the interplay between judicial perspectives on discrimination and the actions of employers, who signal compliance with EEO law, and in doing so, preserve managerial prerogatives.

§9.03 NARROWING THE REACH OF EEO LAW BY PRESERVING MANAGERIAL PREROGATIVES

Several of the books discussed herein note that overt discrimination and implicit bias continue to exist in the American workplace because EEO law has been interpreted narrowly rather than expansively. Sperino and Thomas, for example, argue that a myriad of judicially created frameworks, rules, and inferences restrict the reach and potential of EEO law and result in the dismissal of many deserving discrimination claims before trial.[33] The sociologist Lauren Edelman, however, in her award-winning book *Working Law*, traces back to employers the process that yields narrow judicial interpretations of EEO law, a process she calls "legal endogeneity."[34] Edelman notes that statutory EEO law contains general and ambiguous terms in that prohibitions are issued without an explanation of how compliance may be achieved. Beginning over fifty years ago, this ambiguity allowed organizations themselves—the subjects of regulation—to define the meaning of compliance. This was and continues to be a project of compliance professionals working for employers: those in the human resources management and legal professions.[35]

These professionals, over time, encouraged employers to develop policies and programs that signal attention to EEO law. Such policies and programs, which Edelman calls symbolic structures, include: antidiscrimination policies, antiharassment procedures, diversity training, progressive discipline policies, and formal performance evaluation procedures.[36] Symbolic structures became widespread throughout employing organizations in the decades following the enactment of civil rights law. While one would hope that such structures would cause substantive changes in how organizations function, Edelman finds that they generally do not. Instead, these policies and programs operate mainly symbolically, preserving management's prerogative to manage its workforce as it sees fit and often with minimal disruption of organizational hierarchies, which may track race and gender, for example.

When employees file lawsuits for discrimination, courts, Edelman argues, accept these symbolic structures as evidence that no discrimination took place. She calls this process judicial deference because judges defer to the organizations being sued and their policies and practices. One might assume that plaintiffs' lawyers would be able to

---

32. *Id.*, at 10.
33. *Id.*, at 4.
34. Edelman, *Working Law, supra* note 17, at 12-13, 27-41.
35. *Id.*, at 13-14.
36. *Id.*, at 101, 106-107.

strip away the veneer of neutrality to reveal actual discrimination functioning in organizational life. Drawing in part from my early work,[37] Edelman notes that plaintiffs' lawyers tend to accept the structures as evidence of lack of bias or are unable to sway judges to dig deeper. In fact, notes Edelman, it is employing organizations themselves that construct the meaning of EEO compliance in harmony with business practices and values. This managerialization of civil rights law weakens the transformative potential of law. When the meaning of law and legal compliance is determined by those subject to it, and legislatures and courts defer to those understandings, the effectiveness of the policies and procedures is rendered irrelevant. And when courts actually reference symbolic structures in their written decisions and legal doctrines, "law becomes endogenous...when those symbolic structures are merely symbolic, then legal endogeneity condones managerialization and undermines legal ideals."[38]

Legal scholar Tristin Green in her book *Discrimination Laundering* views the policies and procedures described by Edelman not only as preserving managerial prerogatives but giving rise to what Green calls "organizational innocence."[39] Through a careful reading of EEO case law, she develops this concept by discerning three distinct components. First, she asserts that courts, by which she means judges, tend to believe that top-level decision-makers in organizations are personally unbiased; in other words, these high-level decision-makers do not intend consciously to exclude women and racial and ethnic minorities from equal treatment in the workplace.[40] Courts also, according to Green, see the highest level of management as unlikely to be affected by bias that is subconscious.

Second, courts assume that workplace discrimination is perpetuated mainly by lower-level supervisors in day-to-day discrete actions such as decisions about promotion, pay raises, and assigning job tasks. These lower level managers may be acting from conscious bias or stereotypes operating on a more unconscious level.[41] Third, courts have come to view these biased, lower level bosses as isolated rogues. These rare "bad apples" are not integral to the organization and its climate; rather they act against organizational interests.[42]

Connected to these three components is the belief, held by judges, that courts should hesitate to intervene in managerial decision-making because there is a limit to what organizations can do to prevent and police rogue discriminators. Thus, employers who maintain complaint procedures, investigate instances of harassment or discrimination, take action to discipline or purge the rare discriminator from the organization, and provide harassment and diversity training should not be held legally responsible for the actions of lone supervisors. Having taken all necessary steps to forestall and monitor workplace bias, the organization is, in the view of courts, innocent. In this

---

37. *See* Susan Bisom-Rapp, "Bulletproofing the Workplace: Symbol and Substance in Employment Discrimination Law Practice," 26 Fla. St. U. L. Rev. 959 (1999).
38. *Id.*, at 39.
39. Green, *Discrimination Laundering*, *supra* note 18, at 10.
40. *Id.*, at 40.
41. *Id.*, at 42.
42. *Id.*

way, courts signal to employers that through procedures, policies, and training, they may inoculate their organizations from liability for employment discrimination.[43]

Organizations, in turn, focus their attention on a form over substance approach to creating fair workplaces. As Green notes, courts reticence to intervene and belief in organizational innocence creates "no pressure [for organizations] to do more than take very narrow efforts to reduce discrimination."[44] This shift by courts to protecting employers and preserving managerial decision-making prerogatives rather than viewing EEO law as a tool for transforming the workplace represents a subtle but powerful threat to achieving equal treatment for employees.

Berrey, Nelson, and Nielsen, whose book *Rights on Trial* was discussed above, make the important point that judicial deference to managerial authority cannot be viewed neutrally. For top management is, for the most part, lacking in representation of minorities and women. White men predominate at the highest levels of organizations and the governing systems that tend to exclude, segregate, or limit those for whom EEO law was supposed to be an antidote. Judicial deference to managerial authority within such systems simply preserves the status quo. Thus, "deference...is part of the broader process of reinscription...: the processes by which the...hierarchies that the law was intended to disrupt are reified and rearticulated through law in the workplace and in court."[45] In other words, judicial deference props up the very systems that EEO law was supposed to dismantle.

Indeed, Berrey, Nelson, and Nielsen find that the playing field upon which EEO litigation takes place is tilted very much in favor of employers. They estimate that most employees who have grounds for formal legal action never sue. Those who do sue are unlikely to prevail. Instead, the employee plaintiffs lose or settle their cases for small sums. Only 6% of EEO claims filed result in a trial. The win rate is low. Many plaintiffs represent themselves in litigation because they cannot secure legal counsel. Employers, in contrast, are repeat players and almost always are represented by lawyers. As the author's note, "[i]n short, the formally neutral system of adversarial justice in the United States favors the haves over the have-nots."[46] After half a century, what we find is a system favoring symbolic over substantive compliance, which cannot begin to remedy the intractable problem of inequality in the workplace. The inevitable outcomes of such a system are addressed in section §9.04 below.

§9.04 MISSING DISCRIMINATION THAT OCCURS OVER TIME AND ALLOWING DISADVANTAGE TO CUMULATE

A common complaint about EEO law is that after decades of law on the books much remains to be done. Pay gaps between men and women, and whites and minority races, are still significant. Occupational segregation is evident even though it is created on a de facto rather than de jure basis. Glass ceilings continue to hamper the

---

43. *Id.*, at 47.
44. *Id.*, at 101.
45. Berrey, Nelson, & Nielsen, *Rights on Trial*, supra note 15, at 11.
46. *Id.*, at 13.

promotional opportunities of women and minorities. Responsibility for family care, including care of children and aging parents, continues to cause more women than men to exit from the labor market. Retirement security remains elusive for more women than men and for those who are minority races and ethnicities in comparison to whites.

It is on the latter point that, along with the British coauthor Malcolm Sargeant, we began the book *Lifetime Disadvantage, Discrimination and the Gendered Workforce*. More specifically, in many countries, not just in the U.S., women, especially those who are racial or ethnic minorities, are much more likely than men to fall into poverty during retirement. It was argued that explaining why this happens requires a life course approach. To assist, they developed a Model of Lifetime Disadvantage, which beginning in childhood captures the major factors that on average create unequal outcomes for working women at the end of their careers.[47] One set of factors falls under heading "Gender-based factors."[48] This category concerns phenomena directly connected to social or psychological aspects of gender, such as gender stereotyping and women's traditionally greater roles in family caring activities. The second set of factors is titled "Incremental disadvantage factors."[49] While these factors are connected to gender, that connection is less overt, and the disadvantage they produce increases incrementally over time. Factors in this second category include non-standard working (part-time work, temporary work, etc.) and career interruptions.

Focusing comparatively on the United Kingdom (U.K.) and the U.S., and drawing also from international materials, each factor in light of EEO law and policy that might, if designed and implemented properly, advance equal opportunity and equal treatment is examined. However, it is found that legal and policy efforts consistently fall short, and that the disadvantage that stymies women throughout their lives cumulates over time.

Our model is illustrated in Table 9.1.

Table 9.1 Model of Lifetime Disadvantage

Gender-Based Factors	Incremental Disadvantage Factors
Education and training	Pay inequality
Stereotyping	Occupational segregation
Multiple discrimination	Non-standard working
Caregiving roles	Career breaks
Career outcomes	Retirement and pensions

By modeling women's lifetime disadvantage, the book reveals the complex, interrelated factors that hinder women over the course of their lives, and leave many in poor conditions in retirement compared with men. Such a result is of course not

---

47. Bisom-Rapp & Sargeant, *Lifetime Disadvantage*, supra note 5, at 4.
48. Id.
49. Id.

inevitable. Indeed, an effective, comprehensive regulatory approach could help compensate for these factors. Present legal and policy efforts in the U.K. and the U.S., however, do not sufficiently address women's systemic disadvantage. It has been argued that this is in large part because of a disjointed, incremental approach to law- and policymaking. While governments in both countries are well aware of the problems affecting girls and women during their lifetimes, a piecemeal approach to reform often results in nothing more than tinkering around the margins. Efforts by the state fail to articulate overarching goals, take small rather than grand steps, and produce responses lacking in coordination. Confronting women's lifetime disadvantage, in contrast, requires acknowledging at the outset the outcomes sought and the justifications for them.

That EEO law misses and is unable to disrupt discrimination that plays out over time is a theme tackled by some of the other books discussed herein. Berrey, Nelson, and Nielsen, for example, note that courts over the decades have greatly restricted the legal theories and remedies that most effectively tackle systemic discrimination. These theories and remedies include affirmative action (positive discrimination), disparate impact (indirect discrimination) claims, and class actions. In fact, in the U.S., 93% of the EEO suits filed are brought by a single plaintiff alleging disparate treatment (direct discrimination). This individualization of legal claiming, combined the adversarial nature of the conflict, and the advantages employers hold as repeat players in the legal system, hobble the law's ability to disrupt discrimination on a systemic scale.[50]

Similarly, Sperino and Thomas argue that the myriad of judicially created rules, frameworks, and presumptions in discrimination cases enable judges to discount and undercut evidence of bias. As such, judges fail to consider the evidence before them as a unified whole and miss discrimination that is taking place over time.[51] Finally, Tristin Green notes that judges' perception of organizational innocence enables blindness to organizational structures, work culture, and systems that produce discrimination. Instead, the focus is placed on rogue, low-level bosses who make discrete employment decisions at a single point in time. In short, "[t]he law misses entirely discrimination that accrues over time or is otherwise difficult to identify in a precise moment."[52]

§9.05 CONCLUSION: WHAT IS THE WAY FORWARD WHEN THE GAME HAS CHANGED?

These books were, for the most part, conceived before the election of Donald Trump as President of the U.S. Hence, many of the solutions suggested are wise yet relatively moderate and practical in design. Berrey, Nelson, and Nielsen suggest focusing on ways to facilitate greater access by employees to legal representation, making available bigger enforcement budgets to the federal and state agencies responsible for overseeing EEO laws, improving communication between those agencies and those who file charges against their employers, promoting transparency about employers' workforces

---

50. Berrey, Nelson, & Nielsen, *Rights on Trial*, supra note 15, at 15.
51. Sperino & Thomas, *Unequal*, supra note 19, at 151-151.
52. Green, *Discrimination Laundering*, supra note 18, at 101.

in terms of demographic makeup and pay, among other potential solutions.[53] Sperino and Thomas suggest several amendments to our EEO statutes to increase the chances of expansive rather than narrow statutory interpretation and to abolish or restrict the use of the rules, presumptions, and frameworks presently employed by judges to discern discrimination.[54] Green recommends a system of employer vicarious liability for individual discrimination, which would hold employers strictly liable.[55]

Edelman tackles solutions by saying that the fix for judicial deference to managerial prerogatives and symbolic structures requires that judges refuse to defer. Rather, judges must consider the effectiveness of corporate policies, training, and grievance procedures in particular cases. In the end, she is unsure whether a legal regime with such judges is possible. A sense of pessimism is evident at the close of her book.[56]

Bisom-Rapp and Sargeant find themselves in the Edelman camp recommending big changes and are, at present, somewhat pessimistic about achieving them on the national level. It is believed that a great shift in thinking about equality and how it is achieved is necessary to correct the cumulative disadvantage women of all races and backgrounds suffer during their lives. Since part-and-parcel of our critique is that our governments in the U.K. and the U.S. enact reform in a disjointed, incremental, and ultimately ineffective manner, we are loath to suggest simple legislative changes. Instead, drawing from vulnerability theory, and the work of the American legal scholar Martha Fineman, they recommend a comprehensive, life course approach to regulation.[57]

The authors begin with the idea that the state is responsible for promoting the resilience of individuals when they find themselves in conditions of vulnerability and dependence. Vulnerability, which is inherent in the human condition, is closely related to the idea of dependency, which may be experienced directly, such as when one is young or very old, or is ill, or it may be experienced derivatively, such as when a person is a caregiver of one who is young or very old, or is ill.[58] Those who are derivatively dependent will find that their caregiving roles conflict with other key responsibilities, including those tied to their role in the workforce.[59] Women more frequently than men find themselves in positions of derivative dependence.

In the face of inevitable vulnerability, the role of the state is to promote the resilience of its people. Resilience, in turn, is tied to the way in which societal institutions function—institutions such as the family, corporations, banks, insurance, and the like. The state must set the legal ground rules and monitor outcomes to ensure that resilience is maximized and that no one group has the advantage over others.[60]

---

53. Berrey, Nelson, & Nielsen, *Rights on Trial*, supra note 15, at 272.
54. Sperino & Thomas, *Unequal*, supra note 19, at 164-165.
55. Green, *Discrimination Laundering*, supra note 18, at 151.
56. Edelman, *Working Law*, supra note 17, at 218.
57. Bisom-Rapp & Sargeant, *Lifetime Disadvantage*, supra note 5, at 198.
58. *Id.*, (quoting Martha Albertson Fineman, "'Elderly' as Vulnerable: Rethinking the Nature of Individual and Societal Responsibility," 20 Elder L.J. 71, 84 (2012)).
59. *Id.*
60. *Id.*, at 199 (quoting Martha Albertson Fineman, "The Vulnerable Subject and the Responsive State," 60 Emory L.J. 251, 272 (2010)).

This conception of government responsibility indicts the British and American approach to EEO law and policy regarding the ability of women to plan for and live in retirement. To correct the cumulative disadvantage and discrimination women experience would require a restructuring of societal institutions and law to take into account how many women lead their lives. Yet many of the changes suggested by the author and co-author would be geared to making work more decent and flexible for men as well as women. Thus, the ultimate policy prescription is to craft law and policy with women in mind, which would benefit many men as well.

Their solution is reminiscent of "gender mainstreaming," but to achieve a truly multicultural society of the kind Roger Blanpain envisioned, one would need also to account for men who are racial, ethnic, and religious minorities, the disabled, the LGBTQ community, and the problem of an aging labor force. Perhaps the place to start is to study the challenges associated with gender mainstreaming, which as those in the EU know have yet to be overcome, and build from there.[61]

Such a sweeping set of changes is not easily set into motion. The challenges are formidable at a political moment in which the very premise of diversity, equality, and inclusion is under attack by the forces of nationalism, racism, xenophobia, and nostalgia, in some quarters, for a past with traditional gender roles. Certainly, necessary ingredients for change are grassroots political action and enlightened leadership. Like Bisom-Rapp and Sargeant, Berrey, Nelson, and Nielsen mention the need for social movements to press for a more transformative approach to achieving workplace equality.[62] While it is difficult to set forth a program of action, one possible step is for those who write and engage in research on EEO law-in-action to step out of the university as frequently as possible and interact with policy and opinion-makers. In sum, all must become more involved in politics and public life more generally. This is something Roger Blanpain did on a regular basis throughout his long and illustrious career.[63]

The books reviewed herein are game changing because, when read together, they demonstrate that EEO law and policy have been neutered and rendered ineffective. As such, a call for a radically different approach to achieving equality may be our best hope. At the same moment, Trumpism and its cousins in other countries are challenging the goals and aspirations of the EEO revolution of the second half of the twentieth century. This attempted game change is startlingly regressive and it must be stopped. The author believes that this backward-looking movement inspires those who believe in the equality principle, as passionately as Roger Blanpain did, to take to the streets, maybe run or support someone for political office, and achieve the critical mass necessary to change the game once again.

---

61. *See generally*, Eva Alfama Guillén, Mapping Gender Mainstreaming Implementation Challenges, 4th European Conference on Politics and Gender (Jun. 11–13, 2015) (unpublished manuscript), available at: https://ecpr.eu/Filestore/PaperProposal/0b26bcd7-f62f-4139-a33c-e2903fde1021.pdf.
62. Berrey, Nelson, & Nielsen, *Rights on Trial*, *supra* note 15, at 275.
63. *See* Roger Blanpain, *Memoirs of Roger Blanpain: "What Can I Do For You?"* (Vanden Broele 2009). Part II of Roger Blanpain's memoir offers numerous examples of his engagement with and impact on the public policy issues of the day.

CHAPTER 10
Expansion of Temporary Agency Work Across Borders and the Difficulties for Workers Involved, in Particular in Light of Their Work-Life Balance

Mijke Houwerzijl

§10.01 INTRODUCTION

Until, approximately, the 1980s '*temporary agency work* was practically outlawed. During the 1950s, the International Labour Organisation (ILO) clearly stated (in a request to a question from the Swedish government) that *temporary agency work* was prohibited by ILO Convention n° 96 of 1949 regarding fee-charging placement. Trade unions, of course, were in complete agreement, both because temporary work arrangements undermined the situation of permanent workers and deprived the temporary workers themselves of equal treatment guarantees. Yet persistent employers, always ready to find ways around this prohibition, have gone from strength to strength until today the role of private employment services is offered up to the public as that of an active link between employer and employee and an equal benefit to both.'

This brief sketch of the evolution towards societal acceptance of temporary agency work is taken from the introduction by the late Emeritus Professor Roger Blanpain of the 50th Issue of 'his' Bulletin of comparative labour relations. This Special Issue, published in 2004, was devoted to *Temporary Agency Work and the Information Society*.[1] Now, 14 years and 50 Bulletins later in the 100th Issue of the Bulletin which

---

1. Roger Blanpain, Ronnie Graham (eds), *Temporary Agency Work and the Information Society*, Bulletin of Comparative Labour Relations, Kluwer Law International, 2004.

is commemorating Roger Blanpain, the author reassess the role of temporary employment agencies (TEAs) as fully accepted and integrated manpower providers, in light of today's globalising and Europeanising labour markets.

Whereas the Bulletin celebrates its 100th Issue, the World Employment Confederation (WEC; formerly known as CIETT) recently celebrated its 50th anniversary. According to the WEC, which is representing TEAs from all over the world, they have been shaping the world of work since 1967. In the words of the WEC, 'in the past 50 years the role of labour market enablers has expanded'.[2] According to WEC Europe, citing Eurofound: 'in trying to reach a fair balance between protecting agency workers and enhancing the positive role that agency work may play in the European labour market, the Agency Work industry seems to be at the heart of the Flexicurity debate.'[3]

As listed by WEC, agency work provides flexibility and security for both workers and companies, by:

- Developing more work opportunities for people and creating pathways between unemployment and employment.
- Improving work-life balance by providing additional work patterns, allowing people to work when and where it suits their own wishes.
- Allowing people to work part-time and on temporary jobs to gain extra money.
- Ensuring work security and continuity of social rights for workers, through the portability and transferability of social protection (access to unemployment benefits, social security, pension...).
- Maintaining and developing employability of workers, through training on the job and life-long learning solutions.
- Enabling fast workforce adjustments, therefore maintaining the competitivity of companies.
- Improving companies' market position by responding to changing demands and providing the staff they need for their business without excessive risks or costs.

In this contribution to the 100th Issue of the Bulletin, the perceived advantages of TAW, which played such a decisive role in legitimating the temporary work industry, will be assessed in the context of an increasingly important role of TEAs in facilitating transnational labour mobility. Do cross-border temporary agency workers profit from these advantages of TAW to the same extent as local temporary agency workers? In other words, is cross-border TAW equally beneficial from a worker perspective as agency work within national borders? In light of one of the oldest aims of *bona fide* temporary agency work, namely to improve the work-life balance for employees, the author particularly zooms in on transnational family live of cross-border agency workers. Within the EU, transnational family research is rather scarce and for instance the work-life balance of workers who are regularly posted abroad is an almost completely unexplored issue.

---

2. As 'evidenced' in a youtube clip: https://www.youtube.com/watch?v=wvBVBShhyWY&t=3s.
3. James Arrowsmith, *TAW and Collective Bargaining in the EU*, Eurofound, 2008.

The contribution is structured as follows: the author first explains the (aims of the) relevant rules for TAW in a global and EU context (section §10.02), and then proceed with a sketch of transnational TAW (section §10.03), resulting in a distinction between two types of cross-border agency workers (section §10.04). This is followed by a more specific account of the position of cross-border agency workers in light of work-life balance and the right to family life (section §10.05). The chapter ends with some concluding remarks, including a call to address reconciliation of work and family life in relation to parent workers' temporary and/or circular movement to other EU Member States for work. Arguably, transnational labour mobility as facilitated by TEAs brings the traditional problem of a decent work-life balance at a new level (section §10.06).

§10.02 THE EVOLUTION OF A GLOBAL AND EU REGULATORY FRAMEWORK ON TAW

At a global level, ILO Convention n°181 on private employment agencies has in 1997 replaced ILO Convention n° 96. This marked the end of the 'prohibitive/restrictive' regulatory model for TAW,[4] rather than the provision of a comprehensive regulation of the exact allocation of rights, obligations and responsibilities in the triangular relationship between TEA, agency worker and user company.[5] The Convention n°181 is accompanied by ILO Recommendation n°188 which provides additional guidelines on how best to regulate the sector. The positive correlation between appropriate regulation on agency work and its contribution to improving the performance of labour market has been recognised within the ILO framework: 'As a specific service provided by private employment agencies, if regulated appropriately, temporary agency work contributes to improved functioning of labour markets, fulfils specific needs for both enterprises and workers, and aims at complementing other forms of employment.'[6]

At the European level progress was made at very slow pace. Since the first policy documents on TAW in the 1970s emphasising the need to eliminate the abuses characterising at that time the activities of TEAs,[7] it took until 2008 before the current Temporary Agency Work Directive (TAWD; Directive 2008/104/EC) was adopted. In this process, it was the Court of Justice of the EU (CJEU), which pushed the legitimation of TAW and the need for an accompanying regulatory framework at

---

4. *See* P. Thuy, 'ILO Convention on Private Employment Agencies (no. 181)', in: R. Blanpain (ed.), *Private Employment Agencies*, BCLR, 36, 1999, pp. 77–103.
5. This was left to be dealt with by national legislation. *See* Arts 11 and 12 of Convention no 181.
6. Points of Consensus of ILO Workshop to Promote Ratification of the Private Employment Agencies Convention (2009).
7. As pointed out by Massimiliano Delfino, Interpretation and Enforcement Questions in the EU Temporary Agency Work Regulation. An Italian Point of View, European Labour Law Journal, Volume 2 (2011), No. 3, pp. 297–298, referring to Council Resolution of 21 January 1974, concerning a social action programme, which was the first EC document that referred to temporary agency work among the measures to attain a full and better employment in the Community.

European level by its landmark ruling in 1997 on the incompatibility of public monopolies on employment services with EU competition policy.[8]

Talks on a directive on TAW were launched in 2000 by European trade unions and employers associations. Negotiations went on for a year, but social partners could not agree on equal treatment between agency workers and comparable workers at the user firm regarding basic working and employment conditions, particularly pay. Referring to the 2000 Lisbon commitment to more and better jobs, the European Commission launched its own Draft Directive on TAW in March 2002. Again the key issue of this Draft Directive was the equal treatment between agency workers and people directly hired by the user firm. Again, little progress was made due to the objections of some Member States, in particular the UK and Germany.[9]

In 2007, an EU-wide social dialogue committee for the TAW sector published a Joint Declaration on TAW in light of the flexicurity debate, stressing the following issue: Agency work can facilitate transitions from education and unemployment into work and it *can improve a work-life balance for employees* (emphasis added MH).[10] The social partners also highlighted in their Joint Declaration that TAW was already covered by a number of EU laws, notably the Health and Safety Directive (Directive 91/383/EEC) and the Posting of Workers Directive (PWD; Directive 96/71/EC).[11]

Clearly, it was along the lines of offering an equal benefit to both employers and employee, that the TAWD was discussed and eventually adopted. Five years ago, in 2012, the European sectoral social partners in TAW, WEC Europe (under its old name EuroCiett)[12] and Uni Europa,[13] published a joint declaration confirming and emphasising the positive role of TAW in increasing the chances of agency workers for long-term employment in the labour market as a result of job placement and the possibility of vocational training provided by TEAs.[14] In this respect, they referred to the preamble of the EU Directive on Temporary Agency Work, where it is stated that this form of employment '[...] meets not only undertakings' needs for flexibility but

---

8. *See* Case C-55/96, judgment of 11 December 1997 (Job Centre) and the related Case C-41/90, judgment of 23 April 1991 (*Höfner v. Macroton*).
9. *See* Olga Rymkevitch, 'Prospects for the Regulation of Temporary Agency Work at the EU Level', in R. Blanpain, M. Tiraboschi (eds), *The Global Labour Market. From Globalization to Flexicurity*, BCLR, 65, 2008, pp. 275–292.
10. Also, restrictions and prohibitions on the use of TAW were to be regularly reviewed and when unjustified or disproportional, they were to be removed. Other issues taken up in the Joint Declaration were the fight against unfair competition from fraudulent agencies, a ban on using agency workers to replace workers on strike, the principle of equal treatment, the need for sector-wide dialogue at national level, the right to freedom of association, access to vocational training, and continuity of rights between assignments to improve employment and social protection of agency workers.
11. However, it is important to note that the PWD did not oblige the Member States to give legal recognition to temporary agency work. *See* recital 19 of Directive 96/71/EC.
12. Eurociett, now renamed into World Employment Confederation Europe (WEC Europe) gathers twenty-nine national federations from EU and EFTA countries, and seven of the largest international staffing companies as corporate members. *See* http://www.weceurope.org/.
13. Representing 7 million workers in 330 European trade unions. *See* http://www.uniglobalunion.org/.
14. *See* their joint recommendations, Press release 19.12.12 Temporary Agency Work Facilitates Labour Market Transitions.

also *the need of employees to reconcile their working and private lives.* It thus contributes to job creation and to participation and integration in the labour market' (emphasis added MH).[15]

§10.03 TAW IN THE CONTEXT OF CROSS-BORDER SERVICE PROVISION WITHIN THE EU

Research has shown that there was a rapid increase in the number of labour market intermediaries towards the end of the twentieth century after many EU countries lifted restrictions on TAW. Moreover, next to the importance of TAW as facilitator of transitions on the national labour market, in recent years TEAs play an increasingly important role in 'TAW transitions' across borders of national labour and services markets within the EU. In fact, transnational labour mobility, including the posting and placement of agency workers is rapidly increasing. It was up from 1.60% to 2.4% to 3.3% of the total population of EU nationals in 2014. And the estimates are that this trend will continue. For instance, according to figures provided by the World Economic Forum, 'some 35 million extra workers will be required to fill Europe's employment gap by 2050'.

In the opinion of the WEC: 'Matching labour market supply with demand on a global scale will require well organised intermediaries able to take a professional and coordinated approach and to deliver a successful outcome for all parties. The employment industry is well placed to support and facilitate this. It has an established presence around the world and is familiar with the task of placing people across a global labour market and handling the attendant legal and social issues.'[16] However, recent studies indicate that there may be an overlap between facilitation and exploitation.[17] After the enlargements of the EU in 2004 and 2007 with 10 'low wage' countries from Middle and Eastern Europe, high demand for 'cheap labour' on the demand side combined with scarce information about possibilities to move on the supply side, seems to have encouraged the reliance on migration facilitators, ranging from bona fide temporary agencies and subcontractors to middlemen and gangmasters operating in the shadow economy.[18]

Many research studies have shown, that this new mobile EU-labour force is vulnerable as regards exploitation, especially in the lower segments of the labour markets. Their employers have often strong incentives for 'non-compliance' with

---

15. Directive 2008/104/EC of the European Parliament and of the Council of 19 November 2008 on temporary agency work, preamble para. 11.
16. WEC, *The Future of Work. White paper of the Employment Industry. The Future of Work Issues at stake and policy recommendations from the employment industry*, September 2016, p. 15.
17. Eurofound, 'Regulation of labour market intermediaries and the role of social partners in preventing trafficking of labour', 2016.
18. Jan Cremers, Jon Erik Dølvik & Gerhard Bosch (2007). 'Posting of Workers in the Single Market: Attempts to Prevent Social Dumping and Regime Ccompetition in the EU' *IRJ*, 38, 524-541. < ec.europa.eu/social/BlobServlet?docId = 6677&langId = en > . However, the increasing use of cross-border labour intermediaries also fits into a global trend; Judy Fudge and Kenda Strauss (2013), eds. *Temporary work, agencies, and unfree labour: Insecurity in the new world of work*. Routledge.

labour law, whereas the workers involved often face many barriers to insist on their rights.[19] In some sectors and geographical areas, intermediaries have become strongly associated with migration and cost-reduction as well as flexibility. While the majority of labour market intermediaries are formally registered enterprises, some of them operate informally without being registered. This role of TEAs and recruitment agencies in a cross-border context is an ongoing matter of concern. It has consistently been highlighted that agency workers are exposed to a heightened risk of exploitative working conditions.

Sometimes, intermediaries in other Member States are used with the sole purpose of turning (temporary or seasonal) migration into posting. When, for example, a TEA recruits Polish workers for jobs in the Netherlands, the actual circumstances may not change according to whether the TEA is established in Poland or the Netherlands, but the legal situation does. This creates a clear incentive to look for the easiest and cheapest way (for the employer, the worker or both). Labour law is but one of the points to be taken into consideration; social security, pension and tax law being at least as important. Notably, only a hard core of labour standards may apply mandatorily during the temporary posting in the host country.[20] Next to this, the posted worker stays insured under the social security schemes in the sending state.[21] When posted from 'low wage' to 'high wage' countries, this[22] makes posted workers (far) less costly than locally hired (agency) workers.

§10.04 TWO TYPES OF CROSS-BORDER TEMPORARY AGENCY WORKERS

Legally, we can distinguish two types of cross-border temporary agency workers. The 'recruited temp agency worker' is recruited (for instance by an employment placement agency established) in a 'sending' MS but placed in a user company by a TEA established in the host country. From an EU Law perspective this means the worker is covered by the free movement of workers, enshrined in Article 45 TFEU, and therefore

---

19. See e.g. FRA (2015), *Severe labour exploitation: workers moving within or into the European Union. States' obligations and victims' rights*, Brussels: FRA. http://fra.europa.eu/en/publication/2015/severe-labour-exploitation-workers-moving-within-or-european-union;
Aukje van Hoek & Mijke Houwerzijl, Comparative study on the legal aspects of the posting of workers in the framework of the provision of services in the European Union (Radboud University Nijmegen, 2011).
20. Pursuant to Art. 3 of the PWD.
21. Pursuant to Art. 12 of Regulation 883/2004 on the coordination of national social security systems, which deals with the issue of affiliation to a social security system in case of movement to another Member State. In principle, during the first twenty-four months of posting, the worker remains affiliated to the social security system of the Member State where he normally works.
22. Taxation of workers lies within the competence of Member States. Bilateral agreements exist between most of the Member States in order to avoid double taxation. These agreements set out the rules according to which taxes must be paid either in the country of residence of the worker or in the country of posting. Normally, for posting up to 183 (calendar)days income taxes are paid in the country of residence of the worker. In case of posting beyond 183 days income tax has to be paid in the country where the worker is posted. However, for posted agency workers the tax regime of the host state may apply from day 1.

covered by the labour, social security and tax law in the country of destination, including this country's implementation of the TAWD. Posted agency workers on the other hand are sent to a user firm in the host by a TEA established in a 'sending country'. So here it is the (formal) employer in his role as temporary cross-border service provider who uses the freedom to provide services (Article 56 TFEU).

This legal difference between posted and recruited cross-border temp agency workers is reinforced by different 'narratives': Whereas the narrative of free movement of workers is based on full equal treatment of local and migrant (agency) workers, in contrast, the posted agency worker falls under the heading of EU free movement of services, and is essentially regarded as 'commodity' or 'tool' with which the service provider may provide his services in another Member State.[23] According to the WEC,[24] the posting of (agency) workers offers opportunities for companies to meet economic needs and for workers to explore new professional opportunities. The idea that cross-border mobility is driven by (only) these needs is certainly respectable but is quite disappointing if compared to what is usually mentioned in the national context, in order to promote the TEAs as reputable 'normal employers' (see the list of perceived advantages in section §10.01 above).

For posted agency workers currently the application of the PWD takes precedence over the TAWD when dealing with the cross-border activities of TEAs. The proposal for targeted revision of the PWD of March 2016 however,[25] aims to create a level playing field between posted and non-posted (recruited) agency workers. A proposed new Article 3(1b) PWD renders the terms and conditions under Article 5 TAWD mandatory for posted workers, applying the principle of equal treatment between temporary agency workers and comparable workers of the user undertakings.[26] If this proposal would be adopted, would this create similar advantages for posted agency workers as local agency workers are perceived to have? Does cross-border TAW – apart from employer needs – than also serve the social advancement of (not only high skilled) workers? Will it become a stepping stone for (decent standard) jobs? Will vocational training be facilitated? Would it help posted employees in their need to reconcile their working and private lives? The answer is no. Making the terms and conditions under Article 5 of TAWD mandatory for posted agency workers will not provide them with additional advantages such as being informed of vacant posts, equal access to collective facilities such as child care and measures related to access to training, since these rights are not included in Article 5 TAWD but in Article 6 and further provisions of the directive.

Furthermore, the distinction between workers' movement under Article 45 TFEU and the provision of services under Article 56 TFEU deserves consideration; whereas

---

23. Annette Schrauwen, Mijke Houwerzijl, 'From Competing to Aligned Narratives on (Posted) Mobile Workers Within the EU?', in T. de Lange, C. Rijken (eds), *Towards a Decent Labour Market for Low Waged Migrant Workers*, AUP 2018 (forthcoming).
24. Position paper 21st September 2016.
25. COM (2016) 128.
26. It will make obligatory a practice that is already present in the legislations of fifteen EU Member States, who have – according to the Impact Assessment of the PWD proposal – used the current Art. 3(9) PWD: the principles of equal treatment and equal pay from the first day of assignment.

the PWD does not provide any entitlement to visit or join the posted worker in the host Member State during the period of posting, 'recruited' cross-border agency workers and their family members gain full access to all social and fiscal advantages in the host MS. Apart from widening the range of welfare benefits for children of migrant workers in the meaning of Article 45 TFEU, the CJEU adopted a very proactive approach in relation to enabling children to access and the right to remain in education in the receiving Member State.[27] Hence, being a recruited cross-border agency worker seems from a rights-based perspective much more attractive than being a posted agency worker.[28]

However, as we will see below with respect to family life of transnational agency workers, most research on transnational families is conducted by social scientists and lumps together situations of posting, temporary and circular migration. While plausible that said forms of transnational labour mobility are most often facilitated by TEAs, decisive conclusions for each separate category of temporary (agency) workers will therefore be difficult to draw, apart from the findings of one paper on posted male workers.

§10.05 TRANSNATIONAL AGENCY WORKERS AND THEIR CHILDREN: WHO CARES?

Transnational families[29] used to be treated as a temporary and limited phenomenon with family reunification in the host state as the preferred outcome for all family members. However, now that transnational family arrangements have become prevalent, research from the past decade started with linking (temporary) migration and family studies.[30] Findings show that, due to their parents' migration, children benefit economically and get access to better health and education. However, several studies find that better economic family situations do not necessarily translate to higher well-being for children, as emotional strain may impact negatively on health and school performance. Moreover, also the migrant parents themselves may experience a drop in well-being.[31]

Regarding the situation in the enlarged EU, in 2007 the Soros Foundation largely confirmed these findings. The study covers an estimated 170,000 Romanian children

---

27. For an overview, see H. Stalford, E. Drywood (2009), 'Coming of Age? Children's Rights in the European Union'. *CMLR*, 46, 143–172.
28. At least on paper. Research shows that in practice, both recruited and posted cross-border temporary agency workers experience that rights which cannot be enforced are pretty much worthless. See e.g. L. Berntsen (2015), *Agency of Labour in a Flexible Pan-European Labour Market: A Qualitative Study of Migrant Practices and Trade Union Strategies in the Netherlands* (PhD thesis), University of Groningen and I. Wagner (2015), *Posted Work and Deterritorialization in the European Union: A Study of the German Construction and Meat Industry* (PhD thesis), University of Groningen.
29. Conceived of as families with members living in different nation states.
30. For an overview of transnational family research, see Valentina Mazzucato, Djamila Schans, *Transnational Families and the Well-Being of Children: Conceptual and Methodological Challenges*, Journal of Marriage and the Family, Aug 2011, 73(4): 704–712.
31. Ninna Nyberg Sørensen, Ida Marie Vammen, 'Who Cares? Transnational Families in Debates on Migration and Development', *New Diversities*, 16, 2, 2014.

'left behind' by their parents who went to work, predominantly as strawberry pickers, construction workers and house cleaners in 'old' Member States. In one village examined, more than half of the children of school and preschool age had both parents working abroad, especially in Italy.[32] Dubbed 'migration orphans' or even 'strawberry orphans',[33] most of these children ended up in the care of grandparents or other relatives, however others were finding themselves in group homes and orphanages. Clearly, while migration has brought economic gains – Romanian migrants sent home nearly 7.2 billons in remittances in 2008 – it has also caused a lot of suffering by the relatives and communities in Romania left behind. In 2015, the Romanian singer Voltaj showcased the message in the Eurovision Song Contest 2015 with the song 'De la capăt', referring to three million Romanian migrants who had to leave their children behind in Romania in order to support them by working in other EU Member States. The Song was meant to highlight the detrimental effects on children who grow up without their parents.[34]

On the other hand, the situation of children from Romania and other Central and Eastern European countries who move with their parents in the context of short-term or circular migration is not ideal either. In the 2007 study of the Soros Foundation, the migration flows from Romania to Spain were examined. During 2002–2006, Spain became the second destination for the Romanian migration (25% of all departures). The increases seen after 2000 were spectacular: in 2001, the numbers of Romanian migrants were in the tens of thousands, which became hundreds of thousands a couple of years later. After 2003, the numbers of Romanians 'empatronated' by City Halls in Spain were between 70,000 and 100,000 persons each year, with over 400,000 persons in 2006. Albeit based on incomplete data, in 2006 this included (at least) 54,741 children of 14 years and younger, and 77,202 teenagers between 15 and 19 years old.[35] In light of the predominantly circular migration between the two countries with migrants regularly returning to Romania, the researchers advocate the need to address such temporary situations: 'parents find themselves unable to support their children in Spain, or children fail to adapt. The children may return to Romania for a while, only to try again at a later time. Moved between two worlds, do they stand real chances of adapting to either of them? To what extent and according to which rules will these children complete their education? For which of the two societies will they be prepared when they grow up'?[36]

---

32. Georgiana Păun, 'The Community Dimension of Migration. The Consequences of Economic Migration for Horia', in: Mihaela Ştefănescu et al., *The Effects of Migration: The Children Left Behind*, Soros Foundation, 2007, pp. 27–37.
33. See: www.scotsman.com/news/strawberry-orphans-driven-to-despair-by-their-migrant-mothers-1-1304277.
34. The Song tells the story of a boy in a Romanian village on the Danube river trying to regain contact with his parents who work in Vienna.
35. Monica Şerban, Ioana-Alexandra Mihai, 'Who Do the Children Belong To?, in: Mihaela Ştefănescu et al., *The Effects of Migration: The Children Left Behind*, Soros Foundation, 2007, pp. 34–49.
36. *Ibid.*, p. 49.

Another explorative study was conducted in the Netherlands in 2014,[37] examining the social situation of Polish, Bulgarian and Romanian children aged up to 18 years who are living in the Netherlands.[38] Many of the problems highlighted by professionals (e.g., due to long working hours, poor housing conditions, frequent back-and-forth migration and incomplete families) relate to circular migrants (e.g., seasonal workers), who are often not entered in the population registers. Circumstances such as these have an impact on the well-being of children. Youth health care professionals believe that shuttling back and forth to their homeland makes it more difficult for children to feel at home anywhere, potentially leading to psychological problems (rootlessness). Schools and care professionals report difficulty in communicating with parents (and children) because of their inadequate command of the Dutch language. Another problem in communication with parents is the difficulty in reaching them. Their working hours mean that parents not only have difficulty attending meetings at school or a care agency during the daytime, but may also be difficult to contact by telephone. Schools also point to the high mobility of these groups as an obstacle to accommodating these children. The fact that children (frequently) change schools during the school year creates additional difficulties.

Finally, a study carried out in 2013 by Currie from the perspective of male posted construction workers is interesting. She examines their difficulties to achieve virtually any meaningful experience of family life during their posting.[39] In the words of Currie, 'Periods of time spent away from the family unit, (...) impact on the ability of workers to maintain and develop relationships with family members. (...) Since posting is legally a temporary phenomenon, it could be said that the Union has little obligation to specifically consider the family life of posted workers. However, behind the temporary contracts that see construction workers posted abroad for limited periods of time lies a longevity created by the renewal of those contracts, for example when projects run for longer than expected, and also repeated postings to various and different locations'.[40]

---

37. R. Vogels, M. Gijsberts, M. den Draak (2014), *Poolse, Bulgaarse en Roemeense kinderen in Nederland. Een verkenning van hun leefsituatie*. SCP. In contrast, a follow-up study in 2017 (Ria Vogels, Simone de Roos, Freek Bucx (2017), *From East to West*, SCP) depicted a predominantly positive picture. However, this study was carried out only among migrants entered into the Dutch population registers and it was decided only to survey the parents. For many of them, registering is linked to the intention to remain in the Netherlands for an extended period. As a consequence, the study does not provide a total picture. Research by P.G.M. van der Heijden, M. Cruyff, G. van Gils (2013). *Aantallen geregistreerde en niet-geregistreerde burgers uit moe-landen die in Nederland verblijven. Rapportage schattingen 2009 en 2010*. Utrecht: Universiteit Utrecht, shows that in 2010 an estimated 28% of Poles, 35% of Bulgarians and 12% of Romanians were entered in the personal records database. Hence, it may be assumed that even if the registration rate has increased since 2010, a substantial proportion of migrants from Poland, Bulgaria and Romania are not registered, and could therefore not be included in this study.
38. R. Vogels, M. Gijsberts, M. den Draak (2014), *Polish, Bulgarian and Romanian Children in the Netherlands; English Summary*, pp. 81–85. The study is based on the views of experts and professionals, whose role means they come into contact with problem behaviour. It would seem that many of the problems highlighted by professionals (e.g., due to long working hours, poor housing conditions, frequent back-and-forth migration and incomplete families) relate to circular migrants (e.g., seasonal workers), who are often not entered in the population registers.
39. Currie, S. (2013). 'Men on the Sidelines: The Reconciliation of Work and Family Life Agenda in the Context of Cross-Border Posting'. *Journal of Social Welfare and Family Law*, 35(3), 389–408.
40. *Ibid.*, pp. 390, 396.

Even irrespective of the legal and contractual limitations for posted workers to enjoy family unity, pointed at in section §10.04 above, Currie explores additional non-legal hurdles to the enjoyment of a stable family life. She points to the way in which the workers are housed with very little space or personal privacy, which is not suitable for family visits, even of a short duration. Moreover, both accommodation and transport to the building site are usually arranged by the employer, also since it gives him control over the times at which workers arrive and leave work. As posted workers frequently work very long hours and receive few free days from work, this adds to the inability to enjoy family unity.[41]

While acknowledging that in reality it will seem very far detached from what happens 'on the ground', certainly within the construction sector where there are often problems even in enforcing basic rights of pay, Currie argues that *potentially* periods of family-related leave might be seen as particularly valuable in securing a right for posted workers to return home following, for example, the birth of a child. In light of the growing acknowledgement of reconciliation of work and family life as a fundamental right, she contends that a convincing case can be made to include reconciliation-related rights within the scope of Article 3(1)(f) of the PWD, since this provision also includes protective measures with regard to the terms and conditions of employment of pregnant women or women who have recently given birth. Moreover, a regular break in the working week of three days is suggested as an extremely valuable mechanism through which posted workers might maintain genuine and sustained family contact. Leaving aside the question surrounding the economic viability of frequent trips home, it would *potentially* enable posted workers sufficient time to return home more often, or at least on occasion, during their posting.[42]

§10.06 CONCLUDING REMARKS

In this contribution to the 100th Issue of the Bulletin, the perceived advantages of TAW, which played such a decisive role in legitimating the temporary employment industry, were assessed in the context of an increasingly important role of TEAs in facilitating transnational labour mobility. The question whether cross-border temporary agency workers may profit from advantages of TAW, such as the reconciliation of work and family life, to the same extent as local temporary agency workers was answered in the negative, in light of both the current regulatory framework and the proposed revision of the PWD. Although the silence on the family life of posted (agency) workers in the PWD contrasts markedly with the legal provisions relevant to migrant (agency) workers pursuant to Article 45 TFEU, also the latter category suffers from long working hours, poor housing conditions, frequent back-and-forth migration and incomplete families. Hence, as discussed in section §10.05 above, there are considerable costs attached to posted, temporary and circular transnational labour

---

41. *Ibid.*, p. 402.
42. *Ibid.*, pp. 404, 403.

mobility: both in the situation that children are left behind and when children migrate with parents.

This brings up the question of whose responsibility it is to fill the void of care created by such temporary labour mobility. Labour market intermediaries such as TEAs play an important facilitating role in posted, temporary and circular transnational labour mobility. Therefore, in my view, it would be apt for them and for their employer associations such as the WEC, to do their best to close the gap between the current disadvantages of transnational agency work in comparison to agency work within national borders. Self-evidently, there is a role for regulatory authorities, at national, European and international level to 'nudge' or, if necessary, to force the temporary agency industry to take its responsibility. However, it is questionable whether a kind of win-win transnational flexicurity deal would be feasible. With respect to the right to family life, we should perhaps acknowledge that there are obvious limits to promoting a better reconciliation of work and private life in a transnational context. Enjoying high-quality family life cannot be fully combined with promoting all sorts of insecure transnational temporary labour mobility. Instead, it might entail efforts to curb exploitative forms of said labour mobility and focus on bringing the work to the people instead of the people to the work. After all, transnational temporary agency work as an opportunity and choice, not as a brutal economic necessity, is attractive and desirable for workers.

As a closing remark, such a better balance between economic and social interests in cross-border temporary agency work would also be very much in line with the Commission Juncker's European Pillar of Social Rights. The pillar focuses *inter alia* on equal treatment, stable and adaptable work, fostering work-life balance and the prevention of abuse of precarious forms of labour at national labour markets. Maybe the social pillar could serve as a catalyst to correct the unfair imbalance in the EU *transnational* labour market as well.

CHAPTER 11
Protection Against Dismissal in Contemporary Labour Law

Barbara Kresal

§11.01 INTRODUCTION

Termination of employment relationship remains one of the core issues of labour law.[1] In the context of present day challenges, such as globalization, technological progress and the pressure of international competitiveness with a constant demand – among others – to lower labour costs, there is a need to address questions of how to regulate labour markets and labour relations and what is the role of contemporary labour law and industrial relations in this respect. Although some would argue that stable, standard employment relationships do not fit anymore into the nowadays world of work, characterized by rapid and constant changes, a variety of employment forms, contractualization and deconstruction of the concept of the worker and that, consequently, workers' protection in case of termination of their employment is an outdated topic, this is far from the reality. Work and employment patterns do need to adapt to changes, but at the same time, workers do need secure and reasonably predictable employment engagements with good conditions of work, including adequate protection against dismissal.

---

1. The protection in case of termination of employment, the employment protection and job security is described as 'an essential aspect of the right to work and a major concern of the ILO throughout the history' (ILO, *Employment protection legislation: summary indicators in the area of terminating regular contracts (individual dismissals)*, Geneva 2015, 1); as 'the most salient of fundamental social rights' (J. Kenner, *The EU charter of fundamental rights: A commentary*. Oxford: Hart 2014, p. 832); as the topic which 'should enjoy again the attention it has received in the past' (M. Weiss, 'Job security: A challenge for EU social policy' in N. Contouris and M. Freedland (eds), *Resocialising Europe in a time of crisis* (Cambridge: CUP 2013) p. 289); as 'crucial' and 'one of the most sensitive issues in labour law today' (ILO, *Termination of employment digest*. Geneva: ILO 2000) etc.

These two aspects (flexibility/adaptability to changes and security/predictability) are reconcilable, even complementary; they are not – as too often presented without any reasonable argumentation – conflicting.[2] At the technical, implementation level, it is just a question of good organization and long-term smart management, and at the more fundamental, ideological level, it is a question of how the risks and burdens on one side as well as profits and benefits on the other side are or should be distributed between different stakeholders.

Successful economy and prosperity need – among other conditions – also effective and productive work. Workers are human beings and all human beings need freedom and autonomy for their creativity and development, and there could be no freedom and autonomy without security and long-term life perspective; the society cannot flourish if its progress is not based on decent working and living conditions for all. Adequate protection for workers in case of termination of their employment, whatever their form of employment, i.e., standard or non-standard, is therefore crucial for every society.

This contribution focuses on the termination of employment relationship at the initiative of the employer, against the will of the worker.[3] In this case, there is an evident need for a special legal protection of a dependant and economically weaker and vulnerable contractual party, the worker. Davies emphasizes that the inequality of bargaining power and the need to protect workers' dignity are important arguments in favour of regulating employment relationships.[4] As a rule, loss of employment means loss of main source of income for the workers and their families. Besides, work is not just the basis for earning the (decent) living, it is much more. Therefore, many other negative consequences of the loss of work and employment are mentioned, social and economic, for the worker as well as for the employer, the company, economic entity and for the society at large. Not just short-term, also long-term consequences have to be taken into account. Just to mention some of them, health problems, higher risk of poverty, social exclusion, social unrest… .[5] Beside justified interests of the workers to get adequate protection against dismissal, legal regulation has to consider justified interests of the employers, the needs of the respective company and of the work process. Thus, the issue of termination of employment is a complex matter, and a reasonable equilibrium between interests of the parties involved is often difficult to

---

2. A flexicurity model tried to address this link; however, it is not a sufficient tool and it was often misunderstood or implemented incorrectly, focusing mainly on the flexibility and forgetting about the security aspect. Besides, flexibility and security aspects have been separated and the latter externalized. The link and complementarity of the two aspects should be properly addressed also within the employment relationship itself.
3. Protection against dismissal might be understood too narrowly, limiting the issue only to 'permanent' workers with 'standard' contract of employment for indefinite period. All workers need adequate protection against insecure, precarious employment, since both, non-standard and standard employment patterns can put a worker in precarious situations.
4. A. Davies, 'Regulating atypical work: Beyond equality' in N. Contouris and M. Freedland (eds), *Resocialising Europe in a time of crisis* (Cambridge: CUP 2013) p. 232. On vulnerability *see also* L. Rodgers, *Labour law, vulnerability and the regulation of precarious work* (Cheltenham: Edward Elgar 2016).
5. On socio-economic effects of collective dismissals *see* N. Countouris, S. Deakin, M. Freedland, A. Koukiadaki and J. Prassl, *Report on collective dismissals* (Geneva: ILO 2017), pp. 16, 25–30.

find.[6] Adequate level of workers' protection in case of termination of their employment is therefore a sensitive legal, political as well as social and economic issue.

§11.02 HISTORICAL DEVELOPMENTS AND RECENT TRENDS

Initially, within the capitalist economic system based on free enterprise and market economy, the employment relationship was governed by the rule of the freedom of contract. The workers were given contracts for indefinite period of time, open-ended contracts, as a rule. Yet, at that time, a contract for indefinite period meant weaker legal position for the workers than a fixed-term contract (which was reserved for 'higher-level', qualified positions and usually concluded for a significant length of time). Namely, the worker employed under the standard contract for indefinite period of time could have been dismissed by the employer at any time with a rather short or without any period of notice, and no additional substantive or procedural requirements and restrictions applied.

First protective legislative interventions in the field of labour law did not address the employer's freedom to dismiss workers. Gradually, some rights for the workers dismissed were introduced, for instance few hours of time-off during the period of notice in order to enable the worker to search for a new job and longer periods of notice.

After the First World War, many countries introduced some schemes for the unemployed, either as social insurance or, more often, as social assistance, financed not only by the State or local budgets, but also by the contributions of the employers and employees.[7]

Severance pay was gradually introduced, at first, only for white-collar workers. Next step was to explicitly prohibit a dismissal in certain cases; for instance, a female worker could not be dismissed during a short protected period before and after the confinement. Special protection against dismissals for trade-union representatives was also one of the earlier legal interventions in this field.

---

6. B. Kresal, 'Odpoved pogodbe o zaposlitvi – "flexicurity" ali "securibility"? [Termination of contract of employment – "Flexicurity" or "securibility"?]', *Delavci in delodajalci* 6, No. 2–3 (2006) 148–149.
7. There are two main ways to address the problem of a dismissal, job loss and negative social consequences in this respect: within the labour law (legal rules impose restrictions on the employer's freedom to dismiss and provide for different rights for the employees) and within the social security system (unemployment insurance or similar schemes out of which the dismissed persons are entitled to unemployment benefits, besides, there are different active labour market measures). These two systems should not be seen as alternatives to each other, rather as complementary ways of addressing the problem. Nevertheless, it is often argued that lowering the labour law protection against dismissal can and should be replaced/substituted by stronger protection and support within the unemployment insurance schemes and by more developed active labour market measures. According to this reasoning, weaker support and lower rights within unemployment insurance should vice versa demand a stronger protection against dismissal within labour law. However, such simplification can be misleading, since the two systems should not be considered as alternatives, rather, as already emphasized above, as complementary ways of addressing the issue, each of them having complementary aims, goals, tools and results.

Only after the Second World War, a more comprehensive legal protection in case of dismissal was developed, introducing the concept of a valid/justified reasons for dismissal, additional procedural requirements, special rules for collective dismissals, etc. As late as in 1963, the first international instrument dealing specifically with termination of employment at the initiative of the employer was adopted (the ILO Termination of Employment Recommendation, No. 199), and in 1982, the legally binding convention – the Termination of Employment Convention No. 158 (supplemented by the Recommendation No. 166). This convention is still an up-to-date instrument; however, not many countries have ratified it up until now, only thirty-six, among them only nine EU Member States.[8]

Historical development of legal regulation (at national and international level) of protection of workers in case of termination of their employment can be described as gradual, with late start, slow steps, moderate achievements and retrograde developments in recent years as part of the structural labour law reforms, whereby this trend has even strengthened during and due to the crisis. Or, to put it differently, the recent crisis has often been used as an argument and an excuse to lower – not even yet very well developed – labour law protection against dismissal.

Employment protection legislation (EPL) and the 'rigidity' of labour laws in this respect has often been accused of being the main culprit for inefficient labour markets, higher unemployment, low competitiveness and unattractiveness of national legal environment for foreign investments and, on the other hand, also for the segmentation of the labour market, out-sourcing, contractualization and precarization of labour relations. There are numerous studies and research papers showing, to the contrary, that this is not the case or, at least, that the effects are unclear. The supposed negative effects of labour laws on employment and unemployment may be either very small or non-existent.[9] Different 'rigidity' indexes and similar tools – which have been (mis)used as a strong pressure towards lowering the level of dismissal protection and to support legislative reforms in this direction in many countries – are misleading and of a dubious scientific value. This debate has been going on for decades now; shortcomings and limits of such indexes (e.g., the World Bank's Doing Business, the OECD's EPL index) have been analysed in detail and also acknowledged (to a certain extent) by those developing and promoting them, but still – despite all that – they are

---

8. If compared with some of the most widely ratified ILO Conventions (fundamental conventions), this number is really very low. For instance, the Freedom of Association Convention No. 87 has been ratified by 154 countries, the Forced Labour Convention No. 29 by 178 countries and the Worst Forms of Child Labour Convention No. 138 by 181 countries.
9. S. Deakin, J. Malmberg and P. Sarkar, 'How do labour laws affect unemployment and the labour share of national income? The experience of six OECD countries, 1970–2010', *International Labour Review* 153, No. 1 (2014) 1.

    See also G. Bertola, T. Boeri and S. Cazes, 'Employment protection in industrialized countries: The case for new indicators', *International Labour Review*, 139, No. 1 (2000) 57–72; V. De Stefano, 'A tale of oversimplification and deregulation: The mainstream approach to labour market segmentation and the recent responses to the crisis in European countries', *Industrial Law Journal* 46, No. 2 (2017) 185–207; S. Cazes, S. Khatiwada and M. Malo, *Employment protection and collective bargaining: Beyond the deregulation agenda* (Geneva: ILO 2012); ILO, *Employment protection legislation: Summary indicators in the area of terminating regular contracts (individual dismissals)* (Geneva 2015), and many others.

uncritically used and cited by policy-makers when proposing the next labour law reform.[10]

There are many studies dealing with the effects of EPL on employment and unemployment. The results differ. Deakin et al. note that 'the issue is one which has preoccupied economists and other social scientists for some time, without any clear consensus emerging'.[11] Some studies show that there can be a negative effect of high external flexibility on labour productivity, creativity and innovative practices in the enterprises, etc., whereas worker-protective dismissal laws have the effect of increasing innovation.[12] The important role of 'stable' workforce and adequate employment protection for productivity and good enterprise performance, as well as for the promotion of employer's investments in training is emphasized.[13]

However, despite many arguments in favour of stable, secure employment relationships, it seems that protection against dismissal has remained a 'privilege' of workers with a standard contract of employment, whereas new forms of work are characterized by the absence of protection in case of termination of employment. It seems that, consequently, there is a tense relationship between dismissal protection (and other rights) of regular workers and precariousness of non-standard forms of employment.

All that represents a strong pressure on the regular workers and the general level of their rights. Many emphasize and problematize the conflict of interests between regular and non-standard, precarious workers. But this conflict is not a real one, it is apparent, nevertheless the existing one.[14] On top of that, there is a persistent unemployment which acts as an additional pressure for regular as well as non-standard workers. Activation policies and social welfare reforms, reducing social benefits and,

---

10. For instance, one of the declared goals of the labour market reform in Slovenia in 2013 was to increase flexibility of labour relations, also by simplifying legal regulation of dismissal (certain procedural requirements were abolished, periods of notice shortened, severance payments reduced and other employer's obligations in relation to a dismissal simplified), whereby an explicit reference to the OECD's and WB's 'rigidity' indexes were included into the explanatory notes to the draft law as an important part of the argumentation Same or similar patterns could be seen all over European countries, especially in those more severely hit by the crisis, as well as in other parts of the world.
11. S. Deakin et al., 'How do labour laws affect unemployment and the labour share of national income? The experience of six OECD countries, 1970–2010', *International Labour Review* 153, No. 1 (2014) 1.
12. Tsipouri, L. et al., *Flexibility and Competitiveness: Labour market flexibility, innovation and organisational performance (Flex-Com)* (Brussels: European Commission 2007) pp. 1–7, 13, 26–27; *see also* S. Deakin et al., 'How do labour laws affect unemployment and the labour share of national income? The experience of six OECD countries, 1970–2010', *International Labour Review* 153, No. 1 (2014) 6.
13. P. Auer and S. Cazes (eds), *Employment stability in an age of flexibility – Evidence from industrialized countries* (Geneva: ILO 2003); P. Auer, J. Berg and I. Coulibaly, 'Is a stable workforce good for productivity?', *International Labour Review* 144, No. 3 (2005) 319–343.
14. B. Kresal, 'Mutating or dissolving labour law? The fundamental right to dignity of working people questioned (once again)' in M. Rigaux, J. Buelens and A. Latinne (eds), *From labour law to social competition law?* (Cambridge-Antwerp-Portland: Intersentia 2014) pp. 149–160.

consequently, lowering income security for those not working, make this pressure even stronger.[15]

Generally speaking, there has been a constant growth of flexible and new forms of employment since the end of 1970s and 1980s. They affect in much higher percentage the vulnerable categories of workers, such as migrants, low-skilled workers, the young. Such precarious work is an instrument to influence social competition between precarious workers and workers in a standard employment relationship.[16] Under this pressure, working conditions of the latter are becoming more precarious as well. It can be argued that precariousness is gradually becoming a general feature of employment relations. Not only non-standard work but also the so-called standard employment patterns are more and more insecure, precarious and vulnerable.

However, this is nothing really new. New forms of work and non-standard forms of employment with less or without any adequate legal protection against the loss of employment are in that sense similar and comparable to a standard employment relationship as it was at the beginning, in its 'embryonal' phase. Labour law, including protection against dismissal, was a response to vulnerable, precarious, unacceptable forms of work.

The segmentation on the labour market which creates the distinction between standard and non-standard workers is constantly used as an argument for lowering the protection and rights for regular workers through general labour law reforms. However, the problem of segmentation could better be resolved by raising the level of rights and protection for precarious workers and by limiting the recourse to non-standard forms of work, thus addressing and resolving the real problem, instead of deconstructing the achieved level of protection against unfair dismissal.[17]

§11.03 RELEVANT INTERNATIONAL AND EUROPEAN LEGAL INSTRUMENTS

The level of workers protection in case of a dismissal varies significantly between countries and reflects their different historical development. Not all countries are bound by international standards in this area. As already mentioned, only a few have ratified the ILO Termination of Employment Convention No. 158; not all EU Member States are bound by the relevant provisions of the European Social Charter. As already

---

15. See V. Leskošek, 'Vpliv socialne države na (ne)odvisnost delavcev od tržnih pogojev zaposlovanja [The role of social state for the (non)dependance of workers on labour market conditions]', Časopis za kritiko znanosti 39, No. 247 (2012) 103–112.
16. J. Buelens and J. Pearson (eds), Standard work: An anachronism? (Cambridge-Antwerp-Portland: Intersentia 2012) pp. 3–5.
17. Such an approach seems more reasonable, considering the fact that the precarious work has been widely perceived as problematic. Why gradually pushing also regular workers into such (precarious) situations then?
    Well, the question is: What is perceived as a real problem, differences in rights and protection level or precarious/insecure employment patterns? If it is the latter, then lowering the general level of protection for standard contracts of employment will not resolve the problem at all.

Chapter 11: Protection Against Dismissal in Contemporary Labour Law §11.03

mentioned, the progress in this area has been rather modest up until now and recently under the strong pressure to even lower the achieved level of protection.

A more positive development can be seen in the inclusion of the right of every worker to protection against unjustified dismissal, in accordance with Community law and national laws and practices, into the Charter of Fundamental Rights of the EU (CFREU, Article 30). Weiss points out that this right has been included into the CFREU 'for good reasons'; however 'so far, the concept of job security has been underdeveloped in European employment law' and that 'this is not in line with the fundamental social right as guaranteed by Article 30 of the CFREU'.[18] He strongly argues in favour of a more comprehensive EU regulation on protection against unfair dismissal.[19]

Protection against unfair dismissal is an essential aspect of the right to work which is enshrined in the most important international human rights instruments. Article 23 of the Universal Declaration of Human Rights, Article 6 of the International Covenant on Economic, Social and Cultural Rights (ICESCR) and Article 1 of the European Social Charter are relevant in this respect. According to the General Comment on the right to work, adopted in 2005 by the CESCR under the ICESCR Rights, the failure to protect workers against unlawful dismissal falls within the scope of Article 6 ICESCR and constitutes a violation of the obligation to protect the right to work.[20]

Within the ILO, the above-mentioned ILO Convention No. 158 is of particular importance. The CESCR's General Comment No. 18 explicitly refers to it. The Convention No. 158 introduces the concept of a valid reason and some other substantive and procedural requirements. According to the Convention, 'the employment of a worker shall not be terminated unless there is a valid reason for such termination connected with the capacity or conduct of the worker or based on the operational requirements of the undertaking, establishment or service' (Article 4). Some other ILO conventions are relevant as well: the Workers' Representatives Convention (No. 135) which guarantees to workers' representatives, i.e., trade-union and elected representatives, the effective protection against dismissal; the ILO Maternity Protection Conventions (No. 183 from 2000, and earlier No. 103 from 1952 and No. 3, dating back to 1919) which guarantees adequate protection against dismissal during the pregnancy or absence on maternity leave and during a certain period following the return of the worker back to work; the Discrimination (Employment and Occupation) Convention (No. 111); as well as all conventions dealing with non-standard forms of employment, etc.

Within the Council of Europe, the European Convention on Human Rights and the Revised European Social Charter should be mentioned. According to the ECtHR's interpretation, the right to respect private life (Article 8), the freedom of religious

---

18. M. Weiss, 'Job security: A challenge for EU social policy' in N. Contouris and M. Freedland (eds), *Resocialising Europe in a time of crisis*, Cambridge: CUP 2013), pp. 279, 289.
19. Ibid.
20. Committee on Economic, Social and Cultural Rights (CESCR), The right to work – General Comment No. 18, 24. 11. 2005 (E/C.12/GC/186), paras 11 and 35.

beliefs (Article 9), the freedom of expression (Article 10) and the freedom of association (Article 11), as well as their link with Article 14 on prohibition of discrimination can be relevant in cases of dismissal.[21]

The Revised European Social Charter (RESC), especially its Article 24 on the right to protection in cases of termination of employment, was inspired by the ILO convention No. 158 which is in certain parts literally reproduced in the RESC.[22] Certain other Charter's provisions are relevant as well, such as Article 4§4 (reasonable period of notice), Article 29 (information and consultation in collective redundancy procedures), Article 8§2 (protection of maternity).

At the EU level, besides Article 30 of the CFREU, the EU Directive 98/59 on collective redundancies is the most relevant instrument in this area. However, this directive does not contain any substantive requirements (a concept of a valid reason has not been introduced into the EU law), it just prescribes special procedural requirements in case of collective dismissals. Certain other directives are relevant as well; for instance, on maternity protection, on transfer of undertaking, gender equality and non-discrimination directives, directives on non-standard forms of work.

To summarize, the international labour standards related to the protection of workers against unfair dismissal comprise the following:

(1) Substantive requirements:
   - Valid reason/justified grounds.
   - Certain explicitly enumerated prohibited grounds for termination of employment.
(2) Procedural requirements, such as:
   - Written notification.
   - Opportunity to defend.
   - Right to appeal to an impartial body (judicial review, burden of proof...).
(3) Reasonable period of notice.
(4) Severance/redundancy payment and/or other adequate income protection.
(5) Special, increased protection for certain categories of workers.
(6) Compensation or other appropriate relief (reinstatement) in case of an unjustified dismissal.
(7) Additional requirements in case of collective redundancies:
   - Information and consultation with trade-union/workers' representatives.

---

21. More M. Schmitt, 'The right to protection in cases of termination of employment' in N. Bruun, K. Lörcher, I. Schömann and S. Clauwaert (eds), *The European social charter and the employment relation* (Oxford: Hart 2017), pp. 416–418.
22. Interesting decisions of the European Committee of Social Rights, adopted within the collective complaint's procedure, have to be mentioned, namely, the decisions in:

    Finish Society of Social Rights v. Finland, Complaint No. 107/2014 (decision on the merits 6.9.2016) and
    Finish Society of Social Rights v. Finland, Complaint No. 106/2014 (decision on the merits 6.9.2016).

- Information and involvement of public authority bodies (employment service).

According to international labour standards, the employer's free will should be limited when dismissing an employee. The employer may dismiss an employee only if there is a valid reason justifying a dismissal, whereby such valid reasons can be:

(1) connected with the capacity or conduct of the worker; or
(2) based on the operational requirements of the undertaking, establishment or service.

The most typical categorization of valid/justified reasons includes: the reason of misconduct, the reason of incapacity and the economic (business) reasons.

Besides defining the valid reason as a general rule, certain grounds are explicitly prohibited (e.g., trade-union membership or activity, pregnancy, absence for parental leave, race, colour, sex, age, religion, social origin). Such protection against discriminatory dismissal reinforces a general prohibition of discrimination and legal regulation in this respect.

Very often, the *ultima ratio* rule is mentioned, according to which a dismissal should be considered as a last resort, i.e., reasons justifying a dismissal must be of a relevant weight, serious enough and alternative measures (such as offering another post) should be checked before dismissing an employee.

The employer has to fulfil different procedural requirements, depending on the type of the reason for dismissal. For example, prior to a dismissal, the employer has to warn the employee and give them an opportunity to defend themselves.

The employer has to respect a reasonable period of notice (or compensation in lieu thereof), depending on the reason for dismissal and the length of employee's service with the employer.[23] A dismissed worker should benefit from a severance payment and other income protection. International norms also provide for a special legal protection against dismissal for certain, more vulnerable categories of workers. There are additional special rules for collective dismissals. The right to appeal to an impartial body, such as a court, labour tribunal, arbitration committee or arbitrator, must be guaranteed as well.

§11.04 CONCLUSION

The protection against unfair dismissal is and should remain one of the core issues of labour law. Its effects go beyond the mere protection of workers against the loss of a particular job. In short, adequate legal protection of workers in case of termination of their employment fulfils the following essential functions:

---

23. Exceptionally, the employer may dismiss an employee immediately (summary dismissal), without any period of notice, if there is one of the grounds explicitly laid down by the law, mainly connected with grave misconduct of an employee.

- Protection against insecure, precarious and thus unacceptable employment patterns, by promoting stable, secure and reasonably predictable employment relations with a long-term life perspective.
- It is crucial, a *sine qua non* condition for the effective realization of all other rights of the workers.[24]
- It can be an effective tool against discrimination at work.[25]
- It can add to a more balanced negotiating power between capital and labour.[26]
- It is a reflection of human rights perspective on labour relations.

From the human rights perspective, labour relations are based on and framed within the principle of human dignity. Labour rights have the potential to bring abstract human rights into everyday life of people. They have the potential to empower people with human dignity.[27] But only (i) if labour law guarantees an adequate high level of workers' rights and (ii) if it applies to all situations in which working people are in need of such protection, i.e., including non-standard, precarious workers, and (iii) if workers are sufficiently protected against losing their job, so that they dare to demand their rights in practice.

Bibliography

Auer, P. and Cazes, S. (eds), *Employment stability in an age of flexibility – Evidence from industrialized countries*. Geneva: ILO 2003.

Auer, P., Berg, J. and Coulibaly, I., 'Is a stable workforce good for productivity?', *International Labour Review* 144, No. 3 (2005) 319–343.

Bertola, G., Boeri, T. and Cazes, S., 'Employment protection in industrialized countries: The case for new indicators', *International Labour Review*, 139, No. 1 (2000) 57–72.

Buelens, J. and Pearson, J. (eds), *Standard work: An anachronism?*. Cambridge-Antwerp-Portland: Intersentia 2012.

---

24. If workers do not enjoy adequate protection against dismissal, they might be afraid to claim their rights, demand decent wages, reasonable limitation and distribution of their working time, special protection and rights if they are vulnerable workers, etc.
25. By prohibiting discriminatory dismissals as well as by stronger protection against dismissal for vulnerable categories of workers, such workers are better protected against discriminatory, unfavourable treatment and their overall employment situation can improve. However, special protection should not go beyond what is necessary and should be combined by a strong and effective supervision and enforcement, otherwise there is a risk of a reverse negative effect, i.e., the employers avoid employing such workers.
26. Without adequate legal protection against dismissal, workers might be afraid to unionize and realize their collective labour rights, such as collective bargaining, the right to strike, etc., or become more actively involved in trade-union movement and their activities. Their precarious situation might impede their trade-union engagement or their participation and involvement in workers' representation within the company; adequate protection against dismissal is therefore an important element supporting and promoting the concept of fruitful social dialogue as well as participative labour relations.
27. B. Kresal, 'Mutating or dissolving labour law? The fundamental right to dignity of working people questioned (once again)' in M. Rigaux, J. Buelens and A. Latinne (eds), *From labour law to social competition law?* (Cambridge-Antwerp-Portland: Intersentia, 2014) p. 151.

Cazes, S. Khatiwada, S., and Malo, M., *Employment protection and collective bargaining: Beyond the deregulation agenda.* Geneva: ILO 2012.

Committee on Economic, Social and Cultural Rights (CESCR), The right to work – General Comment No. 18, 24. 11. 2005 (E/C.12/GC/186).

Countouris, N., Deakin, S., Freedland, M., Koukiadaki, A. and Prassl, J., *Report on collective dismissals.* Geneva: ILO 2017.

Davies, A., 'Regulating atypical work: Beyond equality' in N. Contouris and M. Freedland (eds), *Resocialising Europe in a time of crisis.* Cambridge: CUP 2013: pp. 230–249.

Deakin, S., Malmberg, J. and Sarkar, P., 'How do labour laws affect unemployment and the labour share of national income? The experience of six OECD countries, 1970–2010', *International Labour Review* 153, No. 1 (2014) 1–27.

De Stefano, V., 'A tale of oversimplification and deregulation: The mainstream approach to labour market segmentation and the recent responses to the crisis in European countries', *Industrial Law Journal* 46, No. 2 (2017) 185–207.

International Labour Organization *Employment protection legislation: Summary indicators in the area of terminating regular contracts (individual dismissals).* Geneva 2015 (http://www.ilo.org/wcmsp5/groups/public/@ed_protect/@protrav/@travail/documents/publication/wcms_357390.pdf).

International Labour Organization *Termination of employment digest.* Geneva 2000 (http://www.ilo.org/public/libdoc/ilo/2000/100B09_152_engl.pdf).

Kenner, J., *The EU charter of fundamental rights: A commentary.* Oxford: Hart 2014.

Kresal, B., 'Mutating or dissolving labour law? The fundamental right to dignity of working people questioned (once again)' in M. Rigaux, J. Buelens and A. Latinne (eds), *From Labour Law to Social Competition Law?.* Cambridge-Antwerp-Portland: Intersentia 2014: pp. 149–160.

Kresal, B., 'Odpoved pogodbe o zaposlitvi – "flexicurity" ali "securibility"? [Termination of contract of employment – "flexicurity" or "securibility"?]', *Delavci in delodajalci* 6, No. 2–3 (2006) 148–149.

Leskošek, V., 'Vpliv socialne države na (ne)odvisnost delavcev od tržnih pogojev zaposlovanja [The role of social state for the (non)dependance of workers on labour market conditions]', *Časopis za kritiko znanosti* 39, No. 247 (2012) 103–112.

Rodgers, L., *Labour law, vulnerability and the regulation of precarious work.* Cheltenham: Edward Elgar 2016.

Schmitt, M., 'The right to protection in cases of termination of employment' in N. Bruun, K. Lörcher, I. Schömann and S. Clauwaert (eds), *The European social charter and the employment relation.* Oxford: Hart 2017: pp. 412–438.

Tsipouri, L. et al., *Flexibility and competitiveness: Labour market flexibility, innovation and organisational performance (Flex-Com).* Brussels: European Commission 2007 (https://cordis.europa.eu/docs/publications/9088/90882401-6_en.pdf).

Weiss, M., 'Job security: A challenge for EU social policy' in N. Contouris and M. Freedland (eds), *Resocialising Europe in a time of crisis*, Cambridge: CUP 2013, pp. 278–289.

CHAPTER 12
Employee Data Protection in the Transnational Company

Achim Seifert

§12.01 CROSS-BORDER DATA PROCESSING IN THE EMPLOYMENT CONTEXT

One of the main fields of interest Roger Blanpain pursued in his scientific work was the labor law of transnational or—as he called it—multinational companies. His books on the famous Badger Case[1] and Corporate Codes of Conduct[2] in multinational companies impressively bear testimony to this interest in labor relations of companies operating in various countries. It may therefore be justified to choose with the question of employee data protection in the transnational company one specific aspect of labor law of these companies as subject for a contribution to the 100th edition of the *Bulletin of Comparative Labour Law and Industrial Relations* dedicated to Roger Blanpain. However, the following chapter will be using the term "transnational company" instead of "multinational company" since it underlines more clearly that the main characteristic of these companies are cross-border operations as such: the fact that a company is operating in a multitude of countries does not have the same relevance for the subject.

The following Article will focus on the cross-border processing of employee personal data within transnational companies or groups of companies.[3] Cross-border

---
1. Roger Blanpain, The Badger Case and the OECD Guidelines for Multinational Enterprises, 1977.
2. Cf. Roger Blanpain (ed.), Multinational Enterprises and the Challenges of the XXIst Century: The ILO Declaration on Fundamental Principles at Work—Public and Private Corporate Codes of Conduct, 2000; *id.*, Multinational Enterprises and Codes of Conduct: The OECD Guidelines for MNEs in Perspective, 2001.
3. According to Art. 4(19) GDPR, the term "group of companies" means a controlling company and its controlled companies.

processing of employee data becomes increasingly relevant within transnational companies or groups of companies. Some significant examples will suffice in the present context. One important area in this context is cloud computing which is more and more used by HR management: cloud computing enables HR manager of a company or group of companies, for instance, to access from their computers the company's or group's digital personnel files containing relevant (sensitive) personal data of employees from whatever part of the world.[4] By this, HR managers may comb through personnel files of their company or group—even across national borderlines—in order to find employees fit for a specific work or project. Such HR research is facilitated when the transnational company or group has established a company- or group-wide "skill inventory,"[5] comprising important personal data of employees from all over the world such as their skills, education, professional experiences, participation in specific projects, appraisals, misconducts or criminal convictions. In groups, these "skill inventories" are often centralized in one of their subsidiaries to which all relevant personal data of employees need to be transferred from the other companies of the group: in transnational groups of companies, the collection of all these data of the personnel often requires their processing to a company of the group located in another country. Another example for cross-border data transfers is centralized forms of payroll administration for the whole transnational company or group:[6] one option is that the company administers the payroll itself, but often the task is outsourced to an independent contractor to which the necessary employee data need to be transferred; in the latter case, employee personal data will mostly be transferred to a service provider across national borders. Also in the context of compliance strategies, cross-border transfers of employee data within a transnational company or group may take place: in particular, compliance investigations may have the effect that a company's compliance department process data of employees who are subject to them are transmitted across the borders and processed in another country. Furthermore, also in cross-border production chains within vertically integrated transnational companies cross-border transfers of employee data may take place. The increasing integration of production through the digitalization of work favors this development. A last example is matrix organizations as they exist in many transnational companies. These companies or groups are not organized on a country-by-country basis but on the basis of business-units which may be transnational and include various countries: in this event, cross-border transfers of employee data take place such as performance evaluation documents and other data relating to the work performance or to the skills or education.[7]

---

4. Cf. Art. 29 Data Protection Working Party, Opinion 2/2017 on data processing at work, adopted on Jun. 8, 2017, p. 22.
5. On such "skill-inventories" established by (transnational) companies see e.g., Achim Seifert, in: Spiros Simitis (ed.), Kommentar zum Bundesdatenschutzgesetz, 8th edition (2014), § 32, para. 116.
6. Cf. Seifert, in: Simitis (ed.) Bundesdatenschutzgesetz, § 32, para. 120.
7. See e.g., Lokke Moerel, Binding Corporate Rules: Corporate Self-Regulation of Global Data Transfers, Oxford 2012, para. 2.1 with further references.

EU Law has established, with the adoption of Directive 95/46/EC of October 24, 1995 on the protection of individuals with regard to the processing of personal data and on the free movement of such data,[8] a general framework for such cross-border processing of personal data, covering in principle all fields of data processing. The initiatives to adopt a sector-specific Directive on the processing of employee data failed in the late 1990s and the early 2000s.[9] Articles 44 et seq. of the new Regulation (EU) 679/2016 of April 2016 on the protection of natural persons with regard to the processing of personal data and on the free movement of such data, and repealing Directive 95/46/EC (General Data Protection Regulation [GDPR])[10] also only provide a general framework for cross-border data transfers and have only concretized and supplemented the model of Directive 95/46/EC without shifting to another paradigm of data protection regarding cross-border data transfers.

The present chapter gives an overview on the legal framework of the GDPR for cross-border transfers of employee personal data. Its main argument is that the provisions of the GDPR on cross-border data processing are not sufficiently adapted to the employment context and need to be supplemented by more specific rules on employee data protection. Article 88 GDPR only authorizes Member States to provide for more specific rules regarding the employment context but does not aim at protecting employees' personal data in a cross-border context. The chapter analyzes in the first two parts the legal framework provided by the GDPR for cross-border processing of employee data, within the Internal Market as well as to controllers or processors located in third countries. In a third part, emphasis shall be laid on the question whether transnational collective bargaining may contribute to improving employee data protection in cases of cross-border processing of employee personal data.

§12.02 DATA PROCESSING WITHIN THE INTERNAL MARKET

The GDPR harmonizes data processing within the Internal Market. As already mentioned, these general rules also apply to the processing of employee data within the Internal Market. The key provision in this context is Article 6 GDPR determining the "lawfulness of processing." In the employment context, two provisions of Article 6 are of particular interest.

---

8. Cf. Arts 25 et seq. Directive 95/46/EC, O.J.E.C. 1995 L 281/31.
9. Cf. European Commission, Communication "First stage consultation of social partners on the protection of workers' personal data," available at: ec.europa.eu/social/BlobServlet?docId = 2503&langId = en, and *id.*, "Second stage consultation of social partners on the protection of workers' personal data," available at: ec.europa.eu/social/BlobServlet?docId = 2504 &langId = en. For a fuller analysis of these initiatives of the European Commission to adopt a Directive on employee data protection and their failure *see* Spiros Simitis, "Arbeitnehmerdatenschutzgesetz—Realistische Erwartungen oder Lippenbekenntnis?," in: Arbeit und Recht (AuR) 2001, p. 429, at 430 et seq. with further references, and *id.*, Arbeitnehmerdatenschutz, in: Recht der Arbeit (RdA) 2003, Sonderbeilage zu Heft 5, p. 43, at 46 et seq.
10. O.J.E.U. 2016 L 119/1.

[A] Consent of Employees

On the basis of Article 6(1)(a) GDPR, transfer of employee data to another EU Member State (e.g., to a subsidiary of the employer in another Member State) may take place on ground of a consent of the affected employees. The GDPR does not impose written form or another form for the employees' consent. However, the national laws of some Member States require written form for the consent of employees in the processing of their personal data in the employment context.[11] By this, these Member States make use of the opening-clause of the already mentioned Article 88(1) GDPR pursuant to which the Member States may, by law or by collective agreements, provide for more specific rules on data processing in the employment context.

However, normally, such consent of employees is not a viable road for employers to legitimate transfers of employee data to a subsidiary in another European country. One first difficulty to be mastered may be that employers would need the consent of *all* employees to be affected by an envisaged transfer of personal data. This may be difficult to receive: as a matter of fact, it cannot be excluded that some employees refuse to give their consent to a specific processing of their personal data or that they limit the data processing. Furthermore, the consent may be withdrawn by the employee as affected data subject at any moment;[12] from an employer's perspective, the employee consent therefore is a highly fragile instrument.

A third difficulty is that the consent shall be freely given: Article 7(4) GDPR concretizes this requirement by providing that "utmost account shall be taken of whether, *inter alia*, the performance of a contract, including the provision of a service, is conditional on consent to the processing of personal data that is not necessary for the performance of that contract." Pursuant to Recital (43) GDPR, "consent should not provide a valid legal ground for the processing of personal data in a specific case where there is a clear imbalance between the data subject and the controller [...] and it is therefore unlikely that consent was freely given in all the circumstances of that specific situation." As the employment relationship is by definition characterized by such an imbalance of power between employer and employee, employee consent into processing of his or her personal data by the employer may be questioned. Although the GDPR does not exclude per se the consent of the employee as justification for a processing of employee data in the employment context, the rules of the Regulation as well as the provisions of some Member States,[13] adopted on the basis of Article 88(1) GDPR, may result in a legal uncertainty reducing the employer's interest to make recourse to this legal mechanism as there is always the question of proof as to whetherve a given employee consent has been freely given.

Thus, dealing with employee consents in transnational companies justifying cross-border data transmissions may become a challenge for employers and is therefore less attractive as legal basis for the processing of employee data.

---

11. Cf. e.g., S 26(2)(iii) of the Federal Act on Data Protection [*Bundesdatenschutzgesetz*] and Art. L-261-1(1), subpara. 4 of the Labour Code of the Grand-Duchy of Luxembourg.
12. Cf. Art. 7(3) GDPR.
13. *See* the references to German and Luxembourgish law in footnote 11.

[B] Article 6(1)(b) GDPR

As a result of these deficiencies of the consent in the employment context, employers will be much more likely to rely on Article 6(1)(b) GDPR in order to justify transfers of employee data to controllers in other Member States. This provision allows data processing when it is necessary for the performance of a contract to which the data subject (employee) is a party or in order to take steps at the request of the data subject prior to entering into a contract. Under this provision, an employer may be authorized to transfer data of his employees or candidates in hiring processes, e.g., to subsidiaries or contractors located in other EU Member States or in one of the contracting party States to the European Economic Area (EEA).

In case that a transnational company only has dependent subsidiaries in other Member States which do not dispose of a separate legal personality, the company as a whole is controller in the sense of Article 4(7) GDPR and can therefore transfer employee data to departments or other establishments in other Member States. Such transfers are no transmissions and therefore no processing of personal data to thirds in accordance with Article 4(2) GDPR since these data flows take place within the internal organization of one controller, the employer. Thus, the fact that these personal data are crossing national borders of Member States is without relevance in this context.

In the event that the subsidiaries of a transnational group of companies which are located in other Member States have separate legal personality, transfers of employee data to these foreign subsidiaries require a justification. Unlike the draft of the European Parliament,[14] the provisions of the GDPR do not explicitly privilege transmissions of personal data within groups of companies. However, Recital (48) of the GDPR recognizes that controllers which belong to a group of companies "may have a legitimate interest in transmitting personal data within the group for internal administrative purposes, including the processing of [...] employees' personal data." Despite the absence of an explicit rule on data transfers within groups of companies, the GDPR has therefore a tendency to recognize the specific interests of these processors. Nonetheless, each data transmission from one company of the group to another needs therefore to fulfill the requirements of the GDPR.

If the data transfer is a processing under Article 28 GDPR, i.e., the use of employee data under the control and directives of the employing company, it will be allowed under the conditions set out in Articles 28 and 29 GDPR. Thus, the outsourcing of the payroll to another company of the group or an independent service provider, performing under the directives and the control of the employer, regularly is data processing under Article 28 GDPR.[15]

If the data transfer is not a data processing under Article 28 GDPR, it shall meet the requirements of Article 6(1)(b) GDPR. Consequently, only those transmissions of

---

14. Cf. Art. 82(1d) of the draft of the European Parliament, available at: http://www.europarl.europa.eu/sides/getDoc.do?pubRef=-//EP//TEXT%20TA%20P7-TA-2014-0212%200%20DOC%20XML%20V0//en.
15. Cf. Arbeitsbericht der ad-hoc-Arbeitsgruppe "Konzerninterner Datentransfer," p. 3, available at https://www.ldi.nrw.de/mainmenu_Datenschutz/submenu_Datenschutzrecht/Inhalt/Personalwesen/Inhalt/5_Beschaeftigtendatenschutz_Konzern/arbeitspapier_ad_hoc_idv.pdf.

employee data to other companies of the group, located in other EU Member States or in the EEA, may be justified which are necessary for the performance of given employment contracts to which employees of the company are party or in order to take steps at the request of the data subject prior to entering into a contract. In the case of employees who are employed on a group-wide basis and who are often shifting from one subsidiary to another (e.g., in the context of concrete projects) the transmission of their personal data to another company of the group may be necessary for the performance of their employment contract. However, it needs to be verified whether the transmission of employee data to a "skill-inventory" for the whole group is in fact necessary—and not just useful—for the performance of employment contracts in this group. One mechanism to protect employee privacy in these cases might be to limit the number of persons who have access to such "skill-inventories" (e.g., to responsible HR managers) or to pseudonymize or even anonymize personnel files or employee personal data that are in such databases: in case of a legitimate interest (e.g., an employee's skills fit to the profile of a vacant post), the identity of the employee in question may be revealed to persons of HR who are in charge for the relevant recruitment procedure.[16]

§12.03 TRANSFER OF EMPLOYEE PERSONAL DATA TO THIRD COUNTRIES

By far much more problematic than transfers of employee data within the Internal Market are data transfers to controllers or processors located in third countries. It is certainly not exaggerated to consider such data transfers outside the EU as the "Achilles tendon" of European data protection law. In these cases, the main challenge is to ensure that the data protection level of the GDPR, or at least the main principles of the Regulation, are respected in the processing of employee data in third countries. Even though many countries in the world have adopted data protection acts over the last years,[17] there is still no universally agreed minimum standard for employee data protection: The International Labour Organisation (ILO), as the specialized agency of the United Nations (Article 57 Charter of the United Nations) in the field of labor law, has adopted in 1997 only a "Code of Practice on the Protection of workers' Personal

---

16. Cf. Seifert, in: Simitis, Bundesdatenschutzgesetz, § 32, para. 117 with further references.
17. Cf. Commission, Exchanging and Protecting Personal Data in a Globalised World, COM(2017) 7 final, p. 7 with further references; see also United Nations Conference on Trade and Development (UNCTAD), Data Protection Regulations and international data flows: implications for trade and development, New York & Geneva 2016, downloadable at: http://unctad.org/en/PublicationsLibrary/dtlstict2016d1_en.pdf. As far as the regional (European) level is concerned, the Council of Europe has adopted on Jan. 28, 1981 a Convention for the Protection of Individuals with regard to Automatic Processing of Personal Data (European Treaties Series No 108) and has thereby recognized a minimum protection of personal data. For a more in-depth assessment of this Convention cf. Spiros Simitis, Bundesdatenschutzgesetz, 8th edition (2014), Einleitung: Geschichte—Ziele—Prinzipien, paras. 151 et seq.

Data"[18] which does not bind the ILO Member States. But still today, twenty years later and after the adoption of an increasing number of data protection acts on national level, the adoption of a Convention or Recommendation on the protection of employee personal data by the International Labour Conference has not come closer as far as can be seen.[19]

The GDPR provides in its Chapter V ("Transfer of Personal Data to Third Countries or International Organisations") a complex legal framework which tries to safeguard a minimum of data protection for data subjects in the event of data transfers to third countries. It requires from third countries in which the data flows go to ensure the necessary protection of data subjects or from the addressees in the corresponding third countries (companies or public authorities) the necessary data protection guarantees. The system adopted by the GDPR does not differ significantly from that set out in Directive 95/46/EC: generally speaking, the new Regulation takes up most of the mechanisms already recognized by Directive 95/46/EC, in particular by its Article 25-7, but provides a more detailed legal framework for them. The protection of data subjects is partly established by the Commission or at least approved by it or by the competent supervisory authorities in the Member States. In part, the GDPR takes recourse to mechanisms of a "regulated self-regulation."

[A] Data Transfers on the Basis of an Adequacy Decision of the Commission

According to Article 45(1) GDPR, a transfer of personal data to a third country may take place in case of an Adequacy decision of the European Commission. Such decisions recognize that a third country, a territory or one or more specified sectors within this country ensures an adequate level of data protection. The level of adequacy is assessed by taking into account a set of elements such as the rule of law, respect for human rights and fundamental freedoms, the existence and effective functioning of supervisory authorities in the third country and the international commitments the third country concerned has entered into; Article 45(2) GDPR concretizes these elements. Adequacy decisions rely on the assumption that national data protection laws of third countries converge with the standards set out by the GDPR.[20] If there is an adequacy decision concerning a specific third country, data transfers do not require any specific authorization.

As of now, there are only twelve adequacy decisions of the European Commission, concerning *inter alia* Andorra, Argentina, Canada, Switzerland, Guernsey, Israel,

---

18. The Code of Practice is available at the ILO Website under http://www.ilo.org/wcmsp5/groups/public/---ed_protect/---protrav/---safework/documents/normativeinstrument/wcms_107797.pdf.
19. For a brief summary of the ILO's activities in the field of employee data protection, see Jean-Michel Servais, International Labour Law, 3rd revised edition, 2011, para. 680*bis*.
20. On this convergence cf. Commission, Exchanging and Protecting Personal Data in a Globalised World, COM(2017) 7 final, p. 7 with further references.

Jersey and New Zealand.[21] As far as the USA are concerned, the European Commission has initially taken an adequacy decision under Article 25(6) Directive 95/46/EC allowing data transfers from the Internal Market to the USA if the data controller or processor located in the USA has recognized so-called Safe Harbor Privacy Principles issued by the U.S. Department of Commerce and guaranteeing the core data protection principles as enshrined in Directive 95/46/EC.[22] U.S. companies or organizations to which personal data should be transferred were entitled to "self-certify" by sending a letter to the U.S. Department of Commerce through which the organization joins the "Safe Harbor Privacy Principles." However, the Grand Chamber of the CJEU has ruled in the case *Schrems v. Data Protection Commissioner* that this European Commission decision is invalid.[23] In the aftermath of this seminal ruling, the European Commission negotiated with the U.S. Government an "EU-US Privacy Shield" to replace the invalid "Safe Harbor Privacy Principles,"[24] strengthening administrative controls of U.S. Government and comprising the assurance of the U.S. Government that the access of public authorities is subject to clear limitations. It remains to be seen whether this Agreement may effectively eliminate the problems of data safety which have led to the *Schrems*-judgment of the Court of Justice.

In a Communication of January 2017,[25] the European Commission has announced its intention to "prioritize discussions on possible adequacy decisions with key trading partners in East and South-East Asia" (e.g., Japan and Korea) or with India and Latin American countries. However, it may be doubted whether adequacy decisions are in general an effective instrument to ensure employee data protection in cases of data transfers to third countries: they are necessarily generalizing the level of data protection within one given country, one or several of its regions or sectors, but are not able to effectively ensure data protection in one or several given companies in this third country.

---

21. A complete list of the third countries covered by an adequacy decision of the Commission is available at the Commission's Website under: http://ec.europa.eu/justice/data-protection/international-transfers/adequacy/index_en.htm.
22. Commission Decision of Jul. 26, 2000 pursuant to Directive 95/46/EC of the European Parliament and of the Council on the adequacy of the protection provided by the safe harbor privacy principles and related frequently asked questions issued by the US Department of Commerce, O.J.E.C. 2000 L 215/7. For further details on this Commission Decision and its practice *see* e.g., Commission, Communication on the Functioning of the Safe Harbour from the Perspective of EU Citizens and Companies Established in the EU, COM(2013) 847 final.
23. CJEU, judgment of Oct. 6, 2015, case C-362/14 (*Maximilian Schrems v. Data Protection Commissioner*), ECLI:EU:C:2015:650.
24. Commission Implementing Decision (EU) 2016/1250 of Jul. 12, 2016 pursuant to Directive 95/46/EC of the European Parliament and of the Council on the adequacy of the protection provided by the EU-U.S. Privacy Shield, O.J.E.U. 2016 L 207/1. For an assessment of the new Privacy Shield, *see* European Commission, Report on the First Annual Review of the Functioning of the EU-U.S. Privacy Shield, COM(2017) 611 final.
25. Commission, Exchanging and Protecting Personal Data in a Globalised World, COM(2017) 7 final, p. 10.

[B] Appropriate Safeguards

In the absence of an adequacy decision of the Commission, a transfer of personal data (of employees) to third countries may be justified "only if the controller or processor has provided appropriate safeguards, and on condition that enforceable data subject rights and effective legal remedies for data subjects are available."[26] The GDPR provides various mechanisms that may serve for controllers and processors of employee data as mechanisms justifying cross-border data transfers. In this regard, the Regulation picks up the conception of Directive 95/46/EC which may be characterized as a model of "regulated self-regulation"[27] and spells out mechanisms that have for their majority already been—explicitly or implicitly—recognized under Directive 95/46/EC.

[1] Standard Contract Clauses

Standard contract clauses under Article 46(2)(b) and (c) GDPR, comprising the core principles of EU data protection law, may constitute an appropriate safeguard when they are included in contracts between the controller and controllers or processors in third countries to which personal data (of employees) are transferred. Such standard contract clauses need to be approved by the European Commission or by the competent supervisory authorities of the Member States. The instrument is not new. The European Commission has already adopted on the basis of Article 26(4) Directive 95/46/EC "Standard Contract Clauses—Set I" (controller-to-controller transfers),[28] "Standard Contract Clauses—Set II"[29] and "Standard Contract Clauses—Set III" (processors).[30] These model contracts comprise the most important principles of EU data protection law and confer to data subjects individual rights. Pursuant to Article 46(5) GDPR, these Decisions of the European Commission under Article 26(4) Directive 95/46/EC shall remain in force until amended, replaced or repealed, if necessary, by a Commission Decision adopted in accordance with Article 46(2) GDPR.

The problem of these standard contract clauses, adopted by the European Commission, is that they are not an appropriate mechanism to ensure employee data protection in the context of cross-border data transfers within transnational companies or groups of companies. An effective use would require them to be included in all agreements which companies conclude with other companies of the group or with third parties, which may considerably increase transaction costs: their use is therefore

---

26. Cf. Art. 46(1) GDPR.
27. For a fuller analysis of this concept, *see*, e.g., Wolfgang Schulz & Thorsten Held, Regulated Self-regulation as a Form of Modern Government: An Analysis of Case Studies from Media and Telecommunications Law, 2004.
28. Cf. European Commission, Decision 2001/497/EC Standard contractual clauses for the purposes of Art. 26(2) of Directive 95/46/EC for the transfer of personal data to third countries which do not ensure an adequate level of protection (controller–to-controller transfers).
29. European Commission, Decision C(2004)5721 Standard contractual clauses for the transfer of personal data from the Community to third countries (controller-to-controller transfers).
30. European Commission, Decision 2010/87/EU Standard Contract Clauses (processors).

much more complicated than the adoption of Binding Corporate Rules (BCRs) under Article 46 GDPR through which companies may establish a uniform data protection regime for all data transfers in the company or the group.[31] As far as data transfers to the USA are concerned, there still are concerns that surveillance practices in the USA are incompatible with EU law and that EU citizens do not dispose of effective remedies under US law.[32] Furthermore, the standard contract clauses as adopted by the European Commission do not take into account the specific employment context and do not provide specific rules for the protection of employees' personal data in the context of their employment relationship. They do not comprise clauses providing the involvement of employees' representatives (e.g., works councils or company committees) or concretize the legitimate purposes for data transfers to controllers or processors located in third countries. As a result, standard contract clauses, as they exist today, are only in very limited cases an appropriate legal mechanism for employee data protection in case of data transfers to third countries.[33]

[2]   Binding Corporate Rules

Another appropriate safeguard is BCRs under Article 46 GDPR that may compensate a missing adequate level of data protection in a third country to which personal data of employees are transmitted. These BCRs are unilaterally adopted by companies but need to be approved by the competent supervisory authority. Article 47(2) GDPR comprises minimum requirements for BCRs which shall be fulfilled. They normally comprise *inter alia* the commitment of the company to apply the general data protection principles as set out in the GDPR, individual rights of data subjects, liability of the company for any breach of its data protection obligations or complaint procedures for data subjects. Already under Article 26(2) Directive 95/46/EC it was recognized that such BCRs may constitute appropriate safeguards for data transfers to third countries.[34]

These BCRs normally do not comprise specific rules on employee data protection within the company or group of companies. Employees are therefore treated in the same way as other data subjects coming into contact with the company, such as suppliers, purchasers or other contract partners. Even though BCRs guarantee a

---

31. *See infra* §12.03[B][2].
32. Cf. the Irish High Court's request of October 3, 2017 [2016 No. 4809 P.] for a preliminary ruling of the CJEU: the Irish High Court asks *inter alia* whether the Standard Contract Clauses adopted by the European Commission, serving companies such as Facebook as a legal basis for the transfer of customer personal data to the USA are in line with Art. 7 and Art. 8 of the Charter of Fundamental Rights of the EU.
33. Cf. Sebastian Seifert, Der Beschäftigtendatenschutz im transnationalen Konzern, Hamburg 2015, pp. 199 et seq.
34. *See* Simitis, Bundesdatenschutzgesetz, § 4c, para. 59 with further references. The former sec. 4c of the Federal Data Protection Act of Germany, repealed in 2017, even explicitly provided that BCR may constitute appropriate safeguards.

minimum standard of data protection for employees in cases of data transfers to third countries (e.g., complaint rights), more specific rules on employee data protection, taking into account the specific situation of employees (e.g., involvement of employees' representatives) are normally missing in BCRs. However, it would be useful to insert in these BCRs more specific rules on the protection of employee data, as Article 88(1) GDPR, according to which the Member States may, by law or by collective agreements, provide for more specific rules on data processing in the employment context.

[3] Approved Codes of Conduct

Article 46(2)(e) GDPR authorizes data transfers to third countries when they have declared a binding and enforceable commitment to apply the appropriate safeguards, including as regards data subjects' rights, set out in an approved Code of conducts. Such Codes of conduct determining the appropriate safeguards to be respected in case of a data transfer to third countries may be elaborated by associations and other bodies representing categories of controllers or processors.[35] They need the approval of the competent supervisory authority and shall have general validity through a decision of the European Commission.[36] In particular, the latter requirement limits the scope of approved Codes of conduct as appropriate safeguard under Article 46 GDPR considerably. The GDPR recognizes approved Codes of conduct for the first time.[37] It remains to be seen whether this legal mechanism will gain relevance after the coming into force of the GDPR in May 2018.

[4] Certification

A last instrument to ensure appropriate safeguards for data transfers to third countries is "an approved certification mechanism with binding and enforceable commitments of the controller or processor in the third country to apply the appropriate safeguards, including as regards data subjects' rights" ("European Privacy Seal").[38] This mechanism has not been recognized under Directive 95/46/EC. However, certifications may only serve as appropriate safeguards under the condition that it is issued by certification bodies under Article 42 GDPR or by the competent supervisory authority. For the moment, it is not clear whether the "European Privacy Seal" will have a significant impact on (employee) data protection in cases of data transfers to third countries.

---

35. Cf. Art. 40(2) GDPR.
36. Cf. Art. 40(3) and (9) GDPR.
37. For a brief overview on the different initiatives of associations of controllers or processors to prepare such Codes of conduct *see* Friederike Voskamp, Transnationaler Datenschutz: Globale Datenschutzstandards durch Selbstregulierung, 2015, pp. 78 et seq. with further references.
38. Cf. Art. 46(2)(f) GDPR.

§12.04 TOWARD A TRANSNATIONAL COLLECTIVE BARGAINING ON EMPLOYEE DATA TRANSFERS TO THIRD COUNTRIES?

All these legal mechanisms, provided by Articles 44 et seq. GDPR, rely on decisions of the European Commission or unilateral decisions of transnational companies. They do normally not comprise specific rules for the employment context, and employees or their representatives do not have any voice in the elaboration of BCRs, approved Codes of Conduct or approved Certification mechanisms. This is not surprising since the GDPR only provides a general framework for data protection covering different areas of data processing and not a specific instrument of employee data protection.

One strategy to strengthen employee data protection in transnational companies may be that BCRs or approved Codes of conduct, for instance, are collectively negotiated between employees' representatives and the company and thereby adapted to the interests of both sides. There are two forms of transnational collective bargaining which may serve as a basis for such negotiations on employee data protection in transnational companies: in community-wide operating companies or groups of companies under Directive 2009/38/EC,[39] such negotiations may take place between the central management and the European Works Council (§12.04[A]). However, it is also thinkable to negotiate International Framework Agreements (IFAs) on a worldwide scale between transnational companies or groups and global union federations on data protection issues (§12.04[B]).

[A] Employee Data Protection: A New Field for European Works Councils

According to the model of Directive 2009/38/EC,[40] European Works Councils (EWCs) shall improve the right to information and consultation of employees in Community-scale undertakings and Community-scale groups of undertakings.[41] If one takes the provisions of Directive 2009/38/EC as a basis, the right to information and consultation mainly relates to economic and employment questions such as "the structure, economic and financial situation, probable development and production and sales of the Community-scale undertaking or group of undertakings" or "the situation and probable trend of employment, investments, and substantial changes concerning organisation, introduction of new working methods or production processes, transfers of production, mergers, cut-backs or closures of undertakings, establishments or important parts thereof, and collective redundancies."[42] Employee data protection is not explicitly mentioned among these competences of EWCs but is not excluded as subject

---

39. Directive 2009/38/EC of May 6, 2009 on the establishment of a European Works Council or a procedure in Community-scale undertakings and Community-scale groups of undertakings for the purposes of informing and consulting employees (Recast), O.J.E.C. 2009 L 122/28.
40. Also the existing Agreements on the establishing of EWCs focus on information and consultation concerning these questions.
41. Cf. Art. 1(1) Directive 2009/38/EC.
42. Cf. Annexe No 1(a) to Directive 2009/38/EC.

of the information and consultation procedure under Directive 2009/38/EC as long as it is a transnational issue under Article 1(3) and (4) of Directive 2009/38/EC.

It is well known that, despite this limitation of Directive 2009/38/EC to information and consultation,[43] EWCs are increasingly collective bargaining actors and are concluding collective agreements which first and foremost deal with questions of corporate restructuring and its impact on employment.[44] Such European Framework Agreements (EFAs) are in line with Directive 2009/38/EC since the Directive aims at establishing a "dialogue and exchange of views between employees' representatives and central management" about questions relating to the company. Although Directive 2009/38/EC does not explicitly authorize[45] the conclusion of Agreements between EWCs and central management, such Agreements are in accordance with the provisions of the Directive since they correspond to its objective, the improvement of social dialogue in these transnational companies:[46] it would be in contradiction to this main objective of the Directive if it were legally not possible to bring the social dialogue to a successful end, i.e., the conclusion of an agreement between central management and EWCs on issues that have been discussed between them in the information and consultation procedure under Directive 2009/38/EC.

It is interesting to note that the existing agreements between EWCs and central management are only exceptionally dealing with questions of employee data protection, namely with the protection of employees in cases of data transfers to entities in third countries.[47] One exception probably is the "Agreement on Data Protection in the Porr Group at European Level" which has been concluded between the central management of the Austrian construction company and its EWC.[48] The Porr-Agreement entitles the companies belonging to the group to transmit employee data, "within the meaning of the relevant legal provisions," to the HR department or the appropriate payroll account department. Thereby, data transfers are limited to these

---

43. Cf. Art. 1(1) Directive 2009/38/EC.
44. An updated list of transnational company agreements is downloadable at the website of the European Commission under: http://ec.europa.eu/social/main.jsp?catId=978&langId=en. For a more in-depth analysis of thes transnational Agreements from a sociological perspective cf. Stefan Rüb, Hans-Wolfgang Platzer & Torsten Müller, Transnationale Unternehmensvereinbarungen—Zur Neuordnung der Arbeitsbeziehungen in Europa, Berlin 2011; see also Jeremy Waddington, "Was leisten Europäische Betriebsräte? Die Perspektive der Arbeitnehmervertreter," in: WSI-Mitteilungen 2006, pp. 560 et seq., and Valeria Pulignano, "European Integration and Trans-national Employment Regulation: The Company-level Experience of EFAs in the Metal Sector in Europe," in: ELLJ (1) 2010, pp. 81 et seq.
45. The absence of such explicit authorization for Agreements leads some authors to consider that these Agreements infringe Directive 2009/38/EC. See e.g., Marlene Schmidt, Das Arbeitsrecht der Europäischen Gemeinschaft, Baden-Baden 2001, p. 332. The "Ales-Report" speaks in this context of absence of formal legitimacy: cf. Ales, Engblom, Jaspers, Laulom, Sciarra, Sobczak, Valdés Dal-Ré, Transnational Collective Bargaining—Past, Present and Future, 2006, p. 35.
46. In this sense see e.g., Dagmar Schiek, "Europäische Betriebsvereinbarungen," in: Recht der Arbeit (RdA) 2001, p. 218, at 229; cf. also Reingard Zimmer, "European Works Councils as Participants in Europe-wide Collective Agreements," in: ELLJ 2014, 2013, pp. 313 et seq.
47. For a list of the few existing transnational company agreements dealing with employee data protection issues, see the European Commission's Database on transnational company agreements, available at: http://ec.europa.eu/social/main.jsp?catId=978.
48. The Agreement is available at the Website of the European Commission under: http://ec.europa.eu/employment_social/empl_portal/transnational_agreements/Porr_Dataprotection_EN.pdf.

situations. Furthermore, it guarantees to works councils and the EWC the right to access all employee data that have been stored by the companies belonging to the group. Even though the Agreement does not go far beyond existing national and European data protection law, it recognizes that data processing within a transnational company is a legitimate subject for negotiation between central management and the EWC which makes possible to concretize general terms of data protection law.

Another example is the "Agreement on Pre-employment Screening ('Background Checks')" concluded between General Electric Plastics Europe B.V. and its EWC[49] which determines the conditions under which the company may proceed to a pre-employment screening and mainly limits them to the verification of data that already have been submitted by a candidate and to certain "mandatory checks" for all new hires. Indeed, the GE-Agreement does not comprise specific rules on transfers of employee data in the group. Nonetheless, the Agreement is remarkable since it also shows that employee data protection may be a relevant subject for EFAs.

The main problem for such EFAs on data protection issues is that Agreements between central management of a Community-scale company and an EWC normally only cover the establishments located in the EU Member States and not those in third countries. They therefore normally do not apply to subsidiaries outside the EU. However, Article 6(2)(a) of Directive 2009/38/EC opens the door for a globalization of the geographic scope of EWCs when authorizing the parties to an Agreement establishing an EWC to determine "the undertakings of the Community-scale group of undertakings or the establishments of the Community-scale undertaking which are covered by the agreement."[50] EWCs may theoretically act on a global scale. Nonetheless, it seems that there are only few EWC Agreements that also cover subsidiaries in third countries.

Despite this limited scope of EFAs, they may have however an important impact on employee data protection. As a matter of fact, they may determine the cases in which the company shall be entitled to transfer employee data to subsidiaries or processors in third countries and may concretize, for instance, criteria for the selection of processors which will be processing employee personal data. Thus, it may be clarified by collective agreement, under which conditions employee data on skills, data necessary for the payroll or data on employee surveillance may be transferred to a processor in a third country and which requirements this processor needs to fulfill in order to be "hired" by the company. Moreover, the purpose(s) of the data processing to third countries, the use of cloud computing regarding employee data, the way in which the processing of employee data shall take place or questions of safety of personal data to be respected by the transnational company or by its contractors may be clarified by Agreement between the company's central management and its EWC.

---

49. The Agreement is also available at the Website of the European Commission under: http://ec.europa.eu/employment_social/empl_portal/transnational_agreements/Gepe_pre-employmentscreaning_EN.pdf.
50. For a fuller analysis of this provision and the legal practice cf. Achim Seifert, Global Employee Information and Consultation Procedures in Worldwide Enterprises, in: IJCLLIR (24) 2008, p. 327, at 343 et seq. with further examples.

[B] International Framework Agreements

Transnational Collective bargaining may also take place at a worldwide level. It is well-known that a number of (European) transnational companies or groups of companies have concluded so-called IFAs with Global Union Federations such as the International Metalworkers' Federation (IMF), IndustriALL or UNI Global Union.[51] In most of these IFAs, companies commit to respect minimum labor standards in all their worksites worldwide such as the core labor standards as recognized by the ILO Declaration of Fundamental Principles and Rights at Work of June 1998.[52] Some IFAs go further and also guarantee other labor rights such as the right of workers to a living wage or a minimum protection of health and safety at work. A few of them even go so far to establish a worker representation on a worldwide scale.[53]

As far as can be seen, currently there are no IFAs on employee data protection. Despite this absence, employee data protection in transnational companies is a subject which may be dealt with in IFAs. They may set out rules which concretize such vague terms as "necessary for the performance of a contract" (Article 6(2) GDPR). As has already been pointed out with regard to EFAs,[54] such IFAs may determine, for instance, the purpose(s) of a data processing to third countries, the conditions and the cases in which the transfer of employee data to subsidiaries, processors or other third parties in third countries is allowed, the criteria for the selection of processors. They may also give guidance regarding the conditions under which employee consent in the processing of his or her personal data is freely given and therefore in accordance with Article 7 GDPR. No doubt, we are still very far away from a transnational collective bargaining leading to such collectively agreed concrete data protection rules. Nonetheless, employee data protection may be an area with potential for transnational collective bargaining, which may perhaps enhance the conclusion of IFAs in the future.

If such IFAs fulfill the minimum legal requirements of Article 47 GDPR, it is even thinkable to submit them to the competent supervisory authority for approval as BCRs. Even though the GDPR does not mention the possibility of BCRs for specific contexts of data processing such as the employment context, it is not excluded to adopt specific BCR for this area.

Another field of IFAs could be the establishment of a worldwide recognized certification system for employee data protection. This would request however, that the scope of transnational collective bargaining was not limited to the company level, as it is currently the case with the IFAs, but that also international employers' association would be involved in order to ensure a wider scope of application. It is

---

51. For an overview on these IFAs *see* e.g., Isabelle Daugareilh, La responsabilité sociale des entreprises transnationales et les droits fondamentaux de l'homme au travail: le contre-exemple des accords internationaux, in: *id.* (Ed), Mondialisation, travail et droits fondamentaux, Brussels & Paris 2005, pp. 349 et seq.
52. For an assessment of the 1998 Declaration *see* Servais, International Labour Law, paras. 200 et seq. with further references.
53. For a more in-depth analysis of these Agreements *see* Seifert, IJCLLIR (24) 2008, p. 327, at 343 et seq. with examples.
54. Cf. *supra* §12.04[A] with further references.

obvious that such transnational branch-level agreements which concretize the requirements to be fulfilled for transnational data transfers are still rather utopian: at present, there are not even examples or starting points in favor of such a development.

§12.05 CONCLUDING REMARKS

Employee data protection in transnational companies or groups of companies is a highly relevant subject. On many occasions, personal data of employees are transferred to subsidiaries in other countries. Legal problems are particularly raised by data transfers to subsidiaries located in third countries since in these cases the processing of employee data leaves the harmonized European legal framework of the GDPR and is going to be governed by other (national) rules on data protection.

The recently adopted GDPR, as well as Directive 95/46/EC, provides various legal mechanisms to maintain the core principles of EU data protection law for data subjects when their personal data are transferred to controllers or processors in third countries. The European Commission may recognize the adequacy of data protection in a third country, and transnational companies or groups may adopt BCRs, recognize an approved Code of conduct or may use certified systems. All these mechanisms also apply to employee data transfers to third countries. However, they do not take sufficiently into account the specific employment context. Furthermore, employees or their representatives do not have a voice when companies adopt BCRs or when associations of processors adopt a Code of conduct.

The argument of this chapter is that transnational collective bargaining may fill this gap in employee data protection in transnational companies or groups of companies. In particular, EWCs may negotiate agreements with central management of community-wide operating companies or groups of companies under Directive 2009/38/EC, which provide specific rules for employee data protection when employee data are transferred to controllers or processors in third countries. By this, the general terms of the GDPR such as Article 6(1)(b) GDPR could be concretized and adapted to the needs of the employment context. At present, there are only very few EFAs on employee data protection within transnational companies or groups of companies. Nonetheless, it is a promising field for EWCs activities and should be furthered. As far as IFAs are concerned, there is not even one example for a global company- or group-agreement which addresses questions of employee data protection. Perhaps it is necessary that EWCs take the initiative and negotiate such agreements and thereby incite global unions to discover this increasingly important field for transnational collective bargaining.

PART IV Pathways of Labour Law

CHAPTER 13
Regulating Labour Relations and a Changing Society: The Pathways of a Baltic Country – Estonia

Merle Erikson

§13.01 INTRODUCTION

In the development of Estonia, the last thirty years have been revolutionary – it has restored independence, joined international organizations and is adapting to changes due to technological development. These events have challenged both the entire legal system and labour law. The current constitution of Estonia was adopted and entered into force in 1992. The main legal areas of Estonia, including labour law, have been reformed twice by now.[1]

In addition to other aspects, the restoration of independence in 1991 involved the transition from planned economy to market economy and a reunion or accession to international organizations.[2] In recent decades, the advent of computers and the development of information technology have also had a significant impact on the development of society and law.

Proceeding from the above, during the last thirty years there have been three main challenges facing Estonian labour law: the transition to a market economy, an accession to the EU and the development of technology.[3] The aim of this chapter is to

---

1. The first reforms were carried out quickly after the restoration of independence. The next reforms were implemented due to the need to bring Estonian law in line with EU law and developments in society.
2. For example, Estonia joined the United Nations in 1991 and reunited with the ILO in 1992.
3. Due to the same historical background (the occupation by the Soviet Union), the situation has been similar in other Baltic states – Latvia and Lithuania. It should be emphasized, however, that each country has its specific problems, too. For example, for Lithuanian labour law was a big challenge the economic crisis in 2008–2010, but the same cannot be said about Estonia.

examine which is the meaning and impact of all these changes on the regulation of employment relationships. The study is based on Estonian labour law.

§13.02 TRANSITION TO A MARKET ECONOMY

Estonia was occupied by the Soviet Union for fifty years, from 1940 to 1991.[4] It was characteristic of the Soviet regime that the country's economy and social life were led by the Communist Party. It means that production and provision of services took place on the basis of a plan approved by the party. Also, there was no private ownership, all assets belonged to the state what was the single employer.

As regards trade unions, during the Soviet period, the main goal of their activities was not to protect the interests of employees, but to fulfil the programmes of the Communist Party. For the reason that the employer was a state, there was no other party to a social dialogue. A fight for wages with the state was neither appropriate nor purposeful, as the state and employees represented a common interest – the implementation of the party policy.[5]

In the Soviet Estonia, the Labour Code of the Russian Socialist Federalist Soviet Republic was enforced in 1946. In addition, the labour relations were regulated by hundreds of rules adopted by councils, ministries and agencies on the level of both the Soviet Union and Soviet Estonia. Such a very complicated regulation was simplified by the Labour Code of Estonian Soviet Socialist Republic that was adopted in 1972.[6] Although after the enactment of the new Labour Code the regulation of labour relations relied mainly on one act, this act was still based on the general rules provided by the Soviet Union occupying power.

Under the Labour Code, the employee worked on the basis of an employment contract, but since the relations between the parties to the employment contract were very precisely regulated and bureaucratic, they did not have an opportunity to influence the content of the employment relationship. There was no freedom of contract, and the employment relationship was rather a public law relationship in which the recruitment, termination of employment, the amendment of contract, etc. were formalized by an administrative decree.[7]

---

4. During the Second World War (1941–1944), there was the German occupation in Estonia.
5. M. Muda, *Employee Involvement in Estonia*, in Handbook of Employee Involvement in Europe, eds. M. Weiss and M. Seweryński. Kluwer Law International, 2004, p. 9. The functions of Soviet trade unions were dispersing and comprehensive and changed constantly as the party set new goals. Trade unions were implementing state programmes in various areas, engaged in the promotion of cultural, ideological and sport activities, tourism, solving social security and municipal problems. As the entire social life was run through trade unions, a majority of employees belonged to trade unions during the Soviet period. *Ibid.*
6. The Labour Code entered into force on 1 January 1973.
7. Tööõigus. Loengud/Labour Law. Lectures, ed. M. Muda. Fourth revised edition. Tln: Juura, 2008, p. 26.

Due to political and economic changes,[8] it was planned in Estonia to amend the regulation of labour relations already in the late 1980s. Immediately after the restoration of Estonia's independence in 1991, several new labour law provisions were adopted, while the Labour Code of the Soviet Estonia was abolished.[9] All new Acts were drafted and passed very quickly because the fast-developing market economy required new labour laws. Based on the adopted Acts, it was planned to create a labour code after three to four years.[10]

The Estonian first labour law reform that took place at the beginning of the 1990s was conducted on the basis of three main principles. First of all, to extend the scope of labour law,[11] i.e., labour law was to regulate the employment relationships of all persons who were performing work for an employer under the directions and control of the employer, regardless of the ownership relations in the enterprise or organization. Second, the role of the state in the regulation of employment relationships was to be decreased, and the determination of the rights and obligations of the parties to an employment contract by negotiation via collective agreements and individual employment contracts was to be increased. And third, the regulation of employment relationships by rules and regulations of ministries and agencies was to be eliminated.[12]

Following the aforementioned principles, the regulation of labour relations became much clearer and more relevant and it could be applied in market economy conditions. However, the main concept of regulation was still based on the Soviet labour code. Hence, the rights and obligations of the parties to the employment contract had continually been established precisely, the regulation was casuistic and a great attention was paid to meeting the formal requirements. However, from the author's viewpoint, such approach of lawmakers must be approved because the parties to the employment contract who had not used to the principle of contractual freedom would not have been able to apply very abstract norms.

As can be seen from the principles of the first labour law reform, when the new Acts were drafted, neither international labour law norms nor regulation of other (western) countries were taken into account. Nevertheless, as the regulation of new Acts was based on the soviet labour law, there were no problems concerning the conformity of Estonian labour law to the international labour standards. The Soviet Union was a member of the ILO and had ratified several ILO conventions which were

---

8. In the second half of the 1980s, economic reforms had been launched in the Soviet Union, granting the Soviet Republics much greater freedom of decision in many areas.
9. The most important labour law act that determined the overall approach to labour relations regulation was the Employment Contracts Act. Eesti Vabariigi töölepingu seadus (EVTLS)/Republic of Estonia Employment Contracts Act, passed on 15 April 1992 – RT (*Riigi Teataja*/State Gazette) 1992, 15/16, 241; I 2009, 11, 67. This Act is no longer in force as of 1 July 2009. In addition to the Employment Contracts Act, the Wages Act, the Working and Rest Time Act, the Holidays Act and acts regulating collective labour relations were also adopted.
10. I.-M. Orgo, *Labour Law Reform in Re-independent Estonia*, Juridica International Law Review, University of Tartu, 1996, p. 1.
11. Soviet labour law did not extend to members of collective farms and to several other categories of employees.
12. *Supra* n. 10, at 2.

the basis for the drafting of Soviet laws. Thus, the Estonian new Acts were in line with ILO standards.[13]

As mentioned before, Estonia did not proceed from the law of any western country when drawing up new Acts. The question arises why this was not done, because the regulation of other countries would have gotten the idea how labour relations work in the market economy. In the author's opinion, at the time when new Acts were drafted, the law of other countries was ignored due to two reasons. First, the political and economic situation in Estonia was ambiguous, and directions of the development were not clear. Second, as the new rules were needed quickly, lawmakers were not able to deepen other countries' regulation and take it into account when drafting laws.

It can be concluded that the Estonian first labour law reform took place hurriedly and painlessly. Political and economic changes required rapid decision-making and action. This was a reason why the regulation of labour relations in Estonia was based to a considerable extent on the principles of Soviet labour law. However, the new Acts were sufficiently suited to the market economy principles and were well implemented several years, i.e., during the period when the Estonian society adapted to the new situation.[14]

§13.03 ACCESSION TO THE EU

[A] The Formal Aspects of Transposing the EU Law

Quite quickly, after Estonia regained its independence, Estonia took the direction of joining the EU. The association agreement between Estonia and the European Communities and their Member States (the Europe Agreement) entered into force on 12 June 1995. The Europe Agreement imposed an obligation on Estonia to adjust and harmonize its legislation with the EU, particularly in the spheres of commerce and the economy, and in related spheres, including the protection of employees (Articles 68–69).[15]

The conclusion of the Europe Agreement gave an impetus to transpose employees' protection instruments of the EU into Estonian law. As discussed in the previous section §13.02, the Acts adopted at the beginning of the 1990s were planned to be replaced by a labour code within three to four years. The goal of the prospective second labour law reform was to strengthen the regularity of rules and align them with EU labour law. Over the period of 1996 to 2005, eight draft laws regulating employment contracts were issued, but none of them was passed, as the scope of the reform was far

---

13. Since 1992 Estonia has ratified eighteen ILO conventions and this has not entailed the significant changes in (labour law) Acts.
14. For example, the EVTLS that was adopted in 1992 was valid for seventeen years, although at the time of the adoption of that Act it was planned to replace it with the labour code after three to four years.
15. Euroopa Ühenduste ja nende liikmesriikide ning Eesti Vabariigi vaheline assotsieerumisleping (Euroopa leping)/Association Agreement between the European Communities and their Member States and the Republic of Estonia (Europe Agreement) – RT II 1995, 22–27, 120.

from being clear.[16] According to this, as the date for joining the EU was approaching,[17] there was not enough time to carry out a general labour law reform but the existing Acts were amended in the light of the EU law only.

Hence, in order to transpose EU rules into Estonian law, the general concept of the regulation of labour relations was not changed, but the necessary amendments to the specific acts were made. The most important changes were introduced into the EVTLS. It is remarkable that the bill of the Act Amending the EVTLS that harmonized the Estonian regulation with the EU law proceeded in the *Riigikogu* less than a month.[18] Under the Explanatory Statement of Act Amending the EVTLS, that bill transposed principles of eight directives[19] into Estonian law.[20]

Thus, Estonian labour law was harmonized with European labour law principles very quickly. Also, there was no remarkable discussion concerning the transposition of EU rules in the *Riigikogu*. It seems that the most important aspect for the legislator was to comply with the deadline for the transposition of European law. Also, neither trade unions nor employers initiated the discussion. In the authors' view, the latter's

---

16. Only at the end of 2008, the *Riigikogu* (Estonian Parliament) adopted the new Employment Contracts Act (TLS) that entered into force on 1 July 2009 (Töölepingu seadus/Employment Contracts Act, passed on 17 December 2008 – RT I 2009, 5, 35; 28.11.2017, 2; https://www.riigiteataja.ee/en/eli/518122017004/consolide, accessed 20 December 2017). According to the Explanatory Statement of the Bill of the TLS, the new Act builds on the concept of flexicurity. The goal of the TLS was to provide a legal basis for flexible labour arrangements and carry out the extensive reform of Estonian labour relations. Seletuskiri töölepingu seaduse eelnõu juurde/The Explanatory Statement of the Employment Contracts Act, 18 June 2008, p. 2 (available in Estonian at www.riigikogu.ee; accessed 1 November 2017). The TLS abolished previous Wages Act, Working and Rest Time Act, as well as Holidays Act; and incorporated the corresponding rules into the TLS.
17. Estonia became a member of the EU on 1 May 2004.
18. According to the *Riigikogu* website, the corresponding bill was initiated in the parliament on 6 April 2004 and it was adopted on 22 April 2004. The amendments entered into force on 1 May 2004. Information is available in Estonian at www.riigikogu.ee (accessed 1 November 2017).
19. These directives were: 76/207/EEC (on the implementation of the principle of equal treatment for men and women as regards access to employment, vocational training and promotion, and working conditions – OJ L 39, 14.2.1976, pp. 40–42), 91/533/EEC (on an employer's obligation to inform employees of the conditions applicable to the contract or employment relationship – OJ L 288, 18.10.1991, pp. 32–35), 94/33/EC (on the protection of young people at work – OJ L 216, 20.8.1994, pp. 12–20), 97/81/EC (concerning the Framework Agreement on part-time work concluded by UNICE, CEEP and the ETUC – OJ L 14, 20.1.1998, pp. 9–14), 1999/70/EC (concerning the framework agreement on fixed-term work concluded by ETUC, UNICE and CEEP – OJ L 175, 10.7.1999, pp. 43–48), 2000/43/EC (implementing the principle of equal treatment between persons irrespective of racial or ethnic origin – OJ L 180, 19.7.2000, pp. 22–26), 2000/78/EC (establishing a general framework for equal treatment in employment and occupation – OJ L 303, 2.12.2000, pp. 16–22), 2001/23/EC (on the approximation of the laws of the Member States relating to the safeguarding of employees' rights in the event of transfers of undertakings, businesses or parts of undertakings or businesses – OJ L 82, 22.3.2001, pp. 16–20).
20. Seletuskiri EVTLS muutmise seaduse eelnõu juurde/The Explanatory Statement of the Act Amending the EVTLS, 6 April 2004, pp. 5–9. The author explains that Directive 98/59/EC (on the approximation of the laws of the Member States relating to collective redundancies – OJ L 225, 12.8.1998, pp. 16–21) was transposed into the EVTLS earlier, in 2002. Also, in order to harmonize Estonian law with directive 93/104/EEC (concerning certain aspects of the organization of working time – OJ L 307, 13.12.1993, pp. 18–24), the new Working and Rest Time Act was adopted in 2001.

knowledge of the EU labour law and the time frame for the preparation were too limited in order to launch a debate.

Proceeding from the above, in the author's opinion, the transposition of the EU law was more formal. This is also confirmed by the fact that the harmonization was mostly based on texts of directives – commonly, the legislator explored neither the background information about the EU legal principles nor the EC rulings. Probably the reason for this was a temporal factor because, in a relatively short time, hundreds of EU rules had to be transposed into Estonian law. It must be admitted that Estonian labour law was harmonized with the EU law in somewhat inaccurate and superficial manner. However, there are no significant contradictions between Estonian and the EU law.[21]

[B] The Substantive Issues of the Transposition of the EU Law

[1] General Remarks

As previously discussed,[22] the harmonization of Estonian labour law with EU law was formally easy. Also, the content of most of the principles of European law was understandable to Estonian lawyers and practitioners, i.e., these were to a greater or lesser degree similar to Estonian rules (e.g., rules concerning the protection of young people at work; an employer's obligation to inform employees of the conditions applicable to the employment contract; part-time work; fixed-term work; safeguarding of employees' rights in the event of transfers of undertakings). As a general difference, it can be pointed out that before the transposition of directives, in issues regulated by the EU, Estonian law was not as detailed as the directives provided.[23]

Nevertheless, in the author's opinion, there were and are two areas of the EU law that are alien (relatively unknown) to Estonia. These areas are the equal treatment of employees and the employee involvement.

[2] Equal Treatment of Employees

The EU has paid much attention to the guarantee of the equal treatment of employees. Originally, the focus was on the equal treatment of male and female employees.[24] The

---

21. Certain contradictions were reduced by the new TLS that was passed in 2008.
22. See sec. §13.03[A].
23. See also M. Muda, *Improving Estonian Labour Legislation on Integration with Europe*, Juridica International Law Review, University of Tartu, 1996, pp. 109–139; M. Muda, *Application of International Labour Standards in the Regulation of Employment Relationship in Estonia*, Juridica International Law Review, University of Tartu, II, 1997, pp. 112–118.
24. See, for example, Directives 75/117/EEC (on the approximation of the laws of the Member States relating to the application of the principle of equal pay for men and women – OJ L 45, 19.2.1975, pp. 19–20), 76/207/EEC (on the implementation of the principle of equal treatment for men and women as regards access to employment, vocational training and promotion, and working conditions – OJ L 39, 14.2.1976, pp. 40–42), etc. For the present, these directives have been replaced by Directive 2006/54/EC (on the implementation of the principle of equal opportunities and equal treatment of men and women in matters of employment and occupation (recast) – OJ L 204, 26.7.2006, pp. 23–36).

Charter of Fundamental Rights of the EU also emphasizes the equality between women and men in employment relationships.[25] In 2000, the EU adopted rules that prohibit discrimination on other grounds – religion, belief, disability, age, sexual orientation and racial or ethnic origin.[26]

Although before joining the EU several international acts prohibiting discrimination were binding on Estonia,[27] the implementation of the principle of equal treatment was not ensured in practice. The greatest difference existed in the treatment of male and female employees, especially regarding the remuneration for work.[28]

Before accession to the EU, the prohibition of discrimination was not an important issue in Estonian law. No special acts to this effect had been adopted. The general principle of equal treatment was provided for in the Constitution;[29] the application of this principle had also been set forth in the EVTLS and the Wages Act.[30] It must be admitted that the regulation of the issues related to the prohibition against discrimination was insufficient – the corresponding provisions were general and declarative and did not guarantee adequate protection for people.[31] From the author's viewpoint, although the principle of equal treatment of employees was recognized in Estonia already before joining the EU, it was considered a theoretical concept that was not implemented in practice.

In order to comply with the requirements of the EU law and introduce the mentalities and rules of conduct of the contemporary society, in the 2000s, Estonia adopted two specific acts – the Gender Equality Act[32] and the Equal Treatment Act.[33]

---

25. Charter of Fundamental Rights of the European Union – OJ C 326, 26.10.2012, pp. 391–407, Art. 23.
26. Directives 2000/43/EC (implementing the principle of equal treatment between persons irrespective of racial or ethnic origin – OJ L 180, 19.7.2000, pp. 22–26) and 2000/78/EC (establishing a general framework for equal treatment in employment and occupation – OJ L 303, 2.12.2000, pp. 16–22).
27. For example, the United Nations Convention on the Elimination of All Forms of Discrimination Against Women (1979), the United Nations International Covenant on Economic, Social and Cultural Rights (1966), the European Social Charter adopted by the Council of Europe (1961), Convention No. 100 of the ILO concerning Equal Remuneration for Men and Women Workers for Work of Equal Value (1951).
28. Even now, when Estonia has been a member of the EU for over thirteen years, according to the statistics, women's wages are 21% lower than men's wages. The gender pay gap decreased for the third year in a row. Statistics Estonia, 28 April 2017 – News Release No. 45 (http://www.stat.ee/news-release-2017-045; accessed 1 November 2017).
29. According to § 12 (1) of the Constitution, no one shall be discriminated against on the basis of nationality, race, colour, sex, language, origin, religion, political or other opinion, property or social status, or on other grounds. Eesti Vabariigi põhiseadus/The Constitution of the Republic of Estonia, passed on 28 June 1992 – RT 1992, 26, 349; 15.05.2015, 1 (https://www.riigiteataja.ee/en/eli/521052015001/consolide; accessed 20 December 2017).
30. Palgaseadus/Wages Act, passed on 26 January 1994 – RT I 1994, 11, 154; 2008, 56, 315. This Act is no longer in force as of 1 July 2009.
31. *See also* M. Muda, *Prohibition of Discrimination in Labour Relations*, Juridica International Law Review, University of Tartu, IV, 1999, pp. 189–199.
32. Soolise võrdõiguslikkuse seadus/Gender Equality Act, passed on 7 April 2004 – RT I 2004, 27, 181; 07.07.2015, 1 (https://www.riigiteataja.ee/en/eli/521012016001/consolide; accessed 1 November 2017).
33. Võrdse kohtlemise seadus/Equal Treatment Act, passed on 11 December 2008 – RT I 2008, 56, 315; 26.04.2017, 6 (https://www.riigiteataja.ee/en/eli/503052017002/consolide; accessed 1 November 2017).

Notwithstanding that these Acts prohibit discrimination on any basis and establish an exhaustive regulation on the promotion of the principle of equal treatment, the application of that principle is still problematic in Estonia. It is common knowledge that equal treatment is not guaranteed and people do not claim their rights in courts.[34]

In the author's opinion, failure to implement the principle of equal treatment derives to a greater extent from the habits and stereotypes evolved in society and from the lack of awareness and interest and a relatively low quality of life. In Estonia, people began to pay attention to the principle of equal treatment only before accession to the EU. A large number of people are not aware of and/or interested in the problems accompanying equal treatment and creation of equal opportunities. Also, the fear of losing their earnings has made people work at any conditions whatsoever.

Probably, the problems related to discrimination may arise after several years when a certain level of stability has been achieved in the economy and on the labour market, and people start to consider ensuring an increasingly better quality of life.[35] However, the Gender Equality Act and the Equal Treatment Act are still important direction indicators in the Estonian legal system drawing people's attention to and increasing their awareness of the issues related to equal treatment.

[3] Employee Involvement

Employees' influence on decisions to be taken within the company has constantly been increased in Europe. According to several directives,[36] if an employer wants to make decisions that may affect employees, he must inform and consult them before.[37] The rules of these acts base on long traditions of communication that have existed between social partners in the old Member States.

In Estonia, the importance of employees has not been remarkable in shaping employment and social relations. This is particularly due to the historical development of the representative organizations of employees. The first traditional trade unions emerged in Estonia by the 1930s, but their activities were terminated by Estonia's occupation by the Soviet Union in 1940. As previously discussed,[38] the objective of the

---

34. Disputes can also be prevented by the fact that, according to the existing practice, it is not easy to prove that discrimination has occurred in the employment relationship.
35. *See also* M. Muda. *Regulation of Gender Equality as a Fundamental Right in Estonia*, Juridica International Law Review, University of Tartu, VII, 2002, p. 166; *supra* n. 31, at 197.
36. For example, Directives 89/391/EEC (on the introduction of measures to encourage improvements in the safety and health of workers at work – OJ L 183, 29.6.1989, pp. 1–8), 98/59/EC (on the approximation of the laws of the Member States relating to collective redundancies – OJ L 225, 12.8.1998, pp. 16–21), 2001/23/EC (on the approximation of the laws of the Member States relating to the safeguarding of employees' rights in the event of transfers of undertakings, businesses or parts of undertakings or businesses – OJ L 82, 22.3.2001, pp. 16–20), 2002/14/EC (establishing a general framework for informing and consulting employees in the European Community – OJ L 80, 23.3.2002, pp. 29–34), etc.
37. Some recent directives, for example Directive 2001/86/EC (supplementing the Statute for a European company with regard to the involvement of employees – OJ L 294, 10.11.2001, pp. 22–32), establish that, in addition to information and consultation, the involvement of employees includes also participation.
38. *See* sec. §13.02.

trade unions that operated during the Soviet period was not to advocate the rights and interests of employees but to implement the policies of the Communist Party. The restoration of traditional trade unions in Estonia began only in the 1990s and, thus, employees have had an opportunity to participate in the organization of employment affairs only for about the last twenty-five years.[39]

As no particular common law had developed in the area of collective labour relations at the beginning of the 1990s, it was decided to regulate the relations of social partners by law. As of now, several legal acts have been passed that set out the general principles regarding trade unions, employees' trustees, collective agreements and the settlement of collective labour disputes.[40]

Before accession to the EU, the concept of employee involvement was an unfamiliar phenomenon in the Estonian legal order. The entirety of the respective regulation thus rests on EU directives that are correctly transposed into national law, creating a sufficient and appropriate legal basis for employee involvement in enterprise-related decisions.[41]

Although Estonian law provides for a broader competence of the representatives of employees[42] in employment relations, the implementation of these rules is problematic. In practice, informing and consulting of employees is not common. From the author's viewpoint, there are two main causes for that. As previously explained, due to historical reasons, Estonian employees' representatives – mainly trade unions – do not play an important role in shaping employment relationships. Trade union density is low, and their influence in society is small.[43] No employees' representatives[44] have been elected in a great many organizations. But just the existence of strong trade unions ensures the development of collective labour relations, including the successful involvement of employees.

---

39. *Supra* n. 5, at 7–11.
40. Ametiühingute seadus/Trade Unions Act, passed on 14 June 2000 – RT I 2000, 57, 372; 28.04.2017, 1 (https://www.riigiteataja.ee/en/eli/505052017003/consolide; accessed 1 November 2017); töötajate usaldusisiku seadus/Employees' Trustee Act, passed on 13 December 2006 – RT I 2007, 2, 6; 28.04.2017, 1 (https://www.riigiteataja.ee/en/eli/505052017006/consolide; accessed 1 November 2017); kollektiivlepingu seadus/Collective Agreements Act, passed on 14 April 1993 – RT I 1993, 20, 353; 28.04.2017, 1 (https://www.riigiteataja.ee/en/eli/505052017005/consolide; accessed 1 November 2017); kollektiivse töötüli lahendamise seadus/Collective Labour Dispute Resolution Act, passed on 5 May 1993 – RT I 1993, 26, 442; 04.07.2017, 1 (https://www.riigiteataja.ee/en/eli/ee/502112017001/consolide; accessed 20 December 2017). In practice, the relations between employers and employees are quite rarely specified in collective agreements. Only 19% of Estonian employees are covered by a collective agreement. L. Kaldmäe, *'Kollektiivsed töösuhted'*/'Collective Employment Relations' in L. Kaldmäe (ed), *Eesti tööelu-uuring 2015/Estonian Work Life Survey 2015* (Series of the Ministry of Social Affairs 2017/1), p. 78.
41. In employee involvement issues, one of the most important act is the Employees' Trustee Act that transposes Directive 2002/14/EC (establishing a general framework for informing and consulting employees in the European Community – OJ L 80, 23.3.2002, pp. 29–34) into Estonian law.
42. In Estonia, employees participate in collective labour relations via trade unions and employees' trustees who are elected by the general meeting of employees.
43. In 2015, only 4.5% of employees belonged to trade unions and these organizations were active in 6% of entities. L. Kaldmäe, *Supra* n. 40, at 65 and 69.
44. Both representatives of trade union (shop stewards) and employees' trustees.

Even more, informing and consulting does not actually take place in all the organizations where employees' representatives exist. Often the trade union has few members and/or they are incompetent in co-deciding on matters concerning employment relationships and the labour market and the employer's economic activity.[45] As the informing and consulting of employees is a relatively new area in Estonian employment relationships and requires additional knowledge, skills and experiences on the part of the employees' representatives as well as employers, it will probably take years for a constructive dialogue to develop between employees and employers.[46] A prerequisite for this scenario is still the presence of strong employees' representatives which is difficult to anticipate in view of current developments.[47]

§13.04 THE DEVELOPMENT OF TECHNOLOGY

At present, like in many other countries, so in Estonia, the existing nature of employment relationships is influenced by the technological development, especially digitalization. These new trends are changing both the content of work and the organization of work. Working with digital means and using the corresponding opportunities is becoming more and more commonplace. It is quite usual that work is done wherever and whenever,[48] and the service provider and the user of the service meet through an online platform.[49] However, it is not clear which is the nature of respective legal relationship and what guarantees must be guaranteed to the worker. Regulation of this new situation is the current greatest challenge facing labour law.

Since 2016, the need for the new labour law reform has been discussed in Estonia. The key issue of the debate is the impact of new (digital) technologies on the regulation of employment relations. Trade unions are worried about the fact that many persons whose work is organized in a new way (e.g., platform workers, including workbiters',[50] workers whose working time is undetermined) are excluded from the scope of labour law.[51] Employers consider that the regulation of employment relationships (e.g., concerning fixed-term contracts and working time) is too rigid and does not allow

---

45. The situation is better in large-scale industrial undertakings where strong trade union traditions have survived since the Soviet period. *Supra* n. 5, at 19.
46. *See also* M. Muda, *The Impact of European Union Law on Employee Involvement in Estonia*, Juridica International Law Review, University of Tartu, XV, 2008, p. 34.
47. According to the statistics, the number of trade union members is continuously decreasing in Estonia. L. Kaldmäe *Supra* n. 40, at 66.
48. About ICT-based mobile work *see*, for example *New forms of employment*. European Foundation for the Improvement of Living and Working Conditions. Luxembourg: Publications Office of the European Union, 2015, pp. 72–81.
49. About the main features of on-demand workers *see*, for example, V. De Stefano, *The Rise of the 'Just-in-Time Workforce': On-Demand Work, Crowdwork, and Labor Protection in the 'Gig Economy'*, Comparative Labor Law & Policy Journal, 37, Issue 3, 2016.
50. Workbiters' are workers who perform several kinds of work obligations contacting the work provider through an online platform (*see*, for example, https://goworkabit.com/).
51. This information is based on the debates that were carried out in the framework of study about the future of work in Estonia (Tuleviku töö – uued suunad ja lahendused. Lõpparuanne/The Future of Work – New Trends and Solutions. Final Report. Technopolis group and the Centre for Applied Social Sciences of the University of Tartu, 2017. Available in Estonian at http://www.

new forms of employment to be introduced. They are also of the opinion that the current rules do not take into account changed work-related attitudes, desires and needs of new generations.[52]

Thus, employees and employers are waiting for the state to amend the existing regulation of employment relations. In spring 2017, the Ministry of Social Affairs and the Republic of Estonia Government Office commissioned the study about future of work[53] aimed at gaining input on how labour legislation could be changed. However, that analysis did not provide a clear idea of how the current Acts should be amended but rather raised new questions about how to approach problems, for example, whether and how to extend the scope of labour law, create a third category of workers, make the regulation of labour relations more flexible. These questions are fundamental, but Estonian authorities do not have yet an explicit concept how to move forward.[54]

In the author's opinion, although in a small and innovative country like Estonia it is relatively easy to enforce great changes, the implementation of the third labour law reform is most complicated. When previous reforms were carried out, it was possible to build on existing examples, i.e., to modify the Soviet labour law or transpose EU rules, but now, there are no patterns that can be used in order to change the regulation, because other countries also face the same challenges as Estonia. However, it is clear that the current situation cannot last because it hinders the development of economic and employment relations.

§13.05 CONCLUDING REMARKS

The last thirty years have been meaningful for the Estonian state and the legal system. The main challenges facing Estonian labour law during recent decades have been the transition to a market economy, joining the EU, and the development of technology, above all digitalization.

As regards the transition to a market economy, the corresponding labour law reform took place rapidly and painlessly. Political and economic changes required prompt decision-making and action and, thus, the principles of Soviet labour law that were previously in force were largely adapted to market economy rules.

---

sm.ee/sites/default/files/content-editors/Ministeerium_kontaktid/Uuringu_ja_analuusid/Too valdkond/tuleviku_too_-_uued_suunad_ja_lahendused_l6pparuanne.pdf (accessed 1 November 2017).
52. *See* the position of operators (employers), for example, Konkurentsivõime 2.0. Raport Eesti ärikeskkonna konkurentsivõime kasvatamiseks tehtud ettepanekutest/Competitiveness 2.0. Report about proposals made in order to increase the competitiveness of the Estonian business environment. Estonian Ministry of Justice, 2016. Available in Estonian at https://www.just.ee/et/konkurentsivoime-20 (accessed 1 November 2017).
53. *Supra* n. 51. The goal of that study was to find out which new forms of work are used in other countries, which is the corresponding regulation and whether the rules of other countries can be transposed into Estonian law. The study focused on the following forms of work: ICT-based mobile work, employee sharing, intermittent work, on-call work, crowdwork and work on demand via app or internet.
54. At present, it is known that the Ministry of Social Affairs is compiling the document about the future development of labour legislation that will be completed in March 2018.

The accession to the EU did also not cause fundamental changes in the regulation of employment relations but it entailed the emergence of new topics, like the equal treatment of employees and the employee involvement. Estonian society still needs time to adapt to these new concepts.

The biggest challenge facing Estonian labour law has been the technological development that has changed the content of work and the organization of work to a considerable extent. Dealing with this challenge is the most difficult, because other countries are also addressing the same problems and there are no good examples how to reform labour law.

CHAPTER 14
Main Directions of Change in French Industrial Relations and Labor Law

Jacques Rojot

§14.01 INTRODUCTION

The reform of the labor code of September 2017 is taking place within an industrial relations framework characterized by two main features: remaining permanent traits of the French Industrial scene, and, at the same time important changes within that element of continuity.

- A. The permanent traits are well known and illustrated by the graphs in Figures 14.1 to Figure 14.3: a very weak organization rate, the weakest among OECD countries, continuously decreasing since World War II and a deeply divided labor movement, mainly along ideological lines, resulting in increased competition within a declining market share, and for large parts of the labor movement, radical ideologies or behavior.

Figure 14.1   A Weak Rate of Organization

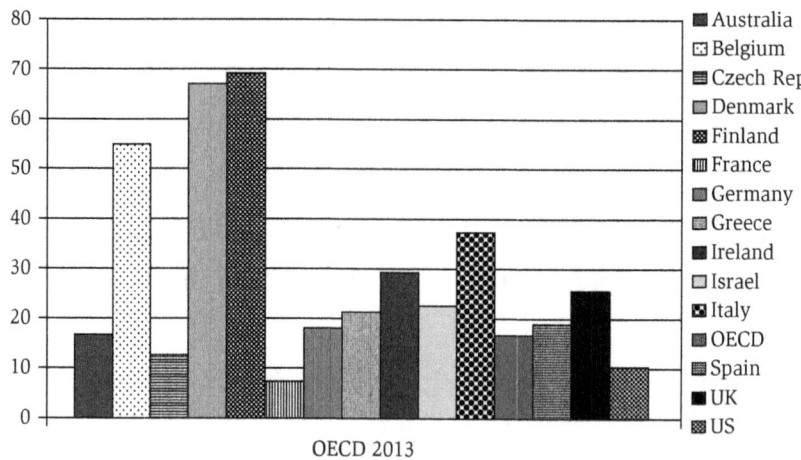

OECD 2013

Figure 14.2   Consistently Weakening

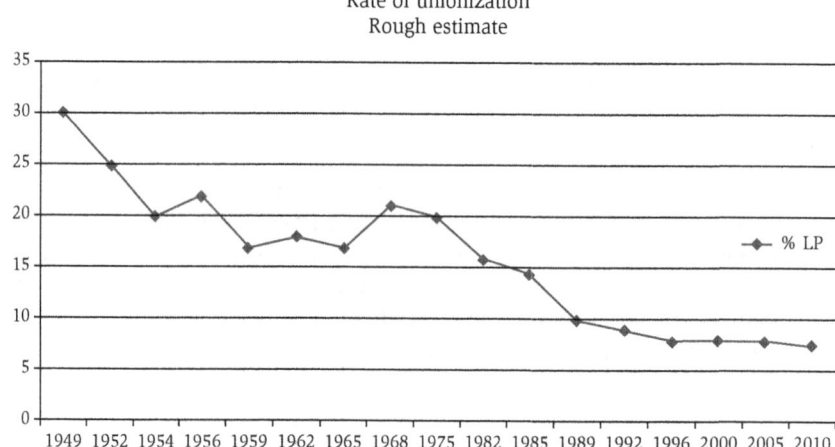

Source: DARES.

Figure 14.3 A Deeply Divided Labor Movement: Elections of Employee Representatives 2017 – All Voters

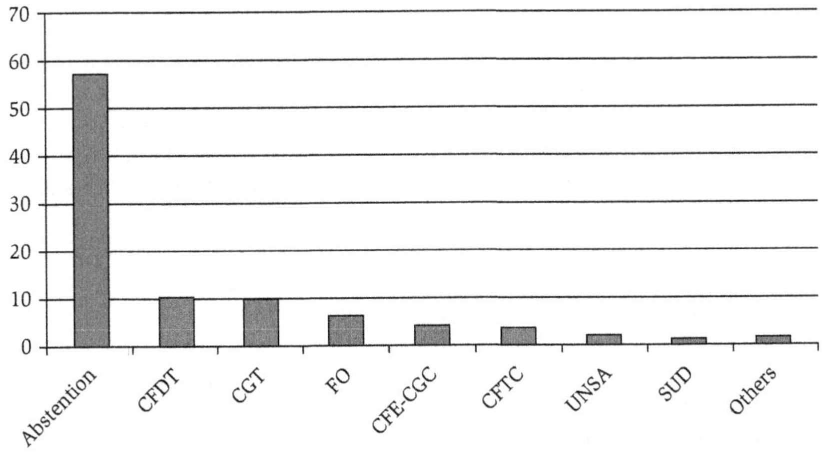

[Bar chart showing percentages of voters: Abstention ~57%, CFDT ~10%, CGT ~10%, FO ~7%, CFE-CGC ~5%, CFTC ~4%, UNSA ~3%, SUD ~2%, Others ~2%]

Source: DARES— % of voters.

B. Within these more or less permanent features, two important changes occurred recently: on the one hand, the system of unions representativeness was deeply overhauled, and on the other hand, the relative ranking of the two main unions in the private sector was upset.

Traditionally, any industry or local union affiliated with the five national union federations listed by an administrative decree was presumed to be representative, and thus able to sign collective agreements, without the possibility of evidence to the contrary. This presumption of representativeness is now suppressed since the application of an Act of 2008 following a negotiation between union federations and employer's associations. It used to be that only a representative union could enjoy the full (but by no means exclusive) rights of representativeness including the negotiation of a collective agreement and a union was either representative or not. The new system establishes three categories of unions by distinguishing two categories and levels among the criteria of representativeness. The unions which do not fulfill the conditions of respect of republican values, independence, financial transparency, a seniority of at least two years are denied any kind of representativeness. They are not considered true unions. Unions which fulfill the conditions are considered bona fide legitimate unions. They enjoy the right to be present on the shop floor in any enterprise, to establish a union section and to appoint a representative of this section as well as a representative to the works council and to sponsor lists of candidates to the elections of employee representatives. However, they cannot appoint a union delegate in order to conduct negotiations and the conclusion of collective agreements. In order to be fully representative, with all the negotiating prerogatives, bona fide unions must also fulfill three additional conditions of representativeness: audience established according to the level of negotiation concerned, meaning that they have achieved a sufficient number of votes in the elections of employee representatives, influence, mainly characterized by the activity and the experience, and the size of membership and dues paid by members. The key to full representativeness and bargaining rights is the audience resulting from the votes of employees in the elections of employee representatives. At the level of the enterprise or establishment, it is set at 10% of the vote in the first ballot of the election of employee representatives. At industry and/or sectoral level, are required a balanced implementation of the union within the sector and 8% of the vote (aggregated by the Ministry of Labour every four years. At national, inter-occupational level, the same principles of balanced implementation in construction, industry and services and the same cutoff point of 8% apply.

Very interestingly, at national level, the results of elections were strikingly similar to the results obtained under the former system (Figure 14.4). At the inter-occupational national level, only five union federations reached the cutoff level of 8% of the vote. They exactly were the same as those holding representativeness under the former system of representativeness by full rights. However, if they had been submitted at the national level to the same enterprise-level cutoff point of 10% of the vote, only three of them would have achieved their former status of national representativeness. In this way, a "gift" was granted to the weaker formerly national unions' representative by rights.

Figure 14.4 Initially Little Change at National Level: Comparison of the Votes Obtained in 2006 to the Election to the Works Councils and the Votes Obtained in 2013 under the New System

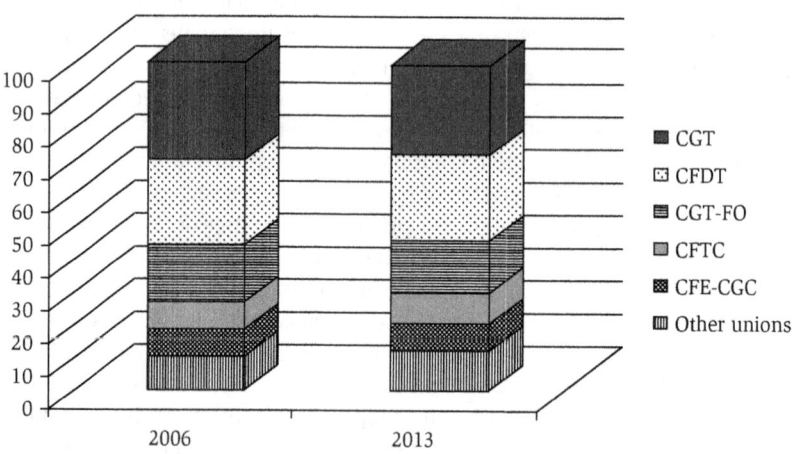

Source: DARES.

However, things were radically different at other levels since national inter-occupational representativeness no longer carries over at industry/sectoral, local or enterprise level, but must be demonstrated by elections results. At sectoral industry level, if the two main unions kept their representativeness in 90% of the sectors (but lost it in respectively 8% and 12%), the weaker ones remained representative only at about one-half and one-third of the sectors. It is even more striking at enterprise and plant level. Many union federations which did not reach the 10% cutoff level thus disappeared locally and lost any control of or presence in employee representative institutions. This constitutes in fact a premium for additional union fragmentation, in an already very divided general picture. It provides also for increased inter-union competition, already bitter, in elections to the employee representative institutions (Figure 14.5). Besides, in multiplant a union can be represented at enterprise level, but not at plant level (or vice versa).

A second very noticeable change was the shift in the balance of power between the two leading union federations. The CFDT passed over the CGT in national representativeness in the private sector.

The shift may appear as small in terms of the percentage of votes, but it is symbolically important. It is the first time since 1895 that the CGT is not the leading union federation in the private sector, even though it remains so in the public sector.

It should be underlined at that opportunity, that most of the public sectors including the civil servants are not concerned by the ordinances, their employment not being regulated under the labor code which, roughly speaking concerns only the private sector. Thus almost 25% of the French workforce is not concerned.

Figure 14.5 Elections of Employee Representatives

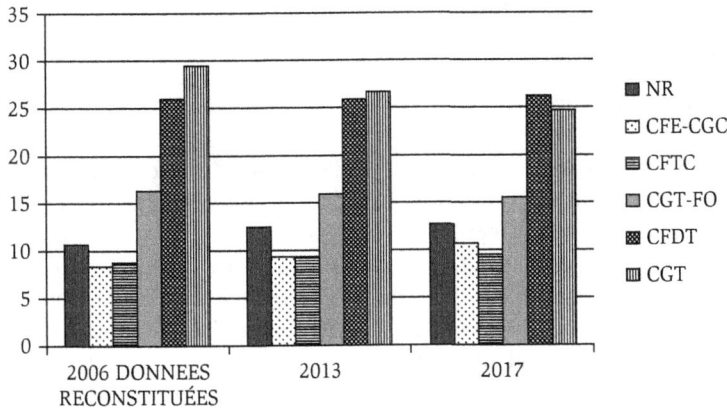

Source: DARES—% of Votes Expressed.

To complete this introduction, it should be noted that the ordinances draw only the general framework for the reforms of the labor code and consequently, and hopefully from the point of view of the government, the reform of the labor market.

On the one hand, the ordinances are to be followed, like all statutes, by decrees of application, taken by the executive branch and dealing with complements and provisions for concrete application to the field. The decrees are to be the object of intense informal negotiations by the Government with the unions and employers representatives, even though, legally they are of the sole competence of the executive branch. They are likely to deeply influence the contents and application of the ordinances (Saint Thomas is alleged to have said that God, or the Devil, is in the details).

On the other hand, some provisions of the ordinances are already or are going to be challenged in national administrative and constitutional courts as well as in international jurisdictions and institutions (notably the ECJ and the ILO)

Finally, the procedure of the ordinances to be briefly described immediately below is subject to a ratification by a vote of Parliament, after a debate, where changes may be introduced by either members of the Parliament or the Government.

Consequently, we can offer below only a very tentative and sketchy description of only the major changes, drawn as they stand at this time and subject to many changes.

It should be added that within the limited space allowed, every effort has been made to keep the explanations as clear and simple as possible. For instances, no specific references to scientific works or theoretical debates have been provided in order to keep the developments as linear as possible, and a brief description of the legal framework within with the provisions of the ordinances take place has been attempted in places. However, a more complete, if even still quite sketchy, description of French industrial relations and labor law recently provided in English reaches 400 pages in length. Therefore a knowledge of, or reference to, existing French labor law and industrial relations will be useful to the reader.

§14.02 THE PROCESS

[A] The Ordinances

The process chosen to reform the Labor code is one of the ordinances. They are provided for in certain circumstances by the Constitution: Parliament gives the executive branch the power to legislate on matters that the constitution normally keeps specifically within the domain granted to Parliament by statutory law (a summa division of the constitution of the Vth republic). Here section 38 of the Constitution is used, the reason is urgency. However, Parliament must first authorize their use and keeps a final right of approval and validation of the ordinances, in a vote still to take place.

This process does not stand as an exception; ordinances under section 38 have been used by the Government many times in the past. They have the legal standing of statutory law, once promulgated.

[B] The Ordinances Constitute Step One in a Series of Important Subjects

They are to be followed by the foreseen and announced radical reforms and complete overhaul of the systems of unemployment compensation, vocational training and pensions.

Unions play an important role in the management of the national systems dealing with these three other domains. Besides, they involve huge amounts of money. EUR 32 billion per year for vocational training alone, out of which are drawn important contributions to the resources of union centers for the role that they play in the management of the relevant system. This may help to explain their relative moderation in the opposition to the ordinances.

[C] An Innovative Consultative Process

Section L1 of the labor code provides that the social partners are to be preliminary consulted (concertation) by the Government before that a reform in the domain of Labor relations (widely understood) be undertaken. However, the consultative process took an innovative form.

It occurred at several levels (President, Prime Minister, Minister for Labor) and was carried out on a one-to-one basis with all of the social partners but separately for each one, several times, in a first preliminary phase

Prior to decision making, it was in a second step followed by furthermore traditional consultations on the text arrived to by the Government after the one-to-one consultation.

§14.03 A POINT OF CONTROVERSY

It has been alleged, from various quarters, that several provisions of the ordinances, giving precedence to the contents of the agreements negotiated at plant level over agreements negotiated at sectoral (branch) level constituted a "reversal of the principles" (inversion des norms) of the sources of law.

This is simply completely inaccurate. The sources of law in France remain fully undisturbed: Constitution, International Treaties, Statutory Law, Decrees.

The legal concept concerned is the "principle of favor" specific to Labor Law. It organizes the relationships between different levels of provisions applicable to situations of labor employment: statutes, Decrees, Collective agreements (at different levels) and the all-important individual contract of employment. Roughly stated, it establishes that negotiation at whatever level could only add benefits and protections for the employee to what existed at the higher level, starting with statutory law.

First, this principle of favor does not have constitutional value and is not considered as a fundamental principle of the Republic, recognized by the preamble of the constitutions of 1946 and 1958. Even if it is considered as a fundamental principle of labor law, statutory law always keeps the power to introduce dispensations and departures from it.

Second, the principle of favor cannot be applied in the area of absolute public policy (ordre public absolu). Provisions more favorable to the employee cannot contradict provisions relative to that domain (of course less favorable provisions are in any case excluded). Such would be the case for instance for provisions regarding the competence of the courts, employment for life, wage indexation on the legally fixed minimum wage, rest in lieu of pay for Labor Day on May first and the like.

Third, the principle of favor remains undisturbed as ever as it concerns the individual contract of employment. The latter cannot, in any circumstances, go against statutory Law or Collective Agreements at whatever levels when it is concluded.

Fourth, exceptions to the principle of favor have for a very long time been provided for in the area of working time, notably within the Acts on the thirty-five hours week of work.

In summary, exceptions to the principle of favor are provided for by the ordinances, as it will be described below, notably in between collective agreements at different levels. However, this was already the case, in some areas and under certain circumstances increasingly so since 1999, by various statutory Acts and in no way constitutes an "inversion of the order of the legal norms."

§14.04 OUTLINE OF THE CONTENTS OF THE REFORM

The five ordinances follow in the wake of preceding Acts, notably in 2015 and 2016 but go much farther. They were promulgated with little opposition other than vocal and among relatively unsuccessful demonstrations called by some of the union federations, but not all of them, and political parties of the extreme left. They indeed go much further than the Act of 2016 called "loi travail", which caused a vast amount of protest and social unrest, violent demonstrations and strikes blocking the country for several days.

They probably represent a major reform of French Labor Law, the first one since a long time.

The main motivation behind the reform as outlined by the prime minister is to bring more flexibility in labor relations in order to increase employment. The goal is to adapt labor law to a new state of things, marked by the diversity of enterprises, sectors of the economy, expectations and careers of the employees.

Three special points have been singled out:

(1) A particular focus on small and medium enterprises (about 50% of French wage earners).
(2) A strong incentive towards collective bargaining.
(3) An objective of simplification.

The complete elements of the reform are too numerous, complex, detailed and encompassing to be fully described here. As indicated above, it will be possible only to give a general description of the most relevant points.

The five ordinances are presented as covering three main blocks of objectives:

(1) A new articulation of the norms of collective bargaining in between statutes, sectors and enterprises.
(2) A renewed social and economic dialog between the social partners.
(3) A promotion of more secure employment relationships.

Practically, they were applicable as soon as they were published, at the end of September, at least for the provisions where a decree of application is not needed. In the unlikely case that the vote of Parliament, necessary and still to take place, rejects their approval, given the government's majority in Parliament, they would cease to be applicable.

[A]   **Collective Bargaining**

It might maybe be argued that it is the first time that Government takes collective bargaining seriously as a general policy. Indeed in the past, many attempts had been tried to promote collective bargaining over the traditional primacy of statutory law in France. However, either they never reached that level, were limited to the specific field of working time or they were implemented half-heartedly in some cases. For instance, the Act on the modernization of the social dialogue of 2007 had made it mandatory for the Government to consult the social partners before proposing to Parliament a new statute in the field of Labor Law and Industrial relations. The following year, in 2008, this was simply forgotten before having Parliament vote a new statute promoting exceptions to the thirty-five hours workweek. Notably, however, since 2004, several acts tried to promote the negotiation of collective agreements. However, their results remained modest. The statistics gathered by the Ministry of Labor (DARES) tend to show that except for peaks for a specific reason (compulsion to negotiate working time agreements, for instance) the number of enterprise level collective agreements remains stable, is mostly constituted of agreements related to wage negotiations and has increased only modestly over a long period.

Now, with the ordinances, the promotion of collective bargaining has presently reached a level unknown heretofore. Several all-important changes are introduced to that order, described below:

(a) A new equilibrium is introduced between sectoral and enterprise level collective agreements
Three categories of topics for bargaining are established. A first category concerns the topics mandatorily bargained at sector level. They include notably the hierarchy of minimum wages, job categorizations, mutualization of funds for vocational training, mutualization of funds for financing joint

action by the social partners, collective complementary health benefits, occupational equality between women and men.

A second category concerns the topics for which the sector can decide to preempt agreements at enterprise level. They include exposure to occupational hazards and risks, employment of handicapped employees, levels of employment at which union delegates should be appointed, bonuses for unhealthy and dangerous work.

For the above two categories sector-level agreements prevail over enterprise level agreements, unless the latter are more favorable to employees.

The third category concerns all other topics and they may bargained for at enterprise level where the agreement when reached prevails over sector-level agreements.

It should be underlined that statutory law prevails over all agreements, of course on matters of absolute public policy and in other areas unless the law itself opens the way to derogatory collective agreements, as has been the case for a long time for working time. In the latter case, statutory law becomes suppletive.

(b) A collective agreement may now determine for a maximum duration of four years the periodicity and contents of the legally compulsory negotiations on mandatory topics, instead of a calendar and order of topics mandated by Statute. Compulsory negotiations include forward-looking management of employment and competences, wages, organization of work, working time, occupational equality between men and women, collective complementary health benefits, employment of handicapped employees.

(c) Majority collective agreements are generalized. In the past, initially, a collective agreement once signed by a single representative union was applicable without any problem of representativeness. Majority collective agreements were introduced since 2008. Now, as already foreseen by the Act "Travail" of 2016 on working time, the generalization beyond working time is brought forward to May instead of September 2018.

Majority collective agreements will thus be the rule for the future. They will have to be signed compulsorily by unions representing more than 50% of employees. Heretofore, collective agreements signed by unions representing 30% of the employees could be applicable if no opposition was raised by unions representing 50% of them. Now the minority agreements signed by unions representing 30% of the employees can be ratified by a referendum of the employees, the organization of which can be initiated by the employer, barring the opposition of unions representing over 50% of the employees. Again it should be underlined that union representativeness to that purpose is decided not on membership but by the votes for the elections of employee representatives.

(d) The four existing kinds of specific collective agreements dealing with safeguard of employment, stability of employment, reduction of working time and internal mobility of employees in the enterprise are unified.

Employees who disagree and do not accept the conditions set up by such a new collective agreement can be dismissed and the dismissal considered for cause, with the relevant procedure to be followed and provisions in favor of the employee applying. An additional 100 hours of training will be financed by the employer in that case.

If signed by unions representing only 30% of employees, the agreements may be submitted to a referendum by the employer and ratified with the majority of the votes by employees.

(e) New areas, formerly covered by statutory law, are opened to collective bargaining, possibly "in pejus" and not only "in melius." In case where no agreement is signed, statutory law applies in a suppletive way:
  - By majority collective agreements, bonuses and allowances may be negotiated at enterprise level (unless they are integrated into the industry level minimum wages agreements or concern certain specific domains, negotiated at sector level.)
  - By industry level collective agreements, it will become possible to modify the duration and conditions of renewal of short-term contract of employments, now established by law only.
  - Besides such agreements, the contract for the duration of a given task, now restricted to the construction industry, for a given building job, may be generalized also by industry level collective agreements, foreseen by the Act of 2016, is now brought forward to May 2018 instead of September.

(f) A presumption of compliance with the Law is created to the benefit of collective agreements. It will be up to the party challenging the legitimacy of the agreement to bring the proof of the unlawfulness of the contents of the agreement, its conditions of validity or the process of negotiating it.

Besides, the delay for challenging judicially a collective agreement is limited to two months.

Finally, in cases when a court declares a collective agreement null and void, the judge is granted the possibility to limit the effects of the decision for the future only, taking in account the consequences over past situations.

[B] Collective Bargaining and Social Dialogue in SMEs

The government takes in stock two facts: the extremely low, if not non-existing rate of organization in SMEs with the presence of union representatives in only 4% of enterprises employing between eleven and fifty employees and the relative failure of the earlier provisions regarding the negotiation with an employee appointed by a union, attempted in earlier Acts. With the goal to give very small, and small and medium enterprises the same right and access to collective bargaining than the large ones, the following provisions are enacted:

(a) Very small enterprises, below eleven employees, are under no legal obligation to proceed to the election of employee representatives. In such enterprises, from now on, the employer will be able to have recourse to a referendum on a project of collective agreement which may cover all themes opened to negotiation at enterprise level. To be applicable, the project of agreement must be approved by a majority of the two-thirds of the employees.

The same provisions apply to enterprises between eleven and twenty employees where no employee representative has been elected.

In enterprises employing between eleven and fifty employees where an employee representative has been elected, the employer may negotiate a collective agreement either with an employee representative or with an employee appointed to that end by a union.

In enterprises over fifty employees, the present rules are not modified. The employer must negotiate a collective agreement first with a union representative. If none exists, he can negotiate with an employee representative appointed to that end by a union. If none exists (or nobody accepts to be appointed by a union), he can then negotiate with an employee representative not appointed by a union. Failing that, if no employee representative accepts to negotiate an agreement, he can negotiate with an employee, not having been elected as an employee representative, but appointed to that end by a union.

In the case of enterprises where no union representative exists, the employer must organize a vote of the employees validating the collective agreement by a majority of employees. This does not apply of course in the case of a required vote of the two thirds in very small enterprises, discussed above.

Industry level collective agreements must from now on include specific provisions regarding SMEs below fifty employees or justify why this is not the case.

(b) A tripartite observatory of social dialogue and collective bargaining in SMEs below fifty employees has been created, with the aim to follow and help collective bargaining. It can be referred to by any party meeting problems in the process of bargaining.

Additionally, it is planned that the Minister in charge of Labor, after consultations proceeds to the reduction of the number of sectors, taking notably in account the sectors where no collective agreement has been concluded since 2009.

[C] Labor Courts

Labor Courts are a specificity of French industrial relations. Created in 1806 they are competent for individual disputes arising from an individual contract of employment. Their original character comes from their composition: they are made only of lay judges, with equal representation from employers and employees. Originally elected on lists presented by employers organizations and unions, since the reform of representativeness of 2008 they are appointed from union lists according to the number of votes gathered in the employee representatives elections (discussed above). The process in front of labor courts if free of any charge and the use of a professional lawyer is not mandatory. Only in case of deadlock, a professional judge is called in to carry the decision. The process in front of the Labor Court is a two-step one: conciliation is attempted, and if it fails a decision is awarded. In fact, more than 90% of cases end by a court decision. Also, it should be noted that the large majority of cases, more than three quarters, deals with dismissals, including challenge to dismissals and compensation for wrongful dismissals. Around 96% of cases are brought by employees.

The unpredictability of Labor Courts decisions, possibly resulting in disastrous financial consequences for small and very small enterprises, was since long exposed by employers' organizations as a major obstacle to hiring employees under a contract of employment for an indeterminate duration. Besides the decisions occurred often in some overloaded labor courts after a long delay, reaching several years in certain cases, when increased by appeals, introducing greater uncertainty, for both employer and employee.

Several provisions aim to remedy to that state of things:

(1) The amount of damages (on top, of course, of severance pay) to which a Labor Court could sentence an employer in case of dismissal without a real and serious cause was heretofore unlimited and decided case by case with wide discrepancies in similar situations, from court to court. It is now framed by the law. Labor Courts' lay judges cannot any longer overstep maximum amounts in their awards and minimums are set up in some cases. This was introduced in order to make foreseeable the financial consequences of a dismissal, particularly for SMEs.
Nowadays, the maximum amount of damages is fixed to one-month wages below one year of seniority. It increases by one month per year until ten years seniority, thereafter by one-half month per year. It cannot exceed twenty months after twenty-nine years seniority. A minimum is also fixed, at one month of wages between one and two years of seniority, three months thereafter. In SMEs below eleven employees, if the same maxima apply, lower minima are provided for. They are fixed at fifteen days of wages after a year seniority increasing up to two months after nine years. Then, at ten years seniority, the normal scale applies.
It is to be noted that this mandatory scale of damages does not apply in cases of violation of a fundamental freedom. For instance such would be the case of "constructive dismissals" when the employee was harassed in order to push him to resignation, all kinds of harassment, discrimination, violation of the right of strike, right to join a union, etc. In those cases a minimum is set and no maximum applies. The damages awarded by the judges may not be inferior to six months wages and are set as before by the judges in consideration of the circumstances of the offense. It is thus to be foreseen by practitioners that most of the caseload in the years to come will fall within that category.

(2) Several other provisions of a more technical nature are taken in order to clarify, simplify and harmonize the present state of the law regarding dismissals, resulting of several layers of statutory law and court decisions. They are too involved in lengthy developments to be discussed in detail here. For instance, among the simpler ones:
   (a) The statute of limitations to seek redress in case of dismissals is harmonized and limited to one year.
   (b) Faulty application of the required form and process of dismissal from the part of the employer cannot be punished by the granting of more than one-month wages of damages. It is no longer due if the employer is recognized justified in having proceeded to the dismissal, even though the process was faulty.
   (c) In the case of dismissals for economic reasons:
      (i) In case of economic dismissal in France by groups operating over several countries, the nature and level of the economic problems faced by the group to justify the dismissals will be considered at the level of their operations in France only, contrarily to present court decisions requiring that world operations be considered.
      (ii) The obligation for enterprises of proposing vacant jobs in the other locations of the enterprise/group to employees made redundant in case of a dismissal for economic reasons is nowadays limited to the national territory, ending the ridiculous situations where enterprises were compelled, under judicial sanctions, to propose jobs, with the relevant level of pay, in faraway developing countries to redundant employees.
   (d) Other related provisions are enacted in a similar spirit:
      (i) Severance pay is raised to ¼ of a month wages per year on seniority (against 1/5 heretofore, an increase of 25%).
      (ii) In order to avoid as far as possible recourse to courts, employers and employees will be granted access to a digitalized version of Labor Law and to an advisory form, listing the rights and duties of each party in case of dismissal.

[D] Collective Breach of Contracts of Employment by Mutual Agreement

A national inter-industry collective agreement of January 2008, enacted into law by an Act of June 25, 2008, created a new way to end the individual contract of employment for an indefinite duration, besides the traditional causes existing in French Law to that end such as dismissal or resignation. It opened the possibility of a breach of contract of employment by mutual agreement between the employer and the individual employee, both wishing to terminate the employment relationship (rupture conventionnelle). Constituting neither a dismissal nor a resignation it must be negotiated between the two parties and cannot be imposed by either one. It does not have to be motivated and is not imputable to either party. The employee having negotiated such a breach of contract has access to unemployment compensation (contrarily to a case of resignation) and receives severance pay in an amount equivalent to a dismissal. Of course, he cannot then sue the employer for dismissal without a real and serious cause. Besides, a procedure must be followed: the employee may be assisted in the negotiation by a third party, can withdraw his agreement within fifteen days and the mutual agreement must be homologated by the departmental direction of labor.

It has become very successful and has become an important cause of the breach of contracts of employment. It is estimated that about 400,000 a year now take place. Besides only 4% are denied homologation by the Departmental Direction of Labor.

The ordinances extend the procedure of mutual agreement to collective breach of employment. Indeed the term "collective" used by the ordinance can be misleading. It is not a "group" process, but more like the opening of a window of opportunity. Enterprises may negotiate by collective agreements homologated by the labor administration a common framework for voluntary breaches of contract of employment. This will be a different legal framework than the one provided for plans of safeguarding of employment. Once a framework to that end has been negotiated, the employees within the categories concerned determined as part of the negotiated agreement may elect to take advantage of breaching their contract of employment. Several provisions and guarantees narrowly frame such agreements as they do for individual cases of voluntary breach of the contract of employment.

[E]   **Simplification of the System of Employee Representatives**

Here also, deep changes are introduced. The structure of employee representation in the enterprise to this day is the result of successive waves of law piling up above each other, all over the twentieth century, particularly after World War II, without much harmonization until very recently and succeeding each other with provisions in the spirit of the politics of newly elected majorities, successively conservative and socialist.

The summa division is between appointed union representatives in the enterprise and elected employee representatives. Union representatives are appointed by local unions, among the employees, by a letter to the employer. Since the Act of 2008, they must have been candidates to the elections of employee representatives on lists having obtained a minimum of 10% of the vote. Their role has not been changed much by the ordinances. Their main function is the negotiation of collective agreements if they are represented in the sense discussed above.

The case of employee representatives is different. They are elected on union-sponsored lists at the first ballot of the elections. If no majority has been reached at the first ballot, nonunion employees may present themselves their candidacy at a second ballot, together with nonelected union sponsored candidates from the first ballot, if there are any.

The two main kinds of elected employee representatives are personnel delegates and employee works council members. Personnel delegates are elected at the establishment level, works councils members at the enterprise level. Their role is to present to the employer the grievances and reclamations of the employees. They are mandatorily elected in enterprises of eleven employees and above. However, if there are no candidates, there are no elections.

Work councils have a general competence of genuine information and consultation on economic matters, however stopping short of codetermination. They have also a role of direct management of the cultural, social and welfare activities in the enterprise, which can amount to impressive budgets in large enterprises. They must be elected in enterprises employing over fifty employees.

Second-degree employee representatives are elected by elected employee representatives into Health, safety and conditions of work committees, central enterprise works councils, group work council, not to mention European works council. They are not directly concerned by the present reform.

A major simplification is introduced. Now, in enterprises above fifty employees existing employee representative instances (personnel delegates, work council, health, safety and conditions of work committee) will be merged within an "economic and social committee" which will carry the existing competences and powers of the existing instances and will be able to seize the courts.

The health, safety and conditions of work committee will remain in enterprises employing more than 300 employees. Below 300 employees, the labor inspectorate may, if it deems necessary to mandate the creation of such a committee.

The powers of the merged institutions are not modified. The questions to be decided by decrees of application which are important ones of much concern to unions are the one of the number of employee representatives issuing from the reform compared to the existing number and the means granted to them, notably in terms of number of paid hours to devote to their representative tasks.

By majority collective agreement, it will be possible to integrate the union delegates in the economic and social committee. The new committee christened then "enterprise council" will have then the capacity to negotiate enterprise level agreements. This constitutes a major change.

[F] Telework

Telework is recognized as applicable by full rights for employees, whereas a modification of the contract of employment and a collective agreement (or a charter elaborated by the employer alone after consultation of the work council) were necessary heretofore. From now on, a simple agreement between employer and employee is sufficient.

Accidents at home during working hours of telework are considered work related and subject to worker's compensation.

Opposition by an employer to telework must be justified.

On this point the reform has been much welcomed, hopefully it is a first step in solving more problems relating to the application of traditional labor law to the specific condition of work of workers in the digital sector and digital workers properly speaking

[G] Other Minor Technical Provisions

Multiple more minor technical simplification provisions of a general nature are also taken. They cannot be outlined here. One should nevertheless be singled out: The preventive individual account for hardship at work is modified and simplified. This account allows employees posted in jobs presenting difficult and particularly hard working conditions to accumulate points allowing either early retirement, part-time work or training. Progressively set in place since 2015 it was considered as an impossibly bureaucratic and cumbersome system by employers, notably in SMEs. Now rechristened "professional account for prevention," it is maintained only for 6 criteria: night work, repetitive work, shift work or work in hyperbaric conditions. Four other criteria are dropped since they were too difficult to be accurately gauged (handling of heavy loads, painful working postings, mechanical vibrations and chemical risks). The latter will open the right to early retirement under the regime of occupational diseases, when diagnosed.

§14.03 IN LIEU OF A CONCLUSION

It is of course impossible to write these early conclusive remarks on what is the tentative state of a major attempted reform. Two remarks are nevertheless possible.

The ordinances are an attempt to introduce a major reform of French Industrial relations. Notably the provisions on collective bargaining and employee representation if successfully adopted in practice are likely to drive to deep changes in union structure and representativeness, as well as individual employers policies.

The ball is now in the hands of the social partners. It is up to them to make use (or not) of the new provisions, within a tradition where collective bargaining has always taken second place to statutory law and State intervention, within a general, if most often silent, consensus. At the time of the Wagner Act, which in 1935 settled collective bargaining as the central pivot of US industrial relations for the half a century which followed, it was famously said that one can drive a horse to the river, but cannot make it drink against its will. The situation here is similar. The tools are ready. It remains to be seen if employers and unions, in France, concretely adopt and make use of them in the potential innovative ways opened.

CHAPTER 15
Tradition and Innovation in Labour Law: The Ambiguous Case of 'Agile Working' in Italy

Michele Tiraboschi

§15.01 LOOKING AT NEW FORMS OF TELEWORK: DRAWING ON ROGER BLANPAIN'S INSIGHTS

Roger Blanpain has been a world-renowned labour law scholar in the truest sense of the word, as such his work and tremendous charisma are widely appreciated and acknowledged. His working method is worth a mention, along with his ability to combine the founding values of labour law with the courage to change. Endeavouring to strike a balance between the need of economic development and workers' protection and promotion, Roger Blanpain taught us not only to preserve tradition but also to place trust in the future and in our responsibility to innovate with labour law.

Ugo Sinzheimer, one of the founding fathers of this discipline, rightly considered labour law as 'the law of the frontier, but also as a frontier of the law'.[1] Aware of this aspect, and of the fact that this branch of law is highly affected by economic and social change, Roger Blanpain acted as a veritable opinion leader. He encouraged us to interpret new facts with curiosity and open-mindedness without being afraid of challenging old certainties when they are no longer in line with ongoing changes, thus urging labour lawyers to define new and ever-changing realities.[2]

---

1. H. Sinzheimer, Über soziologische und dogmatische Methoden in der Arbeitsrechtswissenschaft, in Arbeitsrecht, 1922, p. 187 and ff., non vidi, cit. in G. Vardaro, Contratti collettivi e rapporto individuale di lavoro, Angeli, 1985, p. 27.
2. In this sense *see* the work of another leading figure in Labour Law, cf. G. Giugni, *Introduzione allo studio dell'autonomia collettiva*, Giuffrè, 1977 (but 1960), here p. 20.

Venturing into new territory and moving towards the unknown is not an easy task, even more so in the discipline of labour law which is particularly sensitive to social and economic changes. Altering relevant rules and legal frameworks might negatively affect workers' freedom and safeguards. This risk has long been pointed out, especially in times featuring a number of reforms of national labour legislation and questionable forms of deregulation and re-regulation of the labour market which are difficult to interpret.[3]

Although there are still many scholars who carry out research in the form of solitary investigation with the only purpose of pursuing their own career, others are prepared to stand up and be counted, even when dealing with sensitive and controversial topics. This way of conducting research prioritises reality over theories and is fuelled by an ongoing desire to provide a contribution to the world we live in. I believe the latter was the approach that was dear to Roger Blanpain in his own research, in class[4] or during international conferences, when he urged us to identify those social issues that most directly impact people's lives and addresses them with humility, in an attempt to supply a contribution to make our society 'a more decent one'.[5] Significantly, at the time of evaluating the social sustainability and direction of change, he would say, 'if people do not have a voice, I will raise mine'.

In the view of the above argument, this chapter sets out to examine the recent evolution of Italy's legislation on remote working, and above all the introduction of the 'agile working' scheme. Regarded by lawmakers as a new model to arrange salaried employment, agile working should replace telework, the use of which has been very limited so far, and its unsuitable rules.

Roger Blanpain has made reference to remote working on many occasions. I remember his speech at the European Forum on Telework, which took place on 1 and 2 September 2006 at the Palace of the Royal Flemish Academy in Brussels, the proceedings of which are collected in *the Bulletin of Comparative Labour Relations*.[6] Reflecting on the development of European social law and on whether or not 'voluntary' agreements were binding – e.g., on telework, concluded on 16 July 2002[7] – Roger Blanpain demonstrated his proactive and forward-looking approach, insisting on 'the overall need to consider the revision of existing labour law, given the changing

---

3. For an attempt to examine and analyse labour reforms from 2008 to today, cf. ILO D. Adascalitei, C. Pignatti Morano, *Labour Market Reforms since the Crisis: Drivers and Consequences*, International Labour Office, Research Department, Geneva: ILO, 2015.
4. My memories go back to the 1991-1992 period, when I spent an entire year at the Institute of Labour Law of the Catholic University of Leuven – founded by Roger Blanpain himself – where I had the opportunity to follow his classes.
5. In this sense, I have always found many similarities between the approach of Roger Blanpain and that of Marco Biagi, who in turn inherited his by Federico Mancini, the forefather of Bologna's School of labour law. This feeling was confirmed by an inscription that Mancini wrote on the cover page of a book – *A Theory of Justice* by John Rawls – that he gave to Biagi. I was given this book by Marco a few months before his death, in what appeared to me as a symbolic handover.
6. Cf. R. Blanpain (ed.), *European Framework Agreements and Telework: Law and Practice, A European and Comparative Study*, in *Bulletin of Comparative Labour Relations*, Kluwer, 2007.
7. Cf. R. Blanpain, *The European Social Dialogue and Voluntary Framework Agreements*, in R. Blanpain (ed.), *European Framework Agreements and Telework*, cit., pp. 31-39.

framework'.[8] He had no qualms about moving away from old and ineffective employment safeguards that were still modelled upon the idea of stable employment. In order to ensure the future of labour law and its founding values, Roger Blanpain had a clear purpose in mind, one which relied on devising new forms of protection that considered not only the individual employment contract but also the labour market and measures promoting people's employability.[9] Of course, he fully understood the reluctance and the unwillingness to challenge old certainties and the possible risks faced by labour lawyers when walking down new paths featuring 'even more subtle forms of "liquid" law'.[10]

Italy's new regulation on agile working, and the attempt to move on from telework with the three words of the lawmaker that can turn entire libraries,[11] seem to corroborate Blanpain's valuable recommendations. Accordingly, the present analysis of Italy's new legislation on remote working will be conducted drawing on Blanpain's insights, thus with an open mind and with a willingness to promote social innovation and regulatory change. This approach will serve to address the new great transformation of work,[12] which many think bears all the hallmarks of a Fourth Industrial Revolution.[13] But compliance of these new provisions with European social law will also be assessed, as will the already mentioned balance between the need for innovation and people's protection in an ever-changing labour market.

In this respect, as we will see further on, the new legislation on agile working shows a very high degree of ambiguity in relation to some major aspects – among which is health and safety and working time provisions – and a number of shortcomings as regards the balance between employers' needs and workers' protection. Lawmakers themselves stressed that the new rules aim at promoting flexicurity. Yet this is done but in a distorted way, in that the level of job security offered by telework gives way to flexible forms of agile working, without ensuring adequate proper safeguards to people engaged by employers under this new contractual scheme.

§15.02 THE REGULATION OF AGILE WORKING IN ITALY AS AN INDIRECT AND DEVIOUS RESPONSE TO LEGAL AND TRADE UNION LIMITATIONS TO TELEWORK?

The Italian legislature introduced Act no. 81 on 22 May 2017 to regulate agile working in Italy. We should stress from the onset that – unlike in the past with part-time or on-call work – the wording 'agile working' does not refer to a new employment contract, but to a new type of remote working whereby workers operate off-site on some days and at the employer's premises on other days according to their schedule.

---

8. R. Blanpain, *Introductory Remarks*, in R. Blanpain (ed.), *European Framework Agreements and Telework*, cit., p. 6.
9. R. Blanpain, *Introductory Remarks*, cit., p. 7.
10. Again, R. Blanpain, *Introductory Remarks*, cit., p. 7.
11. Cf. J.H. von Kirchmann, *Die Wertlossigkeil der jurisprudenz als Wissenschaft*, Stutgarnewd, Kohlhammer, 1938.
12. Here, reference is made to K. Polanyi, *The Great Transformation*, Farrar & Rinehart, 1944.
13. Cf. K. Schwab, *The Fourth Industrial Revolution*, World Economic Forum, 2016.

Lawmakers made clear that the objective was to increase work productivity – to be measured through result-based criteria – while improving employees' work-life balance. In other words, the opportunity for workers to choose where and when to work would give them more freedom, therefore reducing absenteeism rates, while at the same time assigning them more responsibility in relation to business objectives, loyalty and performance. The government was convinced of these positive effects brought about by this new way of working. Consequently, it is not surprising that agile working was included among those working arrangements that could benefit from economic incentives in the context of productivity in company-level collective bargaining and could also enjoy tax relief in respect of measures promoting work-life balance put forward within the firm.

Leaving aside these statements of principle, what bears relevance is to understand why Italian lawmakers decided to regulate agile working. This is an interesting point in that, while featuring aspects of performance and result-based work, agile working is expressly and exclusively included by Act no. 81 on 22 May 2017 in the category of salaried employment. Furthermore, it is acknowledged that agile working can be carried out remotely through ICT tools. Yet the new piece of legislation makes no reference to telework, of which agile working could as well represent a sort of development.

Indeed, right after the draft law was submitted before the Parliament, Italian industrial relations actors started to take an interest in agile working by putting forward provisions on an experimental basis.[14] All of this was done pending a number of legal clarifications concerning the new law (which took longer than expected to be formulated) and that were published in *Gazzetta Ufficiale* no. 81 of 22 May 2017.

This significant delay should also come as no surprise because, as stressed in 2015 by the 'Servizio Studi' of Italy's Chamber of Deputies, 'the recourse to simplified and flexible forms of remote working like agile work can be autonomously agreed upon in collective bargaining or in the individual employment contract, irrespective of the existence of a specific provision'.[15] Nevertheless, a rule governing this way of working

---

14. The ADAPT Observatory on smart working points out that as of 13 June 2017 – that is when Act no. 81 of 22 May 2017 was published in the *Gazzetta Ufficiale* – there existed six national collective agreements and twenty-four company-level collective agreements regulating this model of work organisation, though their degree of consistency varied considerably. A similar investigation, that was conducted in January 2016 at the beginning of the parliamentary debate on agile working, revealed that only eight collective agreements concluded at the company level covered this form of employment. The collective agreements concluded both at the national and at the company level that regulated agile working mostly concerned the food sector (Barilla, Ferrero, Nestlè, Parmalat, San Pellegrino), the energy sector (A2A, ENEL, ENI, GDF Suez Energia Italia, Petronas Lubricants Italy, Snam) and the banking and the insurance sectors (Axa, Banca Popolare Etica, Banca del Piemonte, BNP Paribas, Cariparma, Credit Agricole, Intesa San Paolo, Reale Mutua Assicurazioni, Unicredit, Zurich). Some of them were also signed in technology-intensive companies (Gruppo Telespazio/e-Geos, Siemens, Schneider Electric) though in these latter cases they mainly concerned highly qualified staff and agile working is usually governed by internal regulations (Fastweb, Microsoft, Plantronics, Tetra Pack, Tim, Unilever, Vodafone, Whirlpool). Cf. The 'smart working' section of the ADAPT database, available at www.farecontrattazione.it.
15. Camera dei deputati – Servizio Studi, *Disposizioni per la promozione dello smart working A.C. 2014*, Dossier n. 364 – Schede di lettura 3 novembre 2015, p. 2.

would be useful in cases when 'exceptions need to be made to mandatory laws (e.g., those concerning health and safety) or when employers are willing to grant special incentives for work carried out remotely'.[16]

As seen, there are a number of provisions in Italian legislation that already promote, also economically, the use of agile working. Therefore, much curiosity arises as regards the derogations contained in the new law concerning protections granted by current labour law. This holds true if one considers that some of the aspects covered by Act no. 81 of 22 May 2017 – e.g., working time and occupational health and safety – are subject to ad hoc regulation laid down in a number of European directives. Obsolete though they might be – especially because of recent technological innovation in terms of business and work organisation – these rules cannot however be amended by Italian lawmakers, for they are outside their remit.[17]

Underlying this aspect are the reasons prompting Italian lawmakers to go in a direction different from their colleagues in other countries – i.e., shelving telework[18] outright rather than attempting to amend existing legislation governing this form of employment. Equally in this case, they seem to be unaware of the Framework Agreement on Telework of 16 July 2002 and to how it will apply to agile working, though the framework will affect this new form of employment in important respects.

One should not deny that European legislation on telework needs to be adapted to new technologies that make it possible to organise work in a way that was inconceivable until recently.[19] Yet this does not mean to disregard key issues in salaried employment – e.g., working time and occupational health and safety – the contours of which are becoming increasingly blurred in the digital economy and the Internet of Things. On close inspection, state-of-the-art technology has long contributed to the undermining of 'Aristotelian rules' of labour law, namely the place of work (e.g., one's obligation to work on the employer's premises), the time of work (e.g., performing

---

16. Camera dei deputati – Servizio Studi, *Disposizioni per la promozione dello smart working*, cit.
17. In relation to the most controversial aspect of the new provision on agile working, namely the regulation of health and safety at work, EC law is modelled upon medium and large-sized enterprises that are still based on traditional organisational models. On the need to review the concepts of health and safety and their rules safeguarding workers, see M. Weiss, *Digitalizzazione: sfide e prospettive per il diritto del lavoro*, in *Diritto delle Relazioni Industriali*, n. 3/2016, p. 659.
18. Implementing the provisions contained in Art. 57 of *Loi Travail* concerning the reform of the labour market, employers' associations (Medef, CPME e U2P) and trade unions (CFDT, CFE-CGC, CFTC, CGT-FO, CGT) reached an agreement on 23 May 2017 aimed at reviewing legislation on remote working. Cf. the document *Conclusions de la concertation sur le 'developpement du teletravail et du travail a distance'* signed by industrial relations actors on 23 May 2017 and then submitted to the French Minister of Labour on 7 June 2017 for evaluation in the context of the announced labour law reform. As for Spain, research into this topic has recently produced 'a shift from homeworking to remote working'. Ongoing technological innovation has also led Spanish lawmakers to avoid using the concept of 'telework' to prevent the rapid obsolescence of the new wording contained in Art. 13 of the Workers' Statute. Cf. E.M. Sierra Benítez, *La nueva regulación del trabajo a distancia*, in *Revista Internacional y Comparada de Relaciones Laborales y Derecho del Empleo*, 2013, n. 1, pp. 7–35.
19. A review of the different forms of mobile and remote working is provided in the communication of Eurofound, *New Forms of Employment*, Publications Office of the European Union, Luxembourg, 2015, esp. Ch. 6 on *ICT-Based Mobile Work*. See also ILO-Eurofound, *Working Anytime, Anywhere. The Effect on the World of Work*, cit.

work over a single time-period) and the task of work (e.g., engaging in only one type of task at the time).[20] Nevertheless, some doubts can be cast when looking at the surreptitious attempt of the new provision to move beyond the two main features of performance, namely place and time of work. On the one hand, Act no. 81 of 22 May 2017 fails to consider the limitations placed by EU law. On the other hand, the new piece of legislation disregards the problems arising from the persistent centrality of salaried employment, which was further confirmed by Italy's lawmakers at the time of enforcing the implementation decrees of the Jobs Act in Italy. The above takes place within a labour market where less and less relevance is given to instructions, working hours and place of work,[21] mainly because a collaborative dimension has emerged whereby trades, skills and expertise are now brought together depending on objectives, programmes, working phases and projects.

§15.03 AGILE WORKING AND TELEWORK: DEFINITIONS AND LEGAL FRAMEWORK

Italian lawmakers gloss over the issue of differentiating agile working from telework. Indeed, paragraph 1, Article 18 of Law no. 81 of 22 May 2017, defines the scope of application of the new rules on agile working, specifying that 'agile work is performed in part on the employer's premises and *in part remotely, without a fixed workstation*, according to the daily and weekly working time established by law or in collective bargaining' (emphasis added). At the time of providing a definition and a legal framework to this form of employment, emphasis should be placed to the mobile nature of the workstation used by workers outside the company. This is because, following the parliamentary debate accompanying the enactment of the new law, the lack of a fixed work location seems to have been taken as the trait distinguishing agile working from telework.

However, making the absence or the presence of a fixed work location a distinctive trait of agile working or telework is mostly commonplace, which is rooted among industrial relations actors and in the specialised press, with no legislative provision corroborating this view, either in Italian legislation or elsewhere. In this respect, the definition of telework contained in Article 2 of the European Framework Agreement concluded on 16 July 2002 by ETUC, UNICE/UEAPME and CEEP brooks no argument: 'telework is a form of organising and/or performing work, using information technology, in the context of an employment contract/relationship, where work, which

---

20. This point was already dealt with in the past in relation to the organisational models of telework. See B. Veneziani, *Le nuove forme di lavoro*, in R. Blanpain, M. Biagi (a cura di), *Diritto del lavoro e relazioni industriali nei Paesi industrializzati ad economia di mercato. Profili comparati. I. Diritto del lavoro*, Maggioli, 1991, pp. 107–139.
21. Cf. the ILO-Eurofound report already referred to, *Working Anytime, Anywhere. The Effect on the World of Work*, cit. Cf. also C. Degryse, *Digitalisation of the Economy and Its Impact on Labour Markets*, European Trade Union Institute, Working Paper 2016.02 and J. Popma, *The Janus Face of the 'New Ways of Work'. Rise, Risks and Regulation of Nomadic Work*, European Trade Union Institute, Working Paper 2013.07.

could also be performed at the employer's premises, is carried out away from those premises *on a regular basis'* (emphasis added).

Labour law scholars have widely debated the legal nature and effectiveness of these European agreements put forward by Community institutions[22] – such as that signed on 16 July 2002 – that were not incorporated in an EU Directive. We might welcome the view that these agreements[23] either have direct legal effectiveness or that they are legally relevant, in the sense that they produce legal obligations that translate into soft law.[24] If this is the case, we should remember that the European Framework Agreement of 16 July 2002 was faithfully transposed into Italian legislation as specified by the then Article 139, no. 2, of the EC Treaty,[25] by means of the Inter-sectoral Agreement of 9 June 2004.

In turn, the definitions and the provisions contained in the 2004 Inter-sectoral Agreement were included in the most important collective agreements concluded at the industry level, therefore becoming part of Italian legislation. In considering one of the most delicate aspects of agile working, it might be also useful to refer to paragraph 10, Article 3 of Legislative Decree no. 81 of 9 April 2008. It reads as follows: 'The provisions contained in Title VII apply to all workers on salaried employment who work remotely *on a continuous basis* by means of a computer or a telecommunication system. *This also includes* those workers covered by Presidential Decree no. 70 of 8 March 1999 and by the *European Framework Agreement on Telework of 16 July 2002'* (emphasis added).

Consequently, the peculiarity of telework does not lie in the presence of a fixed workstation, but on the fact that work is performed outside the employer's premises *on a continuous basis,*[26] thanks to ICT equipment or tools. This seems to be true if one looks at both EU and national legal sources, since Italian legislation on health and safety makes reference to the definitions contained in the European Framework

---

22. This agreement was reached following the start of formal consultations on the part of the Commission under the then Art. 138 of the EC Treaty. The signatory parties expressly decided not to translate the agreement into a Directive, as was the case for part-time and fixed-term work. In this sense, Art. 12 of the agreement specifies that 'in the context of article 139 of the Treaty, this European framework agreement shall be implemented by the members of UNICE/UEAPME, CEEP and ETUC (and the liaison committee EUROCADRES/ CEC) in accordance with the procedures and practices specific to management and labour in the Member States'.
23. Cf. O. Deinert, *Modes of Implementing European Collective Agreements and Their Impact on Collective Autonomy*, in ILJ, 2003, p. 234.
24. In this sense, *see* the arguments contained in B. Caruso, A. Alaimo, *Il contratto collettivo nell'ordinamento dell'Unione Europea*, in WP C.S.D.L.E. 'Massimo D'Antona'. INT – 87/2011, p. 47, which are shared by the author.
25. See Art. 155, no. 2, of the Treaty on the Functioning of the European Union (consolidated version).
26. Cf. ETUC, *Voluntary Agreement on Telework – ETUC Interpretation Guide*, 2002, where reference is made 'to work performed on a regular basis (one day/week as well as five days a week), irrespective of duration. If telework is not carried out during pre-determined periods, legislation on telework does not apply'. Cf. M. Peruzzi, *Sicurezza e agilità: quale tutela per lo smart worker?*, cit., esp. p. 3, note 7, who points out that the definition of telework used by industrial relations actors differs from the one put forward by the European Commission in the *Report on the implementation of the social partners' Framework Agreement on Telework*, Commission Staff Working Paper, SEC(2008) 2178, Brussels, p. 33) which required workers to work remotely for at least 'a considerable proportion of working time'.

Agreement of 16 July 2002 and not to the Inter-sectoral Agreement of 9 June 2004 through which the former was included in our legal system.

The foregoing consideration raises doubts as to whether Italian lawmakers intended to circumvent the issue of the application of national health and safety rules to workers performing agile working. More to the point, it seems as though the legislative process was affected by a conception of telework[27] that is now passé because the requirement of the fixed workstation was not determined by the law or collective bargaining, but by the use of outdated technologies in place in the past.[28]

Relying on the number of hours worked outside the employer's premises to differentiate between telework and agile working might also be misleading. In its *Report on the implementation of the European social partners' Framework Agreement on Telework,* the European Commission was unequivocal in stressing that the definition contained in the Framework Agreement of 16 July 2002[29] covers 'the three types of telework identified: teleworking from home, mobile teleworking (via portable communication systems) and work in telework centres (outstations, neighbourhood offices, telecottages)' but also 'both permanent and alternating telework, i.e. arrangements whereby the worker spends part of his/her working time at the employer's premises and the rest elsewhere'. Further on in the report, the European Commission confirms another trend regarding telework that has been supported by both relevant research[30] and statistics:[31] the 'alternating telework' working scheme involves 'the largest percentage of teleworkers in most European countries'.[32]

---

27. Cf. J. Messenger, L. Gschwind, *Three Generations of Telework: New ICTs and the (R)evolution from Home Office to Virtual Office,* conference paper for the 17th ILERA World Congress, Cape Town, South Africa, September 2015, esp. p. 2 where the authors insist on the need to deal with the issue of providing a legal definition of telework also considering an historical and interdisciplinary perspective. Cf. also S. Craipeau, *Télétravail: le travail fluide,* cit., pp. 107-120.
28. Cf. J. Messenger, L. Gschwind, *Three Generations of Telework: New ICTs and the (R)evolution from Home Office to Virtual Office,* cit., esp. pp. 15-17, who stress the relevance of telework, at least in the broad definition provided by the European Framework Agreement of 16 July 2002. In Italian literature, *see also* L. Gaeta, *Il telelavoro: legge e contrattazione,* in *DLRI,* 1995, spec. p. 552, who makes reference to 'mobile telework [...] performed without a fixed workstation', somehow anticipating the notions of 'modern Argonaut' and 'digital nomad' that became popular in international labour research thanks to the work of T. Makimoto, D. Manners, *Digital nomad,* Chichester, 1997.
29. European Commission, *Report on the implementation of the European social partners' Framework Agreement on Telework,* Brussels, SEC(2008) 2178, p. 34.
30. Cf. J. Messenger, L. Gschwind, *Three Generations of Telework: New ICTs and the (R)evolution from Home Office to Virtual Office,* cit., esp. p. 13, e the international literature therein.
31. *See* the statistics collected in A. Parent-Thirion, G. Vermeylen, G. van Houten, M. Lyly-Yrjänäinen, I. Biletta, J. Cabrita, *Fifth European Working Conditions Survey,* Luxembourg, Publications Office of the European Union, 2012, according to which '20% of all employees in the European Union are teleworkers, with around 15% partial and around 5% total teleworkers'. Cf. also L. Duxbury, I. Towers, C. Higgins, J.A. Thomas, *From 9 to 5 to 24 and 7: How Technology Redefined the Work Day,* in W.K. Law (ed.), *Information Resources Management: Global Challenges,* Hershey, 2006, pp. 305-332 and M.C. Noonan, J.L. Glass, *The Hard Truth about Telecommuting,* in *Monthly Labor Review,* 2012, pp. 38-45.
32. European Commission, *Report on the implementation of the European social partners' Framework Agreement on Telework,* cit., p. 35.

To corroborate this view, it is sufficient to go through the wide range of international literature on this topic[33] in which the definition of telework is never limited to work carried out from a fixed workstation. Significantly, Jack M. Nilles, who is universally seen as the leading figure in telework research, has pointed out that 'telework covers a wide range of possibilities [...] from the worker who occasionally works at home (our minimum for inclusion is at least one day per month) to those who work at home full-time – and in some cases more than full time'.[34]

§15.04 THE REASONS FOR A NEW PROVISION ON AGILE WORKING

In the previous chapter, we have looked into the definition and the main features of agile working. Based on the foregoing analysis, it is safe to argue that no difference can be seen between this way of working and telework in the Italian legal system, especially if applicable legislation is taken into account. For the sake of precision, we should add that only under two circumstances – which, however, are rarely found in practice – can a distinction be drawn between these working schemes. The first is when work is carried out outside the premises without the use of IT equipment; the second refers to cases in which work is performed both on-site and remotely, though on an occasional basis and with no scheduled hours.

What characterises telework – besides the recourse to ICT tools[35] (even a limited number of them) – is the fact that work is performed remotely on a *regular basis*. This is not equivalent to saying that all work[36] should be done off-site, but that workers carry out their tasks outside the premises routinely[37] and that their assignments and working time are planned according to a weekly, monthly or yearly schedule.

---

33. Cf., the papers collected in R. Blanpain (ed.), *European Framework Agreements and Telework*, cit. See also: L. Mella Méndez (ed.), *Trabajo A Distancia y Teletrabajo – Estudios sobre su régimen jurídico en el derecho español y comparado*, Aranzadi, 2015.
34. Cf. J. M. Nilles, *Telework in the US – Telework America Survey 2000*, International Telework Association and Council, October 2000, p. 14. *See* the classic research by the same author, *Telecommunications and Organizational Decentralization*, published in October 1975 in the *IEEE Transactions on Communications*, volume COM-23, n. 10, pp. 1142–1147. As for labour law research, *see* V. Di Martino, L. Wirth, *Telework: A New Way of Working and Living*, in *International Labour Review*, 1990, n. 5, p. 530 and p. 542 e p. 552, who point out that 'the term "telework" (or "telecommuting", "remote work", "distance work") has been used to cover a variety of situations. [...] Now telework is increasingly used to refer to different combinations of work in central office, at customer sites, in satellite centres or at home. [...] One model which makes the most of what telework has to offer while simultaneously minimising its disadvantages is a combination of telework at home with work in the main or satellite office'.
35. It is sufficient to use a mobile phone or a IPad. Cf. J. Messenger, L. Gschwind, *Three Generations of Telework: New ICTs and the (R)evolution from Home Office to Virtual Office*, cit., p. 3. Cf. also S. Craipeau, *Télétravail: le travail fluide*, cit.
36. On the admissibility of alternating telework, cf. M. Biagi, T. Treu, *Lavoro e* Information Technology: *riflessioni sul caso italiano*, in *Diritto delle Relazioni Industriali*, 2002, spec. p. 12 where reference was already made to the fact that alternating telework was the most widespread form of telework, though it was used informally.
37. Cf. European Foundation for the Improvement of Living and Working Conditions, *Telework in the European Union*, Dublin, 2010, p. 3. After specifying that 'while the definition of telework in the European Framework Agreement is broad in order to cover different forms of telework, it remains open to debate for the industrial relations actors in the Member States which type of

At the international level, the expression 'agile work' has still limited use and usually refers to organisational models devised as a result of work digitalisation.[38] Consequently, all forms of employment in which work is performed remotely fall within the broad notion of telework, as defined by Article 2 of the European Framework Agreement of 16 July 2002. Of course, this is done taking into account the organisational models that make use of technological innovation in order to prevent definitional misunderstanding and confusion as regards applicable legislation.[39]

One question that arises is what has prompted Italian lawmakers to venture into a new and uncertain path and to refer to agile working as a new form of employment. Though pains were taken to draw a distinction between agile working and telework, this difference appears to be more of a theoretical than practical one. As suggested by international experience and authoritative research on this topic, a more viable option would have been that of adapting existing rules to the new forms of telework that resulted from innovative technology.[40]

Formally, Italian legislation specifies that the new provision on agile working is intended to 'boost competitiveness and facilitate reconciliation of work and family life', as international literature also seems to welcome this approach.[41] However, as we have seen with telework,[42] pursuing higher productivity and a better work-life balance does not come automatically and requires the harmonisation of organisational and personal needs. These aspects can be agreed upon by the parties[43] to the employment contract only if legislation or collective agreements provide rules ensuring a proper system of checks and balances. However, looking at Act no. 81 of 22 May 2017, this does not

---

teleworker meets these criteria and, in particular, what quantity of time the term "regular basis' refers to" it rightly points out that 'telework on a "regular basis" could include working away from the employer's premises five days a week as well as one day a week or less, as long as it is performed on a regular basis'.

38. Cf. World Economic Forum, *The Future of Jobs Employment, Skills and Workforce Strategy for the Fourth Industrial Revolution*, Geneva, 2016, p. 30 and Conseil National du Numérique, *Travail emploi numérique – Les nouvelles trahectories*, Rapporto remis à la Ministre du Travail, de l'Emploi, de la Formation professionnelle et du Dialogue social, 2016, p. 56.
39. Cf. J. Messenger, L. Gschwind, *Three Generations of Telework: New ICTs and the (R)evolution from Home Office to Virtual Office*, cit.
40. Cfr. J. Messenger, L. Gscwind, *Three Generations of Telework: New ICTs and the (R)evolution from Home Office to Virtual Office*, cit., passim, who point out the good reasons for using telework rather than other terminology which might give rise to confusion and uncertainty in both literature and legislation.
41. See J. Moreira Dias, Smart Working, in L. Mella Méndez, L. Serrani (a cura di), *Los actuales cambios sociales y laborales: nuevos retos para el mundo del trabajo*, vol. 1, *Cambios tecnológicos y nuevos retos para el mundo del trabajo (Portugal, España, Colombia, Italia, Francia)*, Peter Lang, 2017, pp. 153–184, who however fails to investigate the reasons for new legislation on agile working instead of updating that on telework.
42. Cf. S. Craipeau, *Télétravail: le travail fluide*, cit., p. 110. See also O. Cléach, J.L. Metzger, *Le télétravail des cadres: entre suractivité et apprentissage de nouvelles temporalités*, in *Sociologie du Travail*, 2004, pp. 433–450.
43. As currently regulated by Article 19 of Law no. 81 of 22 May 2017, n. 81.

appear to have been the case – with many commentators even going so far as to talk of 'deceiving forms of work-life balance'.[44]

Recent innovations in remote working have prompted lawmakers in France,[45] and to a small extent in Italy,[46] to acknowledge certain 'newly conceived' rights, such as the right to disconnect. In this latter case, it seems as though workers' previous obligation of being on call[47] – e.g., available for work – had been reversed, especially when considering that we live in a world that is always connected to the internet. The example above shows that making use of state-of-the-art technologies does not always come with a better work-life balance – far from it. The implementation of organisational models enabling one to work anywhere at any time might blur the boundaries between private and professional life, thus increasing the risks of psychosocial conditions and illnesses.[48]

Leaving aside official declarations, the present analysis seems to confirm the suspicions that the new legislation on agile working has been drafted in order to paralyze existing rules regulating remote working at both national and international level will not apply to it. This is particularly true in the event of remote working performed on a regular and continuous basis through a minimum set of ICT tools. Indeed, there exists a widespread conviction among experts and operators in Italy that they are legislation and trade union rules that have traditionally hampered the full development of remote working in our country. On this point, the President of the Observatory on Smart Working, established by Milan's Politecnico, has argued that 'the existing gap between Italy and other European countries in relation to the diffusion of telework can be ascribed to cumbersome and stringent legislation, a short-sighted approach to industrial relations and a hierarchical view of work culture'.

Italy's shortcomings are there for all to see, especially in relation to the implementation of top-down models of work organisation which are still based on compliance with instructions through a 'command-and-control' approach. Significantly, this way of conceiving work has been further acknowledged by means of the decrees

---

44. Cf. A.R. Tinti, *La conciliazione ingannevole. A proposito di lavoro 'agile' e work-life balance*, in *Il Mulino*, 27 maggio 2016, especially when he argues that the new legislation: 'promotes a new idea of work-life balance, regarded as a shared objective and a such it founds everyone's consensus, even though is always a tool to achieve something else'.
45. Cf. L. Fauvarque-Gobin, *La conciliazione vita-lavoro nella Loi travail*, cit., p. 80. The right to disconnect was included in France's Loi Travail of 2016 and now it is also part of Act no. 81 of 22 May 2017. Jean-Emmanuel Ray should be acknowledged for promoting this right. Cf. J-E.-Ray, *Naissance et avis de décèes du droit à la déconnexion: le droit à la vie privée au XXIe siècle*, in *Droit Social*, 2002, pp. 939-944; Id., *Grande accélération et droit à la déconnexion*, in *Droit Social*, 2016, pp. 912-920.
46. Cf., with reference to the parliamentary debate leading to the provision on the right to disconnect in Italy, *see* J. Cervilla Garzón, *Avances en Italia y España hacia la regulación del derecho a la desconexión tecnológica y el nuevo* lavoro agile, in L. Mella Méndez, L. Serrani (a cura di), *Los actuales cambios sociales y laborales: nuevos retos para el mundo del trabajo*, cit., spec. pp. 443-448.
47. On the obligation of being on call, 'through which the worker makes himself available for work to ensure the functioning of the services and the facilities' cf. M. Quaranta, Information communication technology *e orario di lavoro: flessibilità e controllo sindacale*, in *Diritto delle Relazioni Industriali*, 2004, p. 538.
48. *See* J. Popma, *The Janus face of the 'New Ways of Work'*, cit., spec. pp. 13-20.

implementing Act no. 183 of 10 December 2014 (the so-called Jobs Act), as expressly requested by employers.

This state of affairs makes it difficult to explain a recent decision of Italian lawmakers, according to whom the 'agile working' scheme can only be implemented in the form of salaried employment, which by definition is based on command-and-control logics.[49] Furthermore, the proposal to allow workers on self-employment to access this working arrangement was fiercely opposed by the Government. The requests to make agile working regulations more stringent than those governing telework were also rejected. This is despite the fact that the latter is regarded by many labour law scholars[50] simply as a way of organising work of any kind, be it performed through salaried employment, self-employment, quasi-self-employment or even by a firm.

Against this background, which is marked by a work culture and top-down management system peculiar to Fordism, paragraph 1, Article 21 of Act no. 81 of 22 May 2017 seems to strike a discordant note. Specifically, the provision reads as follows: 'the agreement concerning agile working regulates the way the employer exercises their power on work performed outside the premises'. Nevertheless, work carried out off-site through ICT tools should be based on cooperation and trust and should be assessed on output. This is even more so in consideration of the fact that this form of employment takes place 'without any obligation in terms of working time and working hours'.[51] In theory, it is still possible for the employer to exercise their managerial power. Nevertheless, making provisions for mechanisms to supervise the work of those operating remotely appears superfluous and somehow contradictory, especially because this way of working should be evaluated looking at the results produced.

Going through the text of Act no. 81 of 22 May 2017, little reference is made to workers' right to disconnect, the regulation of which is left to the individual parties of the contract and, as such, does not seem to prevent employers' excessive control over staff operating remotely. A more sensible approach – which is also more in line with the overall idea behind agile working[52] – would have been that of entrusting collective bargaining, both at company and at industry level, with striking the right balance

---

49. This takes place knowing that the adoption of remote working provides the occasion to convert employment contracts in salaried employment to collaborations in the form of self-employment. Cf. J. Visser, N. Ramos Martín, *Expert Report on the Implementation of the Social Partner's Framework Agreement on Telework*, Amsterdam Institute for Advanced Labour Studies, 2008, p. 25, who argue that: 'the reorganisation associated with the introduction of telework sometimes represents an opportunity for firms to encourage employees to change their status and to become self-employed, although all that has changed is the way in which the work is performed'.
50. Cf. G. Giugni, *É necessario, subito un altro (tele-)statuto*, in *Telèma*, n. II/1995. See also B. Veneziani, *Le nuove forme di lavoro*, cit., pp. 123–131.
51. Paragraph 1, Art. 18 of Act no. 81 of 22 May 2017.
52. See *Tansformation numérique et vie au travail*, report of 15 September 2015 by M. Bruno Mettling for the French Minister of Labour, who regarded collective bargaining as the right tool to implement the right to disconnection. Cf. F. Jauréguiberry, *Déconnexion volontaire aux technologies de l'information et de la communication*, 2013, where an open-access summary is provided of the DEVOTIC report conducted for the Agence Nationale de Recherche.

between employees' obligations as regards their being on call and their right to disconnect outside working hours, as agreed upon collectively.[53]

A number of experts and engineers engaged in the establishment of smart working lament that there exist many legal constraints hampering the modernisation of employment relationships and the full development of the new industrial revolution. However, it should be pointed out that the question at issue here is not the unconditional defence of old rules because no exceptions can be made to them. Rather, looking at the true function of labour law – which historically safeguards both employee protection and employers' right to production – one might argue that what is seen as technically possible is often legally impracticable.[54]

Labour law is tasked with harmonising the need of economic development and employee protection, all the more so in a time marked by new ways through which human beings generate value. It is also for this reason that one should highlight yet another flaw in Act no. 81 of 22 May 2017. The original draft of this provision contained a clause empowering collective bargaining to lay down measures facilitating workers and employers who were willing to use smart working. Regrettably, that clause was repealed and never saw the light of the day. This occurred despite the wide range of international literature[55] and authoritative works[56] that were unequivocal in regarding collective bargaining as the most likely tool to ensure the proper development of the different forms of remote working performed through ICT tools. Collective bargaining should be used as a tool to regulate smart working because it adheres to reality and serves as an instrument for employee information, consultation and participation at a decentralised level.[57]

Finally, one should not be forgetful that the legal limitations to the use of new technologies are to be ascribed to EU law rather than national law. This holds true for certain aspects of labour law – among others privacy and employee control mechanisms – which affect rules on working time, mandatory insurance against job-related accidents and occupational diseases. EU lawmakers are well aware of these issues, as in the preliminary research carried out for the purpose of amending the working time directive, they acknowledge that digitalisation 'leads to an increasing fragmentation of

---

53. Industrial relations actors promptly took action in France. The result was the enactment of the 2016 *Loi Travail* with the objective of entrusting the social partners the tasks of negotiating the right to disconnection and including this topic in the mandatory negotiation round that takes place annually. Cf. L. Fauvarque-Gobin, *La conciliazione vita-lavoro nella Loi travail*, cit., p. 80.
54. See A. Supiot, *Travail, droit et technique*, in *Droit Social*, 2002, qui spec. pp. 13–14.
55. Cf. V. Di Martino, L. Wirth, *Telework: A New Way of Working and Living*, in *International Labour Review*, 1990, n. 5, spec. pp. 545–547 e p. 547: 'collective agreements, because of their greater flexibility, are particularly suited to regulating the labour conditions of teleworkers'. Cf. also L. Mella Méndez, *Trabajo a Distancia y Teletrabajo. Estudios sobre su régimen jurídico en el Derecho español y comparado*, cit.
56. Cf. *Rapport Mettling*.
57. Cf. M. Weiss, *Digitalizzazione: sfide e prospettive*, cit., pp. 660–661 where reference is made to research conducted by Hans-Böckler-Stiftung on 140 agreements concluded between employers and works councils that 'the use of IT tools is given priority in relation to employee participation'.

work, both with regard to location and to time'[58] requiring us 'to meet the challenges of changing work organisation'.[59]

§15.05 THE RELEVANCE ATTACHED TO EMPLOYEE SUBORDINATION IN A CHANGING WORLD OF WORK: AN UNSOLVED ISSUE

Before concluding this chapter, we should argue that Italian lawmakers have once again failed to keep up with innovation.[60] Besides technical errors and poor attention to detail, one cannot do without noticing the attempt on their behalf to devise a new working scheme (agile working) to circumvent some legal issues posed by telework, which, however, are to be dealt with in the event of any work performed remotely on a regular basis and by means of ICT tools. Importantly, labour law as a discipline has failed to keep abreast of new developments because it has not managed to 'rethink itself and its reasons'[61] or at least to put them on a new footing. To this end, it would have been sufficient to move on from statements of principle and to stop wasting time on ideological battles on the topic of labour flexibility and its relation to the establishment of powers that were peculiar to the twentieth century and were also part of the economic model underlying the legal notion of subordination. Thus, it is not surprising that 'Italian labour law struggles to acknowledge current technological development, positioning itself among those branches of law which fall behind in the modernisation process. Taken as a whole, labour law is still regarded as representing work prior to the technological revolution, manual labour or automatic or mechanical work'.[62]

More to the point, because of today's technologies, working through ICT tools does not simply mean operating outside the employer's premises. What matters now is to fully understand and govern the technological revolution enabling people and devices to connect amongst themselves or through the internet (the so-called Internet of Things).[63] This is such a relevant issue that the search for flexibility includes the 'Internet of People'[64] and concerns 'not only work – and aspects like time, location, remuneration – but the entities interacting on the web and their legal and social

---

58. Cf. Interpretative Communication on Directive 2003/88/EC of the European Parliament and of the Council concerning certain aspects of the organisation of working time (2017/C 165/01), p. C/165/4, which states that 'about 30% of people in employment are working in multiple locations, but only 3% of people are teleworking from home and 8% are exclusively ICT-mobile workers. At the same time, digital technology is opening the way to new possibilities of monitoring working time'.
59. Ibid. Cf. ILO-Eurofound, *Working Anytime, Anywhere. The Effect on the World of Work*, cit., pp. 43–56.
60. See F. Carinci, *Rivoluzione tecnologica e diritto del lavoro: il rapporto individuale*, in *Giornale di Diritto del Lavoro e Relazioni Industriali*, 1985, p. 211. See also G. Vardaro, *Tecnica, tecnologia e ideologia della tecnica nel diritto del lavoro*, in *PD*, 1986, p. 76.
61. U. Romagnoli, *'Noi e loro': diritto del lavoro e nuove tecnologie*, cit., p. 382.
62. Cf. A. Trojsi, *Il comma 7, lettera f), della legge delega n. 183/2014: tra costruzione del Diritto del lavoro dell'era tecnologica e liberalizzazione dei controlli a distanza sui lavoratori*, in M. Rusciano, L. Zoppoli (a cura di), *Jobs Act e contratti di lavoro dopo la legge delega 10 dicembre 2014 n. 183*, WP C.S.D.L.E. 'Massimo D'Antona' – Collective Volumes – 3/2014, p. 118.
63. Cf. AA.VV., *The Internet of Things*, MIT Technology Review Business Report, 2014.
64. Cfr., J. Miranda, N. Mäkitalo, J. Garcia-Alonso, J. Berrocal, T. Mikkonen, C. Canal, J.M. Murillo, *From the Internet of Things to the Internet of People*, in *IEEE Internet Computing*, 2015, pp. 40–47.

roles'.[65] Digitalisation changes the nature of work in important respects and affects it well beyond the physical boundaries of the firm[66] – challenging the traditional distinction between self-employment and salaried employment[67] – although the relevance of the latter has been firmly reasserted by the decrees implementing Act no. 183 of 10 December 2014.

An interesting discussion, which however goes beyond the scope of this chapter, concerns the risks resulting from what has been defined as 'ill-conceived reforms promoting the return of legal socialism' contributing to 'the useless myth that one-day work will become the sweet law of the world'.[68] Nevertheless, we cannot fail to stress both the relevance and the short-sightedness of certain policies aimed at 'making use of the versatility of new technologies to reward the alienated man who works, enabling them to regain some of the time of their life that can be used as they please'.[69] No one can doubt that the twentieth century and the Taylorist approach to work organisation have contributed to interpreting the notion of working time merely as one's physical presence at work. Yet the fourth industrial revolution, while blurring the boundaries between personal and professional life, lays the foundation for workers to manage their own time and work, giving them more freedom and power in terms of decision making.[70] Accordingly, doubts can be cast as regards the choice of lawmakers to deal with agile working only in terms of work-life balance, however relevant this issue can be. Rather, the challenges posed by new technologies to labour law can be overcome by developing a new idea of work and enterprise.

Equally limited is the provision granting workers engaged in agile working 'the right to formal, non-formal or informal learning through their lifetime and to have their skills certified on a regular basis'.[71] This is particularly the case in consideration of a

---

65. P. Tullini, *C'è lavoro sul web?*, in *Labour and Law Issues*, 2015, p. 9.
66. As pointed out by J. Messenger, L. Gschwind, *Three Generations of Telework: New ICTs and the (R)evolution from Home Office to Virtual Office*, cit. The words of T. Makimoto, D. Manners, *Digital Nomad*, Chichester, 1997, become reality: 'that the work of the future would be neither here nor there, but rather constantly on the move'. In the same vein, J. Morgan, *The Future of Work*, Willey, 2014, pp. 14–15 and J. Raso-Delgue, *La empresa virtual: nuevos retos para el Derecho del Trabajo*, in *Revista Internacional y Comparada de Relaciones Laborales y Derecho del Empleo*, 2017, n. 1, pp. 73–107.
67. M. Weiss, *Digitalizzazione: sfide e prospettive per il diritto del lavoro*, cit., pp. 655–663. Cf. G. Valenduc, P. Vendramin, *Work in the Digital Economy: Sorting the Old from the New*, European Trade Union Institute, Working Paper 2016.03, spec. pp. 30–32, where mobile work is regarded as being in between self-employment and salaried employment.
68. U. Romagnoli, *'Noi e loro': diritto del lavoro e nuove tecnologie*, cit., p. 388 who makes reference to L. Fevre, *Lavoro: evoluzione di un termine e di un'idea*, in *Problemi di metodo storico*, Einaudi, 1976.
69. U. Romagnoli, *op. loc. ult. cit*. See also R. De Luca Tamajo, *Il tempo di lavoro (il rapporto individuale di lavoro)*, in *Atti delle giornate di studio di diritto del lavoro*, cit., pp. 3–6.
70. On the importance of giving priority to individuals and their ability to make decisions autonomously, cf. già S. Simitis, *Il diritto del lavoro e la riscoperta dell'individuo*, in *Giornale di Diritto del lavoro e Relazioni Industriali*, 1990, p. 87 and ff.
71. Cf. para. 2, Art. 20 of Act no. 81 of 22 May 2017, which however makes this right dependent on the agreement between the parties without any provision sanctioning possible violations or promoting relevant initiatives. Cf. L. Casano, *Al cuore del lavoro agile: certificazione delle competenze e alfabetizzazione digitale degli adulti*, in E. Dagnino, M. Tiraboschi (a cura di), *Verso il futuro del lavoro. Analisi e spunti su lavoro agile e lavoro autonomo*, cit., pp. 51–55.

possible review of some mandatory rules and certain categories of labour law. In this respect, one problem is the link between modern technologies and professions, in terms of reputation, acknowledgment and status. This also calls for rethinking the terms of the employment contract and the exchanges taking place between the two parties of the individual contract. Does it still refer to making available one's energy in a given timeframe? Or, from now on, should we only speak of competences and skills?

What seems to be important here is that Italian lawmakers avoided dealing with the relevance of subordination – which is a debated issue worldwide – somehow ignoring the recommendations, including those of Roger Blanpain, 'to start from scratch'[72] and to move behind the limitations posed by salaried employment. With old-generation telework, one could still disregard the arguments made by some labour law scholars who linked this form of employment with result-based tasks or with activities that were unrelated to external time constraints.[73] However, it is not possible to ignore technology when it affects skills development and the very way in which work is performed. When this happens, a clash takes place between a command-and-control approach typical of twentieth-century subordination and emerging forms of result and objective-based work,[74] which for the most part is managed by the worker and little interaction is needed with the client or the employer.[75] One might argue that those on salaried employment enjoy higher levels of employment protection and that their work is more organised. It is against this backdrop that Act no. 81 of 22 May 2017 shows some resistance to change, just when an opportunity is given to 'thoroughly review legislation on working time'.[76] In this sense, the provision warns of the risks of subjecting agile workers in salaried employment to the employer's powers, as this might blur the boundaries between private and professional life, therefore challenging the usefulness of this move for the final client.

The truth is that the new forms of telework, which are labelled in a number of ways (e.g., agile working, smart working and so forth) put into question the criteria according to which the time and location where work is performed are assessed, especially in relation to business organisation. Irrespective of the formal definitions provided by lawmakers, some of the work performed through telework or agile working falls outside the contractual obligation concerning the monitoring of one's activity –in terms of either space or time – taking on the characteristic of self-employment. Of course, reference can still be made to working time particularly in

---

72. Cf. R. Blanpain, *The World of Work and Industrial Relations in Developed Market Economies of the XXIth Century. The Age of the Creative Portfolio Worker*, in Blanpain R., Biagi M. (eds), *Non-Standard Work and Industrial Relations*, in *Bulletin of Comparative Labour*, Kluwer, 1999, here p. 41.
73. Cf. R. Flammia, *Telelavoro*, in *Massimario di Giurisprudenza del Lavoro*, 1995, qui p. 638.
74. See M. Biagi, *Competitività e risorse umane: modernizzare la regolazione dei rapporti di lavoro*, in L. Montuschi, M. Tiraboschi, T. Treu (a cura di), *Marco Biagi. Un giurista progettuale*, Giuffrè, 2003, p. 151.
75. Cf. A Supiot, *Les noveaux visages de la subordination*, in *Droit Social*, 2000, p. 231, who talks of a legal metamorphosis of the employer's managerial power.
76. Cf. V. Bavaro, *Il tempo nel contratto di lavoro subordinato*, cit. p. 68 and pp. 216–218 for some reflections on telework and for some elements – e.g., being on call – which contribute to production though they are not considered as being part of working time.

relation to the duration or the regular nature of the work. However, this usually takes place in ways that are similar to result-based work – thus concerning projects, phases or working cycles – rather than interpreting this form of employment simply as workers' energies made available to employers.

To conclude, new legislation on agile working considers technological innovation affecting productive processes and ways of working only to a limited extent. In addition, it does not help us to identify the pieces of this complex puzzle, which is made up of several normative tiles introduced in the past years by the lawmakers (coordinated work, project work, employer-organised work, telework, agile work and so forth). New legislation does not provide a clear picture yet, nor does it contribute to 'solving a number of misunderstandings characterising labour law since its origins'.[77] There exists an awareness that the development of ICT technologies calls for the creation of new conceptual frameworks, contractual and legal strategies that nicely bring together the technicalities and the time needed to perform work. Thirty years after the first reflections on telework made by Italian labour lawyers and following many reforms put in place over time,[78] it seems that little progress has been made on this topic. If anything, the new regulation of agile working seriously undermines the path towards the modernisation of labour law. Like in a board game, we are once again back to square one.

---

77. G. Vardaro, *Tecnica, tecnologia e ideologia della tecnica nel diritto del lavoro*, cit., p. 107 and p. 111.
78. This took place in Italy starting from the 1985 AIDLASS conference on the link between new technology and labour law.

BCLR - BULLETIN OF COMPARATIVE LABOUR RELATIONS

Vol. Author/Title/Year/ISBN

1. Roger Blanpain, *Individual Employment Contracts: Collective Agreements,* 1970.
2. Roger Blanpain, *Social Planning,* 1971 (ISBN 90-312-0018-2).
3. Roger Blanpain, *Guaranteed Income Funds,* 1972 (ISBN 90-312-0019-0).
4. Roger Blanpain, *Employee Participation at the Level of the Enterprise,* 1973 (ISBN 90-312-0020-4).
5. Roger Blanpain, *Vastheid van Betrekking: Staking en Bezetting,* 1974.
6. Roger Blanpain, *Labour Law and Industrial Relations (International Bibliography),* 1975 (ISBN 90-312-0023-9).
7. Roger Blanpain, *Multinational Enterprises,* 1976 (ISBN 90-312-0024-7).
8. Roger Blanpain, *Worker's Participation in the European Company,* 1977 (ISBN 90-312-0044-1).
9. Roger Blanpain, *Women and Labour,* 1978 (ISBN 90-312-0077-8).
10. Roger Blanpain, *European Conference on Labour Law and Industrial Relations: Multinational Enterprises,* 1979 (ISBN 90-312-0091-3).
11. Roger Blanpain, *Job Security and Industrial Relations,* 1980 (ISBN 90-312-0147-2).
12. Roger Blanpain, Greg Bamber & Russell Lansbury, *Technological Change and Industrial Relations: An International Symposium,* 1983 (ISBN 90-312-0205-3).
13. Roger Blanpain, James Janssen van Raay & A. Moulty, *Worker's Participation in the European Community: The Fifth Directive,* 1984 (ISBN 90-654-4187-5).
14. Roger Blanpain, *Equality and Prohibition of Discrimination in Employment,* 1985 (ISBN 90-654-4215-4).
15. Roger Blanpain, *Restructuring Labour in the Enterprise: Law and Practice in France, F.R. of Germany, Italy, Sweden and the United Kingdom,* 1986 (ISBN 90-654-4283-9).
16. Roger Blanpain & E. Kassalow, *Unions and Industrial Relations: Recent Trends and Prospect: A Comparative Treatment,* 1987 (ISBN 90-654-4294-4).
17. Roger Blanpain & Marco Biagi, *Trade Union Democracy and Industrial Relations,* 1988 (ISBN 90-654-4394-0).
18. Roger Blanpain & Jelle Visser, *In Search of Inclusive Unionism,* 1990 (ISBN 90-654-4439-4).
19. Roger Blanpain, *Flexibility and Wages: A Comparative Treatment,* 1990 (ISBN 90-654-4461-0).

20. Roger Blanpain, Stephen Frenkel & Oliver Clarke, *Economic Restructuring and Industrial Relations in Industrialised Countries*, 1990 (ISBN 90-654-4488-2).
21. Roger Blanpain & Friedrich Fürstenberg, *Structure and Strategy in Industrial Relations*, 1991 (ISBN 90-654-4559-5).
22. Roger Blanpain, Amira Galin & Ozer Carmi, *Flexible Work Patterns and Their Impact on Industrial Relations*, 1991 (ISBN 90-654-4572-2).
23. Roger Blanpain, *Workers' Participation: Influence on Management Decision-Making by Labour in the Private Sector*, 1992 (ISBN 90-654-4600-1).
24. Roger Blanpain, Brian Brooks & Chris Engels, *Employed or Self-Employed*, 1992 (ISBN 90-654-4613-3).
25. Roger Blanpain & Tiziano Treu, *Industrial Relations Developments in the Telecommunications Industry*, 1993 (ISBN 90-654-4642-7).
26. Roger Blanpain & Marco Biagi, *Industrial Relations in Small and Medium Sized Enterprises*, 1993 (ISBN 90-654-4696-6).
27. Roger Blanpain & Marco Biagi, *Participative Management and Industrial Relations in a Worldwide Perspective*, 1993 (ISBN 90-654-4769-5).
28. Roger Blanpain, Jacques Rojot & Hoyt N. Wheeler, *Employee Rights and Industrial Justice*, 1994 (ISBN 90-654-4804-7).
29. Roger Blanpain & Ruth Ben-Israel, *Strikes and Lock-Outs in Industrialized Market Economies*, 1994 (ISBN 90-654-4841-1).
30. Roger Blanpain, Kazuo Sugeno & Yasuo Suwa, *The Harmonization of Working Life and Family Life*, 1995 (ISBN 90-411-0064-4).
31. Roger Blanpain & Laszio Nagy, *Labour Law and Industrial Relations in Central and Eastern Europe*, 1996 (ISBN 90-411-0298-1).
32. Roger Blanpain, *Labour Law and Industrial Relations in the European Union*, 1997 (ISBN 90-411-0527-1).
33. Taco Van Peijpe, *Employment Protection under Strain*, 1998 (ISBN 90-411-0528-8).
34. Roger Blanpain, Takashi Araki & Ryuichi Yamakawa, *The Process of Industrialization and the Role of Labour Law in Asia*, 1999 (ISBN 9-041-1104-7-X).
35. Roger Blanpain & Marco Biagi, *Non-standard Work and Industrial Relations*, 1999 (ISBN 90-411-1117-4).
36. Roger Blanpain, *Private Employment Agencies: The Impact of ILO Convention 181 (1997) and the Judgment of the European Court of Justice of 11 December 1997*, 1999 (ISBN 90-411-1118-2).
37. Roger Blanpain, *Multinational Enterprises and the Social Challenges of the XXIst Century: The ILO Declaration on Fundamental* Principles at Work, Public and Private Corporate Codes of Conduct, 2000 (ISBN 90-411-1280-4).
38. Roger Blanpain, Ryuichi Yamakawa & Takashi Araki, *Deregulation and Labour Law: In Search of a Labour Concept for the 21st Century*, 2000 (ISBN 90-411-1370-3).
39. Roger Blanpain, *The Council of Europe and the Social Challenges of the XXIst Century*, 2001 (ISBN 90-411-1543-9).

40. Roger Blanpain, *On-Line Rights for Employees in the Information Society, Use & Monitoring of E-Mail & Internet at Work*, 2002 (ISBN 90-411-1626-5).
41. Roger Blanpain, *The Evolving Employment Relationship and the New Economy: The Role of Labour Law & Industrial Relations*, 2001 (ISBN 90-411-1691-5).
42. Roger Blanpain, *Involvement of Employees in the European Union, Works Councils, Company Statute, Information and Consultation Rights*, 2002 (ISBN 90-411-1760-1).
43. Michele Colucci, *The Impact of the Internet and New Technologies on the Workplace: A Legal Analysis from a Comparative Point of View*, 2002 (ISBN 90-411-1824-1).
44. Roger Blanpain, *White Paper on the Labour Market in Italy: The Quality of European Industrial Relations and Changing Industrial Relations*, 2002 (ISBN 90-411-1841-1).
45. Roger Blanpain, Russell D. Lansbury & Young-Bum Park, *Impact of Globalisation on Employment Relations: A Comparison of the Automobile and Banking Industries in Australia and Korea*, 2002 (ISBN 90-411-1850-0).
46. Roger Blanpain & Antoine Jacobs, *Employee Rights in Bankruptcy: A Comparative-Law Assessment*, 2002 (ISBN 90-411-1942-6).
47. Roger Blanpain, Takashi Araki & Shinya Ouchi, *Corporate Restructuring and the Role of Labour Law*, 2003 (ISBN 90-411-1949-3).
48. Roger Blanpain, *Collective Bargaining, Discrimination, Social Security and European Integration*, 2003 (ISBN 90-411-2010-6).
49. Roger Blanpain & Luis Aparicio-Valdez, *Labour Relations in the Asia- Pacific Countries*, 2004 (ISBN 90-411-2239-7).
50. Roger Blanpain & Ronnie Graham, *Temporary Agency Work and the Information Society*, 2004 (ISBN 90-411-2252-4).
51. Roger Blanpain, *The Actors of Collective Bargaining: A World Report*, 2004 (ISBN 90-411-2253-2).
52. Roger Blanpain & Michele Colucci, *The Globalisation of Labour Standards: The Soft Law Track*, 2004 (ISBN 90-411-2303-2).
53. Roger Blanpain, Takashi Araki & Shinya Ouchi, *Labour Law in Motion: Diversification of the Labour Force & Terms and Conditions of Employment*, 2005 (ISBN 90-411-2315-6).
54. Roger Blanpain, *Smoking and the Workplace*, 2005 (ISBN 90-411-2325-3).
55. Roger Blanpain, *Confronting Globalization: The Quest for a Social Agenda*, 2005 (ISBN 90-411-2381-4).
56. Roger Blanpain, Thomas Blanke & Edgar Rose, *Collective Bargaining Wages in Comparative Perspective: Germany, France, the Netherlands, Sweden and the United Kingdom*, 2005 (ISBN 90-411-2388-1).
57. Roger Blanpain & Anne Numhauser-Henning, *Women in Academia & Equality Law: Aiming High - Falling Short?*, 2006 (ISBN 978-90-411-2427-6).
58. Roger Blanpain, *Freedom of Services in the European Union: Labour and Social Security Law: The Bolkestein Initiative*, 2006 (ISBN 978-90-411-2453-5).
59. Roger Blanpain, Frans Pennings & Nurhan Sural, *Flexibilisation and Modernisation of the Turkish Labour Market*, 2006 (ISBN 978-90-411-2490-X).

60. Roger Blanpain & Boel Flodgren, *Corporate and Employment Perspectives in a Global Business Environment*, 2006 (ISBN 978-90-411-2537-X).
61. Roger Blanpain, Shinya Ouchi & Takashi Araki, *Decentralizing Industrial Relations and The Role of Labor Unions and Employee Representatives*, 2007 (ISBN 978-90-411-2583-3).
62. Roger Blanpain, *European Framework Agreements and Telework: Law and Practice: A European and Comparative Study*, 2007 (ISBN 978-90-411-2560-4).
63. Roger Blanpain, Jim Kitay, Leanne Cutcher & Nick Wailes, *Globalization and Employment Relations in Retail Banking*, 2007 (ISBN 978-90-411-2620-1).
64. Roger Blanpain, Russell Lansbury, Jim Kitay, Nick Wailes & Anja Kirsch, *Globalization and Employment Relations in the Auto Assembly Industry: A Study of Seven Countries*, 2008 (ISBN 978-90-411-2698-6).
65. Roger Blanpain & Michele Tiraboschi, *The Global Labour Market: From Globalization to Flexicurity*, 2008 (ISBN 978-90-411-2722-8).
66. Roger Blanpain, Michele Colucci & Frank Hendrickx, *The Future of Sport in the European Union: Beyond the EU Reform Treaty and the White Paper*, 2008 (ISBN 978-90-411-2761-7).
67. Roger Blanpain, Linda Dickens, *Challenges in European Employment Relations: Employment Regulation, Trade Union Organization, Equality, Flexicurity, Training and New Approaches to Pay*, 2008 (ISBN 978-90-411-2771-6).
68. Roger Blanpain, Hiroya Nakakubo & Takashi Araki, *New Developments in Employment Discrimination Law*, 2008 (ISBN 978-90-411-2782-2).
69. Roger Blanpain, Andrzej Marian wiątkowski, *The Laval and Viking Cases: Freedom of Services and Establishment v. Industrial Conflict in the European Economic Area and Russia*, 2009 (ISBN 978-90-411-2850-8).
70. Roger Blanpain, William Bromwich, Olga Rymkevich, Silvia Spattini, *The Modernization of Labour Law and Industrial Relations in a Comparative Perspective*, 2009 (ISBN 978-90-411-2865-2).
71. Roger Blanpain, Juan Pablo Landa & Brian Langille, *Employment Policies and Multilevel Governance*, 2009 (ISBN 978-90-411-2866-9).
72. Roger Blanpain, European Works Councils; *The European Directive 2009/38/EC of 6 May 2009*, 2009 (ISBN 978-90-411-3208-6).
73. Roger Blanpain, William Bromwich, Olga Rymkevich & Silvia Spattini, *Labour Productivity, Investment in Human Capital and Youth Employment: Comparative Developments and Global Responses*, 2010 (ISBN 978-90-411-3249-9).
74. Greg J. Bamber & Philippe Pochet, *Regulating Employment Relations, Work and Labour Laws: International Comparisons between Key Countries*, 2010 (ISBN 978-90-411-3199-7). General Editor: Roger Blanpain.
75. Roger Blanpain, Desislava Nikolaeva Dimitrova, *Seafarers' Rights in the Globalized Maritime Industry*, 2010 (ISBN 978-90-411-3349-6).
76. Roger Blanpain, Hiroya Nakakubo & Takashi Araki, *Regulation of Fixed- Term Employment Contracts*, 2010 (ISBN 978-90-411-3356-4).

77. Roger Blanpain, William Bromwich, Olga Rymkevich & Iacopo Senatori, *Rethinking Corporate Governance*, 2011 (ISBN 978-90-411-3450-9).
78. Roger Blanpain & Frank Hendrickx, *Labour Law between Change and Tradition: Liber Amicorum Antoine Jacobs*, 2011 (ISBN 978-90-411-3424-0).
79. Roger Blanpain, Thomas Klebe, Marlene Schmidt & Bernd Waas, *Trade Union Rights at the Workplace*, 2012 (ISBN 978-90-411-3460-8).
80. Roger Blanpain, William Bromwich, Olga Rymkevich & Iacopo Senatori, *Labour Markets, Industrial Relations and Human Resources Management: From Recession to Recovery*, 2012 (ISBN 978-90-411-4004-3).
81. Roger Blanpain, Hiroya Nakakubo & Takashi Araki, *Systems of Employee Representation at the Enterprise: A Comparative Study*, 2012 (ISBN 978-90-411-4080-7).
82. Roger Blanpain & Frank Hendrickx, *Temporary Agency Work in the European Union and the United States*, 2013 (ISBN 978-90-411-4769-1).
83. Roger Blanpain, Toker Dereli, Y. Pınar Soykut-Sarıca & Aslı en-Tabaı, *Emerging Patterns of Work and Turkish Labour Market Challenges under Globalization: Readings on Labour and Employment Relations*, 2014 (ISBN 978-90-411-4983-1).
84. Roger Blanpain, Pablo Arellano Ortiz, Marius Olivier & Gijsbert Vonk, *Social Security and Migrant Workers: Selected Studies of Cross-border Social Security Mechanisms*, 2014 (ISBN 978-90-411-4770-7).
85. Roger Blanpain & Nikita Lyutov, *Workers' Representation in Central and Eastern Europe: Challenges and Opportunities for the Works Councils' System*, 2014 (ISBN 978-90-411-4746-2).
86. Roger Blanpain, Ulla Liukkunen & Chen Yifeng, *China and ILO Fundamental Principles and Rights at Works*, 2014 (ISBN 978-90-411-4984-8).
87. Roger Blanpain, *The Use of Languages and Employment Relations*, 2014 (ISBN 978-90-411-5606-8).
88. Roger Blanpain, Hiroya Nakakubo & Takashi Araki, *Protection of Employees' Personal Information and Privacy*, 2014 (ISBN 978-90-411-5608-2).
89. Roger Blanpain, Jan Wouters, Glenn Rayp, Laura Beke & Axel Marx, *Protecting Labour Rights in a Multi-polar Supply Chain and Mobile Global Economy*, 2015 (ISBN 978-90-411-5662-4).
90. Roger Blanpain & Stefania Marassi, *Globalization and Transnational Collective Labour Relations: International and European Framework Agreements at Company Level*, 2015 (ISBN 978-90-411-4748-6).
91. Roger Blanpain, Frank Hendrickx & Petra Herzfeld Olsson, *National Effects of the Implementation of EU Directives on Labour Migration from Third Countries*, 2016 (ISBN 978-90-411-6257-1).
92. Roger Blanpain, Frank Hendrickx & D'Arcy du Toit, *Labour Law and Social Progress: Holding the Line or Shifting the Boundaries?* 2016 (ISBN 978-90-411-6747-7).

93. Roger Blanpain & Frank Hendrickx, *Reasonable Accommodation in the Modern Workplace: Potential and Limits of the Integrative Logics of Labour Law*, 2016 (ISBN 978-90-411-6258-8).
94. Roger Blanpain, Frank Hendrickx & Bernd Waas, *New Forms of Employment in Europe*, 2016 (ISBN 978-90-411-6239-7).
95. Roger Blanpain, Frank Hendrickx, Hiroya Nakakubo & Takashi Araki, *The Notion of Employer in the Era of the Fissured Workplace: Should Labour Law Responsibilities Exceed the Boundary of the Legal Entity?*, 2017 (ISBN 978-90-411-8470-2).
96. Elena Sychenko, *Individual Labour Rights as Human Rights: The Contributions of the European Court of Human Rights to Worker's Rights Protection*, 2017 (ISBN 978-90-411-8629-4).
97. William Bromwich & Olga Rymkevich, *Improving Workplace Quality: New Perspectives and Challenges for Worker Well-Being*, 2017 (ISBN 978-90-411-8628-7).
98. Sarah De Groof, *Work-Life Balance in the Modern Workplace: Interdisciplinary Perspectives from Work-Family Research, Law and Policy*, 2017 (ISBN 978-90-411-8630-0).
99. Sylvaine Laulom, *Collective Bargaining Developments in Times of Crisis*, 2018 (ISBN 978-90-411-8999-8).
100. Frank Hendrickx & Valerio De Stefano, *Game Changers in Labour Law: Shaping the Future of Work*, 2018 (ISBN 978-90-411-9953-9).